400 THREE & FOUR
RECIPES INGREDIENTS

400 RECIPES THREE & FOUR INGREDIENTS

A mouthwatering collection of delicious dishes which need only three or four ingredients to make, all shown step-by-step in 1550 color photographs

JOANNA FARROW & JENNY WHITE

Published by World Publications Group, Inc.
140 Laurel Street
East Bridgewater, MA 02333
www.wrldpub.net

© Anness Publishing Ltd 2005, 2008

Produced by Anness Publishing Ltd
Hermes House, 88–89 Blackfriars Road, London SE1 8HA
tel. 020 7401 2077; fax 020 7633 9499
www.hermeshouse.com; www.annesspublishing.com

If you like the images in this book and would like to investigate using them
for publishing, promotions or advertising, please visit our website
www.practicalpictures.com for more information.

Publisher: Joanna Lorenz
Editorial Director: Judith Simons
Senior Editor: Doreen Gillon
Copy-editors: Bridget Jones and Sally Somers
Photography: Tim Auty, Martin Brigdale, Nicky Dowey, Gus Filgate, Michelle Garrett, Amanda Heywood,
William Lingwood, Craig Robertson, Simon Smith
Home Economist: Jenny White
Home Economist's Assistant: Fergul Connolly
Stylist: Helen Trent
Designer: Paul Oakley
Additional Recipes: Pepita Aris, Alex Barker, Georgina Campbell, Jacqueline Clark, Joanna Farrow, Brian
Glover, Christine Ingram, Becky Johnson, Jane Milton, Jennie Shapter, Marlena Spieler, Linda Tubby, Kate
Whiteman, Jeni Wright

ETHICAL TRADING POLICY

Because of our ongoing ecological investment programme, you, as our customer, can have the pleasure
and reassurance of knowing that a tree is being cultivated on your behalf to naturally replace the
materials used to make the book you are holding. For further information about this scheme, go to
www.annesspublishing.com/trees

ISBN10: 1 57215 151 X
ISBN13: 9781572151512

Previously published as *Best -Ever Three and Four Ingredient Cookbook*

Printed and bound in China

NOTES

Bracketed terms are intended for American readers.

For all recipes, quantities are given in both metric and imperial measures and, where appropriate,
measures are also given in standard cups and spoons. Follow one set, but not a mixture, because they are
not interchangeable.

Standard spoon and cup measures are level.
1 tsp = 5ml, 1 tbsp = 15ml, 1 cup = 250ml/8fl oz

Australian standard tablespoons are 20ml. Australian readers should use 3 tsp in place of 1 tbsp for
measuring small quantities of gelatine, flour, salt etc.

American pints are 16fl oz/2 cups. American readers should use 20fl oz/2.5 cups in place of 1 pint when
measuring liquids.

Electric oven temperatures in this book are for conventional ovens. When using a fan oven, the
temperature will probably need to be reduced by about 10–20°C/20–40°F. Since ovens vary, you should
check with your manufacturer's instruction book for guidance.

Medium (US large) eggs are used unless otherwise stated.

Contents

Cooking with Three and Four Ingredients 6

The Minimalist Kitchen 8
Equipment 10
Minimalist Cooking Techniques 14
Fruit 18
Vegetables 20
Dairy Produce 22
Fish and Shellfish 24
Meat and Poultry 26
Herbs 28
Spices and Aromatics 30
Other Flavourings 34
Kitchen Basics 38
Short-cut Ingredients 42
Making the Basics 44
Making Simple Accompaniments 50
Planning a Menu 54

Breakfasts and Brunches 60

Appetizers 78

Party Snacks 96

Soups 114

Light Lunches 130

Fish and Shellfish 150

Meat 172

Poultry and Game 196

Pasta and Rice 216

Vegetarian Dishes 240

Vegetables and Side Dishes 262

Salads 292

Al Fresco 308

Hot Desserts 324

Cold Desserts 346

Ice Creams and Frozen Desserts 378

Cookies and Sweet Treats 398

Breads 418

Preserves, Pickles, Relishes and Sauces 436

Healthy Juices and Smoothies 454

Drinks 478

Nutritional Information 496
Index 508

Cooking with Three and Four Ingredients

Just because a dish includes only a few ingredients, it doesn't mean you need to compromise on taste and enjoyment. Reducing the number of ingredients you use in a dish has many benefits. Not only does it make shopping easier and quicker, it also means spending less time on preparation because there's less measuring, peeling, scrubbing and chopping to be done. It also allows you to really enjoy the flavours of the few ingredients used. Fresh food tastes fantastic, so why not let the flavours of a few truly fabulous ingredients shine through rather than masking them with the taste of other ingredients?

Keeping it quick, keeping it simple

In today's busy world, time is of the essence – and no one ever seems to have enough of it. When you're trying to cram as much as possible into a single day, often the first thing that falls by the wayside is cooking. When you're busy, the last thing you feel like doing is spending an hour in the supermarket shopping for ingredients, then going home and preparing them before finally cooking a meal. The temptation is to grab a ready-prepared meal to heat up when you get home, or to pick up a takeaway – but sometimes, when you've had a hectic day at work or your kids have been running you ragged, what you really want is to sit down and relax with a tasty home-cooked meal. This book is devoted to helping you do just this.

The idea of making a dish that requires a huge list of ingredients can often put you off before you've even started – the shopping and preparation alone seeming like an unmanageable task. But the good news is that cooking doesn't need to be this way. It's incredibly easy to make delicious dishes using just a few simple ingredients – but the key to success lies in the ingredients you choose, and how you prepare and cook them.

Above and opposite: You need only three ingredients to make this fabulous dish of spaghetti with broccoli and spicy chilli. It tastes delicious and can be made in less than 15 minutes.

Using the right ingredients

The recipes in this book combine basic ingredients such as fruit, vegetables, meat, fish, herbs and spices, but they also make good use of ready-made or pre-prepared products such as curry pastes and pastry. Using these convenient products is a great way to save time, both on preparation and shopping, and can sometimes enhance the final dish in a way that the home-made version may not. For example, puff pastry is enormously difficult to make, while the bought varieties are easy to use, give great results and taste delicious.

When buying basic ingredients, always try to buy the freshest, best quality ones you can to get the maximum flavour. Really fresh ingredients also have the benefit of having a higher nutritional content. If you can buy organic produce, do so. The flavour will be better and you will have the knowledge that they do not contain chemical fertilizers and pesticides.

It is also a good idea to buy fruits and vegetables when they're in season. Although most are available all year round, you can really notice the difference between those that have been ripened naturally and those that have been grown out of season. Strawberries may be available in the middle of winter, but when you cut them open they are often white inside with a slightly waxy texture and none of the sweet, juicy, almost perfumed flavour of the summer fruits. There are so many fabulous ingredients at their peak in their own season that you don't have to buy unseasonal ones. Why buy tired-looking asparagus in autumn when there are plenty of mushrooms, squashes and root vegetables around – all of which can be made into a huge number of delicious, varied meals.

When buying pre-prepared or ready-made ingredients such as stocks for soups or custard to make ice cream, try to buy really good-quality, fresh varieties. When an ingredient is playing an intregral part in a dish, it needs to be well flavoured with a good texture and consistency. If you use a less good product with an inferior flavour, it will really show in the final dish. The same is true of flavouring ingredients such as curry pastes and spicy sauces – go for quality every time and you will reap the benefits.

About this book

Whether you're an experienced cook or an absolute beginner, you'll find the recipes in this book will suit you perfectly. There are dishes for every occasion: juices to quench your thirst; healthy breakfasts and light lunches to make when time is short. There are also fabulous meat, fish and vegetarian dishes to cook when you have more time on your hands or if you're entertaining guests. There is a selection of divine dishes to eat outside when the weather's sunny, and when you need a sweet treat, there are whole chapters devoted to cookies and cakes and sumptuous hot, cold and iced desserts. No matter what the occasion, how much time you have, how many people you need to feed, or what you're in the mood for – you are sure to find the perfect dish within these pages.

Every recipe has an ingredients list of four items or fewer, and the only other things you will need will come from the storecupboard (pantry): oil or butter to cook with and salt and freshly ground black pepper to season the food. In some cases flavoured oils such as garlic-, lemon-, or herb-infused olive oil are used for cooking or drizzling, so it's well worth keeping a small selection of these oils in the storecupboard.

The Minimalist Kitchen

WHEN YOU'RE USING ONLY THREE OR FOUR
INGREDIENTS TO MAKE A DISH, EACH ONE NEEDS TO BE
A STAR PLAYER. THIS CHAPTER GUIDES YOU THROUGH
THE INTRICACIES OF CHOOSING, PREPARING AND
COOKING INGREDIENTS TO ACHIEVE THE BEST RESULTS
AND OFFERS TIPS ON MAXIMIZING FLAVOUR USING
SIMPLE COOKING TECHNIQUES. THERE ARE RECIPES FOR
MAKING BASIC INGREDIENTS SUCH AS FLAVOURED
OILS, STOCKS AND SAUCES, PLUS SUGGESTIONS FOR
SIMPLE ACCOMPANIMENTS AS WELL AS ADVICE ON
MENU PLANNING TO ENSURE SUCCESS EVERY TIME.

Equipment

You don't need a kitchen full of equipment to be a spontaneous and versatile cook. It is quality, not quantity, that counts when you're preparing and cooking food, particularly when choosing essential pieces of equipment such as pans and knives. As long as you look after them, these items should last for many years so are well worth the investment. The following section guides you through the essential items that make cooking as simple and enjoyable as possible, and also offers suggestions on how to improvise if you don't have the right piece of equipment.

Pans and bakeware

Always choose good-quality pans with a solid, heavy base: they retain heat better and are less likely to warp or buckle. Heatproof glass lids are useful because they allow you to check cooking progress without having to uncover the pan repeatedly.

Pans: small, medium and large When cooking large quantities of food, such as pasta or rice, that need to be boiled in a large amount of water, the bigger the pan the better. It does not matter whether the pan is non-stick, but it is useful to have heatproof handles and lids so that the pan can double as a large ovenproof cookpot. A medium-size pan is ideal for cooking sauces and similar mixtures. Ideally, choose a non-stick pan, which will help to prevent thickened sauces sticking and burning. It also makes washing-up easier. The same guidelines apply to a small pan, which is ideal for small quantities.

Above: Choose good-quality, heavy baking sheets because lightweight sheets tend to buckle in the oven.

Frying pan Select a non-stick pan that is shallow enough that you can easily slide a fish slice or metal spatula into it. A pan with an ovenproof handle and lid can be placed in the oven and used as a shallow casserole dish.

Baking sheets Having one or two non-stick baking sheets in the kitchen is invaluable. They can be used for a multitude of tasks such as baking cookies and bread, or they can be placed under full dishes in the oven to catch any drips if the mixture overflows.

Roasting pan A good, heavy roasting pan is essential for roasting large cuts of meat and vegetables. Choose a large pan; you will achieve better results if there is room for heat to circulate as the food cooks. Potatoes, for example, will not crisp well if they are crammed together in a small pan.

Left: It is wise to invest in three good-quality pans of different sizes. Treat them with care and you will get maximum use from them.

Cutting and grinding

Chopping, slicing, cutting, peeling and grinding are all essential aspects of food preparation so it's important to have the right tools for the job.

Chopping board Essential in every kitchen, these may be made of wood or plastic. Wooden boards tend to be heavier and more stable, but they must be thoroughly scrubbed in hot soapy water and properly dried. Plastic boards are easier to clean and better for cutting meat, poultry and fish.

Knives: cook's, vegetable and serrated When buying knives, choose the best ones you can afford. They should feel comfortable in your hand, so try several different types and practise a cutting action before you buy. You will need three different knives. A cook's knife is a good multi-purpose knife. The blade is usually about 18cm/7in long, but you may find that you prefer a slightly longer or shorter blade. A vegetable knife is a small version of the cook's knife and is used for finer cutting. A large serrated knife is essential for slicing bread and ingredients such as tomatoes, which have a hard-to-cut skin compared to the soft flesh underneath.

Vegetable peelers These may have a fixed or swivel blade. Both types will make quick work of peeling vegetables and fruit, with less waste than a small knife.

Graters These come in various shapes and sizes. Box graters have several different cutting blades and are easy to handle. Microplane graters have razor-sharp blades that retain their sharp edges.

Left: The traditional box grater is solid, reliable and easy to handle – with several different grating blades.

Pepper mill Freshly ground black pepper is essential for seasoning. It is worth buying a good pepper mill with strong blades that will not blunt easily.

Measuring equipment

Accurate measuring equipment is essential, particularly when making breads and cakes, which need very precise quantities of ingredients.

Weighing scales These are good for measuring dry ingredients. Digital scales are the most accurate but balance scales that use weights or a sliding weight are also a good choice. Spring scales with a scoop and dial are not usually as precise.

Measuring cups Suitable for dry or liquid ingredients, these standard measures usually come in a set of separate cups for different fractions or portions of a full cup.

Measuring jug/pitcher This is essential for liquids. A heatproof glass jug is useful because it allows hot liquids to be measured and it is easy to check the quantity.

Measuring spoons Table cutlery varies in size, so a set of standard measuring spoons is extremely useful for measuring small quantities.

Below: A heatproof measuring jug and a set of measuring spoons are invaluable for measuring liquids and small quantities.

Looking after knives

Although it may seem like a contradiction, the sharper the knife, the safer it is to use. It takes far more effort to use a blunt knife and this often results in accidents. Try to get into the habit of sharpening your knives regularly because the blunter they become, the more difficult they are to use and the longer it will take to sharpen them. Always wash knives carefully after use and dry them thoroughly to prevent them from discolouring or rusting.

Mixing, rolling and draining

Bowls, spoons, whisks and strainers are all important kitchen items that you can rarely do without.

Mixing bowls You will need one large and one small bowl. Heatproof glass bowls are a good choice because they can be placed over a pan of simmering water to heat delicate sauces and to melt chocolate.

Wooden spoons Inexpensive and essential for stirring and beating, every kitchen should have two or three wooden spoons.

Metal slotted spoon This large spoon with draining holes is very useful for lifting food out of cooking liquid.

Fish slice/metal spatula This is invaluable for lifting delicate fish fillets and other foods out of a pan.

Rolling pin A heavy wooden or marble rolling pin is useful for rolling out pastry. If you don't have one, use a clean, dry, tall glass bottle (such as a wine bottle) instead.

Above: *Metal ballon whisks are great for beating out lumps from mixtures such as sauces.*

Balloon whisk A metal whisk is great for softly whipping cream and whisking sauces to a smooth consistency. Whisks are available in all shapes and sizes. Do not buy an enormous whisk that is difficult to use and will not fit into pans; mini-whisks are not essential – you can use a fork instead.

Sieve/Strainer For sifting flour, icing (confectioners') sugar, cocoa and other dry ingredients, a stainless steel sieve is essential. It can also be used for straining small quantities of cooked vegetables, pasta and rice. Wash and dry a sieve well after use to prevent it becoming clogged and damp.

Colander Choose a free-standing metal colander with feet on the base. This will keep the base of the colander above the liquid that is being drained off. A free-standing design also has the advantage of leaving both hands free to empty heavy pans.

Below: *No kitchen should be without a good selection of wooden cooking utensils for mixing and stirring.*

Electrical appliances

Although not always essential, these can speed up food preparation.

Food processor This fabulous invention can make life a lot easier. It is perfect for processing soft and hard foods and is more versatile than a blender, which is best suited to puréeing very soft foods or liquids.

Hand-held electric whisk A small, hand-held electric whisk or beater is very useful for making cakes, whipping cream and whisking egg whites. Choose an appliance with a powerful motor that will last.

Below: *A food processor is good for chopping and blending.*

Extra equipment

As well as the essential items, some recipes require other items such as tart tins (pans) and cookie cutters. The following are some items you may find you need.

Above: *Cookie cutters come in all kinds of shapes and sizes.*

Cookie cutters These make quick work of cutting out pastry and cookie dough. Metal ones have a sharper cutting edge so are usually preferable to plastic ones. If you don't have cutters, you can use a cup or glass and cut around it, but this takes more time.

Above: *A pastry brush is useful when baking or grilling.*

Pastry brush Made of bristle, with a wooden or plastic handle, this is useful for brushing food lightly with liquid – for example, brushing meat or fish with oil or marinade while grilling (broiling), or brushing pastry with beaten egg or milk.

Cake tins/pans These may have loose bottoms or spring-clip sides to allow easy removal of the cake. Be sure to use the size specified in the recipe.

Muffin tins/pans These consist of six or twelve fairly deep cups in a tray. They can be used for baking muffins, cupcakes, buns, bread rolls and deep tartlets.

Tart or tartlet tins/pans Available with straight or fluted sides, these are not as deep as muffin tins (pans). They come in a variety of sizes, from individual containers to very large tins. They are useful for baking all kinds of sweet and savoury tarts. Loose-bottomed tins are best because the contents are easier to remove.

Skewers These are used for kebabs and other skewered foods. Metal skewers are reusable and practical if you cook over the barbecue frequently, or cook kebabs that need lengthy cooking. Bamboo skewers are disposable and useful for foods that cook quickly – soak them in cold water for 20 minutes before use to stop them burning.

Palette knife/metal spatula This large, flat, round-bladed, blunt knife is great for spreading icing and fillings on cakes, as well as lifting delicate biscuits (cookies) off baking sheets and flipping pancakes.

Griddle pan A good quality, heavy griddle pan is useful for cooking meat and fish. The pan should be very hot before food is placed on it and the surface of the food should be brushed with a little oil to prevent it from sticking, rather than adding oil to the pan.

Wok This traditional Asian pan is larger and deeper than a frying pan, often with a rounded base and curved sides.

Below: *The ridges in the griddle pan allow fat to drain away and create attractive markings on the surface of the food.*

Below: *Double- and single-handled woks are versatile and make a useful addition to any kitchen. They are great for stir-frying, deep-frying, steaming and braising.*

Minimalist Cooking Techniques

When cooking with a limited number of ingredients, the trick is to bring out the flavour of each one. The choice of cooking method is important because it can affect the flavour quite dramatically. Seasonings and aromatics are used to complement and bring out the flavours of the main ingredients, while marinating or macerating help to intensify the relationship between the basic ingredient and the condiments or seasoning. The result is a full, rich flavour.

Cooking methods to maximize flavour

How you cook food can make a real difference to the end result. For example, long-boiled vegetables become soggy and insipid, devoid of nutrients and flavour. In contrast, lightly steaming vegetables, baking fish wrapped in paper or foil parcels, and dry-frying spices are simple techniques that trap and enhance the natural flavour of the food. Some methods also add other flavours during cooking: for example, sprinkling smoking chips on a barbecue gives the food an extra smoky flavour.

Cooking on a barbecue Good-quality lumpwood charcoal will impart its characteristic smoky flavour to the food. A variety of natural or synthetic aromatics can also be added, including hickory, oak, mesquite or applewood chips; woody herbs, such as thyme or rosemary – just the stalks will do; or shells from almonds or walnuts. Soak nutshells in cold water for about 30 minutes before adding them to the barbecue to help them smoke.

Below: *Cooking vegetables, fish or meat over charcoal can help to give the food a wonderful, rich, smoky flavour.*

Above: *Roasting vegetables in the oven really helps to bring out their sweet flavour as the natural sugars caramelize.*

Roasting This is a good method for cooking meat, poultry, fish and vegetables. Long, slow roasting transforms sweet vegetables such as (bell) peppers and parsnips, bringing out a rich, caramelized flavour.

Grilling/broiling This method adds flavour by browning or charring the surface of the food. To achieve a good result the grill (broiler) must be preheated before cooking so that it is as hot as possible when the food is placed under the heat. Grilling is excellent for cheese, fish, poultry and lean meat, such as steak.

Dry-frying Frying with no fat or oil is a useful technique for certain ingredients. Fatty meats such as bacon and pancetta release fat as the meat cooks, providing fat in which to cook the meat and any other ingredients added to the pan. Dry-frying whole spices, such as coriander or cumin seeds, enhances their taste, taking the raw edge off their flavour while making it more intense and rounded. This technique is also known as roasting.

Shallow frying Meat, poultry, fish and vegetables are all delicious pan-fried with a little oil or butter. They can be cooked quickly over a high heat to seal in the flavours, or slowly over a low heat to achieve tender, juicy results.

Deep-frying Meat, poultry, fish, vegetables and even fruit are delicious cooked in hot oil. It is a very quick method and gives rich results. The outside of the food is sealed almost as soon as it hits the oil, forming a crisp exterior that encloses the flavour and juices of the ingredients. Most foods need to be dipped in a protective coating such as batter or breadcrumbs before frying.

Steaming This healthy cooking method is excellent for quick-cooking foods such as vegetables and fish. The natural flavours and nutrients of the food are retained giving moist, tasty results. Few additional ingredients or flavourings are needed when steaming.

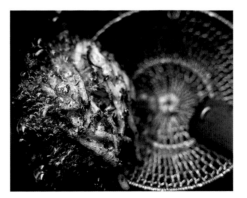

Above: *Deep-frying is a quick way of cooking that produces richly flavoured food with a crisp yet succulent texture.*

Below: *Steaming is a delicate cooking method that is perfect for foods such as dumplings, vegetables and fish.*

Microwaving Vegetables, such as peas and green beans, can be cooked successfully in a microwave. The result is similar to steaming, and traps all the flavour and nutrients. Place the vegetables in a suitable covered container with a little added water, then cook on full power.

Baking in parcels Traditionally known as cooking *en papillote*, this cooking method is a form of steaming. It is perfectly suited to foods such as fish and vegetables. The food is wrapped in baking parchment or foil to make a neat parcel, then baked. The steam and juices from the food are trapped within the parcel as it cooks, capturing the full flavour. Be sure to fold or crumple the edges of the parcel well to ensure that all the steam and juices are retained.

Below: *Fish, such as salmon, is delicious wrapped in a paper parcel with simple flavourings, then baked in the oven.*

Dry-frying whole spices

1 Heat a small frying pan over a medium heat and add the spices. Cook, stirring occasionally, until the spices give off their aroma – take care not to let them burn.

2 Tip the toasted spices into a mortar and roughly crush them with a pestle. (Dry-fry spices freshly, as and when you need them.)

Simple ways of introducing flavour

As well as selecting the cooking method best suited to the ingredients, there are several quick and simple methods of adding flavour using herbs, spices and aromatics. Match the seasoning to the ingredient and go for simple techniques such as marinating, stuffing or coating with a dry spice rub, which will help to intensify the flavours.

Flavours for fish Classic aromatics used for flavouring fish and shellfish include lemon, lime, parsley, dill, fennel and bay leaves. These flavours all have a fresh, intense quality that complements the delicate taste of fish and shellfish without overpowering it. All work well added before, during or after cooking.

• To flavour whole fish, such as trout or mackerel, stuff a few lemon slices and some fresh parsley or basil into the body cavity before cooking. Season with plenty of salt and freshly ground black pepper, then wrap the fish in foil or baking parchment, ensuring the packet is well sealed. Place the fish in an ovenproof dish or on a baking tray and bake until cooked through.

• To marinate chunky fillets of fish, such as cod or salmon, arrange the fish fillets in a dish in a single layer. Drizzle the fish with olive oil, then sprinkle over a little crushed garlic and grated lime rind and squeeze over the lime juice. Cover the dish in clear film (plastic wrap) and leave to marinate in the refrigerator for at least 30 minutes. Grill (broil) lightly until just cooked through.

• To make an unusual, yet delicious, marinade for salmon, arrange the salmon fillets in a single layer in an overproof dish. Drizzle the fillets with a little light olive oil and add a split vanilla pod. Cover and marinate in the refrigerator for a couple of hours before cooking in the oven.

Pepping up meat and poultry Meat and poultry suit both delicate and punchy seasonings. Dry rubs, marinades and sticky glazes are all perfect ways to introduce flavour into the meat and poultry. Marinating the tougher cuts of meat, such as stewing steak, also helps to tenderize them.

• To make a fragrant Cajun spice rub for pork chops, steaks and chicken, mix together 5ml/1 tsp each of dried thyme, dried oregano, finely crushed black peppercorns, salt, crushed cumin seeds and hot paprika. Rub the Cajun spice mix into the raw meat or poultry, then cook over a barbecue or bake until cooked through.

• To marinate red meat, such as beef, lamb or venison, prepare a mixture of two-thirds red wine to one-third olive oil in a shallow non-metallic dish. Stir in some chopped garlic and bruised fresh rosemary sprigs. Add the meat and turn to coat it in the marinade. Cover and chill for at least 2 hours or overnight before cooking.

• To make a mild-spiced sticky mustard glaze for chicken, pork or red meat, mix 45ml/3 tbsp each of Dijon mustard, clear honey and demerara sugar, 2.5ml/^{1}/$_2$ tsp chilli powder, 1.5ml/^{1}/$_4$ tsp ground cloves, and salt and freshly ground black pepper. Cook the poultry or meat over the barbecue or under the grill (broiler) and brush with the glaze about 10 minutes before the end of cooking time.

Below: *Brush on sticky glazes towards the end of cooking time; if the glaze is cooked for too long, it will burn.*

Above: *Adding a drizzle of sesame oil to stir-fried vegetables gives them a wonderfully rich, smoky, nutty flavour.*

Vibrant vegetables Most fresh vegetables have a subtle flavour that needs to be brought out and enhanced. When using delicate cooking methods such as steaming and stir-frying, go for light, fresh flavourings that will enhance the taste of the vegetables. When using more robust cooking methods, such as roasting, choose richer flavours such as garlic and spices.

• To make fragrant, Asian-style steamed vegetables, add a bruised stalk of lemon grass and/or a few kaffir lime leaves to the steaming water, then cook vegetables such as pak choi (bok choy) over the water until just tender. Alternatively, place the aromatics in the steamer under the vegetables and steam as before until just tender.

• To add a rich flavour to stir-fried vegetables, add a splash of sesame oil just before the end of cooking time. (Do not use more than about 5ml/1 tsp because sesame oil has a very strong flavour and can be overpowering.)

• To enhance the taste of naturally sweet vegetables, such as parsnips and carrots, glaze them with honey and mustard before roasting. Mix together 30ml/2 tbsp whole-grain mustard and 45ml/3 tbsp clear honey, and season with salt and ground black pepper. Brush the glaze over the prepared vegetables to coat completely, then roast until sweet and tender.

Fragrant rice and grains Classic accompaniments, such as rice and couscous, can be enhanced by the addition of simple flavourings. Adding herbs, spices and aromatics can help to perk up the rice and grains' subtle flavour. Choose flavourings that will complement the dish that the rice or grains will be served with.

• To make exotic fragrant rice to serve with Asian-style stir-fries and braised dishes, add a whole star anise or a few cardamom pods to a pan of rice before cooking. The rice will absorb the flavour during cooking.

• To make zesty herb rice or couscous, heat a little chopped fresh tarragon and grated lemon rind in olive oil or melted butter until warm, then drizzle the flavoured oil and herbs over freshly cooked rice or couscous.

• To make simple herb rice or couscous, fork plenty of chopped fresh parsley and chives through the cooked grains and drizzle over a little oil just before serving.

Below: *Snipping fresh chives into a bowl of couscous not only adds flavour, but also adds a decorative finish to the side dish.*

Fruit

Widely used in both sweet and savoury dishes, fruit can be used either as a main ingredient or as a flavouring to complement and enhance the taste of other ingredients. The many different varieties offer the cook ample opportunity to create fabulous dishes – whether it's cod fillets with a squeeze of lime juice, a stew of lamb and tangy apricots or a sumptuous dessert made with soft, juicy summer berries.

Orchard fruit

This family of fruit includes apples, pears and quinces, which, depending on the variety, are in season from early summer to late autumn (fall). Choose firm, unblemished fruit and store in a cool dry place.

Apples There are two main categories of apples – eating and cooking. Eating apples have sweet flesh and taste good raw. Many can also be used for cooking; they remain firm making them ideal for pan-frying and open tarts. Cooking apples have a tart flavour and are too sharp to eat raw. When cooked, their flesh tends to break down and become pulpy, making them ideal for sauces and purées.

Pears Most commercially available pears are dessert fruits, just as good for eating as for cooking. They can be pan-fried or used in tarts and pies. They are also excellent poached, especially in a wine syrup.

Quinces Related to the pear, quinces have hard, sour flesh. Cooking and sweetening brings out their delicious, scented flavour. They are worth buying when you find them, and are often used in jellies and sauces.

Stone fruit

Peaches, nectarines, plums, apricots and cherries all belong to this family of fruit which contain a stone (pit) in the

middle. Most stone fruits are at their best through the summer months but some, such as plums, are best through the autumn. Choose firm, smooth-skinned fruit without any blemishes and store in a cool, dry place, preferably the refrigerator. They are used raw or cooked. When eating raw, eat at room temperature.

Above: *Sweet, juicy peaches are delicious served fresh in salads or poached in wine.*

Above: *Fresh raspberries are perfect for breakfast and dessert dishes.*

Soft fruit

These delicate fruits, which include strawberries, raspberries, blackberries, blackcurrants, redcurrants and white currants, need careful handling and storing. Choose brightly coloured fruit and check for signs of grey mould or overripe specimens. Store in the refrigerator for up to 2 days. They are rich in vitamin C.

Citrus fruit

Oranges, lemons, limes, grapefruit, mandarins and satsumas are popular citrus fruits; but there are also hybrids such as clementines. The lemon is probably the most versatile member of the citrus family, with many uses in both savoury and sweet cooking. Citrus fruits are available all year round, with satsumas and clementines at their best in winter. Choose plump fruit that feels heavy. The skin should be bright and not shrivelled. Most citrus fruit is coated with wax to prevent moisture loss, so buy unwaxed fruit when using the rind in a recipe, or scrub the fruit well before use.

Segmenting oranges

1 Cut a slice off the top and bottom of the orange to remove the peel and pith. Stand the fruit on a board and cut off the peel and pith, working around the orange in strips.

2 Hold the orange over a bowl to catch the juices. Cut through one side of a segment, between the flesh and membrane, then cut through the other side of the segment to remove the flesh. Continue removing the segments in this way, leaving behind the clutch of membranes.

Exotic fruit

Once expensive and rarely available, these wonderful fruits are now widely available in supermarkets throughout the year. Eat them fresh or use them in recipes.

Mangoes There are many varieties of this sweet, fragrant, juicy fruit, which are delicious eaten on their own with a squeeze of lime juice, or used in recipes. Choose mangoes that have a fragrant smell, even through the skin, and give slightly when gently squeezed. Store in a cool place, but not the refrigerator, for up to a week.

Pineapple These sweet, tangy, juicy fruits are delicious in fruit salads and desserts. When choosing a pineapple, pull off one of the green leaves at the top – if it comes away easily, the pineapple should be ripe. Store in a cool place, but not the refrigerator, for up to a week.

Kiwi fruit The pale green flesh of kiwi fruit is full of sweet-sharp flavour that goes well with other fruit in salads and is good in various desserts and savoury cooking. Kiwi fruit are rich in vitamin C. Choose fruit with smooth, plump skin and store in the refrigerator for up to 4 days.

Passion fruit These small round fruit have a tough, wrinkled purple-brown skin. A passion fruit should feel heavy if it is nice and juicy. Store in the refrigerator.

Below: *Perfectly ripe pineapples have sweet, tangy flesh with a crisp bite and wonderful fragrance that is quite irresistible.*

Above: *Watermelon has bright pink flesh and a light, delicate flavour that is sweet yet refreshing.*

Other fruit

There are a few fruits that are delicious and very versatile but that don't fit into any particular group.

Rhubarb Tart, pink rhubarb is used in pies, tarts, crumbles and mousses. The stalks are edible but the leaves are poisonous so should be removed before cooking. Rhubarb is available from early spring to mid-summer. Pale, finer-textured pink forced rhubarb is available in January. It has a good colour and flavour, and is considered the best. Choose crisp, firm stalks and store in the refrigerator.

Melons There are two types of melon – dessert melon and watermelon. Charentais, Ogen, cantaloupe, Galia and honeydew melon are all dessert melons, which are in season from summer to winter. Slice them, remove the seeds and enjoy their fragrant flesh. Watermelons have crisp, juicy flesh, studded with dark seeds. They are best served chilled, and are in season from summer to autumn.

Figs Fresh figs with their dense, sweet red flesh are still considered a luxury outside the areas where they are grown. Available in summer, they are delicious raw or cooked and can be used in savoury or sweet dishes. Handle figs carefully and store in the refrigerator for up to 2 days.

Grapes At their best in late summer, there are many varieties of grape, but the seedless ones are popular. Grapes can be used in many ways – served on their own as an accompaniment to cheese; used in fruit salads; or combined with savoury ingredients in salads.

Vegetables

Used in salads and savoury dishes, vegetables are delicious served as the main ingredient in a side dish, or as a flavouring ingredient within a main dish. Take your time when choosing vegetables, selecting healthy-looking specimens that are in season for maximum flavour – you'll really notice the difference.

Root vegetables and potatoes
Grown underground, these vegetables include carrots, parsnips, beetroot and turnips and many varieties of potato. They are very versatile: good for roasting, boiling, steaming and deep-frying. Choose firm vegetables with unblemished skins; avoid withered specimens and green-tinged potatoes, or ones with shoots. Store in a cool, dark place for up to 2 weeks. Scrub well if cooking in their skins.

Cabbages, broccoli and cauliflower
Members of the brassica family, these vegetables are packed with nutrients and good served in many ways.

Cabbage Regardless of variety, cabbage has a distinctive flavour and can be steamed, stir-fried or boiled. The white and red varieties are tight-leafed and ideal for shredding, and can be enjoyed raw in salads such as coleslaw. Green cabbage can be loose or close-leafed, smooth or crinkly and is best cooked. Buy bright, fresh-looking specimens and store in the refrigerator for up to 10 days.

Above: *Fresh, leafy purple sprouting broccoli is delicious steamed, boiled or stir-fried.*

Broccoli With a delicious flavour and crisp texture, broccoli and purple sprouting broccoli can be boiled, steamed and stir-fried. Choose specimens with bright green heads and no sign of yellowing. Store in the refrigerator and use within 4–5 days.

Cauliflower Good cut into florets and served raw with dips, cauliflower can also be boiled or steamed, and is delicious coated in cheese sauce. To ensure even cooking, remove the hard central core, or cut into florets. Choose densely packed heads, avoiding specimens with any black spots, and store in the refrigerator where they will keep for 5–10 days.

Above: *Plump juicy tomatoes have a rich, sweet flavour and are tasty used in salads or cooked in stews and sauces.*

Vegetable fruits
Tomatoes, aubergines, peppers and chillies are actually fruit, although they are generally used as vegetables. They all have a robust flavour and lovely texture and are widely used in Mediterranean-style cooking.

Tomatoes There are numerous varieties of tomatoes, including cherry, plum and beefsteak. They are eaten raw or cooked. Choose plump, bright-red specimens, ideally on the vine, and store in the refrigerator for 5–8 days.

Aubergines/eggplants These can be fried, stewed, brushed with oil and grilled (broiled), or stuffed and baked. Choose firm, plump, smooth-skinned specimens and store in the refrigerator, where they will keep for 5–8 days.

Peppers/bell peppers These may be red, yellow, orange or green, with the green specimens having a fresher, less sweet flavour. Peppers can be grilled, roasted, fried and stewed. Choose firm, unblemished specimens and store in the refrigerator for 5–8 days.

Chillies There are many types of chilli, all with a different taste and heat. As a general rule, the bigger the chilli, the milder it is; green chillies tend to be hotter than red ones.

Leafy green vegetables

There is a wide selection of leafy greens available, which may be used raw in salads or cooked.

Salad leaves There are many different salad leaves, including many types of lettuce. They are delicate and need to be stored in the refrigerator, where most will keep for a few days. Prepare salad leaves at the last minute.

Spinach Tender young spinach leaves are tasty raw. Mature spinach leaves can be fried, boiled or steamed until just wilted; they overcook very easily. Store spinach in the refrigerator for 2–3 days, and wash well before use.

Leafy Asian vegetables Asian vegetables, such as pak choi (bok choy), can be used raw in salads or cooked. Prepare in the same way as cabbage or spinach.

The onion family

This family includes onions, shallots, spring onions (scallions), leeks and garlic. All can be used as flavouring ingredients or cooked on their own. Roasting produces a rich, sweet flavour. Choose firm, unblemished specimens. Store onions in a cool, dry place for up to 2 weeks; store leeks and spring onions in the refrigerator for 2–3 days.

Beans, peas and corn

These are good boiled or steamed and served as a side dish, or used in braised dishes and stir-fries.

Green beans Many varieties of green beans are available throughout the year. Choose firm, fresh-looking beans with a bright green colour; avoid yellowish ones. Store in the refrigerator, where they will keep for up to 5 days.

Peas Fresh peas are generally only available in their pods in the summer. Only buy really fresh ones because their natural sugar content quickly turns to starch, giving them a mealy texture. Frozen peas are often better than fresh ones because they are frozen within a short time of picking and retain all their natural sweetness.

Above: *Fresh green peas are delightfully sweet and tender.*

Above: *Butternut squash has bright orange flesh, a lovely sweet flavour and smooth texture. Roasting brings out its flavour.*

Corn Large corn cobs are good boiled and served with butter, while baby corn are better added to stir-fries. Buy only the freshest specimens when they are in season because stale vegetables can be starchy.

Squashes

These vegetables come in many different shapes and sizes and include courgettes (zucchini); butternut, acorn and spaghetti squashes; and pumpkins and marrows (large zucchini). With the exception of courgettes, all need peeling and seeding before use. They can be cut up and boiled or baked whole. Select smooth, unblemished vegetables with unbroken skin. Most squashes can be stored in a cool place for 1 week, although courgettes should be stored in the refrigerator for 4–5 days.

Mushrooms

Freshly picked mushrooms have a rich, earthy flavour, but are rarely available to most cooks. Chestnut mushrooms are a good alternative; they have more flavour than cultivated mushrooms. Shiitake mushrooms are full-flavoured and delicious in Chinese- and Asian-style dishes.

There are many types of edible wild fungi or mushrooms of different flavours and textures. They tend to have a more intense flavour than cultivated mushrooms and are also more expensive and more difficult to find. Wild mushrooms are seasonal and can generally be found in late summer, autumn (fall) and winter. Choose firm, fleshy specimens and store them in paper bags in a cool place.

Dairy Produce

Milk and milk products, such as yogurt, milk and cheese, are widely used in cooking and can add a delicious richness to many sweet and savoury dishes. Strong-tasting cheeses, such as Gorgonzola or Parmesan, not only contribute a wonderful texture, but also add real bite to many savoury dishes.

Milk, cream and yogurt
These products are widely used in both sweet and savoury dishes, adding a rich, creamy taste and texture.

Milk Full-fat (whole) milk and lower-fat semi-skimmed and skimmed milk is pasteurised and available fresh or in long-life cartons. Buttermilk is a by-product of the butter-making process and is often used in baking.

Cream There are many different types of cream. Double (heavy) cream has a high fat content and can be poured, whipped and heated without curdling. Whipping cream has a lower fat content and can be whipped to give a lighter, less firm texture. Single (light) cream has a lower fat content still and cannot be whipped; it is used for pouring. Clotted cream is very thick and has the highest fat content. Sour cream has the same fat content as single cream, but it is cultured, giving it a thick texture and slightly sour, fresh taste. Crème fraîche is cultured fresh cream, which gives it a slightly sharp, acid taste. It has a fairly thick, spooning texture but it cannot be whipped. It can be heated.

Yogurt Varying in fat content, yogurt may be set or runny, with a thin or creamy texture. It tends to curdle when heated, although Greek (US strained plain) yogurt can be used for cooking.

Above:
Parmesan cheese is
very good for cooking and is also excellent grated
or shaved over pasta, risotto and other dishes.

Butter
There are two main types of butter – salted and unsalted (sweet). Unsalted is better for baking cakes and cookies.

Hard cheeses
These firm, tasty cheeses are good for cooking. They should have a dry rind. Store wrapped in baking parchment in the refrigerator for up to 2 weeks.

Cheddar There are many varieties of this classic sharp cheese – some strong, some mild. Its high fat content and good melting properties make it a great choice for cheese sauces.

Parmesan This cheese comes from the area around Parma in Italy and only cheeses with Parmigiano Reggiano stamped on the rind have this designation. It is a hard, dry cheese with a full, sweet flavour.

Gruyère This Swiss cheese with a dry texture and nutty flavour is good in cooking and for melting over dishes.

Manchego This Spanish ewe's milk cheese has a dry texture and a nutty, buttery taste.

Above: *There are many different types*
of cream, from thick to pourable.

Semi-hard cheeses

These vary in softness depending on the type. Choose cheeses that feel springy and have firm rinds. Wrap in waxed paper and store in the refrigerator for 1–2 weeks.

Fontina This deep golden yellow Italian cheese has a pale brown rind and lots of little holes throughout the cheese. It melts fairly well but is not good for sauces.

Halloumi This salty Greek cheese has a firm, slightly rubbery texture and is perfect for grilling (broiling).

Blue cheese

These strong, often sharp, cheeses usually melt well and are good for cooking and flavouring sauces.

Stilton This strong, sharp cheese melts well into sauces and complements chicken and more robust meats.

Gorgonzola This Italian blue cheese has a rich, piquant flavour with a firm but creamy texture. It melts smoothly and can be used in a wide range of dishes.

Dolcelatte This Italian blue cheese has a milder flavour than Gorgonzola and a soft, creamy texture. It is good with summer fruit and can be used in cooking.

Soft and fresh cheeses

These mild, unripened cheeses should smell fresh. Store in a covered container in the refrigerator for up to 1 week.

Mozzarella This Italian cheese has a soft, elastic texture and mild, milky flavour and is good when melted. Baby balls of mozzarella (bocconcini) are also available.

Above: Stilton has a sharp, tangy flavour and creamy texture. It is good served on its own or used in salads and cooking.

Feta This white, firm Greek cheese has a crumbly texture and sharp, salty flavour. Feta does not melt easily and is not ideal for general cooking but is good used in salads.

Mascarpone This creamy, mild cheese has a high fat content and can be used in sweet and savoury recipes.

White rind cheeses

These creamy cheeses with a firm, white mould rind are delicious used fresh in salads or cooked.

Brie This French cheese is one of the best of the white rind cheeses. The flavour can be mild or extremely strong, tangy and creamy when ripe. Brie can be grilled (broiled), baked or coated in breadcrumbs and deep-fried.

Firm goat's cheese One of the most popular types is shaped in a log, often sold sliced into a white ring. It is excellent for slicing and melting. Soft goat's cheese, without the rind, has a milder flavour.

Eggs

Widely used in sweet and savoury cooking, eggs are incredibly versatile and are perfect for making simple meals such as omelettes or baked eggs.
Hens' eggs These can be boiled, poached, fried, scrambled or baked. They are widely used for baking. Buy the best you can afford – hens reared in better conditions produce better-tasting eggs.
Quails' eggs These small speckled eggs are similar in flavour to hens' eggs. They can be fried, poached or boiled and are useful for canapés.

Left: Mild, milky mozzarella is great used fresh in salads or melted in cooked dishes.

Fish and Shellfish

Full of flavour and quick to cook, fish and shellfish are delicious cooked simply. Always buy really fresh specimens: look for bright-eyed fish with plump flesh and bright, undamaged skin; they should not smell "fishy" but should have a faint aroma of the sea. Good fishmongers will scale, cut and fillet the fish for you. Choose lobsters and crabs that feel heavy for their size. Store fish and shellfish, covered, towards the bottom of the refrigerator, and use within a day of purchase.

Above: *Fresh anchovies are tasty marinated in lemon juice.*

Oily fish

The rich flesh of oily fish is extremely tasty and very good for you. Oily fish are rich in omega 3 fatty acids, which are an essential part of a healthy diet and are said to be good for the heart. Oily fish also contain less fat than most meat or poultry, and the fat is generally unsaturated.

Anchovies When available fresh, anchovies are delicious grilled (broiled) and served with a squeeze of lemon juice. Good-quality salted anchovies are versatile and delicious in many dishes, particularly pasta sauces.

Mackerel These fish have iridescent skin and quite firm, brownish flesh. They can be baked whole, wrapped in baking parchment, with lemon and herbs, or marinated and grilled. The robust flavour of mackerel is enhanced by pungent spices, such as coriander and cumin.

Herring Smaller than mackerel, herring can be treated in much the same way. They are also delicious pickled.

Sardines These small fish are delicious fresh, cooked over a barbecue with lime or lemon juice and herbs.

Rich, meaty fish

This group of firm fish have a meaty texture. Some have a mild flavour, while others such as tuna are more robust.

Monkfish Tasty baked, pan-fried and grilled, this fish is usually sold prepared as monkfish tails, which have a firm, meaty texture and a delicate flavour. Ask the fishmonger to remove all traces of skin and membrane around the fish, as this turns very rubbery on cooking.

Sea bass This is an expensive fish but its flavour is well worth the cost. Try fillets pan-fried in a little butter and served with a squeeze of lime juice.

Tuna Fresh tuna is now more widely available – bluefin is the most prized, followed by yellowfin. It is best served rare. Steaks are best pan-fried for 1–2 minutes each side.

Swordfish Pink-tinged, meaty swordfish is excellent cooked over a barbecue, but be sure not to overcook it because the flesh becomes dry.

Red mullet You can recognise red mullet by the yellow stripe that runs along the body. It is an attractive fish with fine, delicious white flesh. The fillets are good pan-fried with the skin on and served with creamy mashed potato.

White fish

These fish have a firm yet delicate white flesh, excellent cooked simply with subtle or piquant flavouring.

Cod Stocks of cod in the sea are diminishing due to overfishing resulting in a rise in price. Large cod fillet has a firm texture and an almost milky quality to its flesh.

Plaice Cooked whole or as fillets, plaice can be fried, grilled, steamed or baked. It can be slightly bland, so add a piquant sauce or herbs and olive oil to perk it up.

Below: *Tuna steaks are great marinated in oil and lime juice and then grilled.*

Crab These crustaceans are cooked live, plunged into a pan of boiling water, which many people find off-putting. However, crab is also available ready-cooked. A crab yields a small amount of meat for its size, so allow 500g/1¼lb weight of whole crab per person.

Lobster Like crabs, lobsters should be cooked live, so buy ready-cooked lobsters and split in half lengthways to extract the meat. Crack the claws with a hammer to extract the meat in the same way as for crab claws.

Prawns/shrimp There are many types of prawns of different sizes, cooked or raw, in the shell, or peeled. They are delicious pan-fried with chopped garlic and chilli. When large prawns are peeled, the black vein that runs along the back has to be removed and discarded. Brown shrimps must be used for potted shrimps.

Haddock This flaky fish can be used instead of cod or in recipes calling for white fish. Smoked haddock is delicious but avoid the bright yellow dyed variety and go for the paler, undyed version.

Skate This fish has a hard, cartilaginous skeleton and no bones. It is sold as flat wings. Piquant capers are the perfect companion seasoning.

Shellfish

There are several different types of shellfish. Molluscs have either one or two shells. Once dead, they deteriorate rapidly and can cause food poisoning. Because of this, they must always be perfectly fresh and cooked alive. Crustaceans, including crabs, lobsters and prawns (shrimp) have a protective shell that is shed occasionally as the creature grows. Store shellfish in the refrigerator and always use within 1–2 days.

Mussels Sweet, mild-tasting mussels need to be cleaned thoroughly before cooking. Wash or scrub in cold water and pull off any black hairs (the beard) protruding from the shell. Tap any open mussels on a work surface and discard any that do not close straight away, along with any broken shells. When cooked, discard any unopened mussels.

Scallops Tender, delicately flavoured scallops need very little cooking. Simply pan-fry for 1–2 minutes on each side over high heat. Choose scallops with a sweet smell; this indicates freshness. To open, hold the scallop shell, curved side down, and insert the tip of an oyster knife between the two shells. Twist to prise the shells apart, then cut through the muscle holding the scallop in the shell, and remove any muscle and membrane from the meat and coral.

Extracting meat from a cooked crab

1 Lay the crab on its back and twist off the legs and claws. Use a hammer to break open the claws and legs, and pick out the meat.

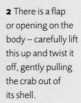

2 There is a flap or opening on the body – carefully lift this up and twist it off, gently pulling the crab out of its shell.

3 Discard the gills from the side of the body and spoon the brown meat from the main body section and from the shell.

Meat and Poultry

If possible, buy organic meat and poultry. It is better to eat less meat of better quality than a larger quantity of cheaper meat. Animals and birds that have been raised in a good environment and fed on quality feed produce better-tasting meat than mass-reared, unhappy livestock. When you are cooking with only a few ingredients, each one needs to have an excellent flavour and texture.

Pork

Comparatively inexpensive, pork is a very versatile meat. It is generally tender and has an excellent flavour.

Shoulder, leg and loin The shoulder or leg is the best cut for roasting. To make good crackling, ensure that the rind is thoroughly dry and rub it generously with sea salt. Loin or shoulder chops are suited to pan-frying or braising.

Belly Traditionally quite fatty, belly pork is good roasted and braised. It is especially tasty with Asian flavourings.

Spare ribs Meaty pork ribs can be delicious marinated and then roasted or barbecued with a sticky glaze.

Pork tenderloin A lean, long piece of meat, the tenderloin can dry out during cooking. Wrap it in bacon to keep it moist before roasting.

Bacon Available smoked or unsmoked. If possible, buy dry-cured bacon. Streaky (fatty) bacon has a higher percentage of fat than back bacon, and can be cooked to a crisp-fried texture. Back bacon has larger rashers (strips) and a balance of lean to fatty areas.

Above: Entrecôte steaks are cut from beef sirloin, have a rich colour and are delicious pan-fried or grilled.

Gammon This smoky meat is available in a whole piece or as steaks. Whole gammon may need soaking before cooking. Steaks can be pan-fried or grilled (broiled).

Pancetta This traditional Italian cured bacon comes in rashers (strips) or cut into dice. It can be pan-fried.

Prosciutto This dry-cured ham is eaten raw, cut into very thin slices. It can be cooked, usually as a topping on dishes or to enclose other ingredients before grilling or roasting.

Beef

This well-flavoured, versatile meat is good for stewing, roasting, grilling (broiling), pan-frying and stir-frying.

Fillet/beef tenderloin, forerib, topside and silverside/pot roast These are best roasted. To make the most of the flavour, serve medium, not well-done.

Steaks Sirloin, T-bone, porterhouse, fillet (beef tenderloin) and sirloin are best pan-fried over a high heat.

Shin or leg/shank, chuck and brisket These cuts can be quite tough and are best stewed slowly to tenderize them and bring out their excellent flavour.

Mince/ground meat This is a very versatile ingredient for meat sauces, chilli con carne, meatballs, pasta dishes, samosas, pies and many other dishes.

Left: Rolled belly of pork is a fatty joint that is succulent either slowly roasted or pot-roasted. Serve with piquant flavours, which go well with the fatty meat.

Lamb

Delicious in roasts and superb grilled (broiled), pan-fried and stewed, lamb is one of the best-loved of all meats.

Best end of neck, leg, shoulder and saddle These are the best cuts for roasting. Best end of neck can be cut into chops. Shoulder contains more fat than leg but it has an excellent flavour. Spring lamb has the best taste.

Chump chops and leg steaks These have a full flavour and can be either grilled (broiled) or pan-fried.

Sausages and offal

Offal refers to all offcuts from the carcass but in everyday use, this usually means liver and kidneys.

Sausages There are many types of fresh sausage from around the world. Depending on the variety, they may be fried, grilled (broiled) or baked.

Liver Pigs', lambs' or calves' liver has a strong flavour and is good pan-fried, with bacon and mashed potato.

Kidneys Lambs' kidneys are lighter in flavour than pigs'. They should be halved and the central core discarded before they are pan-fried or used in stews and pies.

Poultry and game birds

Many people prefer the lighter flavour of poultry and game birds to that of red meat.

Chicken Buy organic or free-range chicken. Choose smooth-skinned, unblemished plump birds.

Carving a roast chicken

1 Leave the bird to rest for 10 minutes, then remove the legs and cut through the joints to make the thigh and drumstick portions.

2 Remove the wings, then carve the meat off the breasts, working down on either side of the breastbone. Use a gentle sawing action.

Poussin These baby chickens are perfect roasted or spatchcocked , then cooked over the barbecue.

Duck Traditionally, duck can be very fatty with a fairly small amount of meat. An average duck will serve two or three people. Duck breasts and legs are a good choice for simple cooking.

Pheasant One pheasant will serve two. The breast meat is fairly dry and needs constant basting during roasting. Choose pheasants that are no older than six months; older birds are tough.

Below from left: *Corn-fed, free-range and organic chickens have a good flavour.*

Herbs

Invaluable in a huge number of sweet and savoury recipes, herbs add flavour, colour and contrast to many dishes. Fresh herbs are widely available and their flavour is superior to that of dried herbs. Many are easy to grow yourself at home – either in the garden or in a pot on the windowsill. You can grow them from seed, or buy them already growing in pots from supermarkets and garden stores.

Robust herbs

These strong-tasting, often pungent herbs are good with meat and well-flavoured dishes. Use in moderation.

Bay leaves These shiny, aromatic leaves can be added to meat dishes, roasts, casseroles and stews before cooking. Roughly tear the leaves before you add them, then remove before serving. They are an essential part of a bouquet garni.

Rosemary This pungent herb is delicious with lamb – insert a few sprigs into slits in the skin of a leg of lamb and the flavour will really penetrate the meat during roasting. For other recipes, use whole leaves or chop them finely.

Above: Rosemary and sage have a robust, pungent flavour that goes well with strongly flavoured, fatty meats such as lamb and pork.

Freezing herbs

This is a great way of preserving fresh herbs because it retains their natural flavour. Use in cooked dishes only. Chop the herbs and place about one tablespoonful in each compartment of an ice cube tray. Pour over water to cover and freeze. To use, simply add a herb ice cube to the pan and stir.

Making a bouquet garni

This classic flavouring for stews, casseroles and soups is very easy to make. Using a piece of string, tie together a fresh bay leaf and a sprig each of parsley and thyme. Alternatively, tie the herbs in a square of muslin (cheesecloth).

Thyme One of the traditional herbs used in a bouquet garni, thyme has small leaves and some types have woody stems. It has a strong, pungent flavour. Add whole sprigs to meat dishes or strip the leaves and use in pasta sauces.

Sage Peppery tasting sage has large, slightly furry leaves. It is a great companion for pork and is excellent with potatoes and also in tomato and garlic pasta dishes. Ravioli served with a little melted butter and warmed sage leaves is particularly delicious. Use in moderation because its flavour can be overpowering if used in excess.

Chives Long slender chives have a distinct onion-like flavour. Chives are best snipped with scissors. They are good in potato salads and egg and dairy dishes.

Oregano One of the few herbs that responds well to drying, oregano is great for tomato-based sauces and with other vegetables. It is also good with chicken.

Lavender This can be used sparingly to complement chicken dishes and also in sweet recipes such as drinks and desserts. The stalks and leaves can be used as well as the flowers, which make a pretty garnish.

Leafy herbs

These delicate, soft-leafed herbs have a fragrant flavour. Use in salads or add towards the end of cooking time.

Basil Widely used in Italian cookery, basil has delicate leaves and should be added at the end of cooking. It has a slightly aniseed flavour that goes well with chicken, fish, all types of vegetables and pasta. It is one of the main ingredients of pesto.

Coriander/cilantro The deep, almost woody, flavour of coriander is superb in spicy dishes. It is good in Thai-style soups and curries, meat and egg dishes, as well as more robustly flavoured fish dishes.

Parsley Flat or curly leafed, parsley is one of the most versatile herbs and adds flavour to most savoury dishes. The flat-leafed variety has a stronger flavour and it can be used as an ingredient in its own right to make soup.

Mint There are many different varieties of mint, including apple mint and spearmint.It grows easily and goes well with lamb, desserts and drinks.

Tarragon This fragrant herb has a strong aniseed flavour and is most often paired with chicken and fish.

Chervil This pretty herb has a mild aniseed flavour that goes well with fish, chicken, cheese and creamy savoury dishes. It is also good in salads.

Below: *Mint has a cool and refreshing flavour and is used in both sweet and savoury dishes.*

Below: *Dill has a sweet, aromatic fragrance and is particularly good used in fish and egg dishes.*

Left: *Delicate, fragrant basil is the perfect flavouring to use with tomatoes.*

Fragrant herbs

These distinctive herbs have a strong, aromatic scent and flavour and suit many different kinds of dishes.

Kaffir lime leaves These dark green leaves are used to impart a citrus flavour to many South-east Asian soups and curries. Add the leaves whole, torn or finely shredded.

Lemon balm With a distinctive lemon flavour and fragrance, this herb complements all ingredients that go well with citrus fruit or juice. Lemon balm makes a good addition to fish, chicken and vegetable dishes as well as sweet drinks and desserts. Use in moderation.

Dill This pretty, feathery herb has a distinctive flavour that is perfect with fish, chicken and egg dishes. It also goes very well with potatoes, courgettes (zucchini) and cucumber. It should be added to dishes just before serving because its mild flavour diminishes with cooking.

Spices and Aromatics

These flavourings play a very important role when cooking with a limited number of ingredients, adding a warmth and roundness of flavour to simple dishes. It is difficult to have every spice to hand, but a few key spices will be enough to create culinary magic. Black pepper is an essential seasoning in every storecupboard; cumin seeds, coriander seeds, dried chillies and turmeric are also good basics.

Above: *Saffron has a delicate fragrance and imparts a pale golden colour to both sweet and savoury dishes.*

Dried spices

Store spices in airtight jars or containers in a cool, dark place. Buy small quantities that will be used up fairly quickly because flavours diminish with age. Check the sell-by dates of the spices in your store cupboard (pantry) and throw away any spices that are old or no longer fragrant; there is little point in using old, tasteless spices to flavour food because the results will not be satisfactory.

Pepper Black pepper is one of the most commonly used spices. It should always be freshly ground because, once ground, it loses its flavour quickly. It is used in almost all savoury recipes but can also be used to flavour shortbread and to bring out the flavour of fruit such as pineapple and strawberries. Green peppercorns have a mild flavour. They are available dried or preserved in brine and are excellent for flavouring pâtés and meat dishes. White pepper is hotter than green, but less aromatic than black.

Chilli flakes Crushed dried red chillies can be added to, or sprinkled over, all kinds of dishes – from stir-fries and grilled (broiled) meats to pasta sauces and pizza.

Cayenne pepper This fiery, piquant spice is made from a dried hot red chilli, so use sparingly. It is excellent in cheese dishes and creamy soups and sauces.

Paprika An essential seasoning for Hungarian goulash and used in many Spanish dishes, paprika is available in a mild and hot form. It has a slightly sweet flavour.

Saffron This expensive spice is the dried stigma of a crocus flower, and is available in strands or ground. Saffron strands have a superior flavour and are best infused in a little hot liquid, such as milk or water, before being added to a recipe. Saffron has a distinct but delicate flavour. It is used sparingly in all kinds of dishes, including paella, curry, risotto, rice pudding and baking. Be wary of very cheap saffron because it is probably not the true spice and will not offer the rich, rounded flavour of the real thing.

Below: *Sweet paprika is the mildest of all the chilli powders and can be used to add a rich flavour and colour to savoury dishes.*

Mustard seeds These may be black, brown or white. They are used to make the condiment mustard and are also used as a flavouring in cooking. Black mustard seeds are added to Indian dishes, for their crunchy texture as well as flavour. Try adding a few mustard seeds to bread dough to give it a spicy kick.

Cumin This warm, pungent spice is widely used in Indian and North African cooking. Cumin works well with meats and a variety of vegetables, particularly robust-tasting sweet potatoes, squashes and cabbage.

Caraway seeds These small dark seeds have a fennel-like flavour. They are very versatile and make a lively addition to savoury breads and sweet cakes, while also complementing strongly flavoured sausage dishes and vegetables such as cabbage.

Fennel seeds These pretty little green seeds have a sweet, aniseed-like flavour that pairs well with chicken and robust fish dishes. It also tastes good in breads.

Coriander Available whole or ground, this warm, aromatic spice is delicious with most meats, particularly lamb. It is widely used in Indian and Asian cooking and is frequently paired with cumin. When combined, ground coriander and cumin make an excellent spice rub.

Below: *Turmeric root is hard and must be ground to make the familiar bright yellow spice used in Indian cooking.*

Above: *Mustard seeds and cumin seeds have a warm, spicy aroma. Buy them whole, then grind them as you need them.*

Turmeric Made from dried turmeric root, the ground spice is bright yellow with a peppery, slightly earthy flavour. It is used in many Indian recipes.

Garam masala This Indian mixture of ground roasted spices is usually made from cumin, coriander, cardamom and black pepper. Ready mixed garam masala is widely available, although the flavour is better when the spices are freshly roasted and ground.

Chinese five spice This is a mixture of ground spices, including anise pepper, cassia, fennel seeds, star anise and cloves. It is used in Chinese cookery, particularly to season pork and chicken dishes. Chinese five spice is a powerful mixture and should be used sparingly.

Salt

Probably the most important of all seasonings, salt is an essential ingredient in almost every cuisine. It has been used for many years, not only to flavour and bring out the taste of other foods, but to preserve them as well. Cured fish and meat, such as salt cod, prosciutto, salt beef and bacon, are preserved in salt to draw out moisture and prevent them from decomposing.

The type of salt used is important – rock salt or sea salt does not have added chemicals, which are often found in table salt. Rock salt is available in crystal form and can be ground in a mill, or refined to cooking salt. Sea salt has a strong, salty taste and it is used in smaller amounts.

Above: *Cinnamon sticks can be used whole in hot drinks, stews and casseroles to add a warm, spicy flavour.*

Green cardamom This fragrant spice is widely used in Indian and North African cooking to flavour both sweet and savoury dishes. The papery green pods enclose little black seeds that are easily scraped out and can be crushed in a mortar with a pestle if required.

Cinnamon This warm spice is available in sticks and ground into powder and has many uses in savoury and sweet recipes. Add sticks to stews, casseroles and other liquid dishes, then remove them before serving. Use ground cinnamon in baking, desserts and drinks.

Ginger The ground, dried spice is particularly useful for baking. For a fresher flavour in savoury recipes and drinks, it is best to use fresh root ginger.

Nutmeg This large aromatic seed has a spicy flavour, which adds a warm spiciness to milk, egg and cream dishes and enhances the flavour of spinach. Nutmeg is available ready ground, but the flavour is far better when the spice is freshly grated. Try sprinkling a little grated nutmeg over milk-based soups before serving.

Mace This spice is the casing of the nutmeg – it has a similar flavour but is slightly milder. Mace is great for flavouring butter for savoury dishes and is an essential ingredient in potted shrimps.

Star anise This pretty, star-shaped spice has a strong aniseed flavour. It is widely used in Chinese and Asian cooking and is a great partner for pork and chicken. It is also good for flavouring rice – simply add a single star anise to the cooking water. It can be used to flavour sweet dishes such as ice creams and jellies.

Allspice This berry has a warm, slightly cinnamon-clove flavour. It is more readily available in its ground form and can be used in both savoury and sweet cooking. It goes particularly well in winter recipes and fruit cake.

Cloves Available whole or ground these dried flower buds are used in savoury and sweet dishes. Ham is particularly tasty studded with whole cloves before baking, while the ground spice is suitable for cakes and cookies. Ground cloves are strong, so use sparingly.

Juniper berries These small, dark-purple berries are the main flavouring in gin. Add a few juniper berries to meaty stews and casseroles to give a fragrant, spicy kick.

Vanilla Dried vanilla pods (beans) are long and black, encasing hundreds of tiny black seeds. Warm the whole pod in milk, or place in a jar of sugar, to allow the flavour to infuse (steep), or split the pods, scrape out the seeds and add to cakes, desserts and ice cream. Natural vanilla extract is distilled from vanilla pods and is a useful alternative to pods. Vanilla extract tends to have a better flavour than vanilla essence, which can be quite overpowering. Some flavourings are not actually vanilla, but a synthetic alternative.

Above: *For the best flavour, grate whole nutmegs as and when you need the spice, using a special small grater.*

Fresh spices and aromatics

These wonderful flavourings are widely used in many dishes and add a rich, round, aromatic taste.

Fresh root ginger This pale-brown root should be peeled and then sliced, shredded, finely chopped or grated as required. It is used in curries, stir-fries, and grilled (broiled) and braised dishes. Choose plump roots and store in the refrigerator for up to 6 weeks. Preserved and crystallized ginger can be used in sweet dishes.

Galangal Similar in appearance to fresh root ginger, but often slimmer and with a pink-purple tinge, galangal is used in Thai and Indonesian cooking. Treat as for fresh root ginger, but store for a maximum of 3 weeks.

Above: *Fresh root ginger has a pungent, zesty flavour that is delicious used in savoury dishes – either raw or cooked.*

Above: *Fresh lemon grass is widely used in Thai cooking.*

Lemon grass This woody pale green stalk is excellent with fish and chicken, and can be used to flavour sweet dishes such as ice cream. Either bruise the bulbous end of the stalk and add whole to curries and soups, or finely slice or chop the end of the stalk and stir into the dish.

Garlic A member of the onion family and therefore often included as a vegetable, garlic also deserves mention as an aromatic for its role in flavouring all kinds of savoury dishes, raw or cooked. The potency of garlic depends on how it has been prepared. Crushed garlic gives the most powerful flavour, while finely chopping, shredding or slicing gives a slightly less strong result. Use garlic to flavour salad dressings or dips, or use whole, peeled cloves to flavour oils or vinegars. (Garlic is renowned for lingering on the breath after consumption; chewing fresh parsley is said to help counteract this.)

Ready-made spice mixes

There is an excellent selection of ready-made spice mixes available that make great short-cut flavouring ingredients for savoury dishes.

Harissa This North Arfrican spice paste is made of chillies, garlic, coriander, caraway, olive oil and other spices. It is delicious with oily fish as well as meat.

Chermoula This is another North African spice paste, which includes coriander, parsley, chilli and saffron.

Cajun seasoning This spice mixture made of black and white pepper, garlic, cumin and paprika is good for rubbing into meat before cooking over a barbecue.

Jerk seasoning This Caribbean spice blend is made of dry spices and goes well with chicken and pork.

Above: *Harissa paste can be used to flavour savoury dishes, such as soups and stews, or as a marinade for meat and fish.*

Other Flavourings

As well as herbs, spices and aromatics, there are a number of basic flavourings that are widely used in both sweet and savoury cooking. Sweeteners, such as sugar and honey, and flavourings, such as chocolate and alcohol, are mainly used in sweet dishes, but they can also be used in savoury dishes. Sauces and condiments, such as soy sauce, can be used to enhance the taste of savoury ingredients.

Sugars and sweet spreads

Refined and raw sugars and sweet spreads such as honey and marmalade can all be used to sweeten and flavour.

Granulated This refined white sugar has large crystals. It is used for sweetening drinks and everyday cooking; it can also be used as a crunchy cookie or cake topping, or stirred into crumble mixtures for extra texture.

Caster/Superfine sugar This fine-grained white sugar is most frequently used in baking. Its fine texture is particularly well suited to making cakes and cookies.

Icing/Confectioners' sugar The finest of all the refined sugars, this sugar has a light, powdery texture. It is used for making icing and sweetening flavoured creams. It is also good for dusting on cakes, desserts and cookies as a decoration.

Below: Sugar cubes and rock sugar are most frequently used to sweeten drinks.

Demerara sugar This golden sugar consists of large crystals with a rich, slightly honeyish flavour. It is great for adding a crunchy texture to cookies.

Brown sugars These dark, unrefined sugars have a rich, caramel flavour. There are different types including light and dark muscovado (brown) sugar and dark brown molasses sugar. The darker the sugar, the more intense its flavour. Always check you are buying unrefined sugar because "brown" sugars are often actually white sugar that has been coloured after refining.

Left: Granulated sugar has larger crystals than caster sugar but both are good for making cakes and desserts.

Below: Golden demerara sugar and soft brown sugar have a moist texture and rich, more rounded flavour.

Honey Clear honey is used to flavour desserts, cakes and cookies as well as savoury dressings. It also makes a good base for barbecue sauces and glazes for chicken or meat.

Marmalade Most often served as a sweet spread, marmalade can also make an interesting ingredient. Try orange marmalade as the base for a quick sauce to serve with duck.

Above: Sweet, golden honey is perfect for flavouring sweet and savoury dishes.

Chocolate

There are many different types of chocolate, each with its own unique flavour. They can all be used in many ways – grated, chopped or melted, and stirred into ice creams, or used for desserts, sauces or in baking. Always choose plain (semisweet) chocolate with at least 70 per cent cocoa solids for a good flavour. Children often prefer the milder flavour of milk chocolate. White chocolate has a low cocoa solids content and is sweet with a very mild flavour. Chocolate spread is also a useful ingredient. It can be melted and stirred into ice cream, custard or drinks, or used in many desserts.

Below: White, dark and milk chocolate are all popularly used in desserts, cookies, cakes, drinks and sweet sauces.

Edible flowers

Many flowers are edible and can be used as ingredients. Roses and violets look delightful frosted and are used to decorate cakes and desserts. Simply brush the clean flower heads or petals with a little egg white, sprinkle with caster (superfine) sugar and leave to dry. Plain rose petals can be used to flavour sugar syrups; rosewater and orange flower water are readily available and convenient and easy to use. Fragrant lavender heads can be left to infuse in cream for about 30 minutes, imparting their flavour.

Flowers can also be used in savoury dishes. Nasturtiums, pansies, marigolds and herb flowers, such as chives, are used to flavour salads.

Coffee

To achieve a strong coffee flavour, use good-quality espresso. You do not need an espresso machine for this because espresso coffee is sold for use in cafetières or filter machines. Make a double-strength brew to flavour desserts, sauces, cakes and cookies.

Almond essence/extract

This distinctive-tasting flavouring is perfect for cakes, cookies and desserts, and is also used for flavouring cream that will be served with fruit desserts. It is very strong, so use sparingly.

Above: Buy good quality espresso coffee beans and grind them freshly to make a really strong brew for flavouring desserts and cakes. Alternatively, use ready-ground espresso coffee.

Alcohol

Wine, spirits, beer and cider add body to both sweet and savoury dishes. Wines and spirits can be used to perk up cooked dishes and to macerate fruits and enliven desserts. Beer and cider are more widely used in savoury dishes such as stews and casseroles.

Wine Fruity red wines can be used to enrich meat dishes, tomato sauces and gravies. Dry white wine goes well with chicken or fish dishes. Sweet white wines and sparkling wines can be used to make jellies and sweet sauces.

Port Ruby port can be added to sauces for red meats – it is richer and sweeter than red wine, so use more sparingly. Port is also suitable for macerating summer fruits.

Sherry Dry, medium or sweet sherry can be used in savoury and sweet recipes. Add a dash to gravies and meat sauces or add a couple of spoonfuls to a rich fruit cake or dessert.

Marsala This Italian fortified wine is used to flavour desserts such as tiramisu and is also good in meat dishes.

Spirits Use rum and brandy for flavouring meat sauces, ice creams and cakes. Clear spirits, such as vodka and gin, can be used for sorbets; add a splash of vodka to tomato-based pasta dishes and fish dishes to give an extra kick. Irish cream liqueurs have a velvet-like texture that is excellent in creams, ice creams and cake fillings. Sweet fruit liqueurs are great used in desserts.

Right: *Almond-flavoured amaretto is delicious in creams and ice creams.*

Above: *Sherry and Marsala are classic flavourings for desserts such as trifle and Italian tiramisu. They are also used in meat dishes and can add a rich, round flavour to meat sauces.*

Preserved fruit and nuts

Above: *Preserved lemons have an intense flavour.*

Preserved lemons A classic in North African cooking, the lemons are preserved whole or in large pieces in a mixture of salt and spices. The chopped peel is usually added to chicken dishes to add an intense, sharp, citrus flavour.

Dried fruit Dried apricots, prunes, figs, currants, sultanas (golden raisins) and raisins can be added to savoury dishes and meat stews to impart a rich, sweet flavour. They are also good for adding flavour and body to sweet desserts, cakes and cookies.

Nuts Almonds, walnuts and pine nuts are useful for savoury dishes such as salads, vegetable dishes, pastes and dips, as well as in desserts and baking.

Coconut milk Thin, creamy coconut milk is made from pulped coconut and is widely used in Thai and Asian cooking, particularly in curries and soups.

Sauces and condiments

Not only are sauces and condiments perfect for serving with main dishes at the table, they are also great for adding extra flavour and bite to simple dishes during cooking.

Mustard Wholegrain mustard containing whole mustard seeds has a sweet, fruity taste and makes a mild, flavourful salad dressing. French Dijon mustard has a fairly sharp, piquant flavour which complements red meat and makes a sharply flavoured dressing. English mustard may be purchased as a dry powder or ready prepared and is excellent added to cheese dishes, or used to enliven bland creamy sauces.

Tomato purée/paste This concentrated purée is an essential in every storecupboard (pantry). It is great for adding flavour, and sometimes body, to sauces and stews.

Passata/bottled strained tomatoes This Italian product, made of sieved tomatoes, has a fairly thin consistency and makes a good base for a tomato sauce.

Tomato ketchup Add a splash of this strong table condiment to tomato sauces for a sweet-sour flavour.

Worcestershire sauce This thin, brown, very spicy sauce brings a piquant flavour to casseroles, stews and soups. It can also be used to perk up cheese dishes.

Below: Wholegrain mustard can be used in dressings and cheese sauces – adding real bite and interest to their flavour.

Right: Dark and light soy sauce are the perfect flavourings for Chinese and Asian dishes.

Below: Sun-dried tomato paste can add extra flavour to tomato sauces, and meat and vegetable soups and stews.

Curry paste There are many ready-made curry pastes, including those for classic Indian and Thai curries. They can also be used to spice up dishes such as burgers.

Sweet chilli sauce You can add this sweet, spicy dipping sauce to stir-fries and braised chicken dishes, and it can be used as a glaze for chicken or prawns before grilling (broiling) or cooking over a barbecue.

Soy sauce Made from fermented soy beans, soy sauce is salty and a little adds a rich, rounded flavour to Asian-style stir-fries, glazes and sauces.

Teriyaki marinade This Japanese marinade has a sweet, salty flavour. Use it to marinate meat, chicken and fish before frying; the leftover marinade will cook down to make a delicious, sticky sauce.

Oyster sauce Add this thick Chinese sauce with a sweet, meaty taste to stir-fries and braised dishes.

Pesto Use fresh pesto, made with basil, garlic, pine nuts and Parmesan cheese, on pasta or to flavour sauces, soups, stews and dressings. There are also variations such as red pesto made with roasted red (bell) peppers.

Kitchen Basics

Keep a well-stocked storecupboard (pantry) and you will be able to cook almost anything at any time. However, this does not mean overloading your storage space with a vast range of ingredients. A selection of well-chosen, essential ingredients is more important than a cupboard full of obscure, out-of-date items that have been used once and then forgotten. The following are some useful basic ingredients that will be invaluable in every kitchen; try to remember to check cupboards regularly and be vigilant about throwing away out-of-date ingredients and replenishing them with fresh ones.

Flour

This is an essential ingredient in every kitchen. There are many different types, which serve many purposes in both sweet and savoury cooking – from baking cakes to thickening gravy and making cheese sauce.

Wheat flours Plain (all-purpose) flour can be used in most recipes, including sauces. Self-raising (self-rising) flour has a raising agent added and is useful for cakes and other baking recipes. Wholemeal flour is available as plain (all-purpose) or self-raising (self-rising). Strong bread flour contains more gluten than plain flour, making it more suitable for making breads.

Right: (Clockwise from top) There are many different types of flour for different purposes, including strong bread flour, French bread flour, self-raising flour and plain flour. For general kitchen use, plain flour is probably the most versatile.

Gluten-free flours For those with an allergy to gluten, which is found in wheat and other grains, gluten-free flour is an invaluable ingredient. It is widely available from most large supermarkets and health food stores.

Cornflour/cornstarch This very fine white flour is useful for thickening sauces and stabilizing egg mixtures, such as custard, to prevent them curdling. A little cornflour is first blended with cold water or another liquid to make a smooth, runny paste, which is then stirred into a hot sauce, soup or stew and boiled until it thickens.

Raising agents Self-raising flour contains raising agents, normally baking powder, which give a light texture to cakes and cookies. You can add baking powder to plain flour to achieve the same result. The baking powder reacts with liquids and heat during cooking and produces carbon-dioxide bubbles, which make the mixture rise.

Oils

Essential both for cooking and adding flavour, there are many different types of oil, all of which have their own character and use in the kitchen. Every cook should have a bottle of oil for cooking, and also oils for drizzling and flavouring.

Olive oil Extra virgin olive oil, made from the first pressing of the olives, has the best, most pronounced flavour and is the most expensive type. It is best reserved for condiments or salad dressings. Ordinary olive oil is generally the third or fourth pressing of the oil and is better used in cooking. Light olive oil is paler and milder in flavour than ordinary olive oil and is ideal for making lightly flavoured salad dressings.

Groundnut/peanut oil This virtually flavourless oil is used for frying, baking and making dressings.

Corn oil Golden-coloured corn oil has a fairly strong flavour and can be used in most types of cooking.

Below: *Flavoured oils are invaluable in the minimalist kitchen – providing extra taste without having to add extra ingredients.*

Left: *Rich, dark sesame oil and spicy chilli oil can be added to stir-fries and dressings to add flavour.*

Vegetable oil This is a blend of oils, usually including corn oil and other vegetable oils. It is quite flavourless and useful in most types of cooking.

Sesame oil Sesame and toasted sesame seed oils both have strong flavours and should be used sparingly when cooking.

Hazelnut and walnut oils Both are quite strongly flavoured and useful as dressings rather than for cooking. They are delicious drizzled over cooked fish, poultry or vegetables, or used in salad dressings.

Flavoured oils There are many types and brands of flavoured oils. Look out for those using a good-quality olive oil as the base.

Chilli oil This is available in various styles – it adds a pleasing spicy kick to all sorts of dishes such as pasta, fish and salads. Add a drizzle just before serving the food.

Garlic oil This is a good alternative to fresh garlic. It has a fairly strong flavour so it should be used with care.

Lemon-infused oil This is excellent with fish, chicken and pasta, and for salad dressings.

Right: *Extra virgin olive oil has a rich, fruity taste and is perfect for drizzling over dishes and making dressings.*

Pasta and noodles

These are invaluable storecupboard (pantry) ingredients that can be used as the base of many hot and cold dishes.

Pasta Dried pasta keeps for months in an airtight container – check the packet for information on keeping quality. There is a wide variety of pasta in all shapes and sizes. Egg pasta is enriched with egg yolks and it has a richer flavour than plain pasta. Generally, the choice depends on personal taste – use whichever type you have in the cupboard. Cook pasta at a rolling boil in plenty of salted water. Fresh pasta cooks very quickly and is available chilled. It can be stored in the refrigerator for several days, or in the freezer for several months.

Above: *Dried pasta is a handy kitchen standby and can be used to make hot, hearty dishes or light, tasty salads.*

Egg noodles Made from wheat flour and eggs, these may be thick, medium or thin. Use them for stir-fries or as an accompaniment to Chinese and Asian dishes.

Below: *Egg noodles have a nutty taste and can be served hot in Asian-style stir-fries and soups, and cold in salads.*

Above:
Polenta is widely used in Italian-style dishes and makes a good alternative to pasta. It can be served as an accompaniment or made into a main dish.

Rice noodles These translucent white noodles are a good alternative to wheat noodles – particularly for those on a gluten-free diet. They are available as broad flat or thin noodles that can be added to stir-fries and soups as well as used cold as the base for salads. Rice noodles are easy to prepare because they don't need to be cooked. Simply soak in boiling water for about 5 minutes, then stir-fry, add to soups or toss with salad ingredients.

Couscous and polenta

Like pasta and noodles, couscous and polenta can be served as an accompaniment or can act as the base of many dishes. They have a mild flavour, and go particularly well with strongly flavoured ingredients.

Couscous Made from durum wheat, couscous is often regarded as a type of pasta. Traditional couscous needed long steaming before serving, but the majority of brands available in supermarkets today are "instant" and need only brief soaking in water. It is the classic accompaniment to Moroccan tagines, but also goes well with all kinds of meat, fish and vegetable stews. It makes an excellent base for salads.

Polenta This is made from finely ground cornmeal. It is cooked with water and either served soft (rather like mashed potato) or left to set and then cut into pieces that can be grilled (broiled) or fried. Quick-cook and ready-made polenta are available in most supermarkets and can be made into simple, hearty dishes. It is best served with flavourful ingredients.

Rice

This versatile grain can be served as an accompaniment, or form the base of both sweet and savoury dishes.

Long-grain rice The narrow grains of white rice cook to a light, fluffy texture and are generally served as an accompaniment to main dishes. They also make a perfect base for other dishes such as stir-fries and salads.

Short-grain rice There are several types of short, stubby, polished rice such as pudding rice and sushi rice. These usually have a high starch content and cook into tender grains that cling together and can be shaped easily.

Thai Jasmine rice This white, slightly sticky rice has a scented flavour. Serve with Thai curries or in stir-fries.

Risotto rice This rice has medium-length polished grains. The grains can absorb a great deal of liquid while still retaining their shape. There are several types of risotto rice, including the popular arborio and carnaroli. When cooking risotto rice, it is imperative to stir it regularly. Liquid or stock should be added periodically throughout cooking to prevent the rice sticking to the pan and burning.

Basmati rice This long-grain rice is widely used in Indian cooking. It is aromatic and cooks to give separated, fluffy grains. Brown basmati rice is also available.

Below: *Canned beans are nutritious and versatile and can be used in hearty stews, healthy salads or tasty dips and pâtés.*

Vegetables, beans and lentils

Dried, canned and bottled vegetables, beans and lentils are very versatile and are a useful storecupboard standby.

Above: *Canned tomatoes are a real storecupboard standby.*

Canned tomatoes Available chopped or whole, canned tomatoes are an essential item in every kitchen. They are very versatile and can be used to make sauces, pasta dishes, pizza toppings, soups and stews. Look out for canned Italian pomodorino tomatoes in a thick juice; they make a superbly rich sauce.

Dried mushrooms Dried wild mushrooms such as porcini and morels are a useful alternative to fresh, seasonal mushrooms, which are not always available. They add a rich flavour to pasta dishes and casseroles.

Bottled antipasti Red (bell) peppers, aubergines (eggplant), mushrooms and artichoke hearts preserved in olive oil with garlic and herbs are a classic Italian appetizer but can make a tasty addition to salads and pasta dishes.

Above: *Juicy black olives add bite to sauces and salads.*

Olives Black and green, olives bring a rich flavour to salads and pasta dishes; they also make a quick and easy appetizer when served with salami and bread.

Red lentils Compared to most other dried beans, red lentils have a relatively short cooking time and are ideal for making a quick and tasty Indian-style dhal.

Canned pulses Dried pulses such as flageolet beans, chickpeas, red kidney beans, cannellini beans and butter (lima) beans have a long shelf-life but require lengthy preparation: soaking overnight and then long boiling. The canned alternatives simply need to be rinsed in cold water, and can then be used in hot dishes or used to make salads.

Short-cut Ingredients

There are some useful products available in supermarkets and food stores that can help you save valuable time in the kitchen. These ingredients are usually pre-prepared in some way, taking the time and effort out of preparation. They provide a quick base for dishes so you will need fewer ingredients and can spend less time on shopping and cooking, and more time relaxing and eating.

Pastry Ready-made pastry is widely available in supermarkets and can make quick work of tarts, pies and filled pastries. Shortcrust, sweet shortcrust, puff and filo pastry can all be purchased frozen or chilled and ready to use. They are usually of excellent quality, giving delicious results. Some pastries are even ready-rolled so all you have to do is open the packet, cut, fold and fill the pastry, and then bake it in the oven until crisp and golden.

Cookie dough Cartons of chocolate chip cookie dough can be useful for many sweet recipes. It can be shaped and baked to make plain cookies or, more imaginatively, they could be coated with a topping or sandwiched together with a chocolate filling or ice cream to make a decadent treat or a sumptuous dessert. The dough can also be rolled thinly and used to line muffin tins (pans) to make a crisp cookie cup to fill with ice cream for dessert. Bitesize pieces of the cookie dough can be stirred into a vanilla ice cream mix to make cookie dough ice cream.

Right (from top to bottom): Ready-made filo, shortcrust, puff and flaky pastries are available fresh and frozen. They can save time when making tarts and pies and give reliably good results.

Marzipan Good quality marzipan is available in most supermarkets. It is perfect for decorating cakes, but it can be used in many other ways as well. Try rolling it out thinly and using it as a tart base under fruit, or chop it into small pieces and add to cookies and cakes.

Custard Fresh ready-made custard is great served hot as an accompaniment to desserts, but it also makes a useful base for ice creams, sauces and soufflés.

Frozen fruit Mixed frozen fruit has already been prepared, ready for making into desserts and sauces. It is available all year round, which means that you can enjoy the sweet taste of summer fruits during the winter when they are out of season. Frozen fruit is often cheaper than fresh.

Above: *Good quality fresh custards are widely available in most supermarkets and make an ideal base for many sweet dishes.*

Above: *Frozen summer berries are available all year round and make a handy alternative to fresh ones in most cooked dishes.*

Cake mixes With the simple addition of an egg and water, these easy-to-use mixes can be turned into a freshly baked cake in no time at all. Scattering the cake mixture with chopped nuts before baking, or sandwiching the cake with cream and fresh summer fruits once it has cooled can transform these simple mixes from an "emergency" storecupboard (pantry) item into a fabulous tea-time treat or delicious dessert with almost no effort.

Batter mixes These are another useful "emergency" product. Simply combine with an egg and water and use to make pancakes for breakfast or dessert, or to coat food before deep-frying.

Pizza base mixes and bread mixes Whereas ready-baked pizza bases tend to be rather cardboard-like, these mixes are excellent and take very little effort to make.

Cakes and cookies Store-bought cakes and cookies can often be used as the base for simple desserts. Dark chocolate brownies can be combined with cream and macerated fruit to create a rich, indulgent dessert, or blended with milk and ice cream to make a decadent milkshake. Broken ginger cookies or sponge fingers can be used as the base for many creamy desserts.

Above: *Crisp ginger cookies can be roughly broken or finely crushed and used as the base for simple desserts such as trifle.*

Pasta sauces Both bottled and fresh pasta sauces are widely available in most supermarkets. Simple tomato and herb sauces are useful for tossing with pasta, spreading over a pizza base or as the base for a quick soup. Ready-made cheese sauces are also versatile – not only good for serving with pasta, but also for topping vegetable gratins, or combining with whisked egg whites and extra grated cheese to make a quick and simple soufflé.

Microwave rice mixes A fairly recent invention, these come in a variety of flavours, including mushroom and pilau. They are extremely useful as the base for quick rice dishes such as kedgeree.

Bags of mixed salad These save time selecting and preparing a variety of leaves. For maximum flavour, choose a bag that includes baby leaves and herbs.

Making the Basics

Having a few ready-made basics, such as stocks, pasta sauces and flavoured oils, can really help with everyday cooking. They can all be bought ready-made in the supermarket, but they are easy to make at home. Stocks take time to prepare, but they can be stored in the freezer for several months. Flavoured oils are easy to make and keep in the same way as ordinary oils so it's well worth having a few in the cupboard. All the basic sauces, dressings, marinades and flavoured creams in this section are simple to make and can be made fresh or in advance.

Flavoured oils

Good quality olive oil can be flavoured with herbs, spices and aromatics to make rich-tasting oils that are perfect for drizzling, making dressings and cooking. Make a couple of different flavoured oils and store in a cool, dark place.

Herb-infused oil Half-fill a jar with washed and dried fresh herbs such as rosemary or basil. Pour over olive oil to cover, then seal the jar and place in a cool, dark place for 3 days. Strain the herb-flavoured oil into a clean jar or bottle and discard the herbs.

Lemon oil Finely pare the rind from 1 lemon, place on kitchen paper, and leave to dry for 1 day. Add the dried rind to a bottle of olive oil and leave to infuse for up to 3 days. Strain the oil into a clean bottle and discard the rind.

Chilli oil Add several dried chillies to a bottle of olive oil and leave to infuse for about 2 weeks before using. If the flavour is not sufficiently pronounced, leave for another week. The chillies can be left in the bottle and give a very decorative effect.

Garlic oil Add several whole garlic cloves to a bottle of olive oil and leave to infuse for about 2 weeks before using. If the flavour is not sufficiently pronounced, leave the oil to infuse for another week, then strain the oil into a clean bottle and store in a cool, dark place.

Stock

You cannot beat the flavour of good home-made stock so it's worth making a large batch and freezing it. To freeze, pour the cooled stock into 600ml/1 pint/2^1/$_2$ cup containers and freeze for up to 2 months.

Chicken stock Put a 1.3kg/3lb chicken carcass into a large pan with 2 peeled and quartered onions, 2 halved carrots, 2 roughly chopped celery sticks, 1 bouquet garni, 1 peeled garlic clove and 5 black peppercorns. Pour in 1.2 litres/2 pints/5 cups cold water to cover the chicken and vegetables and bring to the boil. Reduce the heat, cover and simmer for 4–5 hours, regularly skimming off any scum from the surface. Strain the stock through a sieve lined with kitchen paper and leave to cool.

Beef stock Preheat the oven to 230°C/450°F/Gas 8. Put 1.8kg/4lb beef bones in a roasting pan and roast for 40 minutes, until browned, turning occasionally. Transfer the bones and vegetables to a large pan. Cover with water, add 2 chopped tomatoes and cook as for chicken stock.

Fish stock Put 2 chopped onions, 1.3kg/3lb fish bones and heads, 300ml/^{1}/$_2$ pint/1^1/$_4$ cups white wine, 5 black peppercorns and 1 bouquet garni in a large pan. Pour in 2 litres/3^1/$_2$ pints/9 cups water. Bring to the boil and simmer for 20 minutes, skimming often. Strain the stock.

Vegetable stock Put 900g/2lb chopped vegetables, including onions, leeks, tomatoes, carrots, parsnips and cabbage, in a large pan. Pour in 1.5 litres/2^1/$_2$ pints/6^1/$_4$ cups water. Bring to the boil and simmer for 30 minutes, then strain.

Marinades

These strong-tasting mixes are perfect for adding flavour to meat, poultry, fish and vegetables. Most ingredients should be left to marinate for at least 30 minutes.

Ginger and soy marinade This is perfect for use with chicken and beef. Peel and grate a 2.5cm/1in piece of fresh root ginger and peel and finely chop a large garlic clove. In a small bowl, whisk together 60ml/ 4 tbsp olive oil with 75ml/ 5 tbsp dark soy sauce. Season with freshly ground black pepper and stir in the ginger and garlic.

Rosemary and garlic marinade This is ideal for robust fish, lamb and chicken. Roughly chop the leaves from 3 fresh rosemary sprigs. Finely chop 2 garlic cloves and whisk together with the rosemary, 75ml/5 tbsp olive oil and the juice of 1 lemon.

Lemon grass and lime marinade Use with fish and chicken. Finely chop 1 lemon grass stalk. Whisk together the grated rind and juice of 1 lime with 75ml/5 tbsp olive oil, salt and black pepper and the lemon grass.

Red wine and bay marinade This is ideal for red meat, particularly tougher cuts. Whisk together 150ml/^{1}/$_4$ pint/ ^{2}/$_3$ cup red wine, 1 chopped garlic clove, 2 torn fresh bay leaves and 45ml/3 tbsp olive oil. Season with black pepper.

Below: *Marinades containing red wine are particularly good for tenderizing tougher cuts of meat such as stewing steak.*

Dressings

Freshly made dressings are delicious drizzled over salads but are also tasty served with cooked vegetables and simply cooked fish, meat and poultry. You can make these dressings a few hours in advance and store them in a sealed container in the refrigerator until ready to use. Give them a quick whisk before drizzling over the food.

Honey and wholegrain mustard dressing
Drizzle this sweet, peppery dressing over leafy salads, fish, chicken and red meat dishes or toss with warm new potatoes. Whisk together 15ml/1 tbsp wholegrain mustard, 30ml/2 tbsp white wine vinegar, 15ml/1 tbsp honey and 75ml/5 tbsp extra virgin olive oil and season with salt and ground black pepper.

Orange and tarragon dressing
Serve this fresh, tangy dressing with salads and grilled (broiled) fish. In a small bowl, whisk together the rind and juice of 1 large orange with 45ml/ 3 tbsp olive oil and 15ml/1 tbsp chopped fresh tarragon. Season with salt and plenty of freshly ground black pepper to taste.

Toasted coriander and cumin dressing
Drizzle this warm, spicy dressing over grilled chicken, lamb or beef. Heat a small frying pan and sprinkle in 15ml/1 tbsp each of coriander and cumin seeds. Dry-fry until the seeds release their aromas and start to pop, then crush the seeds using a mortar and pestle. Add 45ml/3 tbsp olive oil, whisk to combine, then leave to infuse for 20 minutes. Season with salt and freshly ground black pepper to taste.

Savoury sauces

Hot and cold savoury sauces lie at the heart of many dishes or can be the finishing touch that makes a meal – tomato sauce tossed with pasta, cheese sauce poured over a vegetable gratin, apple sauce to accompany pork, or a spoonful of mayonnaise with poached salmon. This section covers all the basic sauces: from tomato and pesto sauces to toss with pasta and rich, fruity sauces to serve with meat and poultry to creamy ones such as mayonnaise.

Easy tomato sauce

This versatile sauce can be tossed with pasta, used on a pizza base or served with chicken or fish. Heat 15ml/ 1 tbsp olive oil in a pan, add 1 chopped onion and fry for 3–4 minutes until soft. Add 1 chopped garlic clove and cook for about 1 minute more. Pour in 400g/14oz chopped canned tomatoes and stir in 15ml/1 tbsp tomato purée (paste). Add 30ml/2 tbsp dried oregano and simmer for about 15 minutes, until thickened. Season with salt and pepper.

Mustard cheese sauce

Toss this rich, creamy sauce with pasta, or serve with boiled vegetables or baked white fish. Melt 25g/1oz/2 tbsp butter in a medium pan and stir in 25g/1oz/¹/₄ cup plain (all-purpose) flour. Remove the pan from the heat and stir in 5ml/1 tsp prepared English mustard, then gradually add 200ml/7fl oz/scant 1 cup milk, stirring well to remove any lumps. (If the sauce becomes lumpy, whisk until smooth.) Return the pan to the heat and bring to the boil, stirring constantly. Remove from the heat and stir in 115g/4oz/ 1 cup grated Gruyère or Cheddar cheese. Season to taste with salt and freshly ground black pepper.

Quick satay sauce

Serve this spicy Asian-style sauce with grilled (broiled) chicken, beef or prawns, or toss with freshly cooked egg noodles. Put 30ml/ 2 tbsp crunchy peanut butter in a pan and stir in 150ml/¹/₄ pint/²/₃ cup coconut milk, 45ml/3 tbsp hot water, a pinch of chilli powder and 30ml/2 tbsp light soy sauce. Heat gently and simmer for 1 minute.

Apple sauce Serve with pork. Peel, core and slice 450g/ 1lb cooking apples and place in a pan. Add a splash of water, 15ml/1 tbsp caster (superfine) sugar and a few whole cloves. Cook the apples over a gentle heat, stirring occasionally, until the fruit becomes pulpy.

Quick cranberry sauce Serve with roast chicken or turkey. Put 225g/8oz/2 cups cranberries in a pan with 75g/3oz/scant ¹/₂ cup light muscovado (brown) sugar, 45ml/3 tbsp port and 45ml/3 tbsp orange juice. Bring to the boil, then simmer, uncovered, for 10 minutes, or until the fruit is tender. Stir occasionally to stop it from sticking.

Gooseberry relish Serve this tart relish with oily fish, such as mackerel, or fatty meat such as pork. Put 225g/ 8oz fresh or frozen gooseberries in a pan with 225g/8oz/ generous 1 cup caster (superfine) sugar and 1 star anise. Add a splash of water and a little white wine if desired. Bring to the boil and simmer, uncovered, for 10 minutes, stirring occasionally, until the fruit is soft and pulpy.

Below: Sauces made from tart fruit, such as cranberries, are excellent served with mild or fatty roast poultry and meat.

Traditional pesto This classic Italian sauce is made with basil, garlic, pine nuts and Parmesan cheese but there are many variations. Toss with pasta, stir into mashed potatoes or plain boiled rice, or use to flavour sauces and dressings. Put 50g/2oz fresh basil leaves in a food processor and blend to a paste with 25g/1oz/^{1}/4 cup toasted pine nuts and 2 peeled garlic cloves. With the motor still running, drizzle in 120ml/4fl oz/^{1}/2 cup extra virgin olive oil until the mixture forms a paste. Spoon the pesto into a bowl and stir in 25g/1oz/^{1}/3 cup freshly grated Parmesan cheese. Season to taste with salt and freshly ground black pepper.

Parsley and walnut pesto Put 50g/2oz fresh parsley leaves in a food processor and blend to a paste with 25g/1oz/^{1}/4 cup walnuts and 2 peeled garlic cloves. With the motor still running, drizzle in 120ml/4fl oz/^{1}/2 cup extra virgin olive oil until the mixture forms a paste. Spoon the pesto into a bowl and stir in 25g/1oz/^{1}/3 cup freshly grated Parmesan cheese. Season to taste with salt and freshly ground black pepper.

Gravy

This classic sauce for roast poultry and meat is quick and easy to make. Remove the cooked poultry or meat from the roasting pan, transfer to a serving platter, cover with foil and leave to rest. Spoon off all but about 30ml/2 tbsp of the cooking fat and juices, leaving the sediment in the pan. Place the pan over a low heat and add a splash of white wine for poultry or red wine for meat, stirring in any sediment from the roasting pan. Stir in 30ml/2 tbsp plain (all-purpose) flour and mix to a paste. Remove from the heat and gradually pour in 450ml/^{3}/4 pint/scant 2 cups stock. Return to the heat and stir over a medium heat until the gravy comes to the boil. Simmer for 2–3 minutes, until thickened. Adjust the seasoning and serve.

Rocket pesto Put 50g/2oz fresh rocket (arugula) leaves into a food processor and blend to a paste with 25g/1oz/^{1}/4 cup toasted pine nuts and 2 peeled garlic cloves. With the motor still running, drizzle in 120ml/4fl oz/^{1}/2 cup extra virgin olive oil until the mixture forms a paste. Spoon the pesto into a bowl and stir in 25g/1oz/^{1}/3 cup freshly grated Parmesan cheese. Season to taste with salt and freshly ground black pepper.

Asian-style pesto Try this Asian version of Italian pesto tossed with freshly cooked egg noodles. Put 50g/2oz fresh coriander (cilantro) leaves into a food processor and add 25g/1oz/^{1}/4 cup toasted pine nuts, 2 peeled garlic cloves and 1 roughly chopped, seeded red chilli. Blend until smooth. With the motor still running, drizzle in 120ml/4fl oz/^{1}/2 cup extra virgin olive oil until the mixture forms a paste. Spoon the pesto into a bowl and season to taste with salt and freshly ground black pepper.

Mayonnaise Once you have made your own mayonnaise you will never want to buy it again. Put 2 egg yolks, 10ml/2 tsp lemon juice, 5ml/1 tsp Dijon mustard and some salt and ground black pepper in a food processor. Process briefly to combine, then, with the motor running, drizzle in about 350ml/12fl oz/1^1/2 cups olive oil. The mayonnaise will become thick and pale. Scrape the mayonnaise into a bowl, taste and add more lemon juice and salt and pepper if necessary.

Aioli This classic French garlic mayonnaise is particularly good served with piping hot chips (French fries). Make the mayonnaise as described above, adding 2 peeled garlic cloves to the food processor with the egg yolks.

Lemon mayonnaise This zesty, creamy mayonnnaise complements cold poached fish perfectly. Make the mayonnaise as described above, adding the grated rind of 1 lemon to the food processor with the egg yolks.

Herb mayonnaise Make the plain mayonnaise as described above. Finely chop a handful of fresh herbs, such as basil, coriander (cilantro) and tarragon, then stir into the freshly made mayonnaise.

Savoury dips

These richly flavoured dips are delicious served with tortilla chips, crudités or small savoury crackers, but can also be served as an accompaniment to grilled (broiled) or poached chicken and fish. The creamy dips also make flavourful dressings for salads; you may need to thin them slightly with a squeeze of lemon juice or a little cold water.

Blue cheese dip This sharp, tangy mixture is best served with crunchy crudites. Put 200ml/ 7fl oz/scant 1 cup crème fraîche in a large bowl and add 115g/4oz/1 cup crumbled blue cheese such as stilton. Stir well until the mixture is smooth and creamy. Season with salt and freshly ground black pepper and fold in 30ml/2 tbsp chopped fresh chives.

Sour cream and chive dip This tasty dip is a classic combination and goes particularly well with crudités and savoury crackers. Put 200ml/ 7fl oz/scant 1 cup sour cream in a bowl and add 30ml/2 tbsp snipped fresh chives and a pinch of caster (superfine) sugar. Stir well to mix, then season with salt and plenty of freshly ground black pepper to taste.

Avocado and cumin salsa Serve this spicy Mexican-style salsa with tortilla chips; they're the perfect shape for scooping up the chunky salsa. Peel, stone (pit) and roughly chop 1 ripe avocado. Transfer to a bowl and gently stir in 1 finely chopped fresh red chilli, 15ml/1 tbsp toasted crushed cumin seeds, 1 chopped ripe tomato, the juice of 1 lime, 45ml/3 tbsp olive oil and 30ml/2 tbsp chopped fresh coriander (cilantro). Season and serve immediately.

Sweet sauces

These luscious sauces are perfect spooned over ice cream and can turn a store-bought dessert into an indulgent treat.

Chocolate fudge sauce Put 175ml/6fl oz/³/4 cup double (heavy) cream in a small pan with 45ml/3 tbsp golden (light corn) syrup, 200g/7oz/scant 1 cup light muscovado (brown) sugar and a pinch of salt. Heat gently, stirring, until the sugar has dissolved. Add 75g/3oz/¹/2 cup chopped plain (semisweet) chocolate and stir until melted. Simmer the sauce gently for about 20 minutes, stirring occasionally, until thickened. To keep warm until ready to use, pour into a heatproof bowl, cover and place over a pan of simmering water.

Toffee chocolate sauce Roughly chop 2 Mars bars (chocolate toffee bars) and put them in a pan with 300ml/ ¹/2 pint/1¹/4 cups double (heavy) cream. Stir over a gentle heat until the chocolate bars have melted.

Raspberry and vanilla sauce Scrape the seeds from a vanilla pod into a food processor. Add 200g/7oz/1 cup raspberries and 30ml/2 tbsp icing (confectioners') sugar. Process to a purée, adding a little water to thin, if necessary.

Below: Blended fruit sauces are quick and simple to make and are great drizzled over ice cream and many other desserts.

Flavoured creams

Cream is the perfect accompaniment for any dessert – whether it's a healthy fruit salad, a sumptuous plum tart or a warming baked apple. Flavoured creams are even better and can transform a tasty dessert into a truly luscious one. The ideas below are all incredibly simple and can be prepared in advance and stored in the refrigerator until you are ready to serve.

Rosemary and almond cream This fragrant cream has a lovely texture and is good served with fruit compotes, pies and tarts. Pour 300ml/^{1}/$_2$ pint/ 1^1/$_4$ cups double (heavy) cream into a pan and add 2 fresh rosemary sprigs. Heat the mixture until just about to boil, then remove the pan from the heat and leave the mixture to infuse for 20 minutes. Remove the rosemary from the pan and discard. Pour the cream into a bowl and chill until cold. Whip the cold cream into soft peaks and stir in 30ml/2 tbsp chopped toasted almonds.

Rum and cinnamon cream You can serve this versatile cream with most desserts. It goes particularly well with coffee, chocolate and fruit. Pour 300ml/^{1}/$_2$ pint/1^1/$_4$ cups double (heavy) cream into a pan and add 1 cinnamon stick. Heat the mixture until just about to boil, then remove the pan from the heat and leave to infuse for about 20 minutes. Strain the cream through a fine sieve (strainer) and place in the refrigerator until cold. Whip the cold cream until it stands in soft peaks, then stir in 30ml/2 tbsp rum and 15ml/1 tbsp icing (confectioners') sugar.

Marsala mascarpone This rich, creamy Italian cheese is perfect for serving with grilled (broiled) fruit, tarts and hot desserts. Spoon 200g/7oz/scant 1 cup mascarpone into a large bowl and add 30ml/2 tbsp icing (confectioners') sugar and 45ml/3 tbsp Marsala. Beat the mixture well until smooth and thoroughly combined.

Cardamom cream Warm, spicy cardamom pods make a wonderfully subtle, aromatic cream that is delicious served with fruit salads, compôtes, tarts and pies. It goes particularly well with tropical fruits such as mango. Pour 300ml/ ^{1}/$_2$ pint/1^1/$_4$ cups double (heavy) cream into a pan and add 3 green cardamom pods. Heat the mixture gently until just about to boil, then remove the pan from the heat and leave to infuse for about 20 minutes. Strain the cream through a fine sieve (strainer) and place in the refrigerator until cold. Whip the cold cream until it stands in soft peaks.

Praline cream

1 Put 115g/4oz/^{1}/$_2$ cup sugar and 75ml/5 tbsp water in a small, heavy pan. Stir over a gentle heat until the sugar has dissolved, then boil (not stirring) until golden.

2 Remove from the heat and stir in 50g/2oz/ ^{1}/$_3$ cup whole blanched almonds and tip on to a lightly oiled baking sheet. Leave until hard.

3 Break the hardened nut mixture into smaller pieces and put in a food processor. Process for about 1 minute until finely chopped.

4 In a large bowl, whip 300ml/^{1}/$_2$ pint/1^1/$_4$ cups double (heavy) cream into soft peaks, then stir in the praline and serve immediately.

Making Simple Accompaniments

When you've made a delicious main meal, you need to serve it with equally tasty accompaniments. The following section is full of simple, speedy ideas for fabulous side dishes – from creamy mashed potatoes, fragrant rice and spicy noodles to Italian-style polenta and simple, healthy vegetables.

Mashed potatoes

Potatoes go well with just about any main dish. They can be cooked simply – boiled, steamed, fried or baked – but they are even better mashed with milk and butter to make creamy mashed potatoes. To make even more enticing side dishes, try stirring in different flavourings.

Perfect mashed potatoes Peel 675g/ 1¹/₂lb floury potatoes and cut them into large chunks. Place in a pan of salted boiling water. Return to the boil, then simmer for 15–20 minutes, or until completely tender. Drain the potatoes and return to the pan. Leave over a low heat for a couple of minutes, shaking the pan to drive off any excess moisture. Take the pan off the heat and, using a potato masher, mash the potatoes until smooth. Beat in 45–60ml/3–4 tbsp warm milk and a large knob (pat) of butter, then season with salt and freshly ground black pepper to taste.

Pesto mash This is a simple way to dress up plain mashed potatoes. It gives them real bite and a lovely green-specked appearance. Make mashed potatoes as described above, then stir in 30ml/ 2 tbsp pesto sauce until thoroughly combined.

Mustard mash Make mashed potatoes as above, then stir in 15–30ml/1–2 tbsp wholegrain mustard.

Parmesan and parsley mash Make mashed potatoes as above, then stir in 30ml/2 tbsp freshly grated Parmesan and 15ml/1 tbsp chopped fresh flat leaf parsley.

Apple and thyme mash Serve with pork. Make mashed potatoes as above. Heat 25g/1oz/2 tbsp butter in a pan and add 2 peeled, cored and sliced eating apples. Fry for 4–5 minutes, turning. Roughly mash, then fold into the potatoes, with 15ml/1 tbsp fresh thyme leaves.

Crushed potatoes

This chunky, modern version of mashed potatoes tastes delicious and can be flavoured in different ways.

Crushed potatoes with parsley and lemon Cook 675g/1¹/₂lb new potatoes in salted boiling water for 15–20 minutes, until tender. Drain the potatoes and crush roughly, using a fork. Stir in 30ml/ 2 tbsp extra virgin olive oil, the grated rind and juice of 1 lemon and 30ml/2 tbsp chopped fresh flat leaf parsley. Season with freshly ground black pepper to taste.

Crushed potatoes with garlic and basil Cook 675g/1¹/₂lb new potatoes in a pan of boiling salted water for 15–20 minutes until tender. Drain and crush roughly, using the back of a fork. Stir in 30ml/ 2 tbsp extra virgin olive oil, 2 finely chopped garlic cloves and a handful of torn basil leaves until well combined, then season with ground black pepper to taste.

Crushed potatoes with pine nuts and Parmesan Cook 675g/1¹/₂lb new potatoes in boiling salted water for 15–20 minutes until tender. Drain and crush using a fork. Stir in 30ml/2 tbsp extra virgin olive oil, 30ml/2 tbsp grated Parmesan cheese and 30ml/2 tbsp toasted pine nuts.

Rice

This versatile grain is the staple in many diets around the world. It can be served simply – either boiled or steamed – or can be flavoured or stir-fried with different ingredients to make a tasty, exciting accompaniment to curries, stir-fries, stews and grilled (broiled) meat or fish.

Easy egg-fried rice

Cook 115g/4oz/generous ½ cup long-grain rice in a large pan of boiling water for 10–12 minutes, until tender. Drain well and refresh under cold running water. Spread out on a baking sheet and leave until completely cold. Heat 30ml/2 tbsp sunflower oil in a large frying pan and add 1 finely chopped garlic clove. Cook for 1 minute, then add the rice and stir-fry for 1 minute. Push the rice to the side of the pan and pour 1 beaten egg into the pan. Cook the egg until set, then break up with a fork and stir into the rice. Add a splash of soy sauce, and mix well.

Star anise and cinnamon rice Add 225g/8oz/ generous 1 cup basmati rice to a large pan of salted boiling water. Return to the boil, then reduce the heat and add a cinnamon stick and 2 star anise and simmer gently for 10–15 minutes, until the rice is tender. Drain well and remove the star anise and cinnamon before serving.

Coconut rice Put 225g/8oz/generous 1 cup basmati rice in a pan and pour in a 400ml/14oz can coconut milk. Cover with water, add some salt and bring to the boil. Simmer for 12 minutes, or until the rice is tender. Drain well and serve.

Coriander and spring onion rice

Cook 225g/8oz/generous 1 cup basmati rice in a large pan of salted boiling water for about 12 minutes, or until tender. Drain the rice well and return to the pan. Stir in 3 finely sliced spring onions (scallions) and 1 roughly chopped bunch of fresh coriander (cilantro) until well mixed, then serve immediately.

Noodles

There are many different types of noodles, all of which are quick to cook and make the perfect accompaniment to Chinese- and Asian-style stir-fries and curries. Serve them on their own, or toss them with a few simple flavourings. They can also be served cold as a simple salad.

Spicy peanut noodles

Cook a 250g/9oz packet of egg noodles according to the instructions on the packet, then drain. Heat 15ml/1 tbsp sunflower oil in a wok and add 30ml/2 tbsp crunchy peanut butter. Add a splash of cold water and a dash of soy sauce and stir the mixture over a gentle heat until thoroughly combined. Add the noodles to the pan and toss to coat in the peanut mixture. Sprinkle with fresh coriander (cilantro) to serve.

Chilli and spring onion noodles

Soak 115g/4oz flat rice noodles in cold water for 30 minutes, until softened. Drain well. Heat 30ml/2 tbsp olive oil in a wok or large frying pan. Add 2 finely chopped garlic cloves and 1 seeded and finely chopped red chilli and fry gently for 2 minutes. Slice a bunch of spring onions (scallions) and add to the pan. Cook for a minute or so, then stir in the rice noodles. Season with salt and freshly ground black pepper before serving.

Soy and sesame egg noodles

Cook a 250g/9oz packet of egg noodles according to the instructions on the packet. Drain well and tip the noodles into a large bowl. Drizzle over 30ml/2 tbsp dark soy sauce and 10ml/2 tsp sesame oil, then sprinkle over 15ml/1 tbsp toasted sesame seeds and toss well until thoroughly combined. Serve the noodles hot, or cold as a salad.

Polenta

This classic Italian dish made from cornmeal makes a delicious accompaniment to many dishes and is a useful alternative to the usual potatoes, bread or pasta. It can be served in two ways – either soft, or set and cut into wedges and grilled (broiled) or fried. Soft polenta is rather like mashed potatoes, while the grilled or fried variety has a much firmer texture and lovely crisp shell. Both types can be enjoyed plain, or flavoured with other ingredients such as cheese, herbs and spices. Traditional polenta requires lengthy boiling and constant attention during cooking, but the quick-cook varieties, which are widely available in most large supermarkets, give excellent results and are much simpler and quicker to prepare.

Soft polenta Cook 225g/8oz/2 cups quick-cook polenta according to the instructions on the packet. As soon as the polenta is cooked, stir in about 50g/2oz/¼ cup butter. Season with salt and black pepper to taste, then serve immediately.

Soft polenta with Parmesan and sage Cook 225g/8oz/2 cups quick-cook polenta according to the instructions on the packet. As soon as the polenta is cooked, stir in 115g/4oz/1⅓ cups freshly grated Parmesan cheese and a handful of chopped fresh sage. Stir in a large knob (pat) of butter and season with salt and freshly ground black pepper to taste before serving.

Soft polenta with Cheddar cheese and thyme

Cook 225g/8oz/2 cups quick-cook polenta according to the instructions on the packet. As soon as the polenta is cooked, stir in 50g/2oz/½ cups grated Chedar cheese and 30ml/2 tbsp chopped fresh thyme until thoroughly combined. Stir a large knob (pat) of butter into the cheesy polenta and season with salt and plenty of freshly ground black pepper to taste before serving.

Fried chilli polenta triangles Cook 225g/8oz/2 cups quick-cook polenta according to the instructions on the packet. Stir in 5ml/1 tsp dried chilli flakes, check the seasoning, adding more if necessary, and spread the mixture out on an oiled baking sheet to a thickness of about 1cm/½in. Leave the polenta until cold and completely set, then chill for about 20 minutes. Turn the polenta out on to a board and cut it into large squares, then cut each square into 2 triangles. Heat 30ml/2 tbsp olive oil in a large frying pan. Fry the triangles in the olive oil for 2–3 minutes on each side, until golden, then lift out and briefly drain on kitchen paper before serving.

Grilled polenta with Gorgonzola Cook 225g/8oz/2 cups quick-cook polenta according to the instructions on the packet. Check the seasoning, adding more if necessary, and spread the mixture out on an oiled baking sheet to a thickness of about 1cm/½in. Leave the polenta until cold and completely set, then chill for about 20 minutes. Turn the polenta out on to a board and cut it into large squares, then cut each square into 2 triangles. Pre-heat the grill (broiler) and arrange the polenta triangles on the grill pan. Cook for about 5 minutes, or until golden brown, then turn over and top each triangle with a sliver of Gorgonzola. Cook for a further 5 minutes, or until bubbling.

Below: Wedges of set polenta are great fried and served as an accompaniment to stews, casseroles and other main dishes.

Quick and simple vegetables

Fresh vegetables are an essential part of your everyday diet. They are delicious cooked on their own but they can also be stir-fried with other ingredients. This can be an interesting way of adding flavour and creating colourful, enticing and heathy vegetable dishes.

Stir-fried cabbage with hazelnuts Heat 30ml/2 tbsp sunflower oil in a wok or large frying pan and add 4 roughly chopped rashers (strips) smoked streaky (fatty) bacon. Stir-fry for about 3 minutes, until the bacon starts to turn golden, then add $^1/_2$ shredded green cabbage to the pan. Stir-fry for 3–4 minutes, until the cabbage is just tender. Season with salt and freshly ground black pepper, and stir in 25g/1oz/ $^1/_4$ cup roughly chopped toasted hazelnuts.

Creamy stir-fried Brussels sprouts Heat 15ml/1 tbsp sunflower oil in a wok or large frying pan. Add 1 chopped garlic clove and stir-fry for about 30 seconds. Shred 450g/ 1lb Brussels sprouts and add to the pan. Stir-fry for 3–4 minutes, until just tender. Season with salt and pepper and stir in 30ml/2 tbsp crème fraîche. Warm through for 1 minute before serving.

Honey-fried parsnips and celeriac Peel 250g/ 8oz parsnips and 115g/ 4oz celeriac. Cut both into matchsticks. Heat 30ml/ 2 tbsp olive oil in a wok or large frying pan and add the parsnips and celeriac. Fry over a gentle heat for 6–7 minutes, stirring occasionally, until golden and tender. Season with salt and ground black pepper and stir in 15ml/1 tbsp clear honey. Allow to bubble for 1 minute before serving.

Flavoured breads

Bread makes a simple accompaniment to many meals and is the perfect ready-made side dish when time is short. Look out for part-baked breads that you can finish off in the oven, so you can enjoy the taste of freshly baked bread in a few minutes.

Ciabatta This chewy Italian bread is long and oval in shape and is commonly available in ready-to-bake form. Look out for ciabatta with added sun-dried tomatoes or olives.

Focaccia This flat, dimpled Italian bread is made with olive oil and has a softer texture than ciabatta. It is available plain but is also often flavoured with fresh rosemary and garlic.

Naan Traditionally cooked in a clay oven, this Indian bread is easy to find in supermarkets and makes a tasty accompaniment to curries. It is available plain, and also flavoured with spices.

Chapati This Indian flatbread is less heavy than naan and makes a good alternative. The small, round breads can be a little more difficult to find but are worth searching for.

Above: *Rosemary focaccia has a crumbly texture and is perfect for sandwiches and serving with Italian dishes.*

Planning a Menu

Getting together with friends and family to enjoy good food is one of life's most enjoyable experiences. There's nothing better than inviting friends over to enjoy a leisurely lunch, relaxing dinner or summer barbecue and making sure that everyone has a great time. But just because you are the host, it doesn't mean that you can't enjoy yourself too. Cooking and entertaining should be fun for everybody – including the cook. Try following the suggestions below to ensure your party goes smoothly and that you enjoy the occasion as much as your guests. The key to success is always to plan ahead.

- Make a list of the people you have invited and work out how many you need to cater for. Remember to check if anyone is vegetarian or has special dietary requirements such as an allergy to nuts or dairy products.

- Decide what you are going to make, then make sure you have all the equipment you need. If necessary, buy or borrow the items from a friend. When planning the menu, choose dishes you can cook with confidence and avoid being too adventurous. There's no point in cooking to impress if you can't pull it off.

- Ensure you have enough space in the refrigerator for drinks, ingredients and dishes that need to be chilled. If necessary, have a clear-out and remove any unnecessary items to make space.

- Don't leave shopping for ingredients to the last minute. Buy everything you need the day before. This gives you plenty of time for preparation, and also gives you time to track down ingredients elsewhere if the supermarket or food store is out of stock.

- Try to prepare as much as you can in advance. If some dishes can be made or part-prepared the day before, then it's well worth doing.

- On the day, don't leave everything to the last minute. Prepare in good time, leaving yourself time to relax before your guests arrive.

Healthy breakfast

This healthy breakfast is the perfect way to give your system a boost. It's low in fat, packed with health-giving vitamins and nutrients and offers slow-release energy to keep you going throughout the morning.

Beetroot, ginger and orange juice
This refreshing blend of juices is full of vitamins and nutrients to cleanse and boost the system. Make sure you drink the juice as soon as you've made it because the vitamin content will begin to deplete soon after making.

Zingy papaya, lime and ginger salad
A refreshing fruit salad is the perfect way to start your day. Papaya and ginger are beneficial for the digestion and the tangy flavours of ginger and lime will wake you up with a zing.

Cranachan
The oats in this creamy breakfast dish are packed with slow-release carbohydrates that will sustain you until lunchtime. If you want to be really healthy, use low-fat Greek (US strained plain) yogurt.

Indulgent breakfast

This fabulous combination of dishes is perfect for a lazy weekend breakfast or brunch. You can even prepare the apricot turnovers the night before so you can really take it easy and just enjoy.

Cardamom hot chocolate
This rich, spiced hot chocolate is the perfect way to start a lazy weekend morning. It's particularly good in winter when you want something piping hot.

Apricot turnovers
Make these the night before and keep them in the refrigerator to bake in the morning. If you prefer, you can use rhubarb or raspberry compote in place of apricot.

Smoked salmon and chive omelette
Smoked salmon is a real treat for breakfast and you can buy small packets of smoked salmon quite cheaply. If you don't like fish, try serving Eggs Benedict instead.

Supper for two

For an intimate dinner for two, keep the tone informal. Prepare as much as you can in advance
so that you can relax and enjoy your friend's company when he or she arrives.

Potted shrimps with cayenne pepper
These can be made the day before and kept in the refrigerator – but remember to order fresh shrimps from your fishmonger.

Crème fraîche and coriander chicken
Delicious and quick so your guest will not sit alone while you are cooking!

Green salad
Choose a mixed bag of leaves with plenty of herbs for extra flavour. Whether you dress it or not is up to you.

Coffee Mascarpone creams
These luscious creams can be made ahead and kept in the refrigerator until ready to serve.

Formal entertaining

Although you're taking a more formal approach, it doesn't mean you can't enjoy yourself. To get the party going,
serve a tasty aperitif, such as Quick Bloody Mary, when your guests arrive.

Chicken liver and brandy pâté
This simple appetizer is best made the day before to allow its flavours to develop. Serve with crusty bread or Melba toast.

Sea bass with parsley and lime butter
Remember to order the fish to avoid disappointment and last-minute panic. Ask the fishmonger to fillet and scale it for you.

Green beans with almond and lemon butter
Lightly cook the beans in advance, then warm them through with the almond butter at the last minute.

Crushed potatoes with parsley and lemon

Roast peaches with amaretto
*These peaches make the perfect end to a meal. For the more daring cook, try making passion fruit soufflés.
They need to be made at the last minute, but you can prepare the ramekin dishes in advance.*

Barbecue for 12

When the weather is good, it is fun to go outdoors and cook over the coals. Make everything in advance and keep it in the refrigerator, ready to be cooked on the grill. Serve salads in bowls and let everyone help themselves.

Barbecued sardines with orange and parsley
Ask your fishmonger to get you the freshest sardines possible. Even people who don't think they like sardines will adore these!

Cumin- and coriander-rubbed lamb
Prepare the lamb several hours ahead to let the flavours develop. Let the coals get hot before putting the lamb on the barbecue.

Spring onion flatbreads
These can be made ahead of time if you prefer and served warm or at room temperature.

Roast aubergines with feta and coriander
These are perfect for vegetarian guests but they will also be a hit with meat eaters. You can use different types of cheese such as goat's cheese or halloumi if you prefer.

Potato and caraway seed salad
A potato salad is a barbecue must – caraway seeds give this one a slight edge.

Butter bean, tomato and red onion salad
This is quite a substantial salad, so serve a leafy mix as well. Toss everything together in advance and leave the flavours to develop.

Cuba Libre
Make a big jug with plenty of ice – but remember to offer soft drinks too.

Sunday lunch

This is probably one of the most relaxed and informal meals of the week and is surprisingly easy to make.
Get everyone to help out in the kitchen to make it more relaxing for you.

Roast chicken with black pudding and sage
*Nobody will expect the surprise black pudding stuffing, but it is so delicious they will be back for second helpings.
If you have invited a lot of guests, you will need to roast two chickens.*

Crisp and golden roast potatoes with goose fat and garlic
*Sunday lunch is not Sunday lunch without roast potatoes. Remember to fluff up the outside of the potatoes
when you drain them to get a really crispy result.*

Cheesy creamy leeks
These make a tasty alternative to plain boiled or steamed vegetables. Use sliced large leeks, or whole baby ones.

Plum and almond tart
This impressive tart is easy to make and can be prepared in advance. Serve it warm with generous dollops of clotted cream.

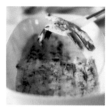

Picnic

Picnics are great fun. Take lots of paper napkins, plates, plastic cups and cutlery. A cool box is invaluable for transporting food and keeping it fresh so if you don't have one, try to borrow one from a friend.

Artichoke and cumin dip
Take this tasty dip in a plastic container and pack breadsticks and raw vegetable crudités for dipping.

Cannellini bean pâté
Serve this as a second dip or spread on wedges of fresh soda bread. Alternatively, use it as a sandwich filling with slices of fresh tomato.

Marinated feta with lemon and oregano
Make this the day before and transport it in a container with a well-fitting lid.

Traditional Irish soda bread
This delicious bread is superb with the feta and the cannellini bean pâté. If you have time, make it on the morning of the picnic.

Pasta with fresh tomatoes and basil
Use small pasta shapes, which are easier to eat. Take a small bottle of olive oil so that you can add an extra drizzle before serving.

Blueberry cake
To make serving easier, cut the cake into wedges before you go, and take along a pot of cream or crème fraîche to serve with it.

Summer al fresco lunch

Al fresco simply means outdoors – and there are few things so enjoyable as eating outside when the sun is shining.

Peperonata
Make this the night before to allow the flavours to develop, and serve with bread and olives.

Fresh crab sandwiches
Little preparation is needed for these glorious sandwiches – but do remember to order the crabs from the fishmonger.

Halloumi and fennel salad
This richly flavoured salad is the perfect partner for crab sandwiches and is ideal if you have the barbecue out.

Watermelon ice
This refreshing, fruity dessert is the perfect way to round off a summer lunch.

Breakfasts and Brunches

NO ONE WANTS THE BOTHER OF LOTS OF INGREDIENTS
AND LENGTHY PREPARATION FOR THEIR FIRST MEAL OF
THE DAY. THIS COLLECTION OF WONDERFULLY SIMPLE
YET DELICIOUS DISHES HAS BEEN CREATED WITH THAT
IN MIND. WHETHER YOU WANT A HEALTHY, VITAMIN-
PACKED FRUIT SALAD FOR BREAKFAST OR AN
INDULGENT SERVING OF EGGS BENEDICT FOR A LAZY
WEEKEND BRUNCH, YOU'RE SURE TO FIND THE PERFECT
RECIPE TO SET YOU UP FOR THE DAY.

Zingy Papaya, Lime and Ginger Salad

This refreshing, fruity salad makes a lovely light breakfast, perfect for the summer months. Choose really ripe, fragrant papayas for the best flavour.

SERVES FOUR

1 Cut the papaya in half lengthways and scoop out the seeds, using a teaspoon. Using a sharp knife, cut the flesh into thin slices and arrange on a platter.

2 Squeeze the lime juice over the papaya and sprinkle with the sliced stem ginger. Serve immediately.

2 large ripe papayas

juice of 1 fresh lime

2 pieces preserved stem ginger, finely sliced

VARIATION

This refreshing fruit salad is delicious made with other tropical fruit. Try using 2 ripe peeled stoned mangoes in place of the papayas.

Cantaloupe Melon
with Grilled Strawberries

If strawberries are slightly underripe, sprinkling them with a little sugar and grilling them will help bring out their flavour.

SERVES FOUR

1 Preheat the grill (broiler) to high. Hull the strawberries and cut them in half. Arrange the fruit in a single layer, cut side up, on a baking sheet or in an ovenproof dish and dust with the icing sugar.

2 Grill (broil) the strawberries for 4–5 minutes, or until the sugar starts to bubble and turn golden.

3 Meanwhile, scoop out the seeds from the half melon using a spoon. Using a sharp knife, remove the skin, then cut the flesh into wedges and arrange on a serving plate with the grilled strawberries. Serve immediately.

115g/4oz/1 cup strawberries

15ml/1 tbsp icing (confectioners') sugar

$^1/_2$ cantaloupe melon

Crunchy Oat Cereal

Serve this tasty crunchy cereal simply with milk or, for a real treat, with yogurt and fresh fruit such as raspberries or blueberries.

SERVES SIX

1 Preheat oven to 160°C/325°F/Gas 3. Mix all the ingredients together and spread on to a large baking tray.

2 Bake for 30–35 minutes, or until golden and crunchy. Leave to cool, then break up into clumps and serve.

200g/7oz/1³/₄ cups jumbo rolled oats

150g/5oz/1¹/₄ cups pecan nuts, roughly chopped

90ml/6 tbsp maple syrup

FROM THE STORECUPBOARD

75g/3oz/6 tbsp butter, melted

COOK'S TIPS
• This crunchy oat cereal will keep in an airtight container for up to two weeks. Store in a cool, dry place.
• You can use other types of nuts if you prefer. Try roughly chopped almonds or hazelnuts instead of pecan nuts, or use a mixture.

Cranachan

This lovely, nutritious breakfast dish is a traditional Scottish recipe, and is delicious served with a generous drizzle of heather honey. It is also absolutely wonderful served with fresh blueberries or blackberries in place of the raspberries.

SERVES FOUR

1 Preheat the grill (broiler) to high. Spread the oat cereal on a baking sheet and place under the hot grill for 3–4 minutes, stirring regularly. Set aside to cool.

2 When the cereal has cooled completely, fold it into the Greek yogurt, then gently fold in 200g/7oz/generous 1 cup of the raspberries, being careful not to crush the berries too much.

3 Spoon the yogurt mixture into four serving glasses or dishes, top with the remaining raspberries and serve immediately.

75g/3oz crunchy oat cereal

600ml/1 pint/2¹/₂ cups Greek (strained plain) yogurt

250g/9oz/1¹/₃ cups raspberries

Porridge

One of the oldest breakfast foods, porridge remains a favourite way to start the day, especially during winter. Brown sugar or honey, cream and a tot of whiskey are treats added for weekend breakfasts and to spoil guests.

SERVES FOUR

1 litre/1³/₄ pints/4 cups water

115g/4oz/1 cup pinhead oatmeal

FROM THE STORECUPBOARD

good pinch of salt

1 Put the water, pinhead oatmeal and salt into a heavy pan and bring to the boil over a medium heat, stirring with a wooden spatula. When the porridge is smooth and beginning to thicken, reduce the heat to a simmer.

2 Cook gently for about 25 minutes, stirring occasionally, until the oatmeal is cooked and the consistency smooth.

3 Serve hot with cold milk and extra salt, if required.

VARIATION

Modern rolled oats can be used, in the proportion 115g/ 4oz/1 cup rolled oats to 750ml/ 1¹/₄ pints/3 cups water, plus a sprinkling of salt. This cooks more quickly than pinhead oatmeal. Simmer, stirring to prevent sticking, for about 5 minutes. Either type of oatmeal can be left to cook overnight in the slow oven of a range.

Eggy Bread Panettone

Thickly sliced stale white bread is usually used for eggy bread, but the slightly dry texture of panettone makes a great alternative. Serve with a selection of fresh summer fruits such as strawberries, raspberries and blackcurrants.

SERVES FOUR

2 large (US extra large) eggs

4 large panettone slices

30ml/2 tbsp caster (superfine) sugar

FROM THE STORECUPBOARD

50g/2oz/¹/₄ cup butter or 30ml/2 tbsp sunflower oil

1 Break the eggs into a bowl and beat with a fork, then tip them into a shallow dish. Dip the panettone slices in the beaten egg, turning them to coat evenly.

2 Heat the butter or oil in a large non-stick frying pan and add the panettone slices. (You will probably have to do this in batches, depending on the size of the pan.) Fry the panettone slices over a medium heat for 2–3 minutes on each side, until golden brown.

3 Remove the panettone slices from the pan and drain on kitchen paper. Cut the slices in half diagonally and dust with the sugar. Serve immediately.

Chocolate Brioche Sandwiches

This luxury breakfast sandwich is a bit of a twist on the classic *pain au chocolat* and beats a boring slice of toast any day. The pale green pistachio nuts work really well with the chocolate spread, adding a satisfying crunch as well as a lovely contrast in colour.

SERVES FOUR

1 Toast the brioche slices until golden on both sides. Spread four of the slices thickly with the chocolate spread and sprinkle over the chopped pistachio nuts in an even layer.

2 Place the remaining brioche slices on top of the chocolate and nuts and press down gently. Using a sharp knife, cut the sandwiches in half diagonally and serve immediately.

8 thick brioche bread slices

120ml/8 tbsp chocolate spread

30ml/2 tbsp shelled pistachio nuts, finely chopped

COOK'S TIP
Brioche is a classic butter-enriched bread from France. It has a wonderful golden colour and slightly sweet taste. It is available in most supermarkets but you can use ordinary white bread if you can't get hold of brioche. Use an uncut loaf rather than a pre-sliced one so that you can cut thick slices.

Roast Bananas with Greek Yogurt and Honey

Roasting bananas like this brings out their natural sweetness. If you are watching the calories, use low-fat Greek yogurt and omit the nuts. Use ripe bananas for maximum flavour. You can also cook bananas in this way over a barbecue and serve them as a simple barbecue dessert drizzled with a little honey.

SERVES FOUR

2 ripe bananas, peeled

500ml/17fl oz/2¹/₄ cups Greek (US strained plain) yogurt with honey

30ml/2 tbsp toasted hazelnuts, roughly chopped

1 Preheat the oven to 200°C/400°F Gas 6. Wrap the bananas in foil and bake for 20 minutes. Leave the bananas to cool completely, then unwrap, place in a small bowl and mash roughly with a fork.

2 Pour the yogurt into a large bowl, add the mashed bananas and gently fold them into the yogurt. Sprinkle with the hazelnuts and serve.

Apricot Turnovers

These sweet and succulent pastries are delicious served with a big cup of milky coffee for a late breakfast or mid-morning treat.

SERVES FOUR

1 Preheat the oven to 190°C/375°F/Gas 5. Roll out the pastry on a lightly floured surface to a 25cm/10in square. Using a sharp knife, cut the pastry into four 13cm/5in squares.

2 Place a tablespoon of the apricot conserve in the middle of each square of pastry. Using a pastry brush, brush the edges of the pastry with a little cold water and fold each square over to form a triangle. Gently press the edges together to seal.

3 Carefully transfer the turnovers to a baking sheet and bake for 15–20 minutes, or until risen and golden. Using a metal spatula, remove the pastries to a wire rack to cool, then dust generously with icing sugar and serve.

225g/8oz ready-made puff pastry, thawed if frozen

60ml/4 tbsp apricot conserve

30ml/2 tbsp icing (confectioners') sugar

Warm Pancakes
with Caramelized Pears

If you can find them, use Williams pears for this recipe because they are juicier than most other varieties. For a really indulgent breakfast, top with a generous spoonful of crème fraîche or fromage frais.

SERVES FOUR

8 ready-made pancakes

4 ripe pears, peeled, cored and thickly sliced

30ml/2 tbsp light muscovado (brown) sugar

FROM THE STORECUPBOARD

50g/2oz/¹/₄ cup butter

1 Preheat the oven to 150°C/330°F/Gas 2. Tightly wrap the pancakes in foil and place in the oven to warm through.

2 Meanwhile, heat the butter in a large frying pan and add the pears. Fry for 2–3 minutes, until the undersides are golden. Turn the pears over and sprinkle with sugar. Cook for a further 2–3 minutes, or until the sugar dissolves and the pan juices become sticky.

3 Remove the pancakes from the oven and take them out of the foil. Divide the pears among the pancakes, placing them in one quarter. Fold each pancake in half over the filling, then into quarters and place two folded pancakes on each plate. Drizzle over any remaining juices and serve immediately.

Smoked Salmon and Chive Omelette

The addition of a generous portion of chopped smoked salmon gives a really luxurious finish to this simple, classic dish. You can use this omelette recipe as the basis of endless variations. Simply replace the salmon and chives with other ingredients such as chopped ham and parsley or grated Cheddar and torn basil leaves.

SERVES TWO

1 Beat the eggs until just combined, then stir in the chives and season with salt and pepper.

2 Heat the butter in a medium-sized frying pan until foamy. Pour in the eggs and cook over a medium heat for 3–4 minutes, drawing the cooked egg from around the edge into the centre of the pan from time to time.

3 At this stage, you can either leave the top of the omelette slightly soft or finish it off under the grill (broiler), depending on how you like your omelette. Top with the smoked salmon, fold the omelette over and cut in half to serve.

4 eggs

15ml/1 tbsp chopped fresh chives

50g/2oz smoked salmon, roughly chopped

FROM THE STORECUPBOARD

knob (pat) of butter

salt and ground black pepper

Quick Kedgeree

Kedgeree is a rice, lentil and onion dish that originally came from India. Fish and eggs were added by the British to make the breakfast dish we know and love today. A garnish of fresh coriander (cilantro) leaves adds extra flavour and colour.

SERVES FOUR

175g/6oz undyed smoked haddock fillet

4 eggs

2 x 250g/9oz packets microwave pilau rice

FROM THE STORECUPBOARD

salt and ground black pepper

1 Preheat the grill (broiler) to medium. Place the smoked haddock on a baking sheet and grill for about 10 minutes, or until cooked through.

2 Meanwhile, place the eggs in a pan of cold water and bring to the boil. Cook for 6–7 minutes, then drain and place under cold running water until cool enough to handle.

3 While the eggs and haddock are cooking, cook the rice according to the instructions on the packet. Shell the eggs and cut into halves or quarters. Flake the fish and gently mix into the rice, with the eggs, taking care not to break up the eggs too much. Spoon on to serving plates, and serve immediately.

Jugged Kippers

The demand for naturally smoked kippers is ever increasing. They are most popular for breakfast, served with scrambled eggs, but they're also good at an old-fashioned high tea. Jugging is the same as poaching, except that the only equipment needed is a jug and kettle. Serve with freshly made bread or toast and a wedge of lemon, if you like.

SERVES FOUR

4 kippers (smoked herrings), preferably naturally smoked, whole or filleted

FROM THE STORECUPBOARD

25g/1oz/2 tbsp butter

ground black pepper

1 Select a jug (pitcher) tall enough for the kippers to be immersed when the water is added. If the heads are still on, remove them.

2 Put the fish into the jug, tails up, and then cover them with boiling water. Leave for about 5 minutes, until tender.

3 Drain well and serve on warmed plates with a knob (pat) of butter and a little black pepper on each kipper.

Scotch Pancakes with Bacon and Maple Syrup

Also known as drop scones, Scotch pancakes are available in most supermarkets. Raisin varieties also work well in this recipe.

SERVES FOUR

8 ready-made Scotch pancakes

8 dry-cured smoked back (lean) bacon rashers (strips)

30ml/2 tbsp maple syrup

1 Preheat the oven to 150°C/330°F/Gas 2. Wrap the pancakes in a sheet of foil and place them in the oven to warm through.

2 Meanwhile, preheat the grill (broiler) and arrange the bacon on a grill pan. Grill (broil) for 3–4 minutes on each side, until crisp.

3 Divide the warmed pancakes between four warmed serving plates and top with the grilled bacon rashers. Drizzle with the maple syrup and serve immediately.

Croque-monsieur

This classic French toastie is delicious served at any time of day, but with a foaming cup of milky coffee it makes a particularly enjoyable brunch dish. Gruyère is traditionally used, but you could use mild Cheddar instead. Prosciutto and Gorgonzola, served with a smear of mustard, also make a fabulous alternative to the classic ham and Gruyère combination.

SERVES FOUR

8 white bread slices

4 large lean ham slices

175g/6oz Gruyère cheese, thinly sliced

FROM THE STORECUPBOARD

a little softened butter

ground black pepper

1 Preheat the grill (broiler). Arrange the bread on the grill rack and toast four slices on both sides and the other four slices on one side only.

2 Butter the slices of bread that have been toasted on both sides and top with the ham, then the cheese, and season with plenty of ground black pepper.

3 Lay the remaining, half-toasted bread slices on top of the cheese, with the untoasted side uppermost. Grill the tops of the sandwiches until golden brown, then cut them in half using a sharp knife and serve immediately.

Eggs Benedict

Use a good quality bought hollandaise sauce for this recipe because it will make all the difference to the end result. Eggs Benedict are delicious served on half a toasted English muffin. Always use organic eggs – they have a superior flavour to eggs from battery hens.

SERVES FOUR

1 Pour cold water into a medium pan to a depth of about 5cm/2in and bring to a gentle simmer. Crack two eggs into the pan and bring back to the simmer. Simmer for 2–3 minutes, until the white is set, but the yolk is still soft.

2 Meanwhile, arrange the ham slices on four serving plates (or on top of four toasted, buttered muffin halves if using). Remove the eggs from the pan using a slotted spoon and place on top of the ham on two of the plates. Cook the remaining eggs in the same way.

3 Spoon the hollandaise sauce over the eggs, sprinkle with salt and pepper and serve immediately.

4 large (US extra large) eggs

4 lean ham slices

60ml/4 tbsp hollandaise sauce

FROM THE STORECUPBOARD

salt and ground black pepper

VARIATION If you prefer eggs cooked all the way through, scramble them instead of poaching. Then spoon over the ham and top with hollandaise sauce as before.

Appetizers

WHEN A SNACK IS CALLED FOR, OR A LITTLE
SOMETHING TO WHET THE APPETITE BEFORE A MAIN
MEAL, YOU WON'T FIND ANYTHING SIMPLER OR MORE
TASTY THAN THE FOLLOWING RECIPES. FROM
MOUTHWATERING DIPS TO DELICIOUS LITTLE EGGS
MIMOSA, THIS CHAPTER IS PACKED WITH SIMPLE, FUSS-
FREE IDEAS THAT YOU WON'T BE ABLE TO RESIST.

Hummus

This classic Middle Eastern chickpea dip is flavoured with garlic and tahini (sesame seed paste).
A little ground cumin can also be added, and olive oil can be stirred in to enrich the hummus, if you like.
It is delicious served with wedges of toasted pitta bread or crudités.

SERVES FOUR TO SIX

1 Using a potato masher or fork, coarsely mash the chickpeas in a mixing bowl. If you like a smoother purée, process the chickpeas in a food processor or blender until a smooth paste is formed.

2 Mix the tahini into the bowl of chickpeas, then stir in the chopped garlic cloves and lemon juice. Season to taste with salt and freshly ground black pepper, and if needed, add a little water. Serve the hummus at room temperature.

400g/14oz can chickpeas, drained

60ml/4 tbsp tahini

2–3 garlic cloves, chopped

juice of ¹/₂–1 lemon

FROM THE
STORECUPBOARD

salt and ground black pepper

Baba Ghanoush

Adjust the amount of aubergine, garlic and lemon juice in this richly flavoured Middle Eastern aubergine dip depending on how creamy, garlicky or tart you want it to be. The dip can served with a garnish of chopped fresh coriander leaves, olives or pickled cucumbers. Hot pepper sauce or a little ground coriander can be added, too.

1 large or 2 medium aubergines (eggplant)

2–4 garlic cloves, chopped

90–150ml/6–10 tbsp tahini

juice of 1 lemon, or to taste

SERVES TWO TO FOUR

1 Place the aubergine(s) directly over the flame of a gas stove or on the coals of a barbecue. Turn the aubergine(s) fairly frequently until deflated and the skin is evenly charred. Remove from the heat with tongs. Alternatively, place under a hot grill (broiler), turning frequently, until charred.

2 Put the aubergine(s) in a plastic bag and seal the top tightly, or place in a bowl and cover with crumpled kitchen paper. Leave to cool for 30–60 minutes.

3 Peel off the blackened skin from the aubergine(s), reserving the juices. Chop the aubergine flesh, either by hand for a coarse texture or in a food processor for a smooth purée. Put the aubergine in a bowl and stir in the reserved juices.

4 Add the garlic and tahini to the aubergine and stir until smooth. Stir in the lemon juice. If the mixture becomes too thick, add 15–30ml/1–2 tbsp water. Spoon into a serving bowl. Serve at room temperature.

Cannellini Bean Pâté

Serve this simple pâté with melba toast or toasted wholegrain bread as an appetizer or snack. A dusting of paprika gives an extra kick. You can also use other types of canned beans such as kidney beans.

SERVES FOUR

1 Put the cannellini beans in a food processor with the olive oil, and process to a chunky paste.

2 Transfer to a bowl and stir in the cheese, parsley and some salt and pepper. Spoon into a serving dish and sprinkle a little paprika on top, if you like.

2 x 400g/14oz cans cannellini beans, drained and rinsed

50g/2oz mature Cheddar cheese, finely grated

30ml/2 tbsp chopped fresh parsley

FROM THE STORECUPBOARD

45ml/3 tbsp olive oil

salt and ground black pepper

COOK'S TIP

Canned beans are usually in a sugar, salt and water solution so always drain and rinse them thoroughly before use – otherwise the finished pâté may be rather too salty.

Chicken Liver and Brandy Pâté

This pâté really could not be simpler to make, and tastes so much better than anything you can buy ready-made in the supermarkets. Serve with crispy Melba toast for an elegant appetizer.

SERVES FOUR

1 Heat the butter in a large frying pan until foamy. Add the chicken livers and cook over a medium heat for 3–4 minutes, or until browned and cooked through.

2 Add the brandy and allow to bubble for a few minutes. Let the mixture cool slightly, then tip into a food processor with the cream and some salt and pepper.

3 Process the mixture until smooth and spoon into ramekin dishes. Level the surface and chill overnight to set. Serve garnished with sprigs of parsley to add a little colour.

350g/12oz chicken livers, trimmed and roughly chopped

30ml/2 tbsp brandy

30ml/2 tbsp double (heavy) cream

FROM THE STORECUPBOARD

50g/2oz/¼ cup butter

salt and ground black pepper

Peperonata

This richly flavoured spicy tomato and sweet red pepper dip is delicious served with crisp Italian-style bread sticks – enjoy it with drinks or as a snack while watching television. It also makes a tasty relish served with grilled chicken and fish dishes. It is delicious served either hot, cold or at room temperature and can be stored in the refrigerator for several days.

SERVES FOUR

1 Heat the oil in a large pan over a low heat and add the sliced peppers. Cook very gently, stirring occasionally for 3–4 minutes.

2 Add the chilli flakes to the pan and cook for 1 minute, then pour in the tomatoes and season. Cook gently for 50 minutes to 1 hour, stirring occasionally.

COOK'S TIP
Long, slow cooking helps to bring out the sweetness of the peppers and tomatoes, so don't be tempted to cheat on the cooking time by cooking over a higher heat.

2 large red (bell) peppers, halved, seeded and sliced

pinch dried chilli flakes

400g/14oz can pomodorino tomatoes

FROM THE STORECUPBOARD

60ml/4 tbsp garlic-infused olive oil

salt and ground black pepper

Artichoke and Cumin Dip

This dip is so easy to make and is unbelievably tasty. Serve with olives, hummus and wedges of pitta bread to make a summery snack selection. Grilled artichokes bottled in oil have a fabulous flavour and can be used instead of canned artichokes. You can also vary the flavourings – try adding chilli powder in place of the cumin and add a handful of basil leaves to the artichokes before blending.

SERVES FOUR

1 Put the artichoke hearts in a food processor with the garlic and ground cumin, and a generous drizzle of olive oil. Process to a smooth purée and season with plenty of salt and ground black pepper to taste.

2 Spoon the purée into a serving bowl and serve with an extra drizzle of olive oil swirled on the top and slices of warm pitta bread for dipping.

2 x 400g/14oz cans artichoke hearts, drained

2 garlic cloves, peeled

2.5ml/½ tsp ground cumin

FROM THE STORECUPBOARD

olive oil

salt and ground black pepper

Sweet and Salty Vegetable Crisps

This delightfully simple snack is perfect to serve with pre-dinner drinks as an informal appetizer. Serve them with a bowl of aioli or a creamy dip such as hummus or taramasalata, and use the crisps to scoop it up. You can cook other sweet root vegetables, such as carrots and sweet potatoes, in the same way. Make a pretty, appetizing snack by making several different types of vegetable crisps, then pile them together in a bowl.

SERVES FOUR

1 Peel the beetroot and, using a mandolin or a vegetable peeler, cut it into very thin slices. Lay the slices on kitchen paper and sprinkle them with sugar and fine salt.

2 Heat 5cm/2in oil in a pan, until a bread cube dropped into the pan turns golden in 1 minute. Cook the slices, in batches, until they float to the surface and turn golden at the edge. Drain on kitchen paper and sprinkle with salt when cool.

1 small fresh beetroot (beet)

caster (superfine) sugar

FROM THE STORECUPBOARD

salt, for sprinkling

olive oil, for frying

Sizzling Prawns

These richly flavoured prawns (shrimp) are a classic Spanish tapas dish, but they also make a perfect appetizer. Traditionally they are brought to the table in little individual earthenware dishes, sizzling frantically in the hot oil with garlic. The addition of fiery chillies gives them an additional kick, but if you prefer a milder appetizer, simply omit the chillies.

SERVES FOUR

1 Split the chillies lengthways and discard the seeds. (Wash your hands with soap and water immediately.)

2 Heat the olive oil in a large frying pan and stir-fry the garlic and chillies for 1 minute, until the garlic begins to turn brown.

3 Add the whole prawns and stir-fry for 3–4 minutes, coating them well with the flavoured oil.

4 Remove the pan from the heat and divide the prawns among four dishes. Spoon over the flavoured oil and serve immediately. (Remember to provide a plate for the heads and shells, plus plenty of napkins.)

1–2 dried chillies (to taste)

3 garlic cloves, finely chopped

16 large raw prawns (shrimp), in the shell

FROM THE STORECUPBOARD

60ml/4 tbsp olive oil

Potted Shrimps
with Cayenne Pepper

Cayenne pepper adds a hint of spiciness to this traditional English seaside favourite. Serve with crusty bread or brown toast. The potted shrimps can be stored in the refrigerator for up to 3 days.

SERVES SIX

2 blades of mace

a pinch of cayenne pepper

600ml/1 pint/2¹/₂ cups peeled brown shrimps

FROM THE STORECUPBOARD

115g/4oz/¹/₂ cup butter, plus extra for greasing

90ml/6 tbsp clarified butter

1 Put the butter, mace and cayenne pepper into a small pan and warm over a gentle heat until melted.

2 Add the peeled shrimps and stir gently until warmed through. Butter six small ramekin dishes.

3 Remove the mace from the shrimp mixture and divide the shrimps and butter evenly between the six ramekins, patting down gently with the back of a spoon. Chill until set.

4 When the butter in the shrimp mixture has set, put the clarified butter in a small pan and melt over a gentle heat. Pour a layer of clarified butter over the top of each ramekin to cover the shrimps and chill again to set.

Marinated Feta
with Lemon and Oregano

The longer the cheese is left to marinate, the better the flavour will be. Serve with tomato and red onion salad and some crisp flatbreads.

SERVES FOUR

200g/7oz Greek feta cheese

1 lemon, cut into wedges

a small handful of fresh oregano sprigs

FROM THE STORECUPBOARD

300ml/¹/₂ pint/1¹/₄ cups extra virgin olive oil

1 Drain the feta and pat dry with kitchen paper. Cut it into cubes and arrange in a non-metallic bowl or dish with the lemon wedges and oregano sprigs.

2 Pour the olive oil over the top and cover with clear film (plastic wrap). Chill for at least 3 hours, then serve with a selection of flat breads and salads.

COOK'S TIP *Feta cheese is a salty, crumbly Greek cheese that is usually bought packed in brine. Use a good quality brand and drain thoroughly before using.*

Mushroom Caviar

The name caviar refers to the dark colour and texture of this dish of chopped mushrooms. Serve the mushroom mixture in individual serving dishes with toasted rye bread rubbed with cut garlic cloves, to accompany. Chopped hard-boiled egg, spring onion and parsley, the traditional garnishes for caviar, can be added as a garnish.

SERVES FOUR

1 Heat the oil in a large pan, add the mushrooms, shallots and garlic, and cook, stirring occasionally, until browned. Season with salt, then continue cooking until the mushrooms give up their liquor.

2 Continue cooking, stirring frequently, until the liquor has evaporated and the mushrooms are brown and dry.

3 Put the mixture in a food processor or blender and process briefly until a chunky paste is formed. Spoon the mushroom caviar into dishes and serve.

450g/1lb mushrooms, coarsely chopped

5–10 shallots, chopped

4 garlic cloves, chopped

FROM THE STORECUPBOARD

45ml/3 tbsp olive or vegetable oil

EXTRAS

For a rich wild mushroom caviar, soak 10–15g/¼–½oz dried porcini in about 120ml/4fl oz/ ½ cup water for about 30 minutes. Add the porcini and their soaking liquid to the browned mushrooms in step 2. Continue as in the recipe. Serve with wedges of lemon, for their tangy juice.

Brandade of Salt Cod

There are many versions of this creamy French salt cod purée: some contain mashed potatoes, others truffles. Serve the brandade with warmed crispbread or crusty bread for a tasty appetizer, or for a light lunch serve the brandade and bread with a tomato and basil salad. You can omit the garlic from the brandade, if you prefer, and serve toasted slices of French bread rubbed with garlic instead.

SERVES SIX

200g/7oz salt cod

250ml/8fl oz/1 cup
extra virgin olive oil

4 garlic cloves, crushed

250ml/8fl oz/1 cup
double (heavy) or
whipping cream

1 Soak the fish in cold water for 24 hours, changing the water frequently. Drain the fish well. Cut the fish into pieces, place in a shallow pan and pour in enough cold water to cover. Heat the water until it is simmering and poach the fish for 8 minutes, until it is just cooked. Drain the fish, then remove the skin and bones.

2 Combine the extra virgin olive oil and crushed garlic cloves in a small pan and heat gently. In another pan, heat the double cream until it just starts to simmer.

3 Put the cod into a food processor, process it briefly, then gradually add alternate amounts of the garlic-flavoured olive oil and cream, while continuing to process the mixture. The aim is to create a purée with the consistency of mashed potato.

4 Season to taste with freshly ground black pepper, then scoop the brandade into a serving bowl or on to individual serving plates and serve with crispbread or crusty bread.

Chopped Egg and Onions

This dish is one of the oldest dishes in Jewish culinary history. It is delicious served sprinkled with chopped parsley and onion rings on crackers, piled on toast, or used as a sandwich or bagel filling. Serve chopped egg and onion as part of a buffet with a selection of dips and toppings.

SERVES FOUR TO SIX

1 Put the eggs in a large pan and cover with cold water. Bring the water to the boil and when it boils, reduce the heat and simmer over a low heat for 10 minutes.

2 Hold the boiled eggs under cold running water (if too hot to handle, place the eggs in a strainer and hold under the running water). When cool, remove the shells from the eggs and discard. Dry the eggs and chop coarsely.

3 Place the chopped eggs in a large bowl, add the onions, season generously with salt and black pepper and mix well. Add enough mayonnaise or chicken fat to bind the mixture together. Stir in the mustard, if using, and chill before serving.

8–10 eggs

6–8 spring onions (scallions) and/or 1 yellow or white onion, very finely chopped, plus extra to garnish

60–90ml/4–6 tbsp mayonnaise or rendered chicken fat

mild French wholegrain mustard, to taste (optional if using mayonnaise)

FROM THE STORECUPBOARD

salt and ground black pepper

Israeli Cheese with Green Olives

In Israel, mild white cheeses spiked with seasonings, such as this one that is flavoured with piquant green olives, are served with drinks and little crackers or toast. It is also very good served for brunch – spread generously on chunks of fresh, crusty bread or bagels.

SERVES FOUR

175–200g/6–7oz soft white (farmer's) cheese

65g/2½ oz feta cheese, preferably sheep's milk, lightly crumbled

20–30 pitted green olives, some chopped, the rest halved or quartered

2–3 large pinches of fresh thyme, plus extra to garnish

1 Place the soft white cheese in a mixing bowl and stir with the back of a spoon or a fork until soft and smooth. Add the crumbled feta cheese and stir the two cheeses together until they are thoroughly combined.

2 Add the chopped, halved and quartered olives and the pinches of fresh thyme to the cheese mixture and mix thoroughly.

3 Spoon the mixture into a bowl, sprinkle with thyme and serve with crackers, toast, chunks of bread or bagels.

Bacon-rolled Enokitake Mushrooms

The Japanese name for this dish is *Obimaki enoki*: an *obi* (belt or sash) is made from bacon and wrapped around enokitake mushrooms before they are grilled. The strong, smoky flavour of the bacon complements the subtle flavour of mushrooms. Small heaps of ground white pepper can be offered with these savouries, if you like.

450g/1lb fresh enokitake mushrooms

6 rindless smoked streaky (fatty) bacon rashers (strips)

4 lemon wedges

SERVES FOUR

1 Cut off the root part of each enokitake cluster 2cm/¾in from the end. Do not separate the stems. Cut the bacon rashers in half lengthways.

2 Divide the enokitake into 12 equal bunches. Take one bunch, then place the middle of the enokitake near the edge of one bacon rasher, with 2.5–4cm/1–1½in of enokitake protruding at each end.

3 Carefully roll up the bunch of enokitake in the bacon. Tuck any straying short stems into the bacon and slide the bacon slightly upwards at each roll to cover about 4cm/1½in of the enokitake. Secure the end of the bacon roll with a cocktail stick (toothpick). Repeat using the remaining enokitake and bacon to make 11 more rolls.

4 Preheat the grill (broiler) to high. Place the enokitake rolls on an oiled wire rack. Grill (broil) both sides until the bacon is crisp and the enokitake start to char. This takes 10–13 minutes.

5 Remove the enokitake rolls and place on a board. Using a fork and knife, chop each roll in half in the middle of the bacon belt. Arrange the top part of the enokitake roll standing upright, the bottom part lying down next to it. Add a wedge of lemon to each portion and serve.

Walnut and Goat's Cheese Bruschetta

The combination of toasted walnuts and melting goat's cheese is lovely in this simple appetizer, served with a pile of salad leaves. Toasting the walnuts helps to enhance their flavour. Walnut bread is readily available in most large supermarkets and makes an interesting alternative to ordinary crusty bread, although this can be used if walnut bread is unavailable.

SERVES FOUR

1 Preheat the grill (broiler). Lightly toast the walnut pieces, then remove and set aside. Put the walnut bread on a foil-lined grill rack and toast on one side. Turn the slices over and drizzle each with 15ml/1 tbsp of the French dressing.

2 Cut the goat's cheese into twelve slices and place three on each piece of bread. Grill (broil) for about 3 minutes, until the cheese is melting and beginning to brown.

3 Transfer the bruschetta to serving plates, sprinkle with the toasted walnuts and drizzle with the remaining French dressing. Serve the bruschetta immediately with salad leaves.

50g/2oz/¹/₂ cup walnut pieces

4 thick slices walnut bread

120ml/4fl oz/¹/₂ cup French dressing

200g/7oz chèvre or other semi-soft goat's cheese

COOK'S TIP Use walnut bread slices from a slender loaf, so that the portions are not too wide. If you can buy only a large loaf, cut the slices in half to make neat, chunky pieces.

Party Snacks

WHEN YOU WANT LITTLE PARTY SNACKS WITH THE
MINIMUM OF FUSS, THINK SIMPLICITY. FROM
MOUTHWATERING CANAPES SUCH AS BLINIS WITH
CAVIAR AND CRÈME FRAÎCHE TO MOREISH SALT COD
AND POTATO FRITTERS, THIS CHAPTER IS PACKED WITH
FUSS-FREE IDEAS THAT YOU WON'T BE ABLE TO RESIST.
SERVE GOLDEN, MELT-IN-THE-MOUTH PARMESAN
TUILES OR GOLDEN GRUYÈRE AND BASIL TORTILLAS
WITH DRINKS, OR ENJOY CRAB AND WATER-CHESTNUT
WONTONS AS AN APPETIZER.

Spanish Salted Almonds

Served with a glass of chilled dry sherry, these delicious salted nuts make a perfect tapas dish or pre-dinner snack.

SERVES FOUR TO SIX

1 Preheat the oven 200°C/400°F/Gas 6. Whisk the egg white in a bowl until it forms stiff peaks.

2 Add the almonds to the egg white, and stir until the nuts are thoroughly coated. Tip the mixture on to a baking sheet and spread out evenly in a single layer.

3 Sprinkle the salt over the almonds and bake for about 15 minutes, or until the egg white and salt are crusty. Leave to cool completely, then serve in bowls with a selection of other nibbles, dips and pâtés.

1 egg white

200g/7oz/generous 1 cup shelled unblanched almonds

a good handful of flaked sea salt

Golden Gruyère and Basil Tortillas

These simple fried tortilla wedges make a great late-night snack with sweet chilli sauce. If you have a few slices of ham or salami in the refrigerator, add these to the tortillas as well.

SERVES TWO

1 Heat the oil in a frying pan, over a medium heat. Add one of the tortillas, arrange the Gruyère cheese slices and basil leaves on top and season with salt and pepper.

2 Place the remaining tortilla on top to make a sandwich and flip the whole thing over with a metal spatula. Cook for a few minutes, until the underneath is golden.

3 Slide the tortilla sandwich on to a chopping board or plate and cut into wedges. Serve immediately.

2 soft flour tortillas

115g/4oz Gruyère cheese, thinly sliced

a handful of fresh basil leaves

FROM THE STORECUPBOARD

15ml/1 tbsp olive oil

salt and ground black pepper

Polenta Chips

These tasty Parmesan-flavoured batons are best served warm from the oven with a spicy, tangy dip. A bowl of Thai chilli dipping sauce or a creamy, chilli-spiked guacamole are perfect for dipping into.

MAKES ABOUT EIGHTY

1 Put 1.5 litres/2½ pints/6¼ cups water into a large heavy pan and bring to the boil. Reduce the heat, add the salt and pour in the polenta in a steady stream, stirring constantly with a wooden spoon. Cook over a low heat for about 5 minutes, stirring, until the mixture thickens and comes away from the sides of the pan.

2 Remove the pan from the heat and add the cheese and butter. Season to taste. Stir well until the mixture is smooth. Pour on to a smooth surface, such as a marble slab or a baking sheet.

3 Using a metal spatula, spread out the polenta to a thickness of 2cm/¾in and shape into a rectangle. Leave to stand for at least 30 minutes until cold. Meanwhile preheat the oven to 200°C/400°F/Gas 6 and lightly oil two or three baking sheets.

4 Cut the polenta slab in half, then carefully cut into even-size strips. Bake for 40–50 minutes, or until dark golden brown and crunchy, turning from time to time. Serve warm.

375g/13oz/3¼ cups instant polenta

150g/5oz/1½ cups freshly grated Parmesan cheese

FROM THE STORECUPBOARD

10ml/2 tsp salt, plus extra

90g/3½oz/7 tbsp butter

10ml/2 tsp cracked black pepper

olive oil, for brushing

Parmesan Tuiles

These lacy tuiles look very impressive and make splendid nibbles for a party, but they couldn't be easier to make. Believe or not, they use only a single ingredient – Parmesan cheese.

MAKES EIGHT TO TEN

1 Preheat the oven to 200°C/400°F/Gas 6. Line two baking sheets with baking parchment. Grate the cheese using a fine grater, pulling it down slowly to make long strands.

2 Spread the grated cheese in 7.5–9cm/3–3½in rounds on the baking parchment, forking it into shape. Do not spread the cheese too thickly; it should just cover the parchment. Bake for 5–7 minutes, or until bubbling and golden brown.

3 Leave the tuiles on the baking sheet for about 30 seconds and then carefully transfer, using a metal spatula, to a wire rack to cool completely. Alternatively, drape over a rolling pin to make a curved shape.

115g/4oz Parmesan cheese

COOK'S TIP

Tuiles can be made into little cup shapes by draping over an upturned egg cup. These little cups can be filled to make tasty treats to serve with drinks. Try a little cream cheese flavoured with herbs.

Yogurt Cheese in Olive Oil

In Greece, sheep's yogurt is hung in muslin to drain off the whey before being patted into balls of soft cheese. Here the cheese is bottled in extra virgin olive oil with dried chillies and fresh herbs to make a wonderful gourmet gift or aromatic appetizer. It is delicious spread on thick slices of toast as a snack or a light lunch.

FILLS TWO 450G/1LB JARS

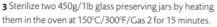

1 Sterilize a 30cm/12in square of muslin (cheesecloth) by soaking it in boiling water. Drain and lay it over a large plate. Season the yogurt with salt and tip on to the centre of the muslin. Bring up the sides of the muslin and tie with string.

2 Hang the bag on a kitchen cupboard handle or suitable position where it can be suspended over a bowl to catch the whey. Leave for 2–3 days until the yogurt stops dripping.

3 Sterilize two 450g/1lb glass preserving jars by heating them in the oven at 150°C/300°F/Gas 2 for 15 minutes.

4 Mix the crushed dried chillies and herbs. Take teaspoonfuls of the cheese and roll into balls with your hands. Lower into the jars, sprinkling each layer with the herb mixture.

5 Pour the oil over the cheese until completely covered. Store in the refrigerator for up to 3 weeks. To serve, spoon the cheese out of the jars with a little of the flavoured olive oil and spread on slices of lightly toasted bread.

1 litre/1¾ pints/4 cups Greek sheep's (US strained plain) yogurt

10ml/2 tsp crushed dried chillies or chilli powder

30ml/2 tbsp chopped fresh herbs, such as rosemary, and thyme or oregano

FROM THE STORECUPBOARD

about 300ml/½ pint/ 1¼ cups extra virgin olive oil, preferably garlic-flavoured

salt and ground black pepper

Eggs Mimosa

Mimosa describes the fine yellow and white grated egg in this dish, which looks very similar to the flower of the same name. The eggs taste delicious when garnished with black pepper and basil leaves. Grated egg yolk can also be used as a garnish for a variety of other savoury dishes, such as sauces, soups and rice dishes.

MAKES TWENTY

1 Reserve two of the hard-boiled eggs and halve the remainder. Carefully remove the yolks with a teaspoon and blend them with the avocados, garlic and oil, adding freshly ground black pepper and salt to taste. Spoon or pipe the mixture into the halved egg whites using a piping (pastry) bag with a 1cm/½in or pipe star nozzle.

2 Sieve the remaining egg whites and sprinkle over the filled eggs. Sieve the yolks and arrange on top. Arrange the filled egg halves on a serving platter.

12 eggs, hard-boiled and peeled

2 ripe avocados, halved and stoned (pitted)

1 garlic clove, crushed

FROM THE STORECUPBOARD

15ml/1 tbsp olive oil

Marinated Smoked Salmon with Lime and Coriander

If you want an elegant appetizer that is really quick to put together, then this is the one for you. The tangy lime juice and aromatic coriander leaves contrast perfectly with the delicate yet distinct flavour of the salmon. Serve with thinly sliced brown bread and butter.

SERVES SIX

200g/7oz smoked salmon

a handful of fresh coriander (cilantro) leaves

grated rind and juice of 1 lime

FROM THE STORECUPBOARD

15ml/1 tbsp extra virgin olive oil

ground black pepper

1 Using a sharp knife or pair of kitchen scissors, cut the salmon into strips and arrange on a serving platter.

2 Sprinkle the coriander leaves and lime rind over the salmon and squeeze over the lime juice. Drizzle with the olive oil and season with black pepper. Cover with clear film (plastic wrap) and chill for 1 hour before serving.

> **COOK'S TIP** You can make this dish up to 1 hour before serving. However, do not leave it for longer than this because the lime juice will discolour the salmon and spoil the look of the dish.

Blinis with Caviar and Crème Fraîche

Classic Russian blinis are made with buckwheat flour, which gives them a very distinctive taste. They are available ready-made in large supermarkets and make a tasty first course or snack to serve with drinks, topped with crème fraîche and caviar. Caviar is expensive, but a very small amount goes a long way and the exquisite flavour is well worth it.

SERVES TWELVE

1 Put the crème fraîche in a bowl and season with salt and ground black pepper to taste. Place a teaspoonful of the mixture on each blini.

2 Top each spoonful of crème fraîche with a teaspoon of caviar and serve immediately.

200g/7oz/scant 1 cup crème fraîche

12 ready-made blinis

60ml/4 tbsp caviar

FROM THE STORECUPBOARD

salt and ground black pepper

> **VARIATION** For a stunning effect, top half the blinis with orange salmon or trout roe and the other half with black caviar.

Marinated Anchovies

These tiny fish tend to lose their freshness very quickly so marinating them in garlic and lemon juice is the perfect way to enjoy them. It is probably the simplest way of preparing these fish, because it requires no cooking. Serve them scattered with parsley for a decorative finish.

SERVES FOUR

225g/8oz fresh anchovies, heads and tails removed, and split open along the belly

juice of 3 lemons

2 garlic cloves, finely chopped

FROM THE STORECUPBOARD

30ml/2 tbsp extra virgin olive oil

flaked sea salt

1 Turn the anchovies on to their bellies, and press down along their spine with your thumb. Using the tip of a small knife, carefully remove the backbones from the fish, and arrange the anchovies skin side down in a single layer on a large plate.

2 Squeeze two-thirds of the lemon juice over the fish and sprinkle them with the salt. Cover and leave to stand for 1–24 hours, basting occasionally with the juices, until the flesh is white and no longer translucent.

3 Transfer the anchovies to a serving plate and drizzle with the olive oil and the remaining lemon juice. Scatter the fish with the chopped garlic, then cover with clear film (plastic wrap) and chill until ready to serve.

Chilli Prawn Skewers

Try to get the freshest prawns you can for this recipe. If you buy whole prawns, you will need to remove the heads and shells, leaving the tail section intact. Serve with extra lime wedges.

SERVES FOUR

1 Place eight bamboo skewers in cold water and leave to soak for at least 10 minutes, then preheat the grill (broiler) to high.

2 Thread a prawn on to each skewer, then a lime wedge, then another prawn. Brush the sweet chilli sauce over the prawns and lime wedges.

3 Arrange the skewers on a baking sheet and grill (broil) for about 2 minutes, turning them once, until cooked through. Serve immediately with more chilli sauce for dipping.

16 giant raw prawns (shrimp), shelled with the tail section left intact

1 lime, cut into 8 wedges

60ml/4 tbsp sweet chilli sauce

Salt Cod and Potato Fritters

These little fritters are extremely easy to make and taste delicious. Serve them simply with a wedge of fresh lemon and some watercress or green salad. Offer a bowl of garlic mayonnaise for dipping.

MAKES ABOUT TWENTY FOUR

450g/1lb salt cod fillets

500g/1¹/₄lb floury potatoes, unpeeled

plain (all-purpose) flour, for coating

FROM THE STORECUPBOARD

vegetable oil, for deep-frying

salt and ground black pepper

1 Put the salt cod in a bowl, pour over cold water and leave to soak for 24 hours, changing the water every 6–8 hours. Drain, rinse and place in a pan of cold water. Slowly bring to the boil and simmer for 5 minutes, then drain and cool. When cooled, remove any bones and skin and mash the fish with a fork.

2 Cook the potatoes in their skins in a pan of salted boiling water for 20–25 minutes, or until just tender. Peel and mash.

3 Add the fish to the potatoes and mix well. Season to taste with salt and pepper. Break off walnut-sized pieces of the mixture and roll into balls. Place on a floured plate, cover and chill for 20–30 minutes. Roll each ball lightly in flour, dusting off any excess.

4 Heat enough oil for deep-frying in a large pan and fry the balls for 5–6 minutes, or until golden. Remove with a slotted spoon and drain on kitchen paper. Serve hot or warm.

Asian-style Crab Cakes

You could serve these patties as a simple supper, or an appetizer for eight people. Use a mixture of white and brown crab meat, as the dark adds a depth of flavour and texture. Serve with sweet chilli sauce.

MAKES SIXTEEN

450g/1lb/2²/₃ cups fresh crab meat, white and brown

15ml/1 tbsp grated fresh root ginger

15–30ml/1–2 tbsp plain (all-purpose) flour

FROM THE STORECUPBOARD

60ml/4 tbsp sunflower oil

salt and ground black pepper

1 Put the crab meat in a bowl and add the ginger, some salt and ground black pepper and the flour. Stir well until thoroughly mixed.

2 Using floured hands, divide the mixture into 16 equal-sized pieces and shape roughly into patties.

3 Heat the sunflower oil in a frying pan and add the patties, four at a time. Cook for 2–3 minutes on each side, until golden. Remove with a metal spatula and leave to drain on kitchen paper for a few minutes.

4 Keep the cooked crab cakes warm while you cook the remaining patties in the same way. Serve immediately.

Crab and Water-chestnut Wontons

Serve these mouthwatering parcels as part of a dim sum selection or with a bowl of soy sauce for dipping as a first course for a Chinese meal. They are also perfect for serving as snacks with drinks at parties as they can be prepared in advance, then steamed at the last minute. Wonton wrappers are available in most Asian food stores and need to be soaked in cold water for a few minutes before use.

SERVES FOUR

1 Finely chop the water chestnuts, mix them with the crab meat and season with salt and pepper.

2 Place about a teaspoonful of the mixture along the centre of each wonton wrapper. Roll up the wontons, tucking in the sides as you go to form a neat parcel.

3 Fill the bottom part of a steamer with boiling water and place the wontons, seam down, in the steamer basket. Sit the basket on top of the water and cover with a tight-fitting lid. Steam for 5–8 minutes, or until the wonton wrappers are tender. Serve hot or warm.

50g/2oz/¹/₃ cup drained, canned water chestnuts

115g/4oz/generous ¹/₂ cup fresh or canned white crab meat

12 wonton wrappers

FROM THE STORECUPBOARD

salt and ground black pepper

Chilli-spiced Chicken Wings

These crispy chicken wings are always the perfect snack for parties and go incredibly well with cold beer! If you like your food spicy, use red hot cayenne pepper in place of the chilli powder. To make a milder version that will be a hit with kids, use sweet paprika in place of the chilli powder. Serve with a fresh tomato and onion salsa for dipping.

SERVES FOUR

12 chicken wings

30ml/2 tbsp plain (all-purpose) flour

15ml/1 tbsp chilli powder

FROM THE STORECUPBOARD

a pinch of salt

sunflower oil, for deep-frying

1 Pat the chicken wings dry with kitchen paper. Mix the flour, chilli powder and salt together and put into a large plastic bag. Add the chicken wings, seal the bag and shake well to coat the chicken wings in the seasoned flour.

2 Heat enough sunflower oil for deep-frying in a large pan and add the chicken wings, three or four at a time. Fry for 8–10 minutes, or until golden and cooked through.

3 Remove the chicken wings with a slotted spoon and drain on kitchen paper. Keep warm in a low oven. Repeat with the remaining chicken wings and serve hot.

Vietnamese Spring Rolls with Pork

You will often find these little spring rolls on the menu in Vietnamese restaurants, called "rice paper rolls". Serve with a chilli dipping sauce.

SERVES FOUR

1 Heat the oil in a frying pan and add the pork. Fry for 5–6 minutes, or until browned. Season well with salt and pepper, stir in the oyster sauce and remove from the heat. Leave to cool.

2 Lay the rice paper wrappers on a clean work surface. Place one-eighth of the pork mixture down one edge of each wrapper. Roll up the wrappers, tucking in the ends as you go to form a roll, and then serve immediately.

350g/12oz/1½ cups minced (ground) pork

30ml/2 tbsp oyster sauce

8 rice-paper roll wrappers

FROM THE STORECUPBOARD

15ml/1 tbsp sunflower oil

salt and ground black pepper

Curried Lamb Samosas

Filo pastry is perfect for making samosas. Once you've mastered folding them, you'll be amazed how quick they are to make.

MAKES TWELVE SAMOSAS

225g/8oz/1 cup minced (ground) lamb

30ml/2 tbsp mild curry paste

12 filo pastry sheets

FROM THE STORECUPBOARD

25g/1oz/2 tbsp butter

salt and ground black pepper

1 Heat a little of the butter in a large pan and add the lamb. Fry for 5–6 minutes, stirring occasionally until browned. Stir in the curry paste and cook for 1–2 minutes. Season and set aside. Preheat the oven to 190°C/375°F/Gas 5.

2 Melt the remaining butter in a pan. Cut the pastry sheets in half lengthways. Brush one strip of pastry with butter, then lay another strip on top and brush with more butter.

3 Place a spoonful of lamb in the corner of the strip and fold over to form a triangle at one end. Keep folding over in the same way to form a triangular package. Brush with butter and place on a baking sheet. Repeat using the remaining pastry. Bake for 15–20 minutes until golden. Serve hot.

Soups

SOUP IS ONE OF THE MOST VERSATILE DISHES AROUND AND
CAN BE SERVED AS AN ELEGANT APPETIZER OR A LIGHT
MEAL. FROM CHILLED SUMMER SOUPS TO WARMING
WINTER BROTHS, THEY ARE INCREDIBLY EASY TO MAKE
AND ONLY NEED A FEW INGREDIENTS AND FLAVOURINGS
TO CREATE FABULOUS, MOUTHWATERING RESULTS.

Avocado Soup

This delicious soup has a fresh, delicate flavour and a wonderful colour. For added zest, add a generous squeeze of lime juice or spoon 15ml/1 tbsp salsa into the soup just before serving. Choose ripe avocados for this soup – they should feel soft when gently pressed. Keep very firm avocados at room temperature for 3–4 days until they soften. To speed ripening, place in a brown paper bag.

SERVES FOUR

1 Cut the avocados in half, remove the peel and lift out the stones (pits). Chop the flesh coarsely and place it in a food processor with 45–60ml/3–4 tbsp of the sour cream. Process until smooth.

2 Heat the chicken stock in a pan. When it is hot, but still below simmering point, stir in the rest of the cream.

3 Gradually stir the avocado mixture into the hot stock. Heat but do not let the mixture approach boiling point.

4 Chop the coriander. Ladle the soup into individual heated bowls and sprinkle each portion with chopped coriander and black pepper. Serve immediately.

2 large ripe avocados

300ml/¹/₂ pint/1¹/₄ cups sour cream

1 litre/1³/₄ pints/4 cups well-flavoured chicken stock

small bunch of fresh coriander (cilantro)

FROM THE STORECUPBOARD

ground black pepper

Vichyssoise

This classic, chilled summer soup of leeks and potatoes was first created in the 1920s by Louis Diat, chef at the New York Ritz-Carlton. He named it after Vichy near his home in France. The soup can be sharpened with lemon juice, enriched with swirls of cream and garnished with chives.

SERVES FOUR TO SIX

1 Melt the unsalted butter in a heavy pan and cook the leeks, covered, for 15–20 minutes, until they are soft but not browned.

2 Add the potato chunks and cook over a low heat, uncovered, for a few minutes.

3 Stir in the stock or water and milk, with salt and pepper to taste. Bring to the boil, then reduce the heat and partly cover the pan. Simmer for 15 minutes, or until the potatoes are soft.

4 Cool, then process the soup until smooth in a blender or food processor. Sieve the soup into a bowl. Taste and adjust the seasoning and add a little iced water if the consistency of the soup seems too thick.

5 Chill the soup for at least 4 hours or until very cold. Taste the chilled soup for seasoning again before serving. Pour the soup into bowls and serve.

600g/1lb 5oz leeks, white parts only, thinly sliced

250g/9oz floury potatoes (such as King Edward or Maris Piper), peeled and cut into chunks

1.5 litres/2½ pints/6½ cups half and half light chicken stock or water and milk

FROM THE STORECUPBOARD

50g/2oz/¼ cup unsalted (sweet) butter

salt and ground black pepper

EXTRAS

To make a fabulous chilled leek and sorrel or watercress soup, add about 50g/2oz/1 cup shredded sorrel to the soup at the end of cooking. Finish and chill as in the main recipe, then serve the soup garnished with a little pile of finely shredded sorrel. The same quantity of watercress can also be used.

Avgolemono

The name of this popular Greek soup means egg and lemon, the two essential ingredients that produce a light, nourishing soup. The soup also contains orzo, which is Greek, rice-shaped pasta, but you can use any small shape. Serve the soup with thin slices of lightly toasted bread and add a garnish of very thin lemon slices for a pretty appearance on special occasions.

SERVES FOUR TO SIX

1 Pour the chicken stock into a large pan and bring to the boil. Add the orzo pasta or other small pasta shapes and cook for 5 minutes, or according to the packet instructions.

2 Beat the eggs until they are frothy, then add the lemon juice and a tablespoon of cold water. Slowly stir in a ladleful of the hot chicken stock, then add one or two more. Remove the pan from the heat, then pour in the egg mixture and stir well. Season to taste with salt and freshly ground black pepper and serve immediately. (Do not let the soup boil once the egg, lemon juice and stock mixture has been added, or it will curdle.)

1.75 litres/3 pints/ 7½ cups chicken stock

115g/4oz/½ cup orzo pasta

3 eggs

juice of 1 large lemon

FROM THE STORECUPBOARD

salt and ground black pepper

Simple Cream of Onion Soup

This wonderfully soothing soup has a deep, buttery flavour that is achieved with only a few ingredients and the minimum of fuss. It makes delicious comfort food on a cold day. Use home-made stock if you have it, or buy fresh stock for the best flavour. Crisp croûtons or chopped chives complement the smooth soup when sprinkled over just before serving.

SERVES FOUR

1kg/2¼lb yellow onions, sliced

1 litre/1¾ pints/4 cups good chicken or vegetable stock

150ml/¼ pint/⅔ cup double (heavy) cream

FROM THE STORECUPBOARD

115g/4oz/ ½ cup unsalted (sweet) butter

salt and ground black pepper

1 Melt 75g/3oz/6 tbsp of the unsalted butter in a large, heavy pan. Set about 200g/7oz of the onions aside and add the rest to the pan. Stir to coat in the butter, then cover and cook very gently for about 30 minutes. The onions should be very soft and tender, but not browned.

2 Add the chicken or vegetable stock, 5ml/1 tsp salt and freshly ground black pepper to taste. Bring to the boil, reduce the heat and simmer for 5 minutes, then remove from the heat.

3 Leave the soup to cool, then process it in a blender or food processor. Return the soup to the rinsed pan.

4 Meanwhile, melt the remaining butter in another pan and cook the remaining onions over a low heat, covered, until soft but not browned. Uncover and continue to cook the onions gently until they turn golden yellow.

5 Add the cream to the soup and reheat it gently until hot, but do not allow it to boil. Taste and adjust the seasoning. Add the buttery onions and stir for 1–2 minutes, then ladle the soup into bowls. Serve the soup immediately.

Cappelletti in Broth

This soup is traditionally served in northern Italy on Santo Stefano (St Stephen's Day, the day after Christmas) and on New Year's Day as a welcome light change from all the special celebration food. Cappelletti are little stuffed pasta shapes that resemble hats.

SERVES FOUR

1.2 litres/2 pints/ 5 cups chicken stock

90–115g/3¹/₂–4oz/ 1 cup fresh or dried cappelletti

about 45ml/3 tbsp finely chopped fresh flat leaf parsley (optional)

about 30ml/2 tbsp freshly grated Parmesan cheese

1 Pour the chicken stock into a large pan and bring to the boil. Drop in the pasta.

2 Stir well and bring back to the boil. Lower the heat to a simmer and cook according to the instructions on the packet, until the pasta is *al dente*, that is, tender but still firm to the bite.

3 Swirl in the finely chopped fresh flat leaf parsley, if using, then taste and adjust the seasoning, if necessary. Ladle into four warmed soup plates, then sprinkle with the freshly grated Parmesan cheese and serve immediately.

COOK'S TIP *If you don't have home-made stock use two 300g/11oz cans of condensed beef consommé, adding water as instructed, or chilled commercial stock.*

Tiny Pasta in Broth

This Italian soup is ideal for a light supper served with ciabatta bread and also makes a delicious first course for an *al fresco* supper. A wide variety of different types of *pastina* or soup pasta are available including stellette (stars), anellini (tiny thin rounds), risoni (rice-shaped) and farfalline (little butterflies). Choose just one shape or a combination of different varieties for an interesting result.

SERVES FOUR

1.2 litres/2 pints/ 5 cups beef stock

75g/3oz/³/₄ cup dried tiny soup pasta

2 pieces bottled roasted red (bell) pepper, about 50g/2oz

coarsely shaved Parmesan cheese

1 Bring the beef stock to the boil in a large pan. Drop in the dried soup pasta. Stir well and bring the stock back to the boil.

2 Reduce the heat so that the soup simmers and cook for 7–8 minutes, or according to the packet instructions, until the pasta is *al dente*, that is, tender but still firm to the bite.

3 Drain the pieces of roasted pepper and dice them finely. Place them in the base of four warmed soup plates. Taste the soup for seasoning before ladling it into the soup plates. Serve immediately, topped with shavings of Parmesan.

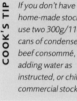

Potato and Roasted Garlic Broth

Roasted garlic takes on a mellow, sweet flavour that is subtle, not overpowering, in this delicious vegetarian soup. Choose floury potatoes for this soup, such as Maris Piper, Estima, Cara or King Edward – they will give the soup a delicious velvety texture. Serve the broth piping hot with melted Cheddar or Gruyère cheese on French bread, as the perfect winter warmer.

SERVES FOUR

1 Preheat the oven to 190°C/375°F/Gas 5. Place the unpeeled garlic bulbs or bulb in a small roasting pan and bake for 30 minutes until soft in the centre.

2 Meanwhile, par-boil the potatoes in a large pan of boiling water for 10 minutes.

3 Simmer the stock in another pan for 5 minutes. Drain the potatoes and add them to the stock.

4 Squeeze the garlic pulp into the soup, reserving a few whole cloves and stir. Simmer for 15 minutes and serve topped with whole garlic cloves and parsley.

2 small or 1 large whole head of garlic (about 20 cloves)

4 medium potatoes (about 500g/1¼lb in total), diced

1.75 litres/3 pints/ 7½ cups good-quality hot vegetable stock

chopped flat leaf parsley, to garnish

Winter Squash Soup with Tomato Salsa

Creamy butternut squash makes good soup with very few additional ingredients. Select a really good bought salsa for this soup and add a sprinkling of chopped fresh oregano or marjoram as a garnish.

1 butternut squash

2 onions, chopped

60–120ml/4–8 tbsp tomato salsa

FROM THE STORECUPBOARD

75ml/5 tbsp garlic-flavoured olive oil

SERVES FOUR TO FIVE

1 Preheat the oven to 220°C/425°F/Gas 7. Halve and seed the butternut squash and place it on a baking sheet and brush with some of the oil and roast for 25 minutes. Reduce the temperature to 190°C/375°F/Gas 5 and cook for 20–25 minutes more, or until it is tender.

2 Heat the remaining oil in a large, heavy pan and cook the chopped onions over a low heat for about 10 minutes, or until softened.

3 Meanwhile, scoop the squash out of its skin, adding it to the pan. Pour in 1.2 litres/ 2 pints/5 cups water and stir in 5ml/1 tsp salt and plenty of black pepper. Bring to the boil, cover and simmer for 10 minutes.

4 Cool the soup slightly, then process it in a blender or food processor to a smooth purée. Alternatively, press the soup through a fine sieve with the back of a spoon. Reheat without boiling, then ladle it into warmed bowls. Top each serving with a spoonful of salsa and serve.

Butter Bean, Sun-dried Tomato and Pesto Soup

This soup is so quick and easy to make: the key is to use a good-quality home-made or bought fresh stock for the best result. Using plenty of pesto and sun-dried tomato purée (paste) gives it a rich, minestrone-like flavour. As an alternative to butter beans, haricot (navy) or cannellini beans will make good substitutes.

SERVES FOUR

1 Put the stock in a pan with the butter beans and bring just to the boil. Reduce the heat and stir in the tomato purée and pesto. Cook gently for 5 minutes.

2 Transfer six ladlefuls of the soup to a blender or food processor, scooping up plenty of the beans. Process until smooth, then return the purée to the pan.

3 Heat gently, stirring frequently, for 5 minutes. Ladle into four warmed soup bowls and serve with warm crusty bread or breadsticks.

900ml/1¹⁄₂ pints/
3³⁄₄ cups chicken or
vegetable stock

2 x 400g/14oz cans
butter (lima) beans,
drained and rinsed

60ml/4 tbsp sun-dried
tomato purée (paste)

75ml/5 tbsp pesto

Stilton and Watercress Soup

A good creamy Stilton and plenty of peppery watercress bring maximum flavour to this rich, smooth soup, which is superlative in small portions. Rocket (arugula) can be used as an alternative to watercress – both leaves are an excellent source of iron. When choosing any salad leaves, look for crisp, fresh leaves and reject any wilted or discoloured greens.

SERVES FOUR TO SIX

1 Pour the stock into a pan and bring almost to the boil. Remove and discard any very large stalks from the watercress. Add the watercress to the pan and simmer gently for 2–3 minutes, until tender.

2 Crumble the cheese into the pan and simmer for 1 minute more, until the cheese has started to melt. Process the soup in a blender or food processor, in batches if necessary, until very smooth. Return the soup to the pan.

3 Stir in the cream and check the seasoning. The soup will probably not need any extra salt, as the blue cheese is already quite salty. Heat the soup gently, without boiling, then ladle it into warm bowls.

600ml/1 pint/2¹⁄₂ cups chicken or vegetable stock

225g/8oz watercress

150g/5oz Stilton or other blue cheese

150ml/¹⁄₄ pint/²⁄₃ cup single (light) cream

Curried Cauliflower Soup

This spicy, creamy soup is perfect for lunch on a cold winter's day served with crusty bread and garnished with fresh coriander (cilantro). You can also make broccoli soup in the same way, using the same weight of broccoli in place of the cauliflower.

SERVES FOUR

750ml/1¼ pints/3 cups milk

1 large cauliflower

15ml/1 tbsp garam masala

FROM THE STORECUPBOARD

salt and ground black pepper

1 Pour the milk into a large pan and place over a medium heat. Cut the cauliflower into florets and add to the milk with the garam masala and season with salt and pepper.

2 Bring the milk to the boil, then reduce the heat, partially cover the pan with a lid and simmer for about 20 minutes, or until the cauliflower is tender.

3 Let the mixture cool for a few minutes, then transfer to a food processor and process until smooth (you may have to do this in two batches). Return the purée to the pan and heat through gently, checking and adjusting the seasoning, and serve immediately.

Tuscan Bean Soup

Cavolo nero is a very dark green cabbage with a nutty flavour from Tuscany and southern Italy. It is ideal for this traditional recipe. It is available in most large supermarkets, but if you can't get it, use Savoy cabbage instead. Serve with ciabatta bread.

SERVES FOUR

2 x 400g/14oz cans chopped tomatoes with herbs

250g/9oz cavolo nero leaves

400g/14oz can cannellini beans

FROM THE STORECUPBOARD

60ml/4 tbsp extra virgin olive oil

salt and ground black pepper

1 Pour the tomatoes into a large pan and add a can of cold water. Season with salt and pepper and bring to the boil, then reduce the heat to a simmer.

2 Roughly shred the cabbage leaves and add them to the pan. Partially cover the pan and simmer gently for about 15 minutes, or until the cabbage is tender.

3 Drain and rinse the cannellini beans, add to the pan and warm through for a few minutes. Check and adjust the seasoning, then ladle the soup into bowls and drizzle each one with a little olive oil and serve.

Pea Soup with Garlic

If you keep peas in the freezer, you can rustle up this delicious soup in minutes. It has a wonderfully sweet taste and smooth texture and is great served with crusty bread and garnished with mint.

SERVES FOUR

1 garlic clove, crushed

900g/2lb/8 cups frozen peas

1.2 litres/2 pints/5 cups chicken stock

FROM THE STORECUPBOARD

25g/1oz/2 tbsp butter

salt and ground black pepper

1 Heat the butter in a large pan and add the garlic. Fry gently for 2–3 minutes, until softened, then add the peas. Cook for 1–2 minutes more, then pour in the stock.

2 Bring the soup to the boil, then reduce the heat to a simmer. Cover the pan and cook for 5–6 minutes, until the peas are tender. Leave to cool slightly, then transfer the mixture to a food processor and process until smooth (you may have to do this in two batches).

3 Return the soup to the rinsed pan and heat through gently. Season with salt and pepper.

Star-gazer Vegetable Soup

If you have the time, it is worth making your own stock for this recipe.

SERVES FOUR

**1 yellow (bell) pepper and
2 large courgettes (zucchini)**

2 large carrots

**900ml/1¹/₂ pints/3³/₄ cups
well-flavoured vegetable stock**

50g/2oz rice vermicelli

FROM THE STORECUPBOARD

salt and ground black pepper

COOK'S TIP

Sauté the leftover vegetable pieces in a little oil and mix with cooked brown rice to make a tasty risotto.

1 Cut the pepper into quarters, removing the seeds and core. Cut the courgettes and carrots lengthways into 5mm/¹/₄in slices.

2 Using tiny pastry cutters, stamp out shapes from the vegetables or use a very sharp knife to cut the sliced vegetables into stars and other decorative shapes.

3 Place the vegetables and stock in a pan and simmer for 10 minutes, until the vegetables are tender. Season to taste with salt and pepper.

4 Meanwhile, place the vermicelli in a bowl, cover with boiling water and set aside for 4 minutes. Drain, then divide among four warmed soup bowls. Ladle over the soup and serve with fresh bread.

Light Lunches

WHAT COULD BE BETTER THAN A TASTY MEAL IN THE
MIDDLE OF THE DAY THAT HAS TAKEN ONLY MINUTES
TO PREPARE AND NEEDS JUST THREE OR FOUR
INGREDIENTS? WHATEVER YOU'RE IN THE MOOD FOR,
WHETHER IT'S A HEALTHY SALAD, A GOURMET
SANDWICH OR A BOWL OF PASTA, THERE'S SOMETHING
HERE FOR YOU. THE RECIPES ARE ALL SO SIMPLE THAT
YOU CAN EASILY REDUCE OR INCREASE THE
PROPORTIONS TO MAKE A QUICK LUNCH FOR ONE,
OR A HEALTHY MEAL FOR THE WHOLE FAMILY.

Baked Eggs with Creamy Leeks

This simple but elegant appetizer is perfect for last-minute entertaining or quick dining. Garnish the baked eggs with crisp, fried fresh sage leaves and serve with warm, fresh crusty bread for a special meal. Small- to medium-sized leeks (less than 2.5cm/1in in diameter) are best for this dish as they have the most tender flavour and only require a short cooking time.

SERVES FOUR

1 Preheat the oven to 190°C/375°F/Gas 5. Generously butter the base and sides of four ramekins.

2 Melt the butter in a frying pan and cook the leeks over a medium heat, stirring frequently, for 3–5 minutes, until softened and translucent, but not browned.

3 Add 45ml/3 tbsp of the cream and cook over a low heat for 5 minutes, until the leeks are very soft and the cream has thickened a little. Season to taste.

4 Place the ramekins in a small roasting pan and divide the leeks among them. Break an egg into each, spoon over the remaining cream and season.

5 Pour boiling water into the roasting pan to come about halfway up the sides of the ramekins. Transfer the pan to the oven and bake in the preheated oven for about 10 minutes, until just set. Serve piping hot.

225g/8oz small leeks, thinly sliced

75–90ml/5–6 tbsp whipping cream

4 small–medium (US medium–large) eggs

FROM THE STORECUPBOARD

15g/¹⁄₂oz/1 tbsp butter, plus extra for greasing

salt and ground black pepper

Red Onion and Olive Pissaladière

For a taste of the Mediterranean, try this French-style pizza – it makes a delicious and easy snack. Cook the sliced red onions slowly until they are caramelized and sweet before piling them into the pastry cases. To prepare the recipe in advance, pile the cooled onions on to the pastry round and chill the pissaladière until you are ready to bake it.

SERVES SIX

1 Preheat the oven to 220°C/425°F/Gas 7. Heat the oil in a large, heavy frying pan and cook the onions gently, stirring frequently, for 15–20 minutes, until they are soft and golden. Season to taste.

2 Roll out the pastry thinly on a floured surface. Cut out a 33cm/13in round and transfer it to a lightly dampened baking sheet.

3 Spread the onions over the pastry in an even layer to within 1cm/½in of the edge. Sprinkle the olives on top. Bake the tart for 20–25 minutes, until the pastry is risen and deep golden. Cut into wedges and serve warm.

500g/1¼lb small red onions, thinly sliced

500g/1¼lb puff pastry, thawed if frozen

75g/3oz/¾ cup small pitted black olives

FROM THE STORECUPBOARD

75ml/5 tbsp extra virgin olive oil

Figs with Prosciutto and Roquefort

Fresh figs are a delicious treat, whether you choose dark purple, yellowy green or green-skinned varieties. When they are ripe, you can split them open with your fingers to reveal the soft, sweet flesh full of edible seeds. In this easy, stylish dish figs and honey balance the richness of the ham and cheese. Serve with warm bread for a simple appetizer before any rich main course.

SERVES FOUR

1 Preheat the grill (broiler). Quarter the figs and place on a foil-lined grill rack. Tear each slice of prosciutto into two or three pieces and crumple them up on the foil beside the figs. Brush the figs with 15ml/1 tbsp of the clear honey and cook under the grill until lightly browned.

2 Crumble the Roquefort cheese and divide among four plates, setting it to one side. Add the honey-grilled figs and ham and pour over any cooking juices caught on the foil. Drizzle the remaining honey over the figs, ham and cheese, and serve seasoned with plenty of freshly ground black pepper.

8 fresh figs

75g/3oz prosciutto

**45ml/3 tbsp
clear honey**

75g/3oz Roquefort cheese

FROM THE STORECUPBOARD

ground black pepper

Pea and Mint Omelette

Serve this deliciously light omelette with crusty bread and a green salad for a fresh and tasty lunch. If you're making the omelette for a summer lunch when peas are in season, use freshly shelled peas instead of frozen ones.

SERVES TWO

1 Cook the peas in a large pan of salted boiling water for 3–4 minutes until tender. Drain well and set aside. Break the eggs into a large bowl and beat with a fork. Season well with salt and pepper, then stir in the peas and chopped mint.

2 Heat the butter in a medium frying pan until foamy. Pour in the egg mixture and cook over a medium heat for 3–4 minutes, drawing in the cooked egg from the edges from time to time, until the mixture is nearly set.

3 Finish off cooking the omelette under a hot grill (broiler) until set and golden. Carefully fold the omelette over, cut it in half and serve immediately.

50g/2oz/¹⁄₂ cup frozen peas

4 eggs

30ml/2 tbsp chopped fresh mint

FROM THE STORECUPBOARD

knob (pat) of butter

salt and ground black pepper

Warm Penne with Fresh Tomatoes and Basil

This dish is fresh, healthy and ready in minutes. It is the perfect way to use up a glut of ripe summer tomatoes.

SERVES FOUR

500g/1¼lb dried penne

5 very ripe plum tomatoes

1 small bunch of fresh basil

FROM THE STORECUPBOARD

60ml/4 tbsp extra virgin olive oil

salt and ground black pepper

1 Cook the pasta in plenty of salted, boiling water according to the instructions on the packet. Meanwhile, roughly chop the tomatoes, pull the basil leaves from their stems and tear up the leaves.

2 Drain the pasta thoroughly and toss with the tomatoes, basil and olive oil. Season with salt and freshly ground black pepper and serve immediately.

COOK'S TIP
If you cannot find ripe tomatoes, roast them to bring out their flavour. Put the tomatoes in a roasting pan, drizzle with oil and roast at 190°C/375°F/ Gas 5 for 20 minutes, then mash roughly.

Broccoli and Chilli Spaghetti

The contrast between the hot chilli and the mild broccoli is delicious and goes perfectly with spaghetti. To add extra flavour and texture, sprinkle the spaghetti and broccoli with toasted pine nuts and grated or shaved Parmesan cheese just before serving.

SERVES FOUR

350g/12oz dried spaghetti

450g/1lb broccoli, cut into small florets

1 fat red chilli, seeded and finely chopped

FROM THE STORECUPBOARD

150ml/¼ pint/²/₃ cup garlic-infused olive oil

salt and ground black pepper

1 Bring a large pan of lightly salted water to the boil. Add the spaghetti and broccoli and cook for 8–10 minutes, until both are tender. Drain thoroughly.

2 Using the back of a fork crush the broccoli roughly, taking care not to mash the spaghetti strands at the same time.

3 Meanwhile, warm the oil and finely chopped chilli in a small pan over a low heat and cook very gently for 5 minutes.

4 Pour the chilli and oil over the spaghetti and broccoli and toss together to combine. Season to taste. Divide between four warmed bowls and serve immediately.

Grilled Aubergine, Mint and Couscous Salad

Packets of flavoured couscous are available in most supermarkets – you can use whichever you like, but garlic and coriander is particularly good for this recipe. Serve with a crisp green salad.

SERVES TWO

1 large aubergine (eggplant)

115g/4oz packet garlic-and-coriander (cilantro) flavoured couscous

30ml/2 tbsp chopped fresh mint

FROM THE STORECUPBOARD

30ml/2 tbsp olive oil

salt and ground black pepper

1 Preheat the grill (broiler) to high. Cut the aubergine into large chunky pieces and toss them with the olive oil. Season with salt and pepper to taste and spread the aubergine pieces on a non-stick baking sheet. Grill for 5–6 minutes, turning occasionally, until golden brown.

2 Meanwhile, prepare the couscous according to the instructions on the packet. Stir the grilled aubergine and chopped mint into the couscous, toss thoroughly and serve immediately.

Marinated Courgette and Flageolet Bean Salad

Serve this healthy salad as a light lunch or as an accompaniment to meat and chicken dishes. It has a wonderful bright green colour and is perfect for a summer lunch.

SERVES FOUR

2 courgettes (zucchini), halved lengthways and sliced

400g/14oz can flageolet beans, drained and rinsed

grated rind and juice of 1 unwaxed lemon

FROM THE STORECUPBOARD

45ml/3 tbsp garlic-infused olive oil

salt and ground black pepper

1 Cook the courgettes in boiling salted water for 2–3 minutes, or until just tender. Drain well and refresh under cold running water.

2 Transfer the drained courgettes into a bowl with the beans and stir in the oil, lemon rind and juice and some salt and pepper. Chill for 30 minutes before serving.

VARIATION *To add extra flavour to the salad add 30ml/2 tbsp chopped fresh herbs before chilling. Basil and mint both have fresh, distinctive flavours that will work very well.*

Roasted Pepper and Hummus Wrap

Wraps make a tasty change to sandwiches and have the bonus that they can be made a few hours in advance without going soggy in the way that bread sandwiches often can. You can introduce all kinds of variation to this basic combination. Try using roasted aubergine (eggplant) in place of the red peppers, or guacamole in place of the hummus. As well as plain flour tortillas, you can also buy flavoured tortillas from most supermarkets.

SERVES TWO

1 large red (bell) pepper, halved and seeded

4 tbsp hummus

2 soft flour tortillas

FROM THE STORECUPBOARD

15ml/1 tbsp olive oil

salt and ground black pepper

1 Preheat the grill (broiler) to high. Brush the pepper halves with the oil and place cut side down on a baking sheet. Grill for 5 minutes, until charred. Put the pepper halves in a sealed plastic bag and leave to cool.

2 When cooled, remove the peppers from the bag and carefully peel away the charred skin and discard. Thinly slice the flesh using a sharp knife.

3 Spread the hummus over the tortillas in a thin, even layer and top with the roasted pepper slices. Season with salt and plenty of ground black pepper, then roll them up and cut in half to serve.

Focaccia with Sardines and Roast Tomatoes

Fresh sardines not only have a lovely flavour and texture, but they are also cheap to buy – so make an economical yet utterly delicious lunch.

SERVES FOUR

20 cherry tomatoes

12 fresh sardine fillets

1 focaccia loaf

FROM THE STORECUPBOARD

45ml/3 tbsp herb-infused olive oil

salt and ground black pepper

1 Preheat the oven to 190°C/375°F/Gas 5. Put the cherry tomatoes in a small roasting pan and drizzle 30ml/2 tbsp of the oil over the top. Season with salt and pepper and roast for 10–15 minutes, or until tender and slightly charred. Remove from the oven and set aside.

2 Preheat the grill (broiler) to high. Brush the sardine fillets with the remaining oil and lay them on a baking sheet. Grill for 4–5 minutes on each side, until cooked through.

3 Split the focaccia in half horizontally and cut each piece in half to give four equal pieces. Toast the cut side under the grill until golden. Top with the sardines and tomatoes and an extra drizzle of oil. Season with black pepper then serve.

Jansson's Temptation

This traditional Swedish gratin is utterly moreish. The name probably does not refer to a specific Jansson but means "everyone's temptation", as Jansson is a common Swedish surname.

SERVES FOUR TO SIX

1 Preheat the oven to 200°C/400°F/Gas 6. Cut the potatoes into thin slices, then cut the slices into matchstick strips. Sprinkle half of them in the base of a greased shallow 1.5 litre/2½ pint/6¼ cup baking dish.

2 Lay half of the onions on top of the potatoes, and season with black pepper. Lay the anchovies on top of the onions, then add the remaining onions and potatoes.

3 Mix the cream with 30ml/2 tbsp cold water and pour over the potatoes and onions. Cover with foil and bake for 1 hour, then reduce the oven temperature to 180°C/350°F/Gas 4 and uncover the dish. Bake for a further 40–50 minutes, or until the potatoes are golden and tender when tested with a knife.

900g/2lb potatoes

2 large, sweet onions, sliced

2 x 50g/2oz cans anchovies in olive oil, drained

450ml/¾ pint/scant 2 cups whipping cream or half and half double (heavy) and single (light) cream

Crisp Fried Whitebait

This must be one of the simplest of all classic fish dishes and it is absolutely delicious with lemon wedges and thinly sliced brown bread and butter. If you prefer, serve the whitebait with a simple lemon and herb dip – mix 150ml/¼ pint/⅔ cup natural (plain) yogurt with the rind of one lemon and 45ml/ 3 tbsp chopped fresh herbs. Serve chilled.

SERVES FOUR

150ml/¹/₄ pint/²/₃ cup milk

115g/4oz/1 cup plain (all-purpose) flour

450g/1lb whitebait

FROM THE STORECUPBOARD

oil, for deep-frying

COOK'S TIP

Most whitebait are sold frozen. Thaw them before use and dry them thoroughly on kitchen paper before flouring.

1 Heat the oil in a large pan or deep-fryer. Put the milk in a shallow bowl and spoon the flour into a paper bag. Season the flour well with salt and pepper.

2 Dip a handful of the whitebait into the bowl of milk, drain them well, then put them into the paper bag. Shake to coat them evenly in the seasoned flour, then transfer to a plate. Repeat until all the fish have been coated. Don't add too many whitebait at once to the bag, or they will stick together.

3 Heat the oil for deep-frying to 190°C/375°F or until a cube of stale bread, dropped into the oil, browns in about 20 seconds. Add a batch of whitebait, preferably in a frying basket, and deep-fry for 2–3 minutes, until crisp and golden brown. Drain and keep hot while you cook the rest. Serve very hot.

Seared Tuna Niçoise

A traditional tuna Niçoise consists of tuna, olives, green beans, potatoes and eggs, but this modern version using fresh tuna is a simplified one – although just as tasty. Serve it with a green salad.

SERVES FOUR

1 Put the tuna steaks in a shallow non-metallic dish. Mix the oil and vinegar together and season with salt and pepper.

2 Pour the mixture over the tuna steaks and turn them to coat in the marinade. Cover and chill for up to 1 hour.

3 Heat a griddle pan until smoking hot. Remove the tuna steaks from the marinade and lay them on the griddle pan. Cook for 2–3 minutes on each side, so that they are still pink in the centre. Remove from the pan and set aside.

4 Meanwhile, cook the eggs in a pan of boiling water for 5–6 minutes, then cool under cold running water. Shell the eggs and cut in half lengthways.

5 Pour the marinade on to the griddle pan and cook until it starts to bubble. Divide the tuna steaks among four serving plates and top each with half an egg. Drizzle the marinade over the top and serve immediately.

4 tuna steaks, about 150g/ 5oz each

30ml/2 tbsp sherry vinegar

2 eggs

FROM THE STORECUPBOARD

45ml/3 tbsp garlic-infused olive oil

salt and ground black pepper

Creamy Parmesan-Baked Eggs

These eggs are delicious as they are but can easily be "dressed up" with additional ingredients. Try adding chopped smoked ham and parsley before you cook them. Serve with thinly sliced bread and butter.

SERVES TWO

1 Preheat the oven to 160°C/325°F/Gas 3. Break the eggs into four ramekin dishes and spoon the cream over the top. Season with salt and ground black pepper and sprinkle the Parmesan cheese on top.

2 Bake the eggs for about 10 minutes, or until they are just set, and serve immediately.

COOK'S TIPS
Serve these rich and creamy eggs with a leafy green salad flavoured with fresh tarragon. For the best results, be sure to serve the eggs as soon as they are cooked.

4 large (US extra large) eggs

60ml/4 tbsp double (heavy) cream

30ml/2 tbsp freshly grated Parmesan cheese

FROM THE STORECUPBOARD

salt and ground black pepper

Toasted Sourdough with Goat's Cheese

Choose a good-quality, firm goat's cheese for this recipe because it needs to keep its shape during cooking. Serve with fresh rocket leaves.

SERVES TWO

2 thick sourdough bread slices

30ml/2 tbsp chilli jam

2 firm goat's cheese slices, about 90g/3½oz each

FROM THE STORECUPBOARD

30ml/2 tbsp garlic-infused olive oil

ground black pepper

1 Preheat the grill (broiler) to high. Brush the sourdough bread on both sides with the oil, and grill (broil) one side until golden. Spread the un-toasted side of each slice with the chilli jam and top with the goat's cheese.

2 Return the bread to the grill and cook for 3–4 minutes, or until the cheese is beginning to melt and turn golden and bubbling. Season with ground black pepper and serve immediately with rocket (arugula) leaves.

Steak and Blue Cheese Sandwiches

Many people like their rib eye steaks cooked quite rare in the centre, but how you like yours is up to you. Add a couple of minutes to the cooking time if you prefer them more well done.

SERVES TWO

1 Bake the ciabatta according to the instructions on the packet. Remove from the oven and leave to rest for a few minutes. Cut the loaf in half and split each half horizontally.

2 Heat a griddle pan until hot. Brush the steaks with the olive oil and lay them on the griddle pan. Cook for 2–3 minutes on each side, depending on the thickness of the steaks.

3 Remove the steaks from the pan and set aside to rest for a few minutes. Cut them in half and place in the sandwiches with the cheese. Season with salt and pepper, and serve.

1 ready-to-bake ciabatta bread

2 rib eye steaks, about 200g/7oz each

115g/4oz Gorgonzola cheese, sliced

FROM THE STORECUPBOARD

15ml/1 tbsp olive oil

salt and ground black pepper

Spicy Chorizo Sausage and Spring Onion Hash

Use up leftover boiled potatoes for this recipe. Fresh chorizo sausages are available from good butchers and Spanish delis.

SERVES FOUR

1 Heat a large frying pan over a medium heat and add the sausages. Cook for 8–10 minutes, turning occasionally, until cooked through. Remove from the pan and set aside.

2 Add the olive oil to the sausage fat in the pan and then add the potatoes. Cook over a low heat for 5–8 minutes, turning occasionally until golden. Meanwhile, cut the sausages into bite-size chunks and add to the pan.

3 Add the spring onions to the pan and cook for a couple more minutes, until they are piping hot. Season with salt and pepper, and serve immediately.

450g/1lb fresh chorizo sausages

450g/1lb cooked potatoes, diced

1 bunch of spring onions (scallions), sliced

FROM THE STORECUPBOARD

15ml/1 tbsp olive oil

salt and ground black pepper

Baked Sweet Potatoes with Leeks and Gorgonzola

This dish tastes wonderful and looks stunning if you buy the beautiful orange-fleshed sweet potatoes.

SERVES FOUR

4 large sweet potatoes, scrubbed

2 large leeks, washed and sliced

115g/4oz Gorgonzola cheese, sliced

FROM THE STORECUPBOARD

30ml/2 tbsp olive oil

salt and ground black pepper

1 Preheat the oven to 190°C/375°F/Gas 5. Dry the sweet potatoes with kitchen paper and rub them all over with 15ml/1 tbsp of the oil. Place them on a baking sheet and sprinkle with salt. Bake for 1 hour, or until tender.

2 Meanwhile, heat the remaining oil in a frying pan and add the sliced leeks. Cook for 3–4 minutes, or until softened and just beginning to turn golden.

3 Cut the potatoes in half lengthways and place them cut side up on the baking sheet. Top with the cooked leeks and season.

4 Lay the cheese slices on top and grill (broil) under a hot grill for 2–3 minutes, until the cheese is bubbling. Serve immediately.

Fish and Shellfish

THE DELICATE TASTE OF FISH AND SHELLFISH IS PERFECTLY
SUITED TO SUBTLE, SIMPLE FLAVOURINGS SUCH AS FRESH
HERBS, CITRUS JUICE, SUCCULENT TOMATOES OR SMOKY
BACON. THE FABULOUS RECIPES IN THIS CHAPTER MAKE
THE MOST OF SIMPLE, SEASONAL INGREDIENTS TO ACHIEVE
TRULY WONDERFUL DISHES.

Mussels in White Wine

This simple yet delicious dish is perfect for informal entertaining. Serve with a big bowl of chips (US fries) to share. To make a variation, cook the mussels in beer instead of wine – they taste fantastic.

SERVES TWO

300ml/¹/₂ pint/1¹/₄ cups dry white wine

1kg/2¹/₄lb mussels, cleaned

45ml/3 tbsp chopped fresh parsley

FROM THE STORECUPBOARD

25g/1oz/2 tbsp butter

salt and ground black pepper

1 Heat the butter in a large pan until foaming, then pour in the wine. Bring to the boil. Discard any open mussels that do not close when sharply tapped, and add the remaining ones to the pan. Cover with a tight-fitting lid and cook over a medium heat for 4–5 minutes, shaking the pan every now and then. By this time, all the mussels should have opened. Discard any that are still closed.

2 Line a large sieve with kitchen paper and strain the mussels and their liquid through it. Transfer the mussels to warmed serving bowls. Pour the liquid into a small pan and bring to the boil. Season with salt and pepper and stir in the parsley. Pour over the mussels and serve immediately.

Crab and Cucumber Wraps

This dish is a modern twist on the ever-popular Chinese classic, crispy Peking duck with pancakes. In this quick and easy version, crisp, refreshing cucumber and full-flavoured dressed crab are delicious with spicy-sweet hoisin sauce in warm tortilla wraps. Serve the wraps as an appetizer for four people, or as a main course for two.

SERVES TWO

1 Cut the cucumber into small even-sized batons. Scoop the dressed crab into a small mixing bowl, add a little freshly ground black pepper and mix lightly to combine.

2 Heat the tortillas gently, one at a time, in a heavy frying pan until they begin to colour on each side.

3 Spread a tortilla with 30ml/2 tbsp hoisin sauce, then sprinkle with one-quarter of the cucumber. Arrange one-quarter of the seasoned crab meat down the centre of each tortilla and roll up. Repeat with the remaining ingredients. Serve immediately.

$^1/_2$ **cucumber**

1 medium dressed crab

4 small wheat tortillas

120ml/8 tbsp hoisin sauce

FROM THE STORECUPBOARD

ground black pepper

Scallops with Fennel and Bacon

This dish is a delicious combination of succulent scallops and crispy bacon, served on a bed of tender fennel and melting mascarpone. If you can't get large scallops (known as king scallops), buy the smaller queen scallops and serve a dozen per person. If you buy scallops in the shell, wash and keep the pretty fan-shaped shells to serve a range of fish dishes in.

SERVES TWO

1 Trim, halve and slice the fennel, reserving and chopping any feathery tops. Blanch the slices in boiling water for about 3 minutes, until softened, then drain.

2 Preheat the grill (broiler) to moderate. Place the fennel in a shallow flameproof dish. Dot with the mascarpone and grill (broil) for about 5 minutes, until the cheese has melted and the fennel is lightly browned.

3 Meanwhile, pat the scallops dry on kitchen paper and season lightly. Cook the bacon in a large, heavy frying pan, until crisp and golden, turning once. Drain and keep warm. Fry the scallops in the bacon fat for 1–2 minutes on each side, until cooked through.

4 Transfer the fennel to serving plates and crumble or snip the bacon into bite size pieces over the top. Pile the scallops on the bacon and sprinkle with any reserved fennel tops.

2 small fennel bulbs

130g/4¹/₂oz/ generous ¹/₂ cup mascarpone cheese

8 large scallops, shelled

75g/3oz thin smoked streaky (fatty) bacon rashers (strips)

Prawn and New Potato Stew

New potatoes with plenty of flavour, such as Jersey Royals, Maris Piper or Nicola, are essential for this effortless stew. Use a good quality jar of tomato and chilli sauce; there are now plenty available in the supermarkets. For a really easy supper dish, serve with warm, crusty bread to mop up the delicious sauce, and a mixed green salad.

SERVES FOUR

675g/1¹/₂lb small new potatoes, scrubbed

15g/¹/₂oz/¹/₂ cup fresh coriander (cilantro)

350g/12oz jar tomato and chilli sauce

300g/11oz cooked peeled prawns (shrimp), thawed and drained if frozen

1 Cook the potatoes in boiling water for 15 minutes, until tender. Drain and return to the pan.

2 Finely chop half the coriander and add to the pan with the tomato and chilli sauce and 90ml/6 tbsp water. Bring to the boil, reduce the heat, cover and simmer gently for 5 minutes.

3 Stir in the prawns and heat briefly until they are warmed through. Do not overheat the prawns or they will quickly shrivel, becoming tough and tasteless. Spoon into shallow bowls and serve sprinkled with the remaining coriander, torn into pieces.

Haddock with Fennel Butter

Fresh fish tastes fabulous cooked in a simple herb butter. Here the liquorice flavour of fennel complements the haddock beautifully to make a simple dish ideal for a dinner party. If you can buy only small haddock fillets, fold them in half before baking, or use cod as an alternative. Serve tiny new potatoes and a herb salad with the fish to make a light, summery main course.

SERVES FOUR

1 Preheat the oven to 220°C/425°F/Gas 7. Season the fish on both sides with salt and pepper. Melt one-quarter of the butter in a frying pan, preferably non-stick, and cook the fish over a medium heat briefly on both sides.

2 Transfer the fish to a shallow ovenproof dish. Cut four wafer-thin slices from the lemon and squeeze the juice from the remainder over the fish. Place the lemon slices on top and then bake for 15–20 minutes, or until the fish is cooked.

3 Meanwhile, melt the remaining butter in the frying pan and add the fennel and a little seasoning.

4 Transfer the cooked fish to plates and pour the cooking juices into the herb butter. Heat gently for a few seconds, then pour the herb butter over the fish. Serve immediately.

675g/1¹/₂ lb haddock fillet, skinned and cut into 4 portions

1 lemon

45ml/3 tbsp coarsely chopped fennel

FROM THE STORECUPBOARD

50g/2oz/¹/₄ cup butter

salt and ground black pepper

Baked Salmon with Caraway Seeds

This classic Czech way of cooking salmon is very easy and gives excellent results. The fish cooks in its own juices, taking on the lovely warm flavour of the caraway seeds. Serve sprinkled with flat leaf parsley and wedges of lemon for squeezing over the fish.

SERVES FOUR

1.8kg/4lb whole salmon, cleaned

2.5–5ml/¹/₂–1 tsp caraway seeds

45ml/3 tbsp lemon juice

FROM THE STORECUPBOARD

115g/4oz/¹/₂ cup butter, melted

1 Preheat the oven to 180°C/350°F/Gas 4. Scale the salmon, remove the head and tail and slice off the fins with a sharp knife, then cut the fish in half lengthways.

2 Place the salmon, skin-side down, in a lightly greased roasting pan. Brush with the melted butter. Season with salt and pepper, sprinkle over the caraway seeds and drizzle with lemon juice.

3 Cover the salmon loosely with foil and bake for 25 minutes. Remove it from the oven, lift off the foil and test the fish. (The flesh should be opaque and flake easily. Return to the oven if necessary.)

4 Remove the foil and carefully lift the fish on to a serving plate. It may be served hot or cold.

Sea Bass in a Salt Crust

Baking fish in a crust of sea salt seals in and enhances its flavour. Any firm fish can be cooked in this way. Decorate with a garnish of seaweed or blanched samphire and lemon slices, and break open the crust at the table to release the glorious aroma. Serve the fish with baby new potatoes roasted with olive oil and a sprinkling of dried rosemary, and steamed green vegetables such as broccoli or green beans.

SERVES FOUR

1 Preheat the oven to 240°C/475°F/Gas 9. Fill the cavity of the fish with the sprigs of fresh fennel, rosemary and thyme, and grind over some of the mixed peppercorns.

2 Spread half the salt in an ovenproof dish (ideally oval) and lay the sea bass on it. Cover the fish all over with a 1cm/½in layer of salt, pressing it down firmly. Moisten the salt lightly by spraying with water from an atomizer. Bake the fish for 30–40 minutes, until the salt crust is just beginning to colour.

3 Bring the sea bass to the table in its salt crust. Use a sharp knife to break open the crust and cut into four portions.

1 sea bass, about 1kg/2¼lb, cleaned and scaled

1 sprig each of fresh fennel, rosemary and thyme

mixed peppercorns

2kg/4½lb coarse sea salt

Roast Cod Wrapped in Prosciutto with Vine Tomatoes

Wrapping chunky fillets of cod in wafer-thin slices of prosciutto keeps the fish succulent and moist, at the same time adding flavour and visual impact. Serve with baby new potatoes and a herb salad for a stylish supper or lunch dish.

SERVES FOUR

1 Preheat the oven to 220°C/425°F/Gas 7. Pat the fish dry on kitchen paper and remove any stray bones. Season.

2 Place one fillet in an ovenproof dish and drizzle 15ml/ 1 tbsp of the oil over it. Cover with the second fillet, laying the thick end on top of the thin end of the lower fillet to create an even shape. Lay the ham over the fish, overlapping the slices to cover the fish in an even layer. Tuck the ends of the ham under the fish and tie it in place at intervals with fine string.

3 Using kitchen scissors, snip the vines into four portions and add to the dish. Drizzle the tomatoes and ham with the remaining oil and season lightly. Roast for 35 minutes, until the tomatoes are lightly coloured and the fish is cooked through. Test the fish by piercing one end of the parcel with the tip of a knife to check that it flakes easily.

4 Slice the fish and transfer the portions to warm plates, adding the tomatoes. Spoon over the cooking juices from the dish and serve immediately.

2 thick skinless cod fillets, each weighing about 375g/13oz

75g/3oz prosciutto, thinly sliced

400g/14oz tomatoes, on the vine

FROM THE STORECUPBOARD

75ml/5 tbsp extra virgin olive oil

salt and ground black pepper

Grilled Hake with Lemon and Chilli

Choose firm hake fillets, as thick as possible. This is an ideal recipe if you are counting the calories, because it is low in fat. Serve with new potatoes and steamed fine green beans. Or, if you're not counting calories, serve with creamy mashed potatoes with plenty of butter stirred in.

SERVES FOUR

4 hake fillets, each 150g/5oz

finely grated rind and juice of 1 unwaxed lemon

15ml/1 tbsp crushed chilli flakes

FROM THE STORECUPBOARD

30ml/2 tbsp olive oil

salt and ground black pepper

1 Preheat the grill (broiler) to high. Brush the hake fillets all over with the olive oil and place them skin side up on a baking sheet.

2 Grill (broil) the fish for 4–5 minutes, until the skin is crispy, then carefully turn them over using a metal spatula.

3 Sprinkle the fillets with the lemon rind and chilli flakes and season with salt and ground black pepper.

4 Grill the fillets for a further 2–3 minutes, or until the hake is cooked through. (Test using the point of a sharp knife; the flesh should flake.) Squeeze over the lemon juice just before serving.

Trout with Grilled Serrano Ham

Traditionally in this Spanish recipe, the trout would have come from mountain streams and been stuffed and wrapped in locally cured ham. One of the beauties of this method is that the skins come off in one piece, leaving the succulent, moist flesh to be eaten with the crisped, salt ham.

SERVES FOUR

1 Extend the belly cavity of each trout, cutting up one side of the backbone. Slip a knife behind the rib bones to loosen them (sometimes just flexing the fish makes them pop up). Snip these off from both sides with scissors, and season the fish well inside.

2 Preheat the grill (broiler) to high, with a shelf in the top position. Line a baking tray with foil and butter it.

3 Working with the fish on the foil, fold a piece of ham into each belly. Use smaller or broken bits of ham for this, and reserve the eight best slices.

4 brown or rainbow trout, about 250g/9oz each, cleaned

16 thin slices Serrano ham, about 200g/7oz

buttered potatoes, to serve (optional)

FROM THE STORECUPBOARD

50g/2oz/¹/₄ cup melted butter, plus extra for greasing

salt and ground black pepper

4 Brush each trout with a little butter, seasoning the outside lightly with salt and pepper. Wrap two ham slices round each one, crossways, tucking the ends into the belly. Grill (broil) the trout for 4 minutes, then carefully turn them over with a metal spatula, rolling them across on the belly so the ham doesn't come loose, and grill for a further 4 minutes.

5 Serve the trout very hot, with any spare butter spooned over the top. Diners should open the trout on their plates, and eat them from the inside, pushing the flesh off the skin.

Tonno con Piselli

This Jewish Italian dish of fresh tuna and peas is especially enjoyed at Passover, which falls in spring. Before the days of the freezer, little peas were only eaten at this time of year when they were in season. At other times of the year chickpeas were used instead – they give a heartier result.

SERVES FOUR

1 Preheat the oven to 190°C/375°F/Gas 5. Sprinkle the tuna steaks on each side with salt and plenty of freshly ground black pepper and place in a shallow ovenproof dish, in a single layer.

2 Bring the tomato sauce to the boil, then add the fresh shelled or frozen peas and chopped fresh flat leaf parsley. Pour the sauce and peas evenly over the fish steaks in the ovenproof dish and bake in the preheated oven, uncovered, for about 20 minutes, or until the fish is tender. Serve the fish, sauce and peas immediately, straight from the dish.

350g/12oz tuna steaks

600ml/1 pint/2¹/₂ cups fresh tomato sauce

350g/12oz/3 cups fresh shelled or frozen peas

45ml/3 tbsp chopped fresh flat leaf parsley

FROM THE STORECUPBOARD

salt and ground black pepper

Filo-wrapped Fish

Select a chunky variety of tomato sauce for this simple but delicious recipe. The choice of fish can be varied according to what is in season and what is freshest on the day of purchase. When working with filo pastry, keep it covered with clear film (plastic wrap) or a damp dishtowel, as once it's exposed to air it dries out quickly and is difficult to handle.

SERVES THREE TO FOUR

130g/4¹/₂oz filo pastry (6–8 large sheets)

about 30ml/2 tbsp 450g/1lb salmon or cod steaks or fillets

550ml/18fl oz/2¹/₂ cups tomato sauce

FROM THE STORECUPBOARD

olive oil, for brushing

1 Preheat the oven to 200°C/400°F/Gas 6. Take a sheet of filo pastry, brush with a little olive oil and cover with a second sheet of pastry. Place a piece of fish on top of the pastry, towards the bottom edge, then top with 1–2 spoonfuls of the tomato sauce, spreading it in an even layer.

2 Roll the fish in the pastry, taking care to enclose the filling completely. Brush with a little olive oil. Arrange on a baking sheet and repeat with the remaining fish and pastry. You should have about half the sauce remaining, to serve with the fish.

3 Bake for 10–15 minutes, or until golden. Meanwhile, reheat the remaining sauce. Serve immediately with the remaining sauce.

Poached Fish in Spicy Tomato Sauce

A selection of white fish fillets are used in this Middle-Eastern dish – cod, haddock, hake or halibut are all good. Serve the fish with flat breads, such as pitta, and a spicy tomato relish. It is also good with couscous or rice and a green salad with a refreshing lemon juice dressing.

SERVES EIGHT

1 Heat the tomato sauce with the harissa and coriander in a large pan. Add seasoning to taste and bring to the boil.

2 Remove the pan from the heat and add the fish to the hot sauce. Return to the heat and bring the sauce to the boil again. Reduce the heat and simmer very gently for about 5 minutes, or until the fish is tender. (Test with a fork: if the flesh flakes easily, then it is cooked.)

3 Taste the sauce and adjust the seasoning, adding more harissa if necessary. Serve hot or warm.

600ml/1 pint/2^1/$_2$ cups fresh tomato sauce

2.5–5ml/^{1}/$_2$–1 tsp harissa

60ml/4 tbsp chopped fresh coriander (cilantro) leaves

1.5kg/3^1/$_4$lb mixed white fish fillets, cut into chunks

FROM THE STORECUPBOARD

salt and ground black pepper

Fish with Tomato and Pine Nuts

Whole fish marinated in lemon juice and cooked with pine nuts in a spicy tomato sauce is a speciality of Jewish cooking, particularly as a festival treat for Rosh Hashanah, the Jewish New Year. The fish may be cooked and served with head and tail on, as here, or if you like, with these removed. A simple garnish of flat leaf parsley improves the appearance of this delicious dish.

SERVES SIX TO EIGHT

1–1.5kg/2^1/$_4$–3^1/$_4$lb fish, such as snapper, cleaned, with head and tail left on

juice of 2 lemons

65g/2^1/$_2$oz/scant ^{3}/$_4$ cup pine nuts, toasted

350ml/12fl oz/1^1/$_2$ cups spicy tomato sauce

FROM THE STORECUPBOARD

salt and ground black pepper

1 Prick the fish all over with a fork and rub with 2.5ml/^{1}/$_2$ tsp salt. Put the fish in a roasting pan or large dish and pour over the lemon juice. Leave to stand for 2 hours.

2 Preheat the oven to 180°C/350°F/Gas 4. Sprinkle half of the pine nuts over the base of an ovenproof dish, top with half of the sauce, then add the fish and its marinade. Add the remaining tomato sauce and the remaining pine nuts.

3 Cover the ovenproof dish tightly with a lid or foil and bake in the preheated oven for 30 minutes, or until the fish is tender. Serve the fish immediately, straight from the dish.

Baked Salmon with Green Sauce

When buying whole salmon, there are several points to consider – the skin should be bright and shiny, the eyes should be bright and the tail should look fresh and moist. Baking the salmon in foil produces a moist result, rather like poaching, but with the ease of baking. Garnish the fish with thin slices of cucumber and dill to conceal any flesh that may look ragged after skinning and serve with lemon wedges.

SERVES SIX TO EIGHT

2–3kg/4¹/₂–6³/₄lb salmon, cleaned with head and tail left on

3–5 spring onions (scallions), thinly sliced

1 lemon, thinly sliced

600ml/1 pint/2¹/₂ cups watercress sauce or herb mayonnaise

FROM THE STORECUPBOARD

salt and ground black pepper

1 Preheat the oven to 180°C/350°F/Gas 4. Rinse the salmon and lay it on a large piece of foil. Stuff the fish with the sliced spring onions and layer the lemon slices inside and around the fish, then sprinkle with plenty of salt and ground black pepper.

2 Loosely fold the foil around the fish and fold the edges over to seal. Bake for about 1 hour.

3 Remove the fish from the oven and leave to stand, still wrapped in the foil, for about 15 minutes, then unwrap the parcel and leave the fish to cool.

4 When the fish is cool, carefully lift it on to a large plate, retaining the lemon slices. Cover the fish tightly with clear film (plastic wrap) and chill for several hours.

5 Before serving, discard the lemon slices from around the fish. Using a blunt knife to lift up the edge of the skin, carefully peel the skin away from the flesh, avoiding tearing the flesh, and pull out any fins at the same time.

6 Chill the watercress sauce or herb mayonnaise before serving. Transfer the fish to a serving platter, garnish with thin cucumber slices if desired, and serve the sauce separately.

VARIATION
Instead of cooking a whole fish, prepare 6–8 salmon steaks. Place each fish steak on an individual square of foil, then top with a slice of onion and a slice of lemon and season generously with salt and ground black pepper. Loosely wrap the foil up around the fish, fold the edges to seal and place the parcels on a baking sheet. Bake the steaks for 10–15 minutes, or until the flesh is opaque. Serve the fish cold with the chilled watercress sauce or herb mayonnaise.

Teriyaki Salmon

Bottles of teriyaki sauce – a lovely rich Japanese glaze – are available in most large supermarkets and Asian stores. Serve the salmon with sticky rice or soba noodles.

SERVES FOUR

1 Put the salmon in a shallow, non-metallic dish and pour over the teriyaki marinade. Cover and chill for 2 hours.

2 Meanwhile, heat the sunflower oil in a small pan and add the ginger. Fry for 1–2 minutes, or until golden and crisp. Remove with a slotted spoon and drain on kitchen paper.

3 Heat a griddle pan until smoking hot. Remove the salmon from the marinade and add, skin side down, to the pan. Cook for 2–3 minutes, then turn over and cook for a further 1–2 minutes, or until cooked through. Remove from the pan and divide among four serving plates. Top the salmon fillets with the crispy fried ginger.

4 Pour the marinade into the pan and cook for 1–2 minutes. Pour over the salmon and serve.

4 salmon fillets, 150g/5oz each

75ml/5 tbsp teriyaki marinade

5cm/2in piece of fresh root ginger, peeled and cut into matchsticks

FROM THE STORECUPBOARD

150ml/¹/₄ pint/²/₃ cup sunflower oil

Roast Mackerel with Spicy Chermoula Paste

Chermoula is a spice mix used widely in Moroccan and North African cooking. It is now readily available in most large supermarkets.

SERVES FOUR

4 whole mackerel, cleaned and gutted

2–3 tbsp chermoula

2 red onions, sliced

FROM THE STORECUPBOARD

75ml/5 tbsp olive oil

salt and ground black pepper

1 Preheat the oven to 190°C/375°F/Gas 5. Place each mackerel on a large sheet of baking parchment. Using a sharp knife, slash each fish several times.

2 In a small bowl, mix the chermoula with the olive oil, and spread over the mackerel, rubbing the mixture into the cuts.

3 Scatter the red onions over the mackerel, and season with salt and pepper. Scrunch the ends of the paper together to seal the fish and place on a baking tray. Bake for 20 minutes, until the mackerel is cooked through. Serve in the paper parcels, to be unwrapped at the table.

Pan-fried Skate Wings with Capers

This sophisticated way of serving skate is perfect for a dinner party. Serve with a light, green salad.

SERVES SIX

1 Heat the butter in a large frying pan and add one of the skate wings. Fry for 4–5 minutes on each side, until golden and cooked through.

2 Using a fish slice (metal spatula) carefully transfer the cooked skate wing to a warmed serving plate and keep warm while you cook each of the remaining skate wings in the same way.

3 Return the pan to the heat and add the lime rind and juice, and capers. Season with salt and freshly ground black pepper to taste and allow to bubble for 1–2 minutes. Spoon a little of the juices and the capers over each skate wing and serve immediately.

6 small skate wings

grated rind and juice of 2 limes

30ml/2 tbsp salted capers, rinsed and drained

FROM THE STORECUPBOARD

50g/2oz/¹⁄₄ cup butter

salt and ground black pepper

Sea Bass with Parsley and Lime Butter

The delicate but firm, sweet flesh of sea bass goes beautifully with citrus flavours. Serve with roast fennel and sautéed diced potatoes.

SERVES SIX

6 sea bass fillets, about 150g/5oz each

grated rind and juice of 1 large lime

30ml/2 tbsp chopped fresh parsley

FROM THE STORECUPBOARD

50g/2oz/¼ cup butter

salt and ground black pepper

1 Heat the butter in a large frying pan and add three of the sea bass fillets, skin side down. Cook for 3–4 minutes, or until the skin is crisp and golden. Flip the fish over and cook for a further 2–3 minutes, or until cooked through.

2 Remove the fillets from the pan with a metal spatula. Place each on a serving plate and keep them warm. Cook the remaining fish in the same way and transfer to serving plates.

3 Add the lime rind and juice to the pan with the parsley, and season with salt and black pepper. Allow to bubble for 1–2 minutes, then pour a little over each fish portion and serve immediately.

Meat

WITH THE SIMPLE ADDITION OF A FEW WELL-CHOSEN
INGREDIENTS, MEAT DISHES CAN BE TRANSFORMED INTO
EXCITING, INNOVATIVE DISHES. FROM STEAK TO PORK,
THIS CHAPTER INCLUDES A WONDERFUL SELECTION OF
DISHES THAT ARE EQUALLY SUITED TO A QUICK FAMILY
SUPPER, A LONG SUNDAY LUNCH OR AN INSPIRED
DINNER PARTY.

Beef Patties with Onions and Peppers

This is a firm family favourite. It is easy to make and delicious, and it can be varied by adding other vegetables, such as sliced red peppers, broccoli or mushrooms. These patties are very versatile and can be served in a variety of ways – with chunky home-made chips (French fries), with crusty bread, or with rice and a ready-made tomato sauce.

SERVES FOUR

1 Place the minced beef, chopped onion and 15ml/1 tbsp garlic-flavoured oil in a bowl and mix well. Season well and form into four large or eight small patties.

2 Heat the remaining oil in a large non-stick pan, then add the patties and cook on both sides until browned. Sprinkle over 15ml/1 tbsp water and add a little seasoning.

3 Cover the patties with the sliced onions and peppers. Sprinkle in another 15ml/1 tbsp water and a little seasoning, then cover the pan. Reduce the heat to very low and braise for 20–30 minutes.

4 When the onions are turning golden brown, remove the pan from the heat. Serve with onions and peppers.

500g/1¼lb lean minced (ground) beef

4 onions, 1 finely chopped and 3 sliced

2–3 green (bell) peppers, seeded and sliced lengthways into strips

FROM THE STORECUPBOARD

30ml/2 tbsp garlic-flavoured olive oil or olive oil

salt and ground black pepper

Steak with Warm Tomato Salsa

A refreshing, tangy salsa of tomatoes, spring onions and balsamic vinegar makes a colourful topping for chunky, pan-fried steaks. Choose rump, sirloin or fillet – whichever is your favourite – and if you do not have a non-stick pan, grill the steak instead for the same length of time. Serve with potato wedges and a mixed leaf salad with a mustard dressing.

SERVES TWO

1 Trim any excess fat from the steaks, then season on both sides with salt and pepper. Heat a non-stick frying pan and cook the steaks for about 3 minutes on each side for medium rare. Cook for a little longer if you like your steak well cooked.

2 Meanwhile, put the tomatoes in a heatproof bowl, cover with boiling water and leave for 1–2 minutes, until the skins start to split. Drain and peel the tomatoes, then halve them and scoop out the seeds. Dice the tomato flesh. Thinly slice the spring onions.

3 Transfer the steaks to plates and keep warm. Add the vegetables, balsamic vinegar, 30ml/2 tbsp water and a little seasoning to the cooking juices in the pan and stir briefly until warm, scraping up any meat residue. Spoon the salsa over the steaks to serve.

2 steaks, about 2cm/³/₄ in thick

4 large plum tomatoes

2 spring onions (scallions)

30ml/2 tbsp balsamic vinegar

FROM THE STORECUPBOARD

salt and ground black pepper

Meatballs in Tomato Sauce

Cook meatballs in their sauce, rather than frying them first, because this helps keep them nice and moist. Serve in the traditional way with spaghetti and shavings of Parmesan cheese.

SERVES FOUR

225g/8oz/1 cup minced (ground) beef

4 Sicilian-style sausages

2 x 400g/14oz cans pomodorino tomatoes

FROM THE STORECUPBOARD

salt and ground black pepper

1 Put the minced beef in a bowl and season with salt and pepper. Remove the sausages from their skins and mix thoroughly into the beef.

2 Shape the mixture into balls about the size of large walnuts and arrange in a single layer in a shallow baking dish. Cover and chill for 30 minutes.

3 Preheat the oven to 180°C/350°F/Gas 4. Process the tomatoes in a food processor until just smooth, and season. Pour over the meatballs, making sure they are all covered.

4 Bake the meatballs for 40 minutes, stirring once or twice until they are cooked through, then serve.

Beef Cooked in Red Wine

Shin of beef is traditionally quite a tough cut that needs long, slow cooking, and marinating the beef in red wine gives a tender result. Sprinkle the stew with rosemary and serve with mashed potatoes.

SERVES FOUR TO SIX

675g/1¹/₂lb boned and cubed shin of beef

3 large garlic cloves, finely chopped

1 bottle fruity red wine

FROM THE STORECUPBOARD

salt and ground black pepper

1 Put the beef in a casserole dish with the garlic and some black pepper, and pour over the red wine. Stir to combine, then cover and chill for at least 12 hours.

2 Preheat the oven to 160°C/325°F/Gas 3. Cover the casserole with a tight-fitting lid and transfer to the oven. Cook for 2 hours, or until the beef is very tender. Season with salt and pepper to taste, and serve piping hot.

VARIATION
Marinate the beef in a mixture of half port and half beef stock instead of the red wine. Port cooks down to produce a lovely rich sauce, but be sure to dilute it with stock because it can be quite overpowering on its own. A half-and-half mixture will give the perfect balance of taste.

Pan-fried Gaelic Steaks

A good steak is always popular and top quality raw materials plus timing are the keys to success. Choose small, thick steaks rather than large, thin ones if you can. Traditional accompaniments include potato chips, fried onions, mushrooms and peas.

SERVES FOUR

4 x 225–350g/8–12oz sirloin steaks, at room temperature

50ml/2fl oz/¼ cup Irish whiskey

300ml/½ pint/1¼ cups double (heavy) cream

FROM THE STORECUPBOARD

15g/1/2oz/1 tbsp butter

5ml/1 tsp oil

salt and ground black pepper

1 Season the steaks with pepper. Heat a heavy pan, over high heat. When it is hot, add the oil and butter. Add the steaks one at a time, to seal the meat quickly. Lower the heat to moderate. Allowing 3–4 minutes for rare, 4–5 minutes for medium or 5–6 minutes for well-done steaks, leave undisturbed for half of the specified cooking time; thick steaks will take longer than thin ones. Turn only once.

2 When the steaks are cooked to your liking, transfer them to warmed plates to keep warm. Pour off the fat from the pan and discard. Add the whiskey and stir to remove the sediment at the base of the pan. Allow the liquid to reduce a little, then add the cream and simmer over low heat for a few minutes, until the cream thickens. Season to taste, pour the sauce around or over the steaks, as preferred, and serve immediately.

Thai-style Rare Beef and Mango Salad

This simplified version of Thai beef salad is especially tasty served with little bowls of fresh coriander (cilantro) leaves, chopped spring onions (scallions) and peanuts for sprinkling at the table.

SERVES FOUR

450g/1lb sirloin steak

45ml/3 tbsp soy sauce

2 mangoes, peeled, stoned (pitted) and finely sliced

FROM THE STORECUPBOARD

45ml/3 tbsp garlic-infused olive oil

ground black pepper

1 Put the steak in a shallow, non-metallic dish and pour over the oil and soy sauce. Season with pepper and turn the steaks to coat in the marinade. Cover and chill for 2 hours.

2 Heat a griddle pan until hot. Remove the steak from the marinade and place on the griddle pan. Cook for 3–5 minutes on each side, moving the steak halfway through if you want a criss-cross pattern.

3 Transfer the steak to a board and leave to rest for 5–10 minutes. Meanwhile, pour the marinade into the pan and cook for a few seconds, then remove from the heat. Thinly slice the steak and arrange on four serving plates with the mangoes. Drizzle over the pan juices to serve.

North African Lamb

This dish is full of contrasting flavours that create a rich, spicy and fruity main course. For best results, use lamb that still retains some fat, as this will help keep the meat moist and succulent during roasting. Serve the lamb with couscous or mixed white and wild rice, sprinkled with chopped coriander (cilantro). Roasted chunks of red and yellow (bell) peppers, aubergine (eggplant) and courgettes (zucchini), cooked in the oven with the lamb, complete the meal.

SERVES FOUR

1 Preheat the oven to 200°C/400°F/Gas 6. Heat a frying pan, preferably non-stick, and cook the lamb on all sides until beginning to brown. Transfer to a roasting pan, reserving any fat in the frying pan.

2 Peel the onions and cut each into six wedges. Toss with the lamb and roast for about 30-40 minutes, until the lamb is cooked through and the onions are deep golden brown.

3 Tip the lamb and onions back into the frying pan. Mix the harissa with 250ml/8fl oz/1 cup boiling water and add to the roasting pan. Scrape up any residue in the pan and pour the mixture over the lamb and onions. Stir in the prunes and heat until just simmering. Cover and simmer for 5 minutes, then serve.

675g/1¹/₂lb lamb fillet or shoulder steaks, cut into chunky pieces

5 small onions

7.5ml/1¹/₂ tsp harissa

115g/4oz ready-to-eat pitted prunes, halved

Lamb Steaks with Redcurrant Glaze

This classic, simple dish is absolutely delicious and is an excellent, quick recipe for cooking on the barbecue. The tangy flavour of redcurrants is a traditional accompaniment to lamb. It is good served with new potatoes and fresh garden peas tossed in butter.

SERVES FOUR

1 Reserve the tips of the rosemary and chop the remaining leaves. Rub the chopped rosemary, salt and pepper all over the lamb.

2 Preheat the grill (broiler). Heat the redcurrant jelly gently in a small pan with 30ml/2 tbsp water. Stir in the vinegar.

3 Place the steaks on a foil-lined grill (broiler) rack and brush with a little of the redcurrant glaze. Cook for about 5 minutes on each side, until deep golden, brushing with more glaze.

4 Transfer the lamb to warmed plates. Tip any juices from the foil into the remaining glaze and heat through. Pour the glaze over the lamb and serve, garnished with the reserved rosemary.

4 large fresh rosemary sprigs

4 lamb leg steaks

75ml/5 tbsp redcurrant jelly

30ml/2 tbsp raspberry or red wine vinegar

FROM THE STORECUPBOARD

salt and ground black pepper

Lamb Chops with a Mint Jelly Crust

Mint and lamb are classic partners, and the breadcrumbs used here add extra texture. Serve the chops with sweet potatoes baked in their skins and some steamed green vegetables.

SERVES FOUR

1 Preheat the oven to 190°C/375°F/Gas 5. Place the lamb chops on a baking sheet and season with plenty of salt and ground black pepper.

2 Put the breadcrumbs and mint jelly in a bowl and mix together to combine. Spoon the breadcrumb mixture on top of the chops, pressing down firmly with the back of a spoon making sure they stick to the chops.

3 Bake the chops for 20–30 minutes, or until they are just cooked through. Serve immediately.

8 lamb chops, about 115g/4oz each

50g/2oz/1 cup fresh white breadcrumbs

30ml/2 tbsp mint jelly

FROM THE STORECUPBOARD

salt and ground black pepper

Marinated Lamb with Oregano and Basil

Lamb leg steaks are chunky with a sweet flavour and go well with oregano and basil. However, you could also use finely chopped rosemary or thyme. Serve with couscous.

SERVES FOUR

1 Put the lamb in a shallow, non-metallic dish. Mix 45ml/3 tbsp of the oil with the oregano, basil and some salt and pepper, reserving some of the herbs for garnish. Pour over the lamb and turn to coat in the marinade. Cover and chill for up to 8 hours.

2 Heat the remaining oil in a large frying pan. Remove the lamb from the marinade and fry for 5–6 minutes on each side, until slightly pink in the centre. Add the marinade and cook for 1–2 minutes until warmed through. Garnish with the reserved herbs and serve.

4 large or 8 small lamb leg steaks

1 small bunch of fresh oregano, roughly chopped

1 small bunch of fresh basil, torn

FROM THE STORECUPBOARD

60ml/4 tbsp garlic-infused olive oil

salt and ground black pepper

Roast Shoulder of Lamb with Whole Garlic Cloves

The potatoes catch the lamb fat as it cooks, giving garlicky, juicy results. Return the potatoes to the oven to keep warm while you leave the lamb to rest before carving. Serve with seasonal vegetables.

SERVES FOUR TO SIX

675g/1¹/₂lb waxy potatoes, peeled and cut into large dice

12 garlic cloves, unpeeled

1 whole shoulder of lamb

FROM THE STORECUPBOARD

45ml/3 tbsp olive oil

salt and ground black pepper

1 Preheat the oven to 180°C/350°F/Gas 4. Put the potatoes and garlic cloves into a large roasting pan and season with salt and pepper. Pour over 30ml/2 tbsp of the oil and toss the potatoes and garlic to coat.

2 Place a rack over the roasting pan, so that it is not touching the potatoes. Place the lamb on the rack and drizzle over the remaining oil. Season with salt and pepper.

3 Roast the lamb and potatoes for 2–2¹/₂ hours, or until the lamb is cooked through. Halfway through the cooking time, carefully take the lamb and the rack off the roasting pan and turn the potatoes to ensure even cooking.

Roast Leg of Lamb with Rosemary and Garlic

This is a classic combination of flavours, and always popular. Serve as a traditional Sunday lunch with roast potatoes and vegetables. Leaving the lamb to rest before carving ensures a tender result.

SERVES FOUR TO SIX

1 leg of lamb, approx 1.8kg/4lb

2 garlic cloves, finely sliced

leaves from 2 sprigs of fresh rosemary

FROM THE STORECUPBOARD

30ml/2 tbsp olive oil

salt and ground black pepper

1 Preheat the oven to 190°C/375°F/Gas 5. Using a small sharp knife, make slits at 4cm/1^1/$_2$in intervals over the lamb, deep enough to hold a piece of garlic. Push the garlic and rosemary leaves into the slits.

2 Drizzle the olive oil over the top of the lamb and season with plenty of salt and ground black pepper. Roast for 25 minutes per 450g/1lb of lamb, plus another 25 minutes.

3 Remove the lamb from the oven and leave to rest for about 15 minutes before carving.

Sweet-and-sour Lamb

Buy lamb loin chops from your butcher and ask him to French trim them for you. Serve with steamed carrots or green beans.

SERVES FOUR

8 French-trimmed lamb loin chops

90ml/6 tbsp balsamic vinegar

30ml/2 tbsp caster (superfine) sugar

FROM THE STORECUPBOARD

30ml/2 tbsp olive oil

salt and ground black pepper

1 Put the lamb chops in a shallow, non-metallic dish and drizzle over the balsamic vinegar. Sprinkle with the sugar and season with salt and black pepper. Turn the chops to coat in the mixture, then cover with clear film (plastic wrap) and chill for 20 minutes.

2 Heat the olive oil in a large frying pan and add the chops, reserving the marinade. Cook for 3–4 minutes on each side.

3 Pour the marinade into the pan and leave to bubble for about 2 minutes, or until reduced slightly. Remove from the pan and serve immediately.

Roast Lamb with Figs

Lamb fillet is an expensive cut of meat, but because it is very lean there is very little waste. To make a more economical version of this dish, use leg of lamb instead. It has a stronger flavour but is equally good. Serve with steamed green beans.

SERVES SIX

1kg/2¹/₄lb lamb fillet

9 fresh figs

150ml/¹/₄ pint/²/₃ cup ruby port

FROM THE STORECUPBOARD

30ml/2 tbsp olive oil

salt and ground black pepper

1 Preheat the oven to 190°/375°F/Gas 5. Heat the oil in a roasting pan over a medium heat. Add the lamb fillet and sear on all sides until evenly browned.

2 Cut the figs in half and arrange around the lamb. Season the lamb with salt and ground black pepper and roast for 30 minutes. Pour the port over the figs.

3 Return the lamb to the oven and roast for a further 30–45 minutes. The meat should still be slightly pink in the middle so be careful not to overcook.

4 Transfer the lamb to a board and leave to rest for about 5 minutes. Carve into slices and serve.

Paprika Pork

This chunky, goulash-style dish is rich with peppers and paprika. Grilling the peppers before adding them to the meat really brings out their sweet, vibrant flavour. Rice or buttered boiled potatoes go particularly well with the rich pork.

SERVES FOUR

2 red, 1 yellow and 1 green (bell) pepper, seeded

500g/1¼lb lean pork fillet (tenderloin)

45ml/3 tbsp paprika

300g/11oz jar or tub of tomato sauce with herbs or garlic

FROM THE STORECUPBOARD

salt and ground black pepper

1 Preheat the grill (broiler). Cut the peppers into thick strips and sprinkle in a single layer on a foil-lined grill rack. Cook under the grill for 20–25 minutes, until the edges of the strips are lightly charred.

2 Meanwhile, cut the pork into chunks. Season and cook in a frying pan for about 5 minutes, until beginning to brown.

3 Transfer the meat to a heavy pan and add the paprika, tomato sauce, 300ml/½ pint/1¼ cups water and a little seasoning. Bring to the boil, reduce the heat, cover and simmer gently for 30 minutes.

4 Add the grilled (broiled) peppers and cook for a further 10–15 minutes, until the meat is tender. Taste for seasoning and serve immediately.

Pork Kebabs

The word kebab comes from Arabic and means on a skewer. Use pork fillet (tenderloin) for these kebabs because it is lean and tender, and cooks very quickly. They are good served with rice, or stuffed into warmed pitta bread with some shredded lettuce leaves.

SERVES FOUR

500g/1¼lb lean pork fillet (tenderloin)

8 large, thick spring onions (scallions), trimmed

120ml/4fl oz/½ cup barbecue sauce

1 lemon

1 Cut the pork into 2.5cm/1in cubes. Cut the spring onions into 2.5cm/1in long sticks.

2 Preheat the grill (broiler) to high. Oil the wire rack and spread out the pork cubes on it. Grill (broil) the pork until the juices drip, then dip the pieces in the barbecue sauce and put back on the grill. Grill for 30 seconds on each side, repeating the dipping process twice more. Set aside and keep warm.

3 Gently grill (broil) the spring onions until soft and slightly brown outside. Do not dip in the barbecue sauce. Thread about four pieces of pork and three spring onion pieces on to each of eight bamboo skewers.

4 Arrange the skewers on a platter. Cut the lemon into wedges and squeeze a little lemon juice over each skewer. Serve immediately, offering the remaining lemon wedges separately.

COOK'S TIP
If you are cooking the pork on a barbecue, soak the skewers overnight in water. This prevents them burning. Keep the skewer handles away from the fire and turn them frequently.

Fragrant Lemon Grass and Ginger Pork Patties

Lemon grass lends a fragrant citrus flavour to pork, enhanced by the fresh zing of ginger. Serve the patties in burger buns with thick slices of juicy tomato, crisp, refreshing lettuce and a splash of chilli sauce.

SERVES FOUR

450g/1lb/2 cups minced (ground) pork

15ml/1 tbsp fresh root ginger, grated

1 lemon grass stalk

FROM THE STORECUPBOARD

30ml/2 tbsp sunflower oil

salt and ground black pepper

1 Put the pork in a bowl and stir in the ginger. Season with salt and pepper. Remove the tough outer layers from the lemon grass stalk and discard. Chop the centre part as finely as possible and mix into the pork. Shape into four patties and chill for about 20 minutes.

2 Heat the oil in a large, non-stick frying pan and add the patties. Fry for 3–4 minutes on each side over a gentle heat, until cooked through. Remove from the pan with a metal spatula and drain on kitchen paper, then serve.

Pan-fried Gammon with Cider

Gammon and cider are a delicious combination with the sweet, tangy flavour of cider complementing the gammon perfectly. Serve with mustard mashed potatoes.

SERVES FOUR

4 gammon steaks (smoked or cured ham), 225g/8oz each

150ml/^{1}/$_4$ pint/^{2}/$_3$ cup dry (hard) cider

45ml/3 tbsp double (heavy) cream

FROM THE STORECUPBOARD

30ml/2 tbsp sunflower oil

salt and ground black pepper

1 Heat the oil in a large frying pan until hot. Neatly snip the rind on the gammon steaks to stop them curling up and add them to the pan.

2 Cook the steaks for 3–4 minutes on each side, then pour in the cider. Allow to boil for a couple of minutes, then stir in the cream and cook for 1–2 minutes, or until thickened. Season with salt and pepper, and serve immediately.

Caramelized Onion and Sausage Tarte Tatin

Toulouse sausages have a garlicky flavour and meaty texture that is delicious with fried onions. Serve with a green salad of bitter leaves.

SERVES FOUR

450g/1lb Toulouse sausages

2 large onions, sliced

250g/9oz ready-made puff pastry, thawed if frozen

FROM THE STORECUPBOARD

45ml/3 tbsp sunflower oil

salt and ground black pepper

1 Heat the oil in a 23cm/9in non-stick frying pan with an ovenproof handle, and add the sausages. Cook over a gentle heat, turning occasionally, for 7–10 minutes, or until golden and cooked through. Remove from the pan and set aside.

2 Preheat the oven to 190°C/375°F/Gas 5. Pour the remaining oil into the frying pan and add the onions. Season with salt and pepper and cook over a gentle heat for 10 minutes, stirring occasionally, until caramelized and tender.

3 Slice each sausage into four or five chunks and stir into the onions. Remove from the heat and set aside.

4 Roll out the puff pastry and cut out a circle slightly larger than the frying pan. Lay the pastry over the sausages and onions, tucking the edges in all the way around. Bake for 20 minutes, or until the pastry is risen and golden. Turn out on to a board, pastry side down, cut into wedges and serve.

Roast Pork with Juniper Berries and Bay

Juniper berries have a strong, pungent taste and are a great flavouring for rich, fatty meats such as pork, while bay leaves add a lovely aroma. Serve with roast potatoes and lightly cooked leafy green vegetables.

SERVES FOUR TO SIX

1kg/2¼lb boned leg of pork

5 fresh bay leaves

6 juniper berries

FROM THE STORECUPBOARD

15ml/1 tbsp olive oil

salt and ground black pepper

1 Preheat the oven to 180°C/350°F/Gas 4. Open out the pork and season with plenty of salt and black pepper.

2 Lay the bay leaves on the pork and sprinkle over the juniper berries. Carefully roll up the pork to enclose the bay leaves and juniper berries and tie with string to secure.

3 Rub the skin with the oil and then rub in plenty of salt. Roast the pork for 20 minutes per 450g/1lb, plus an extra 20 minutes.

4 Remove the pork from the oven and leave to rest for about 10 minutes before carving, then serve immediately.

Sticky Glazed Pork Ribs

These spare ribs have a lovely sweet-and-sour flavour and are always as popular with children as they are with adults, making them the perfect choice for a family meal. They're also great for cooking over a barbecue; make sure you leave them to marinate for at least 30 minutes before cooking. To enjoy sticky ribs at their best you need to get stuck in and eat them with your fingers, so make sure you serve them with plenty of paper napkins.

SERVES FOUR

1 Preheat the oven to 190°C/375°F/Gas 5. Put the spare ribs in a roasting pan and season well with plenty of salt and ground black pepper.

2 In a small bowl, mix together the honey and soy sauce and pour over the ribs. Turn the ribs several times, spooning over the mixture until thoroughly coated.

3 Bake the spare ribs for 30 minutes, then increase the oven temperature to 220°C/425°F/Gas 7 and cook for a further 10 minutes, or until the honey and soy sauce marinade turns into a thick, sticky glaze.

900g/2lb pork spare ribs

75ml/5 tbsp clear honey

75ml/5 tbsp light soy sauce

FROM THE STORECUPBOARD

salt and ground black pepper

Chinese Spiced Pork Chops

Five-spice powder is a fantastic ingredient for perking up dishes and adding a good depth of flavour. The five different spices – Szechuan pepper, cinnamon, cloves, fennel seeds and star anise – are perfectly balanced, with the aniseed flavour of star anise predominating. Serve the chops with lightly steamed pak choi (bok choy) and plain boiled rice.

SERVES FOUR

4 large pork chops, about 200g/7oz each

15ml/1 tbsp Chinese five-spice powder

30ml/2 tbsp soy sauce

FROM THE STORECUPBOARD

30ml/2 tbsp garlic-infused olive oil

1 Arrange the pork chops in a single layer in a non-metallic roasting pan or baking dish.

2 Sprinkle the five-spice powder over the chops, then drizzle over the soy sauce and garlic infused oil. (Alternatively, mix together the garlic-infused olive oil, soy sauce and five-spice powder, and pour over the chops.)

3 Using your hands, rub the mixture into the meat. Cover the dish with clear film (plastic wrap) and chill for 2 hours.

4 Preheat the oven to 160°C/325°F/Gas 3. Uncover the dish and bake for 30–40 minutes, or until the pork is cooked through and tender. Serve immediately.

Poultry and Game

WITH THE SIMPLE ADDITION OF A FEW WELL-CHOSEN
INGREDIENTS, POULTRY CAN BE TRANSFORMED INTO
EXCITING, INNOVATIVE DISHES. FROM DUCK TO PHEASANT,
THIS CHAPTER INCLUDES A WONDERFUL SELECTION OF
DISHES THAT ARE EQUALLY SUITED TO A QUICK FAMILY
SUPPER OR A DINNER PARTY.

Pot-roasted Chicken with Preserved Lemons

Roasting chicken and potatoes in this way gives an interesting variety of textures. The chicken and potatoes on the top crisp up, while underneath they stay soft and juicy. Serve with steamed carrots or curly kale.

SERVES FOUR TO SIX

675g/1¹/₂lb potatoes, unpeeled and cut into chunks

6–8 pieces of preserved lemon

1.3kg/3lb corn-fed chicken, jointed

FROM THE STORECUPBOARD

30ml/2 tbsp olive oil

salt and ground black pepper

1 Preheat the oven to 190°C/375°F/Gas 5. Drizzle the olive oil into the bottom of a large roasting pan. Spread the chunks of potato in a single layer in the pan and tuck in the pieces of preserved lemon.

2 Pour about 1cm/¹/₂in of cold water into the roasting pan. Arrange the chicken pieces on top and season with plenty of salt and black pepper. Roast for 45 minutes–1 hour, or until the chicken is cooked through, and serve.

Honey Mustard Chicken

Chicken thighs have a rich flavour, but if you want to cut down on fat, use four chicken breast portions instead and cook for 20–25 minutes. Serve with a chunky tomato and red onion salad.

SERVES FOUR

1 Preheat the oven to 190°C/375°F/Gas 5. Put the chicken thighs in a single layer in a roasting pan.

2 Mix together the mustard and honey, season with salt and ground black pepper to taste and brush the mixture all over the chicken thighs.

3 Cook for 25–30 minutes, brushing the chicken with the pan juices occasionally, until cooked through. (To check the chicken is cooked through, skewer it with a sharp knife; the juices should run clear.)

8 chicken thighs

60ml/4 tbsp wholegrain mustard

60ml/4 tbsp clear honey

FROM THE STORECUPBOARD

salt and ground black pepper

Drunken Chicken

In this traditional Chinese dish, cooked chicken is marinated in sherry, fresh root ginger and spring onions for several days. Because of the lengthy preparation time, it is important to use a very fresh bird from a reputable supplier. Fresh herbs can be added as an additional garnish, if you like.

SERVES FOUR TO SIX

1 Rinse and dry the chicken inside and out. Place the ginger and spring onions in the body cavity. Put the chicken in a large pan or flameproof casserole and just cover with water. Bring to the boil, skim off any scum and cook for 15 minutes.

2 Turn off the heat, cover the pan or casserole tightly and leave the chicken in the cooking liquid for 3–4 hours, by which time it will be cooked. Drain well, reserving the stock. Pour 300ml/½ pint/1¼ cups of the stock into a jug (pitcher).

3 Remove the skin and cut the chicken into neat pieces. Divide each leg into a drumstick and thigh. Make two more portions from the wings and some of the breast. Finally, cut away the remainder of the breast pieces (still on the bone) and divide each piece into two even-size portions.

4 Arrange the chicken portions in a shallow dish. Rub salt into the chicken and cover with clear film (plastic wrap). Leave in a cool place for several hours or overnight in the refrigerator.

5 Later, lift off any fat from the stock, add the sherry and pour over the chicken. Cover again and leave in the refrigerator to marinate for 2–3 days, turning occasionally.

6 When ready to serve, cut the chicken through the bone into chunky pieces and arrange on a large serving platter. Garnish the chicken with spring onion shreds.

1 chicken, about 1.3kg/3lb

1cm/½in piece of fresh root ginger, thinly sliced

2 spring onions (scallions), trimmed, plus extra to garnish

300ml/½ pint/1¼ cups dry sherry

FROM THE STORECUPBOARD

salt

VARIATION
To serve as a cocktail snack, take the meat off the bones, cut it into bitesize pieces, then spear each piece on a cocktail stick (toothpick).

Soy-marinated Chicken

Two simple flavours, soy sauce and orange, combine to make this mouthwatering dish. Serving the chicken on a bed of asparagus turns the dish into a special treat. Wilted spinach or shredded greens work well as an everyday alternative. Boiled egg noodles or steamed white rice make a good accompaniment.

SERVES FOUR

4 skinless, chicken breast fillets

1 large orange

30ml/2 tbsp dark soy sauce

400g/14oz medium asparagus spears

1 Slash each chicken portion diagonally and place them in a single layer in a shallow, ovenproof dish. Halve the orange, squeeze the juice from one half and mix it with the soy sauce. Pour this over the chicken. Cut the remaining orange into wedges and place these on the chicken. Cover and leave to marinate for several hours.

2 Preheat the oven to 180°C/350°F/Gas 4. Turn the chicken over and bake, uncovered, for 20 minutes. Turn the chicken over again and bake for a further 15 minutes, or until cooked through.

3 Meanwhile, cut off any tough ends from the asparagus and place in a frying pan. Pour in enough boiling water just to cover and cook gently for 3–4 minutes, until just tender. Drain and arrange on warmed plates, then top with the chicken and orange wedges. Spoon over the cooking juices. Serve immediately.

Stir-fried Chicken with Thai Basil

Thai basil, sometimes called holy basil, has purple-tinged leaves and a more pronounced, slightly aniseedy flavour than the usual varieties. It is available in most Asian food stores but if you can't find any, use a handful of ordinary basil instead. Serve this fragrant stir-fry with plain steamed rice or boiled noodles and soy sauce on the side.

SERVES FOUR

1 Using a sharp knife, slice the chicken breast portions into strips. Halve the peppers, remove the seeds, then cut each piece of pepper into strips.

2 Heat the oil in a wok or large frying pan. Add the chicken and red peppers and stir-fry over a high heat for about 3 minutes, until the chicken is golden and cooked through. Season with salt and ground black pepper.

3 Roughly tear up the basil leaves, add to the chicken and peppers and toss briefly to combine. Serve immediately.

4 skinless chicken breast fillets, cut into strips

2 red (bell) peppers

1 small bunch of fresh Thai basil

FROM THE STORECUPBOARD

30ml/2 tbsp garlic-infused olive oil

salt and ground black pepper

Crème Fraîche and Coriander Chicken

Boneless chicken thighs are used for this recipe but you can substitute breast portions if you like. Be generous with the coriander leaves, as they have a wonderful fragrant flavour, or use chopped parsley instead. Serve with creamy mashed potatoes. To make a lower fat version of this dish, use chicken breast portions and low-fat crème fraîche.

SERVES FOUR

6 skinless chicken thigh fillets

60ml/4 tbsp crème fraîche

1 small bunch of fresh coriander (cilantro), roughly chopped

FROM THE STORECUPBOARD

15ml/1 tbsp sunflower oil

salt and ground black pepper

1 Cut each chicken thigh into three or four pieces. Heat the oil in a large frying pan, add the chicken and cook for about 6 minutes, turning occasionally, until cooked through.

2 Add the crème fraîche to the pan and stir until melted, then allow to bubble for 1–2 minutes.

3 Add the chopped coriander to the chicken and stir to combine. Season with salt and ground black pepper to taste, and serve immediately.

Chicken Escalopes with Lemon and Serrano Ham

Chicken escalopes are flattened chicken breast fillets – they cook quicker than normal breast portions and absorb flavours more readily. In this light summery dish, the chicken absorbs the delicious flavours of the ham and lemon. It can be assembled in advance, so is good for entertaining.

SERVES FOUR

1 Preheat the oven to 180°C/350°F/Gas 4. Beat the butter with plenty of freshly ground black pepper and set aside. Place the chicken portions on a large sheet of clear film (plastic wrap), spacing them well apart. Cover with a second sheet, then beat with a rolling pin until the portions are half their original thickness.

2 Transfer the chicken to a large, shallow ovenproof dish and crumple a slice of ham on top of each. Cut eight thin slices from the lemon and place two on each slice of ham.

3 Dot with the pepper butter and bake for about 30 minutes, until the chicken is cooked. Transfer to serving plates and spoon over any juices from the dish.

4 skinless chicken breast fillets

4 slices Serrano ham

1 lemon

FROM THE STORECUPBOARD

40g/1½oz/3 tbsp butter, softened

salt and ground black pepper

Roast Chicken with Herb Cheese, Chilli and Lime Stuffing

Whether you are entertaining guests or cooking a family meal, a tasty chicken is a sure winner every time. This is a modern twist on the classic roast chicken – the stuffing is forced under the chicken skin, which helps to produce a wonderfully flavoured, succulent flesh.

SERVES FIVE TO SIX

1 Preheat the oven to 200°C/400°F/Gas 6. Using first the point of a knife and then your fingers, separate the skin from the meat across the chicken breast and over the tops of the legs. Use the knife to loosen the first piece of skin, then carefully run your fingers underneath, taking care not to tear the skin.

2 Grate the lime and beat the rind into the cream cheese together with the chopped chilli. Pack the cream cheese stuffing under the skin, using a teaspoon, until fairly evenly distributed. Push the skin back into place, then smooth your hands over it to spread the stuffing in an even layer.

3 Put the chicken in a roasting pan and squeeze the juice from the lime over the top. Roast for 1½ hours, or until the juices run clear when the thickest part of the thigh is pierced with a skewer. If necessary, cover the chicken with foil towards the end of cooking if the top starts to become too browned.

4 Carve the chicken and arrange on a warmed serving platter. Spoon the pan juices over it and serve immediately.

1.8kg/4lb chicken

1 lime

115g/4oz/½ cup cream cheese with herbs and garlic

1 mild fresh red chilli, seeded and finely chopped

Tandoori Chicken

If you have time, prepare this dish when you get up in the morning, so that it's ready to cook for supper. Serve with a red onion and cucumber salad and warmed naan bread.

SERVES FOUR

4 skinless chicken breast fillets and 4 skinless chicken thigh fillets

200ml/7fl oz/scant 1 cup Greek (US strained plain) yogurt

45ml/3 tbsp tandoori curry paste

FROM THE STORECUPBOARD

salt and ground black pepper

1 Using a sharp knife, slash the chicken breasts and thighs and place in a shallow, non-metallic dish.

2 Put the curry paste and yogurt in a bowl and mix together. Season with salt and pepper, then pour over the chicken and toss to coat well. Cover the dish with clear film (plastic wrap) and chill for at least 8 hours.

3 Preheat the oven to 190ºC/375ºF/Gas 5. Remove the clear film from the chicken and transfer the dish to the oven. Bake for 20–30 minutes, or until the chicken is cooked through. Serve immediately.

Roast Chicken with Black Pudding and Sage

The combination of juicy roast chicken and black pudding is wonderful. Serve as part of a Sunday roast or simply with a salad.

SERVES FOUR

1 medium oven-ready chicken

115g/4oz black pudding (blood sausage), skinned

30ml/2 tbsp fresh sage leaves

FROM THE STORECUPBOARD

25g/1oz/2 tbsp softened butter

salt and ground black pepper

1 Preheat the oven to 190°C/375°F/Gas 5. Carefully push your fingers between the skin and the flesh at the neck end of the bird to loosen it, making sure you don't tear the skin.

2 Shape the black pudding into a flat, roundish shape, to fit the space between the skin and the breast meat. Push it under the skin with half the sage leaves.

3 Smooth the skin back and tuck underneath. Tie the legs together and place the chicken in a roasting pan. Spread the butter over the breast and thighs, and season. Sprinkle over the remaining sage leaves and roast for $1\frac{1}{2}$ hours, or until the chicken is cooked through. Remove to a board and leave to rest for 10 minutes before carving.

Spatchcock Poussins with Herb Butter

Spatchcock is said to be a distortion of an 18th-century Irish expression "dispatch cock" for providing an unexpected guest with a quick and simple meal. A young chicken was prepared without frills or fuss by being split, flattened and fried or grilled.

SERVES TWO

2 poussins, each weighing about 450g/1lb

2 garlic cloves, crushed

45ml/3 tbsp chopped mixed fresh herbs, such as flat leaf parsley, sage, rosemary and thyme

FROM THE STORECUPBOARD

75g/3oz/6 tbsp butter, softened

salt and ground black pepper

1 To spatchcock a poussin, place it breast down on a chopping board and split it along the back. Open out the bird and turn it over, so that the breast side is uppermost. Press the bird as flat as possible, then thread two metal skewers through it, across the breast and thigh, to keep it flat. Repeat with the second poussin and place the skewered birds on a large grill pan.

2 Add the crushed garlic and chopped mixed herbs to the butter with plenty of seasoning, and then beat well. Dot the butter over the spatchcock poussins.

3 Preheat the grill to high and cook the poussins for 30 minutes, turning them over halfway through. Turn again and baste with the cooking juices, then cook for a further 5–7 minutes on each side.

Chilli-spiced Poussin

When you are short of time these spicy poussins make a quick alternative to a traditional roast. Serve with a leafy salad.

SERVES FOUR

2 poussins, 675g/1¹/₂lb each

15ml/1 tbsp chilli powder

15ml/1 tbsp ground cumin

FROM THE STORECUPBOARD

45ml/3 tbsp olive oil

salt and ground black pepper

1 Spatchcock one poussin: remove the wishbone and split the bird along each side of the backbone and remove it. Press down on the breastbone to flatten the bird. Push a metal skewer through the wings and breast to keep the bird flat, then push a second skewer through the thighs and breast. Spatchcock the second poussin in the same way.

2 Combine the chilli, cumin, oil and seasoning. Brush over the poussins. Preheat the grill (broiler). Lay the birds, skin side down, on a grill rack and grill (broil) for 15 minutes. Turn over and grill for a further 15 minutes until cooked through.

3 Remove the skewers and split each bird in half along the breastbone. Serve drizzled with the pan juices.

Turkey Patties

So much better than store-bought burgers, these light patties are delicious served hamburger-style in split and toasted buns with relish, salad leaves and chunky fries. They can also be made using minced chicken, lamb, pork or beef. If you are making them for children, shape the mixture into 12 equal-sized rounds and serve in mini-rolls or in rounds stamped out from sliced bread.

SERVES SIX

1 Mix together the turkey, onion, thyme, 15ml/1 tbsp of the oil and seasoning. Cover and chill for up to 4 hours to let the flavours infuse (steep), then divide the mixture into six equal portions and shape into round patties.

2 Preheat a griddle pan. Brush the patties with half of the remaining lime-flavoured olive oil, then place them on the pan and cook for 10–12 minutes. Turn the patties over, brush with more oil, and cook for 10–12 minutes on the second side, or until cooked right through. Serve the patties immediately.

675g/1¹/₂lb minced (ground) turkey

1 small red onion, finely chopped

small handful of fresh thyme leaves

FROM THE STORECUPBOARD

30ml/2 tbsp lime-flavoured olive oil

Guinea Fowl with Whisky Sauce

Served with creamy, sweet mashed potato and lightly boiled whole baby leeks, guinea fowl is magnificent with a rich, creamy whisky sauce. If you don't like the flavour of whisky, then substitute brandy, Madeira or Marsala. Or, to make a non-alcoholic version, use freshly squeezed orange juice instead. Garnish with fresh thyme sprigs or other fresh herbs.

SERVES FOUR

2 guinea fowl, each weighing about 1kg/2^1/4lb

90ml/6 tbsp whisky

**150ml/^{1}/4 pint/^{2}/3 cup well-flavoured
chicken stock**

**150ml/^{1}/4 pint/^{2}/3 cup double
(heavy) cream**

FROM THE STORECUPBOARD

salt and ground black pepper

1 Preheat the oven to 200°C/400°F/Gas 6. Brown the guinea fowl on all sides in a roasting pan on the hob (stove-top), then turn it breast uppermost and transfer the pan to the oven. Roast for about 1 hour, until the guinea fowl are golden and cooked through. Transfer the guinea fowl to a warmed serving dish, cover with foil and keep warm.

2 Pour off the excess fat from the pan, then heat the juices on the hob and stir in the whisky. Bring to the boil and cook until reduced. Add the stock and cream and simmer again until reduced slightly. Strain and season to taste.

3 Carve the guinea fowl and serve on individual plates, arranged around the chosen vegetable accompaniments. Sprinkle with plenty of freshly ground black pepper. Spoon a little of the sauce over each portion and serve the rest separately.

Pheasant Cooked in Port with Mushrooms

This warming dish is delicious served with mashed root vegetables and shredded cabbage or leeks. Marinating the pheasant in port helps to moisten and tenderize the meat, which can often be slightly dry. If you prefer, marinate the pheasant in a full-bodied red wine and use button (white) mushrooms.

SERVES FOUR

2 pheasants, cut into portions

300ml/¹/₂ pint/1¹/₄ cups port

300g/11oz chestnut mushrooms, halved if large

FROM THE STORECUPBOARD

50g/2oz/¹/₄ cup butter

salt and ground black pepper

1 Place the pheasant in a bowl and pour over the port. Cover and marinate for 3–4 hours or overnight, turning the portions occasionally.

2 Drain the meat thoroughly, reserving the marinade. Pat the portions dry on kitchen paper and season lightly with salt and pepper. Melt three-quarters of the butter in a frying pan and cook the pheasant portions on all sides for about 5 minutes, until deep golden. Drain well, transfer to a plate, then cook the mushrooms in the fat remaining in the pan for 3 minutes.

3 Return the pheasant to the pan and pour in the reserved marinade with 200ml/7fl oz/scant 1 cup water. Bring to the boil, reduce the heat and cover, then simmer gently for about 45 minutes, until the pheasant is tender.

4 Using a slotted spoon, carefully remove the pheasant portions and mushrooms from the frying pan and keep warm. Bring the cooking juices to the boil and boil vigorously for 3–5 minutes, until they are reduced and slightly thickened. Strain the juices through a fine sieve and return them to the pan. Whisk in the remaining butter over a gentle heat until it has melted, season to taste, then pour the juices over the pheasant and mushrooms and serve.

Roast Pheasant with Sherry and Mustard Sauce

Use only young pheasants for roasting – older birds are too tough and only suitable for casseroles. Serve with potatoes braised in wine with garlic and onions, Brussel sprouts and bread sauce.

SERVES FOUR

2 young oven-ready pheasants

200ml/7fl oz/scant 1 cup sherry

15ml/1 tbsp Dijon mustard

FROM THE STORECUPBOARD

50g/2oz/¹/₄ cup softened butter

salt and ground black pepper

1 Preheat the oven to 200°C/400°F/Gas 6. Put the pheasants in a roasting pan and spread the butter all over both birds. Season with salt and pepper.

2 Roast the pheasants for 50 minutes, basting often to stop the birds from drying out. When the pheasants are cooked, take them out of the pan and leave to rest on a board, covered with foil.

3 Meanwhile, place the roasting pan over a medium heat. Add the sherry and season with salt and pepper. Simmer for 5 minutes, until the sherry has slightly reduced, then stir in the mustard. Carve the pheasants and serve with the sherry and mustard sauce.

Marmalade and Soy Roast Duck

Sweet-and-sour flavours, such as marmalade and soy sauce, complement the rich, fatty taste of duck beautifully. Serve these robustly flavoured duck breast portions with simple accompaniments such as steamed sticky rice and lightly cooked pak choi (bok choy).

SERVES SIX

6 duck breast portions

45ml/3 tbsp fine-cut marmalade

45ml/3 tbsp light soy sauce

FROM THE STORECUPBOARD

salt and ground black pepper

1 Preheat the oven 190°C/375°F/Gas 5. Place the duck breasts skin side up on a grill (broiler) rack and place in the sink. Pour boiling water all over the duck. This shrinks the skin and helps it crisp during cooking. Pat the duck dry with kitchen paper and transfer to a roasting pan.

2 Combine the marmalade and soy sauce, and brush over the duck. Season with a little salt and some black pepper and roast for 20–25 minutes, basting occasionally with the marmalade mixture in the pan.

3 Remove the duck breasts from the oven and leave to rest for 5 minutes. Slice the duck breasts and serve drizzled with any juices left in the pan.

Duck with Plum Sauce

Sharp plums cut the rich flavour of duck wonderfully well in this updated version of an old English dish. Duck is often considered to be a fatty meat but modern breeding methods have made leaner ducks widely available. For an easy dinner party main course, serve the duck with creamy mashed potatoes and celeriac and steamed broccoli.

SERVES FOUR

4 duck quarters

1 large red onion, finely chopped

500g/1¼lb ripe plums, stoned (pitted) and quartered

30ml/2 tbsp redcurrant jelly

1 Prick the duck skin all over with a fork to release the fat during cooking and help give a crisp result, then place the portions in a heavy frying pan, skin side down.

2 Cook the duck pieces for 10 minutes on each side, or until golden brown and cooked right through. Remove the duck from the frying pan using a slotted spoon and keep warm.

3 Pour away all but 30ml/2 tbsp of the duck fat, then stir-fry the onion for 5 minutes, or until golden. Add the plums and cook for 5 minutes, stirring frequently. Add the jelly and mix well.

4 Replace the duck portions and cook for a further 5 minutes, or until thoroughly reheated. Serve immediately.

COOK'S TIP *It is important that the plums used in this dish are very ripe, otherwise the mixture will be too dry and the sauce will be extremely sharp.*

Pasta and Rice

PASTA AND RICE ARE THE PERFECT STAPLES UPON WHICH

TO BASE SIMPLE, TASTY MEALS. YOU NEED ONLY A FEW

INGREDIENTS TO RUSTLE UP DELICIOUS DISHES, FROM A

SIMPLE MIDWEEK SUPPER TO MORE ELEGANT DISHES FOR

ENTERTAINING. WHETHER YOU CHOOSE A SUBSTANTIAL

BOWL OF PASTA OR A FRAGRANT SEAFOOD RISOTTO –

THE RECIPES IN THIS CHAPTER ARE SURE TO DELIGHT.

Minty Courgette Linguine

Sweet, mild courgettes and refreshing mint are a great combination and are delicious with pasta. Dried linguine has been used here but you can use any type of pasta you like. Couscous also works well in place of pasta if you prefer.

SERVES FOUR

450g/1lb dried linguine

4 small courgettes (zucchini), sliced

1 small bunch of fresh mint, roughly chopped

FROM THE STORECUPBOARD

75ml/5 tbsp garlic-infused olive oil

salt and ground black pepper

1 Cook the linguine in plenty of salted, boiling water according to the instructions on the packet.

2 Meanwhile, heat 45ml/3 tbsp of the oil in a large frying pan and add the courgettes. Fry for 2–3 minutes, stirring occasionally, until they are tender and golden.

3 Drain the pasta well and toss with the courgettes and chopped mint. Season with salt and pepper, drizzle over the remaining oil and serve immediately.

Pasta with Roast Tomatoes and Goat's Cheese

Roasting tomatoes brings out their flavour and sweetness, which contrasts perfectly with the sharp taste and creamy texture of goat's cheese. Serve with a crisp green salad flavoured with herbs.

SERVES FOUR

8 large ripe tomatoes

450g/1lb any dried pasta shapes

200g/7oz firm goat's cheese, crumbled

FROM THE STORECUPBOARD

60ml/4 tbsp garlic-infused olive oil

salt and ground black pepper

1 Preheat the oven to 190°C/375°F/Gas 5. Place the tomatoes in a roasting pan and drizzle over 30ml/2 tbsp of the oil. Season well with salt and pepper and roast for 20–25 minutes, or until soft and slightly charred.

2 Meanwhile, cook the pasta in plenty of salted, boiling water, according to the instructions on the packet. Drain well and return to the pan.

3 Roughly mash the tomatoes with a fork, and stir the contents of the roasting pan into the pasta. Gently stir in the goat's cheese and the remaining oil and serve.

Linguine with Anchovies and Capers

This is a fantastic storecupboard recipe. Use salted capers if you can find them, as they have a better flavour than the bottled ones, but remember that you need to rinse them thoroughly before using. Be sure to chop the anchovies finely so that they "melt" into the sauce.

SERVES FOUR

450g/1lb dried linguine

8 anchovy fillets, drained

30ml/2 tbsp salted capers, thoroughly rinsed and drained

FROM THE STORECUPBOARD

75ml/5 tbsp garlic-infused olive oil

salt and ground black pepper

1 Cook the linguine in plenty of salted, boiling water according to the instructions on the packet.

2 Meanwhile, finely chop the anchovy fillets and place in a small pan with the oil and some black pepper. Heat very gently for 5 minutes, stirring occasionally, until the anchovies start to disintegrate.

3 Drain the pasta thoroughly and toss with the anchovies, oil and capers. Season with a little salt and plenty of black pepper to taste. Divide between warmed bowls and serve immediately.

Home-made Potato Gnocchi

These classic Italian potato dumplings are very simple to make – it just requires a little patience when it comes to shaping them. Serve them as soon as they are cooked, tossed in melted butter and fresh sage leaves, sprinkled with grated Parmesan cheese and plenty of black pepper. They make a fabulous alternative to pasta.

SERVES TWO

900g/2lb floury potatoes, cut into large chunks

2 eggs, beaten

150–175g/5–6oz/1¼–1½ cups plain (all-purpose) flour

FROM THE STORECUPBOARD

10ml/2 tsp salt

1 Cook the potatoes in salted, boiling water for 15 minutes, until tender. Drain well and return to the pan, set it over a low heat and dry the potatoes for 1–2 minutes.

2 Mash the potatoes until smooth, then gradually stir in the eggs and salt. Work in enough flour to form a soft dough.

3 Break off small pieces of the dough and roll into balls, using floured hands. Press the back of a fork into each ball to make indentations. Repeat until all the dough has been used. Leave the gnocchi to rest for 15–20 minutes before cooking.

4 Bring a large pan of water to a gentle boil. Add the gnocchi, about ten at a time, and cook for 3–4 minutes, or until they float to the surface. Drain thoroughly and serve as soon as all the gnocchi have been cooked.

VARIATION To make herb-flavoured gnocchi, add 45ml/3 tbsp chopped fresh herbs, such as basil, parsley and sage, to the potato and flour dough and combine well. Serve with butter and grated Parmesan.

Spaghettini with Roasted Garlic

If you have never tried roasting garlic, then this is the recipe that will convert you to its delicious mellowed sweetness. Spaghettini is very fine spaghetti, but any long thin pasta can be used in this dish – try spaghetti, linguine, tagliatelle or capellini. This simple pasta dish is very good served with a mixed leaf salad dressed with lemon juice and extra virgin olive oil.

SERVES FOUR

1 Preheat the oven to 180°C/350°F/Gas 4. Place the garlic in an oiled roasting pan and roast it for 30 minutes.

2 Leave the garlic to cool, then lay it on its side and slice off the top one-third with a sharp knife.

3 Hold the garlic over a bowl and dig out the flesh from each clove with the point of the knife. When all the flesh has been added to the bowl, pour in the oil and add plenty of black pepper. Mix well.

4 Cook the pasta in a pan of salted boiling water according to the instructions on the packet. Drain the pasta and return it to the clean pan. Pour in the oil and garlic mixture and toss the pasta vigorously over a medium heat until all the strands are thoroughly coated. Serve immediately, with shavings of Parmesan.

1 whole head of garlic

400g/14oz fresh or dried spaghettini

coarsely shaved Parmesan cheese

FROM THE STORECUPBOARD

120ml/4fl oz/^{1}/$_2$ cup extra virgin olive oil

salt and ground black pepper

Spaghetti with Lemon

This is the dish to make when you get home and find there's nothing to eat. If you keep spaghetti and olive oil in the store cupboard (pantry), and garlic and lemons in the vegetable rack, you can prepare this delicious meal in minutes. You can also add some freshly grated Parmesan cheese if you have some.

SERVES FOUR

1 Cook the pasta in a pan of salted boiling water according to the instructions on the packet, then drain well and return to the pan.

2 Pour the olive oil and lemon juice over the cooked pasta, sprinkle in the slivers of garlic and add seasoning to taste. Toss the pasta over a medium to high heat for 1–2 minutes. Serve immediately in four warmed bowls.

350g/12oz dried spaghetti

juice of 1 large lemon

2 garlic cloves, cut into very thin slivers

FROM THE STORECUPBOARD

90ml/6 tbsp extra virgin olive oil

salt and ground black pepper

COOK'S TIP Spaghetti is the best type of pasta for this recipe, because the olive oil and lemon juice cling to its long thin strands. If you are out of spaghetti, use another dried long pasta shape instead, such as spaghettini, linguine or tagliatelle.

Linguine with Rocket

This fashionable first course is very quick and easy to make at home. Rocket has an excellent peppery flavour which combines beautifully with the rich, creamy tang of fresh Parmesan cheese. Fresh Parmesan keeps well in the refrigerator for up to a month – the dried variety is a very poor substitute and bears little resemblance to the real thing.

SERVES FOUR

1 Cook the pasta in a large pan of boiling water according to the instructions on the packet, then drain thoroughly.

2 Heat about 60ml/4 tbsp of the olive oil in the pasta pan, then add the drained pasta, followed by the rocket. Toss over a medium to high heat for 1–2 minutes, or until the rocket is just wilted, then remove the pan from the heat.

3 Tip the pasta and rocket into a large, warmed bowl. Add half the freshly grated Parmesan and the remaining olive oil. Add a little salt and black pepper to taste.

4 Toss the mixture quickly to mix. Serve immediately, sprinkled with the remaining Parmesan.

350g/12oz fresh or dried linguine

1 large bunch rocket (arugula), about 150g/5oz, stalks removed, shredded or torn

75g/3oz/1 cup freshly grated Parmesan cheese

FROM THE STORECUPBOARD

120ml/4fl oz/½ cup extra virgin olive oil

salt and ground black pepper

Tagliatelle with Vegetable Ribbons

Narrow strips of courgette and carrot mingle well with tagliatelle to resemble coloured pasta. Serve as a side dish, or sprinkle with freshly grated Parmesan cheese for a light appetizer or vegetarian main course. Garlic flavoured olive oil is used in this dish – flavoured oils such as rosemary, chilli or basil are widely available and are a quick way of adding flavour to pasta.

SERVES FOUR

2 large courgettes (zucchini)

2 large carrots

250g/9oz fresh egg tagliatelle

FROM THE STORECUPBOARD

60ml/4 tbsp garlic flavoured olive oil

salt and ground black pepper

1 With a vegetable peeler, cut the courgettes and carrots into long thin ribbons. Bring a large pan of salted water to the boil, then add the courgette and carrot ribbons. Bring the water back to the boil and boil for 30 seconds, then drain and set aside.

2 Cook the tagliatelle according to the instructions on the packet. Drain the pasta and return it to the pan. Add the vegetable ribbons, garlic flavoured oil and seasoning and toss over a medium to high heat until the pasta and vegetables are glistening with oil. Serve the pasta immediately.

Spaghetti with Raw Tomato and Ricotta Sauce

This wonderfully simple uncooked sauce goes well with many different kinds of freshly cooked pasta, both long strands such as spaghetti, tagliatelle or linguini, and short shapes such as macaroni, rigatoni or penne. It is always at its best in summer when made with rich, sweet plum tomatoes that have ripened on the vine in the sun and have their fullest flavour.

SERVES FOUR

500g/1¹/₄lb ripe Italian plum tomatoes

350g/12oz dried spaghetti or pasta of your choice

115g/4oz ricotta salata cheese, diced

FROM THE STORECUPBOARD

75ml/5 tbsp garlic-flavoured olive oil

salt and ground black pepper

1 Coarsely chop the plum tomatoes, removing the cores and as many of the seeds as you can.

2 Put the tomatoes and oil in a bowl, adding salt and pepper to taste, and stir well. Cover and leave at room temperature for 1–2 hours to let the flavours mingle.

3 Cook the spaghetti or your chosen pasta according to the packet instructions, then drain well.

4 Taste the sauce to check the seasoning before tossing it with the hot pasta. Sprinkle with the cheese and serve immediately.

Farfalle with Tuna

Bought tomato sauce and canned tuna are endlessly versatile for making weekday suppers. A variety of herbs can be added to simple pasta dishes like this one – choose from basil, marjoram or oregano – and use fresh herbs, as the short cooking time does not allow the flavour of dried herbs to develop fully. Add a garnish of fresh oregano to this dish if you happen to have some.

SERVES FOUR

1 Cook the pasta in a large pan of lightly salted boiling water according to the instructions on the packet. Meanwhile, heat the tomato sauce in a separate pan and add the olives.

2 Drain the canned tuna and flake it with a fork. Add the tuna to the sauce with about 60ml/4 tbsp of the hot water used for cooking the pasta. Taste and adjust the seasoning.

3 Drain the pasta thoroughly and tip it into a large, warmed serving bowl. Pour the tuna sauce over the top and toss lightly to mix. Serve immediately.

400g/14oz/3^1/$_2$ cups dried farfalle

600ml/1 pint/2^1/$_2$ cups tomato sauce

175g/6oz can tuna in olive oil

8–10 pitted black olives, cut into rings

FROM THE STORECUPBOARD

salt and ground black pepper

Fettuccine all'Alfredo

This simple recipe was invented by a Roman restaurateur called Alfredo, who became famous for serving it with a gold fork and spoon. Today's busy cooks will find cartons of long-life cream invaluable for this type of recipe. If you can't get fettucine, any long ribbon-like pasta can be used in this dish – try tagliatelle or slightly wider pappardelle instead.

SERVES FOUR

1 Melt the butter in a large pan. Add the cream and bring it to the boil. Simmer for 5 minutes, stirring constantly, then add the Parmesan cheese, with salt and freshly ground black pepper to taste, and turn off the heat under the pan.

2 Bring a large pan of salted water to the boil. Drop in the pasta all at once and quickly bring the water back to the boil, stirring occasionally. Cook the pasta for 2–3 minutes, or according to the instructions on the packet. Drain well.

3 Turn on the heat under the pan of cream to low, add the cooked pasta all at once and toss until it is well coated in the sauce. Taste the sauce for seasoning. Serve immediately, with extra grated Parmesan handed around separately.

200ml/7fl oz/scant 1 cup double (heavy) cream

50g/2oz/²/₃ cup freshly grated Parmesan cheese, plus extra to serve

350g/12oz fresh fettuccine

FROM THE STORECUPBOARD

50g/2oz/¹/₄ cup butter

salt and ground black pepper

Pansotti with Walnut Sauce

Walnuts and cream make a rich and luscious sauce for stuffed pasta, particularly the types filled with cheese and herbs. Serve this indulgent dish with warm walnut bread and a light, fruity white wine.

SERVES FOUR

1 Put the walnuts and garlic oil in a food processor and process to a paste, adding up to 120ml/4fl oz/½ cup warm water through the feeder tube to slacken the consistency. Spoon the mixture into a large bowl and add the cream. Beat well to mix, then season to taste with salt and black pepper.

2 Cook the pansotti or stuffed pasta in a large pan of salted boiling water for 4–5 minutes, or according to the instructions on the packet. Meanwhile, put the walnut sauce in a large warmed bowl and add a ladleful of the pasta cooking water to thin it.

3 Drain the pasta and tip it into the bowl of walnut sauce. Toss well, then serve immediately.

90g/3¹/₂oz/scant 1 cup shelled walnuts

120ml/4fl oz/¹/₂ cup double (heavy) cream

350g/12oz cheese and herb-filled pansotti or other stuffed pasta

FROM THE STORECUPBOARD

60ml/4 tbsp garlic-flavoured olive oil

salt and ground black pepper

Fettuccine with Butter and Parmesan

Very few ingredients are needed to make up this incredibly simple dish. It comes from northern Italy, where butter and cheese are the most popular ingredients for serving with pasta. Children love it.

SERVES FOUR

1 Cook the pasta in a pan of salted boiling water according to the instructions on the packet. Drain thoroughly, then tip into a warmed bowl.

2 Add the butter and Parmesan a third at a time, tossing the pasta after each addition until it is evenly coated. Season to taste and serve.

400g/14oz fresh or dried fettuccine

115g/4oz/1¹/₃ cups freshly grated Parmesan cheese

FROM THE STORECUPBOARD

50g/2oz/¹/₄ cup unsalted butter, cubed

salt and ground black pepper

Penne with Cream and Smoked Salmon

This modern way of serving pasta is popular all over Italy and in many Italian restaurants. The three essential ingredients combine beautifully, and the dish is very quick and easy to make.

SERVES FOUR

1 Cook the pasta in a saucepan of salted boiling water according to the instructions on the packet.

2 Meanwhile, using kitchen scissors, cut the smoked salmon into thin strips, about 5mm/¼in wide. Strip the leaves from the thyme sprigs.

3 Melt the butter in a large saucepan. Stir in the cream with about a quarter of the salmon and thyme leaves, then season with pepper. Heat gently for 3–4 minutes, stirring all the time. Do not allow to boil. Taste the sauce for seasoning.

4 Drain the pasta and toss it in the cream and salmon sauce. Divide among four warmed bowls and top with the remaining salmon and thyme leaves. Serve immediately.

350g/12oz/3 cups dried penne

115g/4oz thinly sliced smoked salmon

2–3 fresh thyme sprigs

150ml/¼ pint/⅔ cup extra-thick single cream

FROM THE STORECUPBOARD

25g/1oz/2 tbsp butter

salt and ground black pepper

Oven-baked Porcini Risotto

This risotto is easy to make because you don't have to stand over it stirring constantly as it cooks, as you do with a traditional risotto.

SERVES FOUR

25g/1oz/¹/₂ cup dried porcini mushrooms

1 onion, finely chopped

225g/8oz/generous 1 cup risotto rice

FROM THE STORECUPBOARD

30ml/2 tbsp garlic-infused olive oil

salt and ground black pepper

1 Put the mushrooms in a heatproof bowl and pour over 750ml/1¹/₄ pints/3 cups boiling water. Leave to soak for 30 minutes. Drain the mushrooms through a sieve lined with kitchen paper, reserving the soaking liquor. Rinse the mushrooms thoroughly under running water to remove any grit, and dry on kitchen paper.

2 Preheat the oven to 180°C/350°F/Gas 4. Heat the oil in a roasting pan on the hob and add the onion. Cook for 2–3 minutes, or until softened but not coloured.

3 Add the rice and stir for 1–2 minutes, then add the mushrooms and stir. Pour in the mushroom liquor and mix well. Season with salt and pepper, and cover with foil.

4 Bake in the oven for 30 minutes, stirring occasionally, until all the stock has been absorbed and the rice is tender. Divide between warm serving bowls and serve immediately.

Persian Baked Rice

In this Persian-style dish, rice is cooked slowly over a low heat so that a crust forms on the bottom. The mild flavours of saffron and almonds go perfectly together. This dish is an ideal accompaniment for lamb.

SERVES FOUR

450g/1lb basmati rice

a good pinch of saffron strands

50g/2oz/^{1}/$_2$ cup flaked (sliced) almonds

FROM THE STORECUPBOARD

50g/2oz/^{1}/$_4$ cup butter

salt and ground black pepper

1 Cook the rice in a pan of boiling salted water for 5 minutes, then drain thoroughly. Meanwhile, put the saffron in a small bowl with 30ml/2 tbsp warm water and leave to infuse for at least 5 minutes.

2 Heat the butter in a large flameproof pan and add the almonds. Cook over a medium heat for 2–3 minutes, or until golden, stirring occasionally. Add the rice and stir well, then stir in the saffron and its liquid, plus 1 litre/1^3/$_4$ pints/ 4 cups water. Season and cover with a tight-fitting lid.

3 Cook over a very low heat for 30 minutes, or until the rice is tender and a crust has formed on the bottom of the pan. Fork up the rice to mix in the crust before serving.

Rosemary Risotto with Borlotti Beans

Select a high-quality risotto in a subtle flavour as the base for this recipe.
The savoury beans, heady rosemary and creamy mascarpone will transform
a simple product into a feast. For an even more authentic risotto flavour,
substitute half the water with dry white wine. Serve with a simple salad of
rocket (arugula) and Parmesan shavings dressed with balsamic vinegar and
plenty of freshly ground black pepper.

SERVES THREE TO FOUR

400g/14oz can borlotti beans

275g/10oz packet vegetable or chicken risotto

60ml/4 tbsp mascarpone cheese

5ml/1 tsp finely chopped fresh rosemary

1 Drain the beans, rinse under cold water and drain again. Process
about two-thirds of the beans to a fairly coarse purée in a food
processor or blender. Set the remaining beans aside.

2 Make up the risotto according to the packet instructions, using
the suggested quantity of water.

3 Immediately the rice is cooked, stir in the bean purée. Add
the reserved beans, with the mascarpone and rosemary. Stir
thoroughly, then cover and leave to stand for about 5 minutes
so that the risotto absorbs the flavours fully.

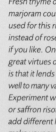

VARIATION

*Fresh thyme or
marjoram could be
used for this risotto
instead of rosemary,
if you like. One of the
great virtues of risotto
is that it lends itself
well to many variations.
Experiment with plain
or saffron risotto and
add different herbs to
make your own
speciality dish.*

Pancetta and Broad Bean Risotto

This moist risotto makes a satisfying, balanced meal, especially when served with cooked fresh seasonal vegetables or a mixed green salad. Add some chopped fresh herbs and Parmesan shavings as a garnish, if you like. Pancetta is dry cured pork and is the Italian equivalent of streaky (fatty) bacon – either can be used in this recipe.

SERVES FOUR

1 Place the pancetta in a non-stick or heavy pan and cook gently, stirring occasionally, for about 5 minutes, until the fat runs.

2 Add the risotto rice to the pan and cook for 1 minute, stirring constantly. Add a ladleful of the simmering stock and cook, stirring constantly, until the liquid has been absorbed.

3 Continue adding the simmering stock, a ladleful at a time, until the rice is tender, and almost all the liquid has been absorbed. This will take 30–35 minutes.

4 Meanwhile, cook the broad beans in a pan of lightly salted, boiling water for about 3 minutes until tender. Drain well and stir into the risotto. Season to taste. Spoon into a bowl and serve.

175g/6oz smoked pancetta, diced

350g/12oz/1³/₄ cups risotto rice

1.5 litres/2¹/₂ pints/ 6¹/₄ cups simmering herb stock

225g/8oz/2 cups frozen baby broad (fava) beans

FROM THE STORECUPBOARD

salt and ground black pepper

COOK'S TIP
If the broad beans are large, or if you prefer skinned beans, remove the outer skin after cooking them.

Mussel Risotto

The addition of freshly cooked mussels, aromatic coriander and a little cream to a packet of instant risotto can turn a simple meal into a decadent treat. Serve with a side salad for a splendid supper. Other types of cooked shellfish, such as clams or prawns (shrimp), can be used instead of mussels.

SERVES THREE TO FOUR

1 Scrub the mussels, discarding any that do not close when sharply tapped. Place in a large pan. Add 120ml/4fl oz/½ cup water and seasoning, then bring to the boil. Cover the pan and cook the mussels, shaking the pan occasionally, for 4–5 minutes, until they have opened. Drain, reserving the liquid and discarding any that have not opened. Shell most of the mussels, reserving a few in their shells for garnish. Strain the mussel liquid.

2 Make up the packet risotto according to the instructions, using the cooking liquid from the mussels and making it up to the required volume with water.

3 When the risotto is about three-quarters cooked, add the mussels to the pan. Add the coriander and re-cover the pan without stirring in these ingredients.

4 Remove the risotto from the heat, stir in the cream, cover and leave to rest for a few minutes. Spoon into a warmed serving dish, garnish with the reserved mussels in their shells, and serve.

900g/2lb fresh mussels

275g/10oz packet risotto

30ml/2 tbsp chopped fresh coriander (cilantro)

30ml/2 tbsp double (heavy) cream

FROM THE STORECUPBOARD

salt and ground black pepper

COOK'S TIP

For a super-quick mussel risotto, use cooked mussels in their shells – the type sold vacuum packed ready to reheat. Just reheat them according to the packet instructions and add to the made risotto with the coriander and cream.

Crab Risotto

This simple risotto has a subtle flavour that makes the most of delicate crab. It makes a tempting main course or appetizer. It is important to use a good quality risotto rice, which will give a deliciously creamy result, but the cooked grains are still firm to the bite.

SERVES THREE TO FOUR

2 large cooked crabs

275g/10oz/1¹/₂ cups risotto rice

1.2 litres/2 pints/5 cups simmering fish stock

30ml/2 tbsp mixed finely chopped fresh herbs such as chives, tarragon and parsley

FROM THE STORECUPBOARD

salt and ground black pepper

1 One at a time, hold the crabs and hit the underside with the heel of your hand. This should loosen the shell from the body. Using your thumbs, push against the body and pull away from the shell. Remove and discard the intestines and the grey gills.

2 Break off the claws and legs, then use a hammer or crackers to break them open. Using a pick, remove the meat from the claws and legs. Place the meat on a plate.

3 Using a skewer, pick out the white meat from the body cavities and place with the claw and leg meat, reserving a little white meat to garnish. Scoop out the brown meat from the shell and add to the rest of the crab meat.

4 Place the rice in a pan and add one-quarter of the stock. Bring to the boil and cook, stirring, until the liquid has been absorbed. Adding a ladleful of stock at a time, cook, stirring, until about two-thirds of the stock has been absorbed. Stir in the crab meat and herbs, and continue cooking, adding the remaining stock.

5 When the rice is almost cooked, remove it from the heat and adjust the seasoning. Cover and leave to stand for 3 minutes. Serve garnished with the reserved white crab meat.

Coconut Rice

This rich dish is usually served with a tangy papaya salad to balance the sweetness of the coconut milk and sugar. It is one of those comforting treats that everyone enjoys.

SERVES FOUR TO SIX

1 Place the measured water, coconut milk, salt and sugar in a heavy pan. Wash the rice in cold water until it runs clear.

2 Add the jasmine rice, cover tightly with a lid and bring to the boil over a medium heat. Reduce the heat to low and simmer gently, without lifting the lid unnecessarily, for 15–20 minutes, until the rice is tender and cooked through. Test it by biting a grain.

3 Turn off the heat and leave the rice to rest in the pan, still covered with the lid, for a further 5–10 minutes.

4 Gently fluff up the rice grains with chopsticks or a fork before transferring it to a warmed dish and serving.

250ml/8fl oz/1 cup water

475ml/16fl oz/2 cups coconut milk

30ml/2 tbsp granulated sugar

450g/1lb/2²/₃ cups jasmine rice

FROM THE STORECUPBOARD

2.5ml/¹/₂ tsp salt

COOK'S TIP For a special occasion serve in a halved papaya and garnish with thin shreds of fresh coconut.

Savoury Ground Rice

Savoury ground rice is often served as an accompaniment to soups and stews in West Africa.

SERVES FOUR

1 Place the water in a saucepan. Pour in the milk, bring to the boil and add the salt and parsley.

2 Add the butter or margarine and the ground rice, stirring with a wooden spoon to prevent the rice from becoming lumpy.

3 Cover the pan and cook over a low heat for about 15 minutes, beating the mixture every 2 minutes to prevent the formation of lumps.

4 To test if the rice is cooked, rub a pinch of the mixture between your fingers: if it feels smooth and fairly dry, it is ready. Serve hot.

300ml/¹/₂ pint/1¹/₄ cups **water**

300ml/¹/₂ pint/1¹/₄ cups milk

15ml/1 tbsp chopped fresh parsley

25g/1oz/2 tbsp butter or margarine

275g/10oz/1²/₃ cups ground rice

FROM THE STORECUPBOARD

salt

COOK'S TIP
Ground rice is a creamy white colour, with a grainy texture. Although often used in sweet dishes, it is a tasty grain to serve with savoury dishes too. The addition of milk gives a creamier flavour if preferred.

Vegetarian
Dishes

FRESH-TASTING VEGETABLES, MILD EGGS,

RICH AND CREAMY CHEESES AND AROMATIC HERBS

AND SPICES ARE GREAT PARTNERS AND CAN BE COMBINED

TO MAKE A DELICIOUS ARRAY OF VEGETARIAN MAIN

MEALS. ENJOY WONDERFUL DISHES SUCH AS BAKED

STUFFED VEGETABLES, RICHLY FLAVOURED TARTS

AND LIGHT-AS-AIR SOUFFLÉS.

Aubergines with Cheese Sauce

This wonderfully simple dish of aubergines in cheese sauce is delicious hot and the perfect dish to assemble ahead of time ready for baking at the last minute. Kashkaval cheese is particularly good in this recipe – it is a hard yellow cheese made from sheep's milk and is originally from the Balkans. Serve with lots of crusty bread to mop up the delicious aubergine-flavoured cheese sauce.

SERVES FOUR TO SIX

1 Layer the aubergine slices in a bowl or colander, sprinkling each layer with salt, and leave to drain for at least 30 minutes. Rinse well, then pat dry with kitchen paper.

2 Heat the oil in a frying pan, then cook the aubergine slices until golden brown on both sides. Remove from the pan and set aside.

3 Preheat the oven to 180°C/350°F/Gas 4. Mix most of the grated cheese into the savoury white or béchamel sauce, reserving a little to sprinkle on top of the finished dish.

4 Arrange a layer of the aubergines in an ovenproof dish, then pour over some sauce. Repeat, ending with sauce. Sprinkle with the reserved cheese. Bake for 35–40 minutes until golden.

2 large aubergines (eggplants), cut into 5mm/¼ in thick slices

400g/14oz/3½ cups grated cheese, such as kashkaval, Gruyère, or a mixture of Parmesan and Cheddar

600ml/1 pint/2½ cups savoury white sauce or béchamel sauce

FROM THE STORECUPBOARD

about 60ml/4 tbsp olive oil

salt and ground black pepper

Mushroom Stroganoff

This creamy mixed mushroom sauce is ideal for a dinner party. Serve it with toasted buckwheat, brown rice or a mixture of wild rices and garnish with snipped chives. For best results, choose a variety of different mushrooms – wild mushrooms such as chanterelles, ceps and morels add a delicious flavour and texture to the stroganoff, as well as adding colour and producing a decorative appearance.

SERVES FOUR

900g/2lb mixed mushrooms, cut into bitesize pieces, including ²/₃ button (white) mushrooms and ¹/₃ assorted wild or unusual mushrooms

350ml/12fl oz/1¹/₂ cups white wine sauce

250ml/8fl oz/1 cup sour cream

FROM THE STORECUPBOARD

25g/1oz/2 tbsp butter

salt and ground black pepper

1 Melt the butter in a pan and quickly cook the mushrooms, in batches, over a high heat, until brown. Transfer the mushrooms to a bowl after cooking each batch.

2 Add the sauce to the juices remaining in the pan and bring to the boil, stirring. Reduce the heat and replace the mushrooms with any juices from the bowl. Stir well and heat for a few seconds, then remove from the heat.

3 Stir the sour cream into the cooked mushroom mixture and season to taste with salt and lots of freshly ground black pepper. Heat through gently for a few seconds, if necessary, then transfer to warm plates and serve immediately.

Red Onion and Goat's Cheese Pastries

These attractive little tartlets couldn't be easier to make. Garnish them with fresh thyme sprigs and serve with a selection of salad leaves and a tomato and basil salad for a light lunch or quick supper. A wide variety of different types of goat's cheeses are available – the creamy log-shaped types without a rind are most suitable for these pastries. Ordinary onions can be used instead of red, if you prefer.

SERVES FOUR

1 Heat the oil in a large, heavy frying pan, add the onions and cook over a gentle heat for 10 minutes, or until softened, stirring occasionally to prevent them from browning. Add seasoning to taste and cook for a further 2 minutes. Remove the pan from the heat and leave to cool.

2 Preheat the oven to 220°C/425°F/Gas 7. Unroll the puff pastry and using a 15cm/6in plate as a guide, cut out four rounds. Place the pastry rounds on a dampened baking sheet and, using the point of a sharp knife, score a border, 2cm/¾in inside the edge of each pastry round.

3 Divide the onions among the pastry rounds and top with the goat's cheese. Bake for 25–30 minutes until golden brown.

450g/1lb red onions, sliced

425g/15oz packet ready-rolled puff pastry

115g/4oz/1 cup goat's cheese, cubed

FROM THE STORECUPBOARD

15ml/1 tbsp olive oil

salt and ground black pepper

EXTRAS *To make richer-flavoured pastries ring the changes by spreading the pastry base with red or green pesto or tapenade before you top with the goat's cheese and cooked onions.*

Baked Leek and Potato Gratin

Potatoes baked in a creamy cheese sauce make the ultimate comfort dish, whether served as an accompaniment to pork or fish dishes or, as here, with plenty of leeks and melted cheese as a main course. When preparing leeks, separate the leaves and rinse them thoroughly under cold running water, as soil and grit often get caught between the layers.

SERVES FOUR TO SIX

1 Preheat the oven to 180°C/350°F/Gas 4. Cook the potatoes in plenty of lightly salted, boiling water for 3 minutes, until slightly softened, then drain. Cut the leeks into 1cm/½in lengths and blanch them in boiling water for 1 minute, until softened, then drain.

2 Turn half the potatoes into a shallow, ovenproof dish and spread them out to the edge. Cover with two-thirds of the leeks, then add the remaining potatoes. Tuck the slices of cheese and the remaining leeks in among the top layer of potatoes. Season and pour the cream over.

3 Bake for 1 hour, until tender and golden. Cover with foil if the top starts to overbrown before the potatoes are tender.

900g/2lb medium potatoes, thinly sliced

2 large leeks, trimmed

200g/7oz ripe Brie or Camembert cheese, sliced

450ml/³/₄ pint/scant 2 cups single (light) cream

FROM THE STORECUPBOARD

salt and ground black pepper

Mushroom Polenta

This simple recipe uses freshly made polenta, but for an even easier version you can substitute ready-made polenta and slice it straight into the dish, ready for baking. The cheesy mushroom topping is also delicious on toasted herb or sun-dried tomato bread as a light lunch or supper. Any combination of mushrooms will work – try a mixture of button (white) and wild mushrooms as an alternative.

SERVES FOUR

1 Line a 28 x 18cm/11 x 7in shallow baking tin (pan) with baking parchment. Bring 1 litre/1¾ pints/4 cups water with 5ml/1 tsp salt to the boil in a large pan. Add the polenta in a steady stream, stirring constantly. Bring back to the boil, stirring, and cook for 5 minutes, until thick and smooth. Turn the polenta into the prepared tin and spread it out into an even layer. Leave to cool.

2 Preheat the oven to 200°C/400°F/Gas 6. Melt the butter in a frying pan and cook the mushrooms for 3–5 minutes, until golden. Season with salt and lots of freshly ground black pepper.

3 Turn out the polenta on to a chopping board. Peel away the parchment and cut the polenta into large squares. Pile the squares into a shallow, ovenproof dish. Sprinkle with half the cheese, then pile the mushrooms on top and pour over their buttery juices. Sprinkle with the remaining cheese and bake for about 20 minutes, until the cheese is melting and pale golden.

250g/9oz/1¹/₂ cups quick-cook polenta

50g/2oz/¹/₄ cup butter

400g/14oz chestnut mushrooms, sliced

175g/6oz/1¹/₂ cups grated Gruyère cheese

FROM THE STORECUPBOARD

salt and ground black pepper

Tomato and Tapenade Tarts

These delicious individual tarts look and taste fantastic, despite the fact that they demand very little time or effort. The mascarpone cheese topping melts as it cooks to make a smooth, creamy sauce. Cherry tomatoes have a delicious sweet flavour with a low acidity, but plum tomatoes or vine-ripened tomatoes are also suitable for these tarts and will give delicious results. Red pesto can be used instead of the tapenade if you prefer a subtler flavour.

SERVES FOUR

1 Preheat the oven to 220°C/425°F/Gas 7. Lightly grease a large baking sheet and sprinkle it with water. Roll out the pastry on a lightly floured surface and cut out four 16cm/6½in rounds, using a bowl or small plate as a guide.

2 Transfer the pastry rounds to the prepared baking sheet. Using the tip of a sharp knife, mark a shallow cut 1cm/½in in from the edge of each round to form a rim.

3 Reserve half the tapenade and spread the rest over the pastry rounds, keeping the paste inside the marked rim. Cut half the tomatoes in half. Pile all the tomatoes, whole and halved, on the pastry, again keeping them inside the rim. Season lightly.

4 Bake for 20 minutes, until the pastry is well risen and golden. Dot with the remaining tapenade. Spoon a little mascarpone on the centre of the tomatoes and season with black pepper. Bake for a further 10 minutes, until the mascarpone has melted to make a sauce. Serve the tarts warm.

500g/1¼lb puff pastry, thawed if frozen

60ml/4 tbsp black or green olive tapenade

500g/1¼lb cherry tomatoes

90g/3½oz/scant ½ cup mascarpone cheese

FROM THE STORECUPBOARD

salt and ground black pepper

Stuffed Baby Squash

It is worth making the most of baby squash while they are in season. Use any varieties you can find and do not worry too much about choosing vegetables of uniform size, as an assortment of different types and sizes looks attractive. The baked vegetables can easily be shared out at the table. Serve with warm sun-dried tomato bread and a ready-made spicy tomato sauce for a hearty autumn supper.

SERVES FOUR

1 Preheat the oven to 190°C/375°F/Gas 5. Pierce the squash in with the tip of a knife. Bake for 30 minutes, until the squash are tender. Leave until cool enough to handle.

2 Meanwhile, cook the rice in salted, boiling water for 12 minutes, until tender, then drain. Slice a lid off the top of each squash and scoop out and discard the seeds. Scoop out and chop the flesh.

3 Heat the oil in a frying pan and cook the chopped squash for 5 minutes. Reserve 60ml/4 tbsp of the cheese, add the remainder to the pan with the rice and a little salt. Mix well.

4 Pile the mixture into the squash shells and place in a dish. Sprinkle with the remaining cheese and bake for 20 minutes.

4 small squash, each about 350g/12oz

200g/7oz/1 cup mixed wild and basmati rice

150g/5oz/1¼ cups grated Gruyère cheese

FROM THE STORECUPBOARD

60ml/4 tbsp chilli and garlic oil

salt and ground black pepper

Roasted Peppers with Halloumi and Pine Nuts

Halloumi cheese is creamy-tasting and has a firm texture and salty flavour that contrast well with the succulent sweet peppers. This is a good dish to assemble in advance. Halloumi is usually served cooked and lends itself well to barbecuing, frying or grilling (broiling). When heated the exterior hardens while the interior softens and is similar to mozzarella cheese.

SERVES FOUR

1 Preheat the oven to 220°C/425°F/Gas 7. Halve the red peppers, leaving the stalks intact, and discard the seeds. Seed and coarsely chop the orange or yellow peppers. Place the red pepper halves on a baking sheet and fill with the chopped peppers. Drizzle with half the garlic or herb olive oil and bake for 25 minutes, until the edges of the peppers are beginning to char.

2 Dice the cheese and tuck in among the chopped peppers. Sprinkle with the pine nuts and drizzle with the remaining oil. Bake for a further 15 minutes, until well browned. Serve warm.

4 red and 2 orange or yellow (bell) peppers

250g/9oz halloumi cheese

50g/2oz/$^{1}/_{2}$ cup pine nuts

FROM THE STORECUPBOARD

60ml/4 tbsp garlic or herb olive oil

salt and ground black pepper

Spicy Chickpea Samosas

A blend of crushed chickpeas and coriander sauce makes an interesting alternative to the more familiar meat or vegetable fillings in these little pastries. The samosas look pretty garnished with fresh coriander leaves and finely sliced onion and are delicious served with a simple dip made from Greek (US strained plain) yogurt and chopped fresh mint leaves.

MAKES EIGHTEEN

1 Preheat the oven to 220°C/425°F/Gas 7. Process half the chickpeas to a paste in a food processor. Tip the paste into a bowl and add the whole chickpeas, the hara masala or coriander sauce, and a little salt. Mix until well combined.

2 Lay a sheet of filo pastry on a work surface and cut into three strips. Brush the strips with a little of the oil. Place a dessertspoon of the filling at one end of a strip. Turn one corner diagonally over the filling to meet the long edge. Continue folding the filling and the pastry along the length of the strip, keeping the triangular shape. Transfer to a baking sheet and repeat with the remaining filling and pastry.

3 Brush the pastries with any remaining oil and bake for 15 minutes, until the pastry is golden. Cool before serving.

2 x 400g/14oz cans chickpeas, drained and rinsed

120ml/4fl oz/^{1}/$_2$ cup hara masala or coriander (cilantro) sauce

275g/10oz filo pastry

FROM THE STORECUPBOARD

60ml/4 tbsp chilli and garlic oil

salt and ground black pepper

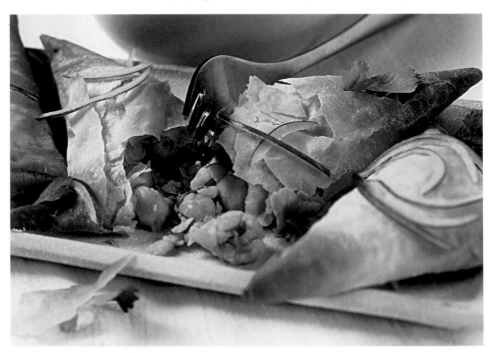

Tofu and Pepper Kebabs

A simple coating of ground, dry-roasted peanuts pressed on to cubed tofu provides plenty of additional flavour along with the peppers. Use metal or bamboo skewers for the kebabs – if you use bamboo, then soak them in cold water for 30 minutes before using to prevent them from scorching during cooking. The kebabs can also be cooked on a barbecue, if you prefer.

SERVES FOUR

1 Pat the tofu dry on kitchen paper and then cut it into small cubes. Grind the peanuts in a blender or food processor and transfer to a plate. Turn the tofu cubes in the ground nuts to coat.

2 Preheat the grill (broiler) to moderate. Halve and seed the peppers, and cut them into large chunks. Thread the chunks of pepper on to four large skewers with the tofu cubes and place on a foil-lined grill rack.

3 Grill (broil) the kebabs, turning frequently, for 10–12 minutes, or until the peppers and peanuts are beginning to brown. Transfer the kebabs to plates and serve with the dipping sauce.

250g/9oz firm tofu

50g/2oz/¹/₂ cup dry-roasted peanuts

2 red and 2 green (bell) peppers

60ml/4 tbsp sweet chilli dipping sauce

FROM THE STORECUPBOARD

salt and ground black pepper

Mixed Bean and Tomato Chilli

Here, mixed beans, fiery red chilli and plenty of freshly chopped coriander are simmered in a tomato sauce to make a delicious vegetarian chilli. Always a popular dish, chilli can be served with a variety of accompaniments – choose from baked potatoes, baked rice, crusty bread or tortillas. Garnish with slices of tomato, chopped celery or sweet (bell) pepper and top with natural (plain) yogurt.

SERVES FOUR

1 Pour the tomato sauce and mixed beans into a pan. Seed and thinly slice the chilli, then add it to the pan. Reserve a little of the coriander, chop the remainder and add it to the pan.

2 Bring the mixture to the boil, reduce the heat, cover and simmer gently for 10 minutes. Stir the mixture occasionally and add a dash of water if the sauce starts to dry out.

3 Ladle the chilli into warmed individual serving bowls and top with a spoonful of yogurt to serve.

400g/14oz jar tomato and herb sauce

2 x 400g/14oz cans mixed beans, drained and rinsed

1 fresh red chilli

large handful of fresh coriander (cilantro)

FROM THE STORECUPBOARD

salt and ground black pepper

Cheese and Tomato Soufflés

Using a ready-made cheese sauce takes the effort out of soufflé making. The key to success when making soufflés is to whisk the egg whites thoroughly to incorporate as much air as possible. During the cooking time don't open the oven door – the cold draught could cause the delicate mixture to collapse.

SERVES SIX

1 Preheat the oven to 200°C/400°F/Gas 6. Turn the cheese sauce into a bowl. Thinly slice the sun-dried tomatoes and add to the bowl with 90g/3½oz/generous 1 cup of the Parmesan, the egg yolks and seasoning. Stir until well combined.

2 Brush the base and sides of six 200ml/7fl oz/scant 1 cup ramekins with the oil and then coat the insides of the dishes with half the remaining cheese, tilting them until evenly covered.

3 Whisk the egg whites in a clean bowl until stiff. Use a large metal spoon to stir one-quarter of the egg whites into the sauce, then fold in the remainder. Spoon the mixture into the prepared dishes and sprinkle with the remaining Parmesan cheese. Place on a baking sheet and bake for 15–18 minutes, until well risen and golden. Serve the soufflés as soon as you remove them from the oven.

350g/12oz tub fresh cheese sauce

50g/2oz sun-dried tomatoes in olive oil, drained, plus 10ml/ 2 tsp of the oil

130g/4¹/₂oz/1¹/₃ cups grated Parmesan cheese

4 large (US extra large) eggs, separated

FROM THE STORECUPBOARD

salt and ground black pepper

Classic Margherita Pizza

Bought pizza base mixes are a great storecupboard stand-by. A Margherita Pizza makes a lovely simple supper, but of course you can add any extra toppings you like. Prosciutto and rocket (arugula) make a great addition – just add them to the pizza after it is cooked.

SERVES TWO

half a 300g/11oz packet pizza base mix

45ml/3 tbsp ready-made tomato and basil sauce

150g/5oz mozzarella, sliced

FROM THE STORECUPBOARD

15ml/1 tbsp herb-infused olive oil

salt and ground black pepper

1 Make the pizza base mix according to the instructions on the packet. Brush the base with a little of the olive oil and spread over the tomato and basil sauce, not quite to the edges.

2 Arrange the slices of mozzarella on top of the pizza and bake for 25–30 minutes, or until golden.

3 Drizzle the remaining oil on top of the pizza, season with salt and black pepper and serve immediately, garnished with fresh basil leaves.

Cheesy Leek and Couscous Cake

The tangy flavour of sharp Cheddar cheese goes perfectly with the sweet taste of leeks. The cheese melts into the couscous and helps it stick together, making a firm cake that's easy to cut into wedges. Serve with a crisp green salad.

SERVES FOUR

300g/11oz couscous

2 leeks, sliced

200g/7oz mature Cheddar or Monterey Jack, grated

FROM THE STORECUPBOARD

45ml/3 tbsp olive oil

salt and ground black pepper

VARIATION *There are endless variations on this tangy, tasty cake but choose a cheese that melts well because it will help the cake to stick together. Try using caramelized onions and blue cheese in place of the leeks and Cheddar.*

1 Put the couscous in a large heatproof bowl and pour over 450ml/³⁄₄ pint/scant 2 cups boiling water. Cover and set aside for about 15 minutes, or until all the water has been absorbed.

2 Heat 15ml/1 tbsp of the oil in a 23cm/9in non-stick frying pan. Add the leeks and cook over a medium heat for 4–5 minutes, stirring occasionally, until tender and golden.

3 Remove the leeks with a slotted spoon and stir them into the couscous. Add the grated cheese and some salt and pepper and stir through. Heat the remaining oil in the pan and tip in the couscous and leek mixture. Pat down firmly to form a cake and cook over a fairly gentle heat for 15 minutes, or until the underside is crisp and golden.

4 Slide the couscous cake onto a plate, then invert it back into the pan to cook the other side. Cook for a further 5–8 minutes, or until golden, then remove from the heat. Slide on to a board and serve cut into wedges.

Potato and Onion Tortilla

This deep-set omelette with sliced potatoes and onions is the best-known Spanish tortilla and makes a deliciously simple meal when served with a leafy salad and crusty bread. Tortilla are often made with a variety of ingredients – chopped red or yellow (bell) peppers, cooked peas, corn, or grated Cheddar or Gruyère cheese can all be added to the mixture in step 2, if you like.

SERVES FOUR TO SIX

800g/1³/₄lb medium potatoes

2 onions, thinly sliced

6 eggs

FROM THE STORECUPBOARD

100ml/3¹/₂fl oz/scant ¹/₂ cup extra virgin olive oil

salt and ground black pepper

1 Thinly slice the potatoes. Heat 75ml/5 tbsp of the oil in a frying pan and cook the potatoes, turning frequently, for 10 minutes. Add the onions and seasoning, and continue to cook for a further 10 minutes, until the vegetables are tender.

2 Meanwhile, beat the eggs in a large bowl with a little seasoning. Tip the potatoes and onions into the eggs and mix gently. Leave to stand for 10 minutes.

3 Wipe out the pan with kitchen paper and heat the remaining oil in it. Pour the egg mixture into the pan and spread it out in an even layer. Cover and cook over a very gentle heat for 20 minutes, until the eggs are just set. Serve cut into wedges.

Spiced Lentils

The combination of lentils, tomatoes and cheese is widely used in Mediterranean cooking. The tang of feta cheese complements the slightly earthy flavour of the attractive dark lentils. True Puy lentils come from the region of France, Le Puy, which has a unique climate and volcanic soil in which they thrive.

SERVES FOUR

250g/9oz/1¹/₂ cups Puy lentils

200g/7oz feta cheese

75ml/5 tbsp sun-dried tomato purée (paste)

small handful of fresh chervil or flat leaf parsley, chopped, plus extra to garnish

FROM THE STORECUPBOARD

salt and ground black pepper

1 Place the lentils in a heavy pan with 600ml/1 pint/2½ cups water. Bring to the boil, reduce the heat and cover the pan. Simmer gently for about 20 minutes, until the lentils are just tender and most of the water has been absorbed.

2 Crumble half the feta cheese into the pan. Add the sun-dried tomato purée, chopped chervil or flat leaf parsley and a little salt and freshly ground black pepper. Heat through for 1 minute.

3 Transfer the lentil mixture and juices to warmed plates or bowls. Crumble the remaining feta cheese on top and sprinkle with the fresh herbs to garnish. Serve hot.

Roast Acorn Squash with Spinach and Gorgonzola

Roasting squash brings out its sweetness, here offset by tangy cheese. Acorn squash has been used here, but any type of squash will give delicious results.

SERVES FOUR

4 acorn squash

250g/9oz baby spinach leaves, washed

200g/7oz Gorgonzola cheese, sliced

FROM THE STORECUPBOARD

45ml/3 tbsp garlic-infused olive oil

salt and ground black pepper

1 Preheat the oven to 190°C/375°F/Gas 5. Cut the tops off the squash, and scoop out and discard the seeds. Place the squash, cut side up, in a roasting pan and drizzle with 30ml/ 2 tbsp of the oil. Season with salt and pepper and bake for 30–40 minutes, or until tender.

2 Heat the remaining oil in a large frying pan and add the spinach leaves. Cook over a medium heat for 2–3 minutes, until the leaves are just wilted. Season with salt and pepper and divide between the squash halves.

3 Top with the Gorgonzola and return to the oven for 10 minutes, or until the cheese has melted. Season with ground black pepper and serve.

Creamy Red Lentil Dhal

This makes a tasty winter supper for vegetarians and meat eaters alike. Serve with naan bread, coconut cream and fresh coriander (cilantro) leaves. The coconut cream gives this dish a really rich taste.

SERVES FOUR

500g/1¼lb/2 cups red lentils

15ml/1 tbsp hot curry paste

FROM THE STORECUPBOARD

15ml/1 tbsp sunflower oil

salt and ground black pepper

1 Heat the oil in a large pan and add the lentils. Fry for 1–2 minutes, stirring continuously, then stir in the curry paste and 600ml/1 pint/2½ cups boiling water.

2 Bring the mixture to the boil, then reduce the heat to a gentle simmer. Cover the pan and cook for 15 minutes, stirring occasionally, until the lentils are tender and the mixture has thickened.

3 Season the dhal with plenty of salt and ground black pepper to taste, and serve piping hot.

Wild Mushroom and Fontina Tart

Use any types of wild mushrooms you like in this tart – chanterelles, morels, horns of plenty and ceps all have wonderful flavours. It makes an impressive vegetarian main course, served with a green salad.

SERVES SIX

225g/8oz ready-made shortcrust pastry, thawed if frozen

350g/12oz/5 cups mixed wild mushrooms, sliced if large

150g/5oz Fontina cheese, sliced

FROM THE STORECUPBOARD

50g/2oz/¹/₄ cup butter

salt and ground black pepper

1 Preheat the oven to 190°C/375°F/Gas 5. Roll out the pastry and use to a line a 23cm/9in loose-bottomed flan tin (tart pan). Chill the pastry for 30 minutes, then bake blind for 15 minutes. Set aside.

2 Heat the butter in a large frying pan until foaming. Add the mushrooms and season with salt and ground black pepper. Cook over a medium heat for 4–5 minutes, moving the mushrooms about and turning them occasionally with a wooden spoon, until golden.

3 Arrange the mushrooms in the cooked pastry case with the Fontina. Return the tart to the oven for 10 minutes, or until the cheese is golden and bubbling. Serve hot.

Parmigiana di Melanzane

This flavoursome Italian dish can be served as a vegetarian main course, or as an accompaniment to meat or chicken dishes. For a delicious variation, layer a few artichoke hearts between the slices of aubergine.

SERVES EIGHT

900g/2lb aubergines (eggplants), sliced lengthways

600ml/1 pint/2¹/₂ cups garlic and herb passata (bottled strained tomatoes)

115g/4oz/1¹/₄ cups freshly grated Parmesan cheese

FROM THE STORECUPBOARD

60ml/4 tbsp olive oil

salt and ground black pepper

1 Preheat the grill (broiler) to high. Brush the aubergine slices with the oil and season with salt and pepper to taste. Arrange them in a single layer on a grill pan and grill (broil) for 4–5 minutes on each side, until golden and tender. (You will have to do this in batches.)

2 Preheat the oven to 190°C/375°F/Gas 5. Spoon a little passata into a large baking dish. Arrange a single layer of aubergine slices over the top and sprinkle with some grated Parmesan cheese. Repeat the layers of passata, aubergine and Parmesan until all the ingredients have been used up, finishing with a good sprinkling of Parmesan. Bake for 20–25 minutes, or until golden and bubbling.

Vegetables and Side Dishes

A FEW CAREFULLY CHOSEN INGREDIENTS CAN BE BROUGHT

TOGETHER TO CREATE MOUTHWATERING SIDE DISHES

AND ACCOMPANIMENTS THAT WILL COMPLEMENT AND

ENHANCE ANY MAIN DISH. THIS COLLECTION OF TASTY

AND COLOURFUL COMBINATIONS OF VEGETABLES MAKES

HEALTHY EATING A TEMPTING TREAT.

Japanese-style Spinach with Toasted Sesame Seeds

This Japanese speciality, known as *O-hitashi*, has been served as a side dish on dining tables in Japan for centuries. Seasonal green vegetables are simply blanched and cooled and formed into little towers. With a little help from soy sauce and sesame seeds, they reveal their true flavour. Serve the spinach towers with simply cooked chicken, or fish such as salmon or tuna.

SERVES FOUR

1 Blanch the spinach leaves in boiling water for 15 seconds. For Japanese-type spinach, hold the leafy part and slip the stems into the pan. After 15 seconds, drop in the leaves and cook for 20 seconds.

2 Drain immediately and place the spinach under running water. Squeeze out all the excess water by hand. Now what looked like a large amount of spinach has become a ball, roughly the size of an orange. Mix the shoyu and water, then pour on to the spinach. Mix well and leave to cool.

3 Meanwhile, put the sesame seeds in a dry frying pan and stir or toss until they start to pop. Remove from the heat and leave to cool.

4 Drain the spinach and squeeze out the excess sauce with your hands. Form the spinach into a log shape of about 4cm/1½in in diameter on a chopping board. Squeeze again to make it firm. With a sharp knife, cut it across into four cylinders.

5 Place the spinach cylinders on a large plate or individual dishes. Sprinkle with the toasted sesame seeds and serve.

450g/1lb fresh young spinach

30ml/2 tbsp shoyu

30ml/2 tbsp water

15ml/1 tbsp sesame seeds

COOK'S TIP *Japanese spinach, the long-leaf type with the stalks and pink root intact, is best, but you can use ordinary young spinach leaves, or any soft and deep-green salad leaves – such as watercress, rocket (arugula) or lamb's lettuce.*

Braised Lettuce and Peas with Spring Onions

This light vegetable dish is based on the classic French method of braising peas with lettuce and spring onions in butter, and is delicious served with simply grilled fish or roast or grilled duck. A sprinkling of chopped fresh mint makes a fresh, flavoursome and extremely pretty garnish. Other legumes such as broad (fava) beans, mangetouts (snow peas) and sugar snap peas can be used instead of peas to create a delicious variation.

SERVES FOUR

50g/2oz/¹/₄ cup butter

4 Little Gem (Bibb) lettuces, halved lengthways

2 bunches spring onions (scallions), trimmed

400g/14oz shelled peas (about 1kg/2¹/₄lb in pods)

FROM THE STORECUPBOARD

salt and ground black pepper

1 Melt half the butter in a wide, heavy pan over a low heat. Add the lettuces and spring onions.

2 Turn the vegetables in the butter, then sprinkle in salt and plenty of freshly ground black pepper. Cover, and cook the vegetables very gently for 5 minutes, stirring once.

3 Add the peas and turn them in the buttery juices. Pour in 120ml/4fl oz/¹/₂ cup water, then cover and cook over a gentle heat for a further 5 minutes. Uncover and increase the heat to reduce the liquid to a few tablespoons.

4 Stir in the remaining butter and adjust the seasoning. Transfer to a warmed serving dish and serve immediately.

EXTRA *Braise about 250g/9oz baby carrots with the lettuce.*

Asparagus with Lemon Sauce

Sometimes less is more: here a simple egg and lemon dressing brings out the best in asparagus. Serve the asparagus as an appetizer or side dish; alternatively, enjoy it for a light supper, with bread and butter to mop up the juices. When buying asparagus, look for bright coloured firm spears with tight buds – avoid those with tough woody stems. Choose roughly even-sized spears for uniform cooking.

SERVES FOUR

1 Cook the bundle of asparagus in a tall pan of lightly salted, boiling water for 7–10 minutes.

2 Drain well and arrange the asparagus in a serving dish. Reserve 200ml/7fl oz/scant 1 cup of the cooking liquid.

3 Blend the cornflour with the cooled, reserved cooking liquid and place in a pan. Bring to the boil, stirring constantly, and cook over a gentle heat until the sauce thickens slightly. Remove the pan from the heat and leave to cool.

4 Beat the egg yolks with the lemon juice and stir into the cooled sauce. Cook over a low heat, stirring constantly, until the sauce is thick. Be careful not to overheat the sauce or it may curdle. As soon as the sauce has thickened, remove the pan from the heat and continue stirring for 1 minute. Taste and season with salt. Leave the sauce to cool slightly.

5 Stir the cooled lemon sauce, then pour a little over the cooked asparagus. Cover and chill in the refrigerator for at least 2 hours before serving with the rest of the sauce.

675g/1¹/₂lb asparagus, tough ends removed, and tied in a bundle

15ml/1 tbsp cornflour (cornstarch)

2 egg yolks

juice of 1¹/₂ lemons

FROM THE STORECUPBOARD

salt and ground black pepper

COOK'S TIP

For a slightly less tangy sauce, add a little caster (superfine) sugar with the salt in step 4.

Caramelized Shallots

Sweet, golden shallots are good with all sorts of main dishes, including poultry or meat. Shallots have a less distinctive aroma than common onions and a milder flavour; they are also considered to be easier to digest. These caramelized shallots are also excellent with braised or roasted chestnuts, carrots or chunks of butternut squash. You may like to garnish the shallots with sprigs of fresh thyme before serving.

SERVES FOUR TO SIX

1 Heat the butter or oil in a large frying pan and add the shallots or onions in a single layer. Cook gently, turning occasionally, until they are lightly browned.

2 Sprinkle the sugar over the shallots and cook gently, turning the shallots in the juices, until the sugar begins to caramelize. Add the wine or port and let the mixture bubble for 4–5 minutes.

3 Add 150ml/¼ pint/⅔ cup water and seasoning. Cover and cook for 5 minutes, then remove the lid and cook until the liquid evaporates and the shallots are tender and glazed. Adjust the seasoning before serving.

500g/1¼lb shallots or small onions, peeled with root ends intact

15ml/1 tbsp golden caster (superfine) sugar

30ml/2 tbsp red or white wine or port

FROM THE STORECUPBOARD

50g/2oz/¼ cup butter or 60ml/4 tbsp olive oil

salt and ground black pepper

Green Beans with Almond Butter and Lemon

The mild flavour of the almonds in this dish makes it a perfect accompaniment for baked or grilled oily fish such as trout or mackerel.

SERVES FOUR

350g/12oz green beans, trimmed

50g/2oz/¹/₃ cup whole blanched almonds

grated rind and juice of 1 unwaxed lemon

FROM THE STORECUPBOARD

50g/2oz/¹/₄ cup butter

salt and ground black pepper

1 Cook the beans in a pan of salted boiling water for about 3 minutes, or until just tender. Drain well. Meanwhile, melt the butter in a large frying pan until foamy.

2 Add the almonds to the pan and cook, stirring occasionally, for 2–3 minutes, or until golden. Remove from the heat and toss with the beans, lemon rind and juice, and season.

VARIATION *This salad is delicious made with different types of nuts. Use the same quantity of roughly chopped shelled walnuts or blanched hazelnuts in place of the almonds.*

Garlicky Green Salad with Raspberry Dressing

Adding a splash of raspberry vinegar to the dressing enlivens a simple green salad, turning it into a sophisticated side dish.

SERVES FOUR

2 garlic cloves, finely sliced

4 handfuls of green salad leaves

15ml/1 tbsp raspberry vinegar

FROM THE STORECUPBOARD

45ml/3 tbsp olive oil

salt and ground black pepper

1 Heat the oil in a small pan and add the garlic. Fry gently for 1–2 minutes, or until just golden, being careful not to burn the garlic. Remove the garlic with a slotted spoon and drain on kitchen paper. Pour the oil into a small bowl.

2 Arrange the salad leaves in a serving bowl. Whisk the raspberry vinegar into the reserved oil and season with salt and ground black pepper.

3 Pour the garlic dressing over the salad leaves and toss to combine. Sprinkle over the fried garlic slices and serve.

Cauliflower with Garlic Crumbs

This simple dish makes a great accompaniment to any meat or fish dish. When buying cauliflower look for creamy white coloured florets with the inner green leaves curled round the flower. Discard cauliflowers with discoloured patches or yellow leaves. As an alternative, try using broccoli florets instead of the cauliflower. Broccoli should have a fresh appearance: avoid yellowing specimens and those that feel soft or are wilting.

SERVES FOUR TO SIX

1 Steam or boil the cauliflower in salted water until just tender. Drain and leave to cool.

2 Heat 60–75ml/4–5 tbsp of the olive or vegetable oil in a pan, add the breadcrumbs and cook over a medium heat, tossing and turning, until browned and crisp. Add the garlic, turn once or twice, then remove from the pan and set aside.

3 Heat the remaining oil in the pan, then add the cauliflower, mashing and breaking it up a little as it lightly browns in the oil. (Do not overcook but just cook until lightly browned.)

4 Add the garlic breadcrumbs to the pan and cook, stirring, until well combined, with some of the cauliflower still holding its shape. Season and serve hot or warm.

1 large cauliflower, cut into bitesize florets

130g/4^{1}/$_{2}$oz/2^{1}/$_{4}$ cups dry white or wholemeal (whole-wheat) breadcrumbs

3–5 garlic cloves, thinly sliced or chopped

FROM THE STORECUPBOARD

90–120ml/6–8 tbsp olive or vegetable oil

salt and ground black pepper

COOK'S TIP

Serve this garlicky cauliflower dish as they do in Italy, with cooked pasta, such as spaghetti.

Summer Squash and Baby New Potatoes in Warm Dill Sour Cream

Fresh vegetables and fragrant dill are delicious tossed in a simple sour cream or yogurt sauce. Choose small squash with bright skins that are free from blemishes and bruises. To make a simpler potato salad, pour the dill sour cream over warm cooked potatoes. Serve either version of the potato salad with poached salmon or chargrilled chicken.

SERVES FOUR

1 Cut the squash into pieces about the same size as the potatoes. Put the potatoes in a pan and add water to cover and a pinch of salt. Bring to the boil, then simmer for about 10 minutes, until almost tender. Add the squash and continue to cook until the vegetables are just tender, then drain.

2 Put the vegetables into a wide, shallow pan and gently stir in the finely chopped fresh dill and chives.

3 Remove the pan from the heat and stir in the sour cream or yogurt. Return to the heat and heat gently until warm. Season and serve.

400g/14oz mixed squash, such as yellow and green courgettes (zucchini), and green patty pan

400g/14oz baby new potatoes

1 large handful mixed fresh dill and chives, finely chopped

300ml/¹/₂ pint/1¹/₄ cups sour cream or Greek (US strained plain) yogurt

FROM THE STORECUPBOARD

salt and ground black pepper

Minty Broad Beans with Lemon

Young, tender broad beans have a sweet, mild taste and are delicious served in a simple salad. Take advantage of them when they're in season and make them into this fresh, zesty dish. Green peas – either fresh or frozen – are also delicious served in the same way, but you don't need to peel off their already tender skins.

SERVES FOUR

450g/1lb broad (fava) beans, thawed if frozen

grated rind and juice of 1 unwaxed lemon

1 small bunch of fresh mint, roughly chopped

FROM THE STORECUPBOARD

30ml/2 tbsp garlic-infused olive oil

salt and ground black pepper

1 Using your fingers, slip the grey skins off the broad beans and discard – this takes a little time but the result is well worthwhile. Cook the beans in salted boiling water for 3–4 minutes, or until just tender.

2 Drain well and toss with the oil, lemon rind and juice, and mint. Season with salt and pepper, and serve immediately.

COOK'S TIP

When using fresh broad beans, it is easier to cook them first, then run them under cold water before slipping off their skins. Quickly blanch the skinned beans in boiling water to re-heat them.

Gingered Carrot Salad

This fresh and zesty salad is ideal served as an accompaniment to simple grilled chicken or fish. Some food processors have an attachment that can be used to cut the carrots into batons, which makes quick work of the preparation, but even cutting them by hand doesn't take too long. Fresh root ginger goes perfectly with sweet carrots, and the tiny black poppy seeds not only add taste and texture, but also look stunning against the bright orange of the carrots.

SERVES FOUR

350g/12oz carrots, peeled and cut into fine matchsticks

2.5cm/1in piece of fresh root ginger, peeled and grated

15ml/1 tbsp poppy seeds

FROM THE STORECUPBOARD

30ml/2 tbsp garlic-infused olive oil

salt and ground black pepper

1 Put the carrots in a bowl and stir in the oil and grated ginger. Cover and chill for at least 30 minutes, to allow the flavours to develop.

2 Season the salad with salt and pepper to taste. Stir in the poppy seeds just before serving.

VARIATION

To make a parsnip and sesame seed salad, replace the carrots with parsnips and blanch in boiling salted water for 1 minute before combining with the oil and ginger. Replace the poppy seeds with the same quantity of sesame seeds.

Baked Winter Squash with Tomatoes

Acorn, butternut or Hubbard squash can all be used in this simple recipe. Serve the squash as a light main course, with warm crusty bread, or as a side dish for grilled meat or poultry. Canned chopped tomatoes with herbs are used in this recipe. A variety of flavoured canned tomatoes are now available including garlic, onion and olive – they are ideal for adding a combination of flavours when time is short.

SERVES FOUR TO SIX

1 Preheat the oven to 160°C/325°F/Gas 3. Heat the oil in a pan and cook the pumpkin or squash slices, in batches, until golden brown, removing them from the pan as they are cooked.

2 Add the tomatoes and cook over a medium-high heat until the mixture is of a sauce consistency. Stir in the rosemary and season to taste with salt and pepper.

3 Layer the pumpkin slices and tomatoes in an ovenproof dish, ending with a layer of tomatoes. Bake for 35 minutes, or until the top is lightly glazed and beginning to turn golden brown, and the pumpkin is tender. Serve immediately.

1kg/2¼lb pumpkin or orange winter squash, peeled and sliced

2 x 400g/14oz cans chopped tomatoes with herbs

2–3 rosemary sprigs, stems removed and leaves chopped

FROM THE STORECUPBOARD

45ml/3 tbsp garlic-flavoured olive oil

salt and ground black pepper

Stewed Okra with Tomatoes and Coriander

This is a favourite Middle-Eastern way to prepare okra. Add wedges of lemon as a garnish so that their juice can be squeezed over the vegetables to taste. Okra, also known as lady's fingers, are narrow green lantern-shaped pods. They contain a row of seeds that ooze a viscous liquid when cooked. This liquid acts as a natural thickener in a variety of curries and soups.

SERVES FOUR TO SIX

1 Heat the tomatoes and the cinnamon, cumin and cloves with half the coriander in a pan, then season to taste with salt and freshly ground black pepper and bring to the boil.

2 Add the okra and cook, stirring constantly, for 1–2 minutes. Reduce the heat to low, then simmer, stirring occasionally, for 20–30 minutes, until the okra is tender.

3 Taste for spicing and seasoning, and adjust if necessary, adding more of any one spice, salt or pepper to taste. Stir in the remaining coriander. Serve hot, warm or cold.

400g/14oz can chopped tomatoes with onions and garlic

generous pinch each of ground cinnamon, cumin and cloves

90ml/6 tbsp chopped fresh coriander (cilantro) leaves

800g/1³⁄₄lb okra

FROM THE STORECUPBOARD

salt and ground black pepper

Roast Asparagus
with Crispy Prosciutto

Choose tender, fine asparagus for this recipe, as it cooks through quickly in the oven without losing its flavour or texture.

SERVES FOUR

350g/12oz fine asparagus spears, trimmed

1 small handful of fresh basil leaves

4 prosciutto slices

FROM THE STORECUPBOARD

30ml/2 tbsp olive oil

salt and ground black pepper

1 Preheat the oven to 190°C/375°F/Gas 5. Put the asparagus in a roasting pan and drizzle with the olive oil. Sprinkle over the basil and season with salt and ground black pepper. Gently stir to coat in the oil, then spread the asparagus in a single layer.

2 Lay the slices of prosciutto on top of the asparagus and cook for 10–15 minutes, or until the prosciutto is crisp and the asparagus is just tender. Serve immediately.

Garlicky Roasties

Potatoes roasted in their skins retain a deep, earthy taste (and, as a bonus, absorb less fat too) while the garlic mellows on cooking to give a pungent but not overly-strong taste to serve alongside or squeezed over as a garnish.

SERVES FOUR

1 Preheat the oven to 240°C/475°F/Gas 9. Place the potatoes in a pan of cold water and bring to the boil. Drain.

2 Combine the oils in a roasting tin and place in the oven to get really hot. Add the potatoes and garlic and coat in oil.

3 Sprinkle with salt and roast for 10 minutes. Reduce the heat to 200°C/400°F/Gas 6. Continue roasting, basting occasionally, for 30–40 minutes.

4 Serve each portion with several cloves of garlic.

1kg/2¼lb small floury potatoes

10ml/2 tsp walnut oil

2 whole garlic bulbs, unpeeled

FROM THE STORECUPBOARD

60–75ml/4–5 tbsp sunflower oil

salt and ground black pepper

Leek Fritters

These crispy fried morsels are best served at room temperature, with a good squeeze of lemon juice and a sprinkling of salt and freshly grated nutmeg. Matzo meal, a traditional Jewish ingredient, is used in these fritters: it is made from crumbled matzo, an unleavened bread, similar to water biscuits. Matzo meal is used in a similar way to breadcrumbs, which can also be used to make these fritters.

SERVES FOUR

1 Cook the leeks in salted boiling water for 5 minutes, or until just tender and bright green. Drain well and leave to cool.

2 Chop the leeks coarsely. Put in a bowl and combine with the matzo meal, eggs and seasoning.

3 Heat 5mm/¼in oil in a frying pan. Using two tablespoons, carefully spoon the leek mixture into the hot oil. Cook over a medium-high heat until golden brown on the underside, then turn and cook the second side. Drain on kitchen paper. Add more oil if needed and heat before cooking more mixture.

4 large leeks, total weight about 1kg/2¹/₄lb, thickly sliced

120–175ml/4–6fl oz/¹/₂–³/₄ cup coarse matzo meal

2 eggs, lightly beaten

FROM THE STORECUPBOARD

olive or vegetable oil, for shallow frying

salt and ground black pepper

Deep-fried Artichokes

This is an Italian speciality, named *carciofi alla giudia*. The artichokes are baked, then pressed to open them and plunged into hot oil, where their leaves twist and brown, turning the artichokes into crispy flowers. Serve with lamb or pork steaks.

SERVES FOUR

2–3 lemons, halved

4–8 small young globe artichokes

olive or vegetable oil, for deep-frying

1 Fill a large bowl with cold water and stir in the juice of one or two of the lemons. Trim and discard the stems of the artichokes, then trim off their tough ends and remove all the tough outer leaves until you reach the pale pointed centre. Carefully open the leaves of one of the artichokes by pressing it against the table or poking them open. Trim the tops if they are sharp.

2 If there is any choke inside the artichoke, remove it with a melon baller or small pointed spoon. Put the artichoke in the acidulated water and prepare the remaining artichokes in the same way.

3 Put the artichokes in a large pan and pour over water to cover. Bring to the boil, reduce the heat and simmer for 10–15 minutes, or until partly cooked. If they are small, cook them for only 10 minutes. Drain the artichokes and leave upside down until cool enough to handle. Press them open gently, being careful not to break them apart.

4 Fill a pan with oil to a depth of 5–7.5cm/2–3in and heat. Add one or two artichokes at a time, with the leaves uppermost, and press down with a spoon to open up the leaves. Fry for 5–8 minutes, turning, until golden and crisp. Remove from the pan, and drain on kitchen paper. Serve immediately, with the remaining lemon cut into wedges.

COOK'S TIP *Select immature artichokes, before their chokes have formed. If you like, you can prepare and boil them ahead and deep-fry just before serving.*

Stir-fried Broccoli with Soy Sauce and Sesame Seeds

Purple sprouting broccoli has been used for this recipe, but when it is not available an ordinary variety of broccoli, such as calabrese, will also work very well.

SERVES TWO

225g/8oz purple sprouting broccoli

15ml/1 tbsp soy sauce

15ml/1 tbsp toasted sesame seeds

FROM THE STORECUPBOARD

15ml/1 tbsp olive oil

salt and ground black pepper

1 Using a sharp knife, cut off and discard any thick stems from the broccoli and cut the broccoli into long, thin florets.

2 Heat the olive oil in a wok or large frying pan and add the broccoli. Stir-fry for 3–4 minutes, or until tender, adding a splash of water if the pan becomes too dry.

3 Add the soy sauce to the broccoli, then season with salt and ground black pepper to taste. Add sesame seeds, toss to combine and serve immediately.

Stir-fried Brussels Sprouts with Bacon and Caraway Seeds

This is a great way of cooking Brussels sprouts, helping to retain their sweet flavour and crunchy texture. Stir-frying guarantees that there will not be a single soggy sprout in sight, which is often what puts people off these fabulous vegetables.

SERVES FOUR

1 Using a sharp knife, cut the Brussels sprouts into fine shreds and set aside. Heat the oil in a wok or large frying pan and add the bacon. Cook for 1–2 minutes, or until the bacon is beginning to turn golden.

2 Add the shredded sprouts to the wok or pan and stir-fry for 1–2 minutes, or until lightly cooked.

3 Season the sprouts with salt and ground black pepper to taste and stir in the caraway seeds. Cook for a further 30 seconds, then serve immediately.

450g/1lb Brussels sprouts, trimmed and washed

2 streaky (fatty) bacon rashers (strips), finely chopped

10ml/2 tsp caraway seeds, lightly crushed

FROM THE STORECUPBOARD

30ml/2 tbsp sunflower oil

salt and ground black pepper

Bocconcini with Fennel and Basil

These tiny balls of mozzarella are best when they're perfectly fresh. They should be milky and soft when you cut into them. Buy them from an Italian delicatessen or a good cheese shop.

SERVES SIX

1 Drain the bocconcini well and place in a bowl. Stir in the olive oil, fennel seeds and basil, and season with salt and pepper. Cover and chill for 1 hour.

2 Remove the bowl from the refrigerator and leave to stand for about 30 minutes for the cheese to return to room temperature before serving.

COOK'S TIP
Bocconcini are mini mozzarella balls, each one hand-stretched and rolled, then preserved in brine. If you can't find bocconcini, use ordinary mozzarella cut into bitesize pieces.

450g/1lb bocconcini mozzarella

5ml/1 tsp fennel seeds, lightly crushed

a small bunch of fresh basil leaves, roughly torn

FROM THE STORECUPBOARD

45ml/3 tbsp extra virgin olive oil

salt and ground black pepper

Noodles with Sesame - roasted Spring Onions

You can use any kind of noodles for this Asian-style dish. Rice noodles look and taste particularly good, but egg noodles work very well too. Serve with fish and chicken dishes.

SERVES FOUR

1 bunch of spring onions (scallions), trimmed

225g/8oz flat rice noodles

30ml/2 tbsp oyster sauce

FROM THE STORECUPBOARD

30ml/2 tbsp sesame oil

salt and ground black pepper

1 Preheat the oven to 200°C/400°F/Gas 6. Cut the spring onions into three pieces, then put them in a small roasting pan and season with salt and pepper.

2 Drizzle the sesame oil over the spring onions and roast for 10 minutes, until they are slightly charred and tender. Set aside.

3 Cook the noodles according to the instructions on the packet and drain thoroughly. Toss with the spring onions and oyster sauce, and season with ground black pepper. Serve immediately.

Spicy Potato Wedges

These wedges are easy to make and can be served on their own with a garlic mayonnaise dip or as an accompaniment to meat or fish dishes. To make extra-hot potato wedges, use chilli powder instead of paprika.

SERVES FOUR

675g/1¹/₂lb floury potatoes, such as Maris Piper

10ml/2 tsp paprika

5ml/1 tsp ground cumin

FROM THE STORECUPBOARD

45ml/3 tbsp olive oil

salt and ground black pepper

1 Preheat the oven to 190°C/375°F/Gas 5. Using a sharp knife, cut the potatoes into chunky wedges and place in a roasting pan.

2 In a small bowl, combine the olive oil with the paprika and cumin and season with plenty of salt and ground black pepper. Pour the mixture over the potatoes and toss well to coat thoroughly.

3 Spread the potatoes in a single layer in the roasting pan and bake for 30–40 minutes, or until golden brown and tender. Serve immediately.

Crisp and Golden Roast Potatoes with Goose Fat and Garlic

Goose fat gives the best flavour to roast potatoes and is now widely available in cans in supermarkets. However, if you can't find goose fat, or you want to make a vegetarian version of these potatoes, use a large knob (pat) of butter or 15ml/1 tbsp olive oil instead. If you like, add a couple of bay leaves to the potatoes before roasting; they impart a lovely flavour.

SERVES FOUR

675g/1¹/₂lb floury potatoes, such as Maris Piper, peeled

30ml/2 tbsp goose fat

12 garlic cloves, unpeeled

FROM THE STORECUPBOARD

salt and ground black pepper

1 Preheat the oven to 190°C/375°F/Gas 5. Cut the potatoes into large chunks and cook in a pan of salted, boiling water for 5 minutes. Drain well and give the colander a good shake to fluff up the edges of the potatoes. Return the potatoes to the pan and place it over a low heat for 1 minute to steam off any excess water.

2 Meanwhile, spoon the goose fat into a roasting pan and place in the oven until hot, about 5 minutes. Add the potatoes to the pan with the garlic and turn to coat in the fat. Season well with salt and ground black pepper and roast for 40–50 minutes, turning occasionally, until the potatoes are golden and tender.

Tomato and Aubergine Gratin

This colourful, Mediterranean dish makes the perfect partner to grilled, pan-fried or baked meat or poultry. If you prefer, thinly sliced courgettes (zucchini) can be used in this dish instead of the aubergines. Grill the courgettes for 10–15 minutes. Choose plum tomatoes if you can – they have fewer seeds than most round tomatoes, so are less watery and are ideal for cooking.

SERVES FOUR TO SIX

1 Preheat the grill (broiler). Thinly slice the aubergines and arrange them in a single layer on a foil-lined grill rack. Brush the aubergine slices with some of the oil and grill (broil) for 15–20 minutes, turning once, until golden on both sides. Brush the second side with more oil after turning the slices.

2 Preheat the oven to 200°C/400°F/Gas 6. Toss the aubergine and tomato slices together in a bowl with a little seasoning, then pile them into a shallow, ovenproof dish. Drizzle with any remaining olive oil and sprinkle with the grated Parmesan cheese. Bake for 20 minutes, until the cheese is golden and the vegetables are hot. Serve the gratin immediately.

2 medium aubergines (eggplants), about 500g/1¼lb

400g/14oz ripe tomatoes, sliced

40g/1½oz/½ cup freshly grated Parmesan cheese

FROM THE STORECUPBOARD

90ml/6 tbsp olive oil

salt and ground black pepper

Bubble and Squeak

Whether you have leftovers or cook this old-fashioned classic from fresh, be sure to give it a really good "squeak" in the pan so it turns a rich honey brown. Serve as an accompaniment to grilled pork chops or fried eggs, or simply serve with warm bread for a quick supper. If you prefer, cook the bubble and squeak in individual-sized portions – divide into four and form into patties before cooking.

SERVES FOUR

1 Heat 30ml/2 tbsp of the bacon fat or oil in a heavy frying pan. Add the onion and cook over a medium heat, stirring frequently, until softened but not browned.

2 In a bowl, mix together the potatoes and cooked cabbage or sprouts and season with salt and plenty of pepper to taste.

3 Add the vegetables to the pan with the cooked onions, stir well, then press the vegetable mixture into a large, even cake.

4 Cook over a medium heat for about 15 minutes, until the cake is browned underneath.

5 Invert a large plate over the pan, and, holding it tightly against the pan, turn them both over together. Lift off the frying pan, return it to the heat and add the remaining bacon fat or oil. When hot, slide the cake back into the pan, browned side uppermost.

6 Cook over a medium heat for 10 minutes, or until the underside is golden brown. Serve hot, in wedges.

60ml/4 tbsp bacon fat or vegetable oil

1 medium onion, chopped

450g/1lb floury potatoes, cooked and mashed

225g/8oz cooked cabbage or Brussels sprouts, chopped

FROM THE STORECUPBOARD

salt and ground black pepper

Cheesy Creamy Leeks

This is quite a rich accompaniment that could easily be served as a meal in itself with brown rice or couscous. Cheddar cheese has been used here for a slightly stronger flavour, but you could use a milder Swiss cheese, such as Gruyère, if you like.

SERVES 4

4 large leeks or 12 baby leeks, trimmed and washed

150ml/¹⁄₄ pint/²⁄₃ cup double (heavy) cream

75g/3oz mature Cheddar or Monterey Jack cheese, grated

FROM THE STORECUPBOARD

15ml/1 tbsp olive oil

salt and ground black pepper

1 Preheat the grill (broiler) to high. If using large leeks, slice them lengthways. Heat the oil in a large frying pan and add the leeks. Season with salt and pepper and cook for about 4 minutes, stirring occasionally, until starting to turn golden.

2 Pour the cream into the pan and stir until well combined. Allow to bubble gently for a few minutes.

3 Preheat the grill (broiler). Transfer the creamy leeks to a shallow ovenproof dish and sprinkle with the cheese. Grill for 4–5 minutes, or until the cheese is golden brown and bubbling and serve immediately.

Creamy Polenta with Dolcelatte

Soft-cooked polenta is a tasty accompaniment to meat dishes and makes a delicious change from the usual potatoes or rice. It can also be enjoyed on its own as a hearty snack.

SERVES FOUR TO SIX

900ml/1¹/₂ pints/3³/₄ cups milk

115g/4oz/1 cup instant polenta

115g/4oz Dolcelatte cheese

FROM THE STORECUPBOARD

60ml/4 tbsp extra virgin olive oil

salt and ground black pepper

1 Pour the milk into a large pan and bring to the boil, then add a good pinch of salt. Remove the pan from the heat and pour in the polenta in a slow, steady stream, stirring constantly to combine.

2 Return the pan to a low heat and simmer gently, stirring constantly, for 5 minutes. Remove the pan from the heat and stir in the olive oil.

3 Spoon the polenta into a serving dish and crumble the cheese over the top. Season with more ground black pepper and serve immediately.

Fennel, Potato and Garlic Mash

This flavoursome mash of potato, fennel and garlic goes well with practically all main dishes, whether fish, poultry or meat. Floury varieties of potato such as Pentland Squire, King Edward or Marfona are best for mashing as they produce a light fluffy result. Waxy potatoes are more suitable for baking, or for salads, as they produce a dense, rather starchy mash.

SERVES FOUR

1 Boil the potatoes in water for 20 minutes, until tender.

2 Meanwhile, trim and chop the fennel, reserving any feathery tops. Chop the tops and set them aside. Heat 30ml/ 2 tbsp of the oil in a pan. Add the fennel, cover and cook over a low heat for 20–30 minutes, until soft but not browned.

3 Drain and mash the potatoes. Purée the fennel in a food mill or blender and beat it into the potato with the remaining oil.

4 Warm the milk or cream and beat sufficient into the potato and fennel to make a creamy, light mixture. Season to taste and reheat gently, then beat in any chopped fennel tops. Serve immediately.

800g/1³/₄lb potatoes, cut into chunks

2 large fennel bulbs

120–150ml/4–5fl oz/ ¹/₂–²/₃ cup milk or single (light) cream

FROM THE STORECUPBOARD

90ml/6 tbsp garlic-flavoured olive oil

salt and ground black pepper

Champ

This traditional Irish dish of potatoes and green or spring onions is enriched with a wickedly indulgent amount of butter – for complete indulgence, replace 60ml/4 tbsp of the milk with crème fraîche or buttermilk. Serve the champ as an accompaniment to beef or lamb stew for a warming and hearty winter meal.

SERVES FOUR

1 Boil the potatoes in lightly salted water for 20–25 minutes, or until they are tender. Drain and mash the potatoes with a fork until smooth.

2 Place the milk, spring onions and half the butter in a small pan and set over a low heat until just simmering. Cook for 2–3 minutes, until the butter has melted and the spring onions have softened.

3 Beat the milk mixture into the mashed potato using a wooden spoon until the mixture is light and fluffy. Reheat gently, adding seasoning to taste.

4 Turn the potato into a warmed serving dish and make a well in the centre with a spoon. Place the remaining butter in the well and let it melt. Serve immediately, sprinkled with extra spring onion.

1kg/2¼lb potatoes, cut into chunks

300ml/½ pint/1¼ cups milk

1 bunch spring onions (scallions), thinly sliced, plus extra to garnish

115g/4oz/½ cup salted butter

FROM THE STORECUPBOARD

salt and ground black pepper

EXTRAS

To make colcannon, another Irish speciality, follow the main recipe, using half the butter. Cook about 500g/1¼lb finely shredded green cabbage or kale in a little water until just tender, drain thoroughly and then beat into the creamed potato. This is delicious served with sausages and grilled (broiled) ham or bacon. The colcannon may also be fried in butter and then browned under the grill (broiler).

Salads

WHETHER SERVED AS A MAIN COURSE OR AN
ACCOMPANIMENT, SALADS ARE ALWAYS A REFRESHING
AND WELCOME CHANGE. THE MOST SUCCESSFUL ARE
COMPOSED OF ONLY A FEW INGREDIENTS – COOKED OR
RAW – WHOSE COLOURS, TEXTURES AND FLAVOURS
COMPLEMENT AND BALANCE PERFECTLY.

Sour Cucumber with Fresh Dill

This is half pickle, half salad, and totally delicious served with pumpernickel or other coarse, dark, full-flavoured bread, as a light meal or an appetizer. Choose smooth-skinned, smallish cucumbers for this recipe as larger ones tend to be less tender, with tough skins and bitter indigestible seeds. If you can only buy a large cucumber, peel it before slicing.

SERVES FOUR

1 In a large mixing bowl, combine together the thinly sliced cucumbers and the thinly sliced onion. Season the vegetables with salt and toss together until they are thoroughly combined. Leave the mixture to stand in a cool place for 5–10 minutes.

2 Add the cider vinegar, 30–45ml/2–3 tbsp water and the chopped fresh dill to the cucumber and onion mixture. Toss all the ingredients together until well combined, then chill in the refrigerator for a few hours, or until ready to serve.

2 small cucumbers, thinly sliced

3 onions, thinly sliced

75–90ml/5–6 tbsp cider vinegar

30–45ml/2–3 tbsp chopped fresh dill

FROM THE STORECUPBOARD

salt and ground black pepper

Beetroot with Fresh Mint

This simple and decorative beetroot salad can be served as part of a selection of salads, as an appetizer, or as an accompaniment to grilled or roasted pork or lamb. Balsamic vinegar is a rich, dark vinegar with a mellow, deep flavour. It can be used to dress a variety of salad ingredients and is particularly good drizzled over a tomato and basil salad.

SERVES FOUR

1 Slice the beetroot or cut into even-size dice with a sharp knife. Put the beetroot in a bowl. Add the balsamic vinegar, olive oil and a pinch of salt and toss together to combine.

2 Add half the thinly shredded fresh mint to the salad and toss lightly until thoroughly combined. Place the salad in the refrigerator and chill for about 1 hour. Serve garnished with the remaining thinly shredded mint leaves.

EXTRAS *To make Tunisian beetroot, add a little harissa to taste and substitute chopped fresh coriander (cilantro) for the shredded mint.*

4–6 cooked beetroot (beet)

15–30ml/1–2 tbsp balsamic vinegar

1 bunch fresh mint, leaves stripped and thinly shredded

FROM THE STORECUPBOARD

30ml/2 tbsp olive oil

salt and ground black pepper

Globe Artichokes with Green Beans and Garlic Dressing

Piquant garlic dressing or creamy aioli go perfectly with these lightly-cooked vegetables. Serve lemon wedges with the artichokes so that their juice may be squeezed over to taste. The vegetables can also be garnished with finely shredded lemon rind. Artichokes should feel heavy for their size – make sure that the inner leaves are wrapped tightly round the choke and the heart inside.

SERVES FOUR TO SIX

225g/8oz green beans

3 small globe artichokes

250ml/8fl oz/1 cup garlic dressing or aioli

FROM THE STORECUPBOARD

15ml/1 tbsp lemon-flavoured olive oil

salt and ground black pepper

1 Cook the beans in boiling water for 1–2 minutes, until slightly softened. Drain well.

2 Trim the artichoke stalks close to the base. Cook them in a large pan of salted water for about 30 minutes, or until you can easily pull away a leaf from the base. Drain well.

3 Using a sharp knife, halve them lengthways and ease out their chokes using a teaspoon.

4 Arrange the artichokes and beans on serving plates and drizzle with the oil. Season with coarse salt and a little pepper. Spoon the garlic dressing or aioli into the hearts and serve warm.

5 To eat the artichokes, pull the leaves from the base one at a time and use to scoop a little of the dressing. It is only the fleshy end of each leaf that is eaten as well as the base, bottom or "fond".

Halloumi and Grape Salad

Firm and salty halloumi cheese is a great standby ingredient for turning a simple salad into a special dish. In this recipe it is tossed with sweet, juicy grapes, which complement its flavour and texture. Fresh young thyme leaves and dill taste especially good mixed with the salad. Serve with a crusty walnut or sun-dried tomato bread for a light lunch.

SERVES FOUR

1 Toss together the salad leaves and fresh herb sprigs and the green and black grapes, then transfer to a large serving plate.

2 Thinly slice the halloumi cheese. Heat a large non-stick frying pan. Add the sliced halloumi cheese and cook briefly until it just starts to turn golden brown on the underside. Turn the cheese with a fish slice or metal spatula and cook the other side until it is golden brown.

3 Arrange the fried cheese over the salad on the plate. Pour over the oil and lemon juice or vinegar dressing and serve immediately while the cheese is still hot.

150g/5oz mixed salad leaves and tender fresh herb sprigs

175g/6oz mixed seedless green and black grapes

250g/9oz halloumi cheese

75ml/5 tbsp oil and lemon juice or vinegar dressing

Watermelon and Feta Salad

The combination of sweet watermelon with salty feta cheese is inspired by Turkish tradition. The salad may be served plain and light, on a leafy base, or with a herbed vinaigrette dressing drizzled over. It is perfect served as an appetizer. Feta cheese is salty because it is preserved in brine – but the salt is not supposed to overpower the taste of the cheese.

SERVES FOUR

4 slices watermelon, chilled

130g/4¹/₂oz feta cheese, preferably sheep's milk feta, cut into bitesize pieces

handful of mixed seeds, such as lightly toasted pumpkin seeds and sunflower seeds

10–15 black olives

1 Cut the rind off the watermelon and remove as many seeds as possible. Cut the flesh into triangular-shaped chunks.

2 Mix the watermelon, feta cheese, mixed seeds and black olives. Cover and chill the salad for 30 minutes before serving.

COOK'S TIP *The best choice of olives for this recipe are plump black Mediterranean ones, such as kalamata, other shiny, brined varieties or dry-cured black olives.*

Tomato, Bean and Fried Basil Salad

Infusing basil in hot oil brings out its wonderful, aromatic flavour, which works so well in almost any tomato dish. Various canned beans or chickpeas can be used instead of mixed beans in this simple dish, as they all taste good and make a wholesome salad to serve as an accompaniment or a satisfying snack with some warm, grainy bread.

SERVES FOUR

1 Reserve one-third of the basil leaves for garnish, then tear the remainder into pieces. Pour the olive oil into a small pan. Add the torn basil and heat gently for 1 minute, until the basil sizzles and begins to colour.

2 Place the halved cherry tomatoes and beans in a bowl. Pour in the basil oil and add a little salt and plenty of freshly ground black pepper. Toss the ingredients together gently, cover and leave to marinate at room temperature for at least 30 minutes. Serve the salad sprinkled with the remaining basil leaves.

15g/¹/₂oz/¹/₂ cup fresh basil leaves

300g/11oz cherry tomatoes, halved

400g/14oz can mixed beans, drained and rinsed

FROM THE STORECUPBOARD

75ml/5 tbsp extra virgin olive oil

salt and ground black pepper

Moroccan Date, Orange and Carrot Salad

Take exotic fresh dates and marry them with everyday ingredients, such as carrots and oranges, to make this deliciously different salad. The salad looks really pretty arranged on a base of sweet Little Gem (Bibb) lettuce leaves. This fruity salad is excellent served with chargrilled lamb steaks, or with skewered lamb.

SERVES FOUR

3 carrots

3 oranges

115g/4oz fresh dates, stoned (pitted) and cut lengthways into eighths

25g/1oz/¹/₄ cup toasted whole almonds, chopped

FROM THE STORECUPBOARD

salt and ground black pepper

1 Grate the carrots and place in a mound in a serving dish, or on four individual plates.

2 Peel and segment two of the oranges and arrange the orange segments around the carrot. Season with salt and freshly ground black pepper. Pile the dates on top, then sprinkle with the chopped, toasted almonds.

3 Squeeze the juice from the remaining orange and sprinkle it over the salad. Chill in the refrigerator for an hour before serving.

Pink Grapefruit and Avocado Salad

Smooth, creamy avocado and zesty citrus fruit are perfect partners in an attractive, refreshing salad. Pink grapefruit are tangy but not too sharp, or try large oranges for a sweeter flavour. Avocados turn brown quickly when exposed to the air: the acidic grapefruit juice will prevent this from occurring, so combine the ingredients as soon as the avocados have been sliced.

SERVES FOUR

1 Slice the top and bottom off a grapefruit, then cut off all the peel and pith from around the side. Working over a small bowl to catch the juices, cut out the segments from between the membranes and place them in a separate bowl. Squeeze any juices remaining in the membranes into the bowl, then discard them. Repeat with the remaining grapefruit.

2 Halve, stone (pit) and peel the avocados. Slice the flesh and add it to the grapefruit segments. Whisk a little salt and then the chilli oil into the grapefruit juice.

3 Pile the rocket leaves on to four serving plates and top with the grapefruit segments and avocado. Pour over the dressing and serve.

2 pink grapefruit

2 ripe avocados

90g/3¹/₂oz rocket (arugula)

FROM THE STORECUPBOARD

30ml/2 tbsp chilli oil

salt and ground black pepper

Turnip Salad in Sour Cream

Usually served cooked, raw young tender turnips have a tangy, slightly peppery flavour. Serve this as an accompaniment for grilled poultry or meat. It is also delicious as a light appetizer, garnished with parsley and paprika, and served with warmed flat breads such as pitta or naan. Garnish the salad with fresh flat leaf parsley and paprika, if you like.

SERVES FOUR

1 Thinly slice or coarsely grate the turnips. Alternatively, thinly slice half the turnips and grate the remaining half. Put in a bowl.

2 Add the onion and vinegar and season to taste with salt and plenty of freshly ground black pepper. Toss together, then stir in the sour cream. Chill well before serving.

VARIATIONS *Large white radishes can be used instead of turnips and crème fraîche can be substituted for the sour cream. The salad is good with a selection of salads and cold dishes for a light lunch or long and leisurely supper.*

2–4 young, tender turnips, peeled

$1/4$–$1/2$ onion, finely chopped

2–3 drops white wine vinegar, or to taste

60–90ml/4–6 tbsp sour cream

FROM THE STORECUPBOARD

salt and ground black pepper

Moroccan Carrot Salad

In this intriguing salad from North Africa, the carrots are lightly cooked before being tossed in a cumin and coriander vinaigrette. Cumin is widely used in Indian and Mexican cooking, as well as North African cuisines. It has a strong and spicy aroma and a warm pungent flavour that goes particularly well with root vegetables. This salad is a perfect accompaniment for both everyday or special meals.

SERVES FOUR TO SIX

3–4 carrots, thinly sliced

1.5ml/¹/₄ tsp ground cumin, or to taste

60ml/4 tbsp garlic-flavoured oil and vinegar dressing

30ml/2 tbsp chopped fresh coriander (cilantro) leaves or a mixture of coriander and parsley

FROM THE STORECUPBOARD

salt and ground black pepper

1 Cook the thinly sliced carrots by either steaming or boiling in lightly salted water until they are just tender but not soft. Drain the carrots, leave for a few minutes to dry and cool, then put into a mixing bowl.

2 Add the cumin, garlic dressing and herbs. Season to taste and chill well before serving. Check the seasoning just before serving and add more ground cumin, salt or black pepper, if required.

Warm Chorizo and Spinach Salad

Spanish chorizo sausage contributes an intense spiciness to any ingredient with which it is cooked. In this hearty warm salad, spinach has sufficient flavour to compete with the chorizo. Watercress or rocket (arugula) could be used instead of the spinach, if you prefer. For an added dimension use a flavoured olive oil – rosemary, garlic or chilli oil would work perfectly. Serve the salad with warm crusty bread to soak up all the delicious cooking juices.

SERVES FOUR

1 Discard any tough stalks from the spinach. Pour the oil into a large frying pan and add the sausage. Cook gently for 3 minutes, until the sausage slices start to shrivel slightly and colour.

2 Add the spinach leaves and remove the pan from the heat. Toss the spinach in the warm oil until it just starts to wilt. Add the sherry vinegar and a little seasoning. Toss the ingredients briefly, then serve immediately, while still warm.

225g/8oz baby spinach leaves

150g/5oz chorizo sausage, very thinly sliced

30ml/2 tbsp sherry vinegar

FROM THE STORECUPBOARD

90ml/6 tbsp olive oil

salt and ground black pepper

Potato and Olive Salad

This delicious salad is simple and zesty – the perfect choice for lunch, as an accompaniment, or as an appetizer. Similar in appearance to flat leaf parsley, fresh coriander has a distinctive pungent, almost spicy flavour. It is widely used in India, the Middle and Far East and in eastern Mediterranean countries. This potato salad is particularly good served as part of a brunch.

SERVES FOUR

8 large new potatoes

45–60ml/3–4 tbsp garlic-flavoured oil and vinegar dressing

60–90ml/4–6 tbsp chopped fresh herbs, such as coriander (cilantro) and chives

10–15 dry-fleshed black Mediterranean olives

FROM THE STORECUPBOARD

salt and ground black pepper

1 Cut the new potatoes into chunks. Put them in a pan, pour in water to cover and add a pinch of salt. Bring to the boil, then reduce the heat and cook gently for about 10 minutes, or until the potatoes are just tender. Drain well and leave in a colander to dry thoroughly and cool slightly.

2 When they are cool enough to handle, chop the potatoes and put them in a serving bowl.

3 Drizzle the garlic dressing over the potatoes. Toss well and sprinkle with the coriander and chives, and black olives. Chill in the refrigerator for at least 1 hour before serving.

EXTRAS *Add a pinch of ground cumin or a sprinkling of roasted whole cumin seeds to spice up the salad.*

Asparagus, Bacon and Leaf Salad

This excellent salad turns a plain roast chicken or simple grilled fish into an interesting meal, especially when served with buttered new potatoes. It also makes an appetizing first course or light lunch. A wide range of different salad leaves are readily available – frisée has feathery, curly, slightly bitter tasting leaves and is a member of the chicory family. Frisée leaves range in colour from yellow-white to yellow-green.

SERVES FOUR

1 Trim off any tough stalk ends from the asparagus and cut the spears into three, setting the tender tips aside. Heat a 1cm/½in depth of water in a frying pan until simmering. Reserve the asparagus tips and cook the remainder of the spears in the water for about 3 minutes, until almost tender. Add the tips and cook for 1 minute more. Drain and refresh under cold, running water.

2 Dry-fry the bacon until crisp and then set it aside to cool. Use kitchen scissors to snip it into bitesize pieces. Place the frisée or mixed leaf salad in a bowl and add the bacon.

3 Add the asparagus and a little black pepper to the salad. Pour the dressing over and toss the salad lightly, then serve.

500g/1¼lb medium asparagus spears

130g/4½oz thin-cut smoked back (lean) bacon

250g/9oz frisée lettuce leaves or mixed leaf salad

100ml/3½fl oz/scant ½ cup French dressing

FROM THE STORECUPBOARD

salt and ground black pepper

Anchovy and Roasted Pepper Salad

Sweet peppers, salty anchovies and plenty of garlic make an intensely flavoured salad that is delicious with meat, poultry or cheese. It also makes a tasty snack with olive bread. If you find that canned anchovies are too salty for your liking, you can reduce their saltiness by soaking them in milk for 20 minutes. Drain off the oil first and after soaking drain and rinse them in cold water.

SERVES FOUR

2 red, 2 orange and 2 yellow (bell) peppers, halved and seeded

50g/2oz can anchovies in olive oil

2 garlic cloves

45ml/3 tbsp balsamic vinegar

FROM THE STORECUPBOARD

salt and ground black pepper

1 Preheat the oven to 200°C/400°F/Gas 6. Place the peppers, cut side down, in a roasting pan. Roast for 30-40 minutes, until the skins are charred. Transfer the peppers to a bowl, cover with clear film (plastic wrap) and leave for 15 minutes.

2 Peel the peppers, then cut them into chunky strips. Drain the anchovies and halve the fillets lengthways.

3 Slice the garlic as thinly as possible and place it in a large bowl. Stir in the olive oil, vinegar and a little pepper. Add the peppers and anchovies and use a spoon and fork to fold the ingredients together. Cover and chill until ready to serve.

Al Fresco

EATING OUTSIDE, WHETHER IT'S A PICNIC, A FAMILY
LUNCH IN THE GARDEN OR A BARBECUE, IS ONE OF THE
GREAT PLEASURES OF SUMMER. THERE'S SOMETHING
QUINTESSENTIALLY RELAXING ABOUT EATING OUT IN
THE OPEN AND THIS CHAPTER IS PACKED WITH SIMPLE,
NO-FUSS RECIPES THAT ARE PERFECT FOR HOT, LAZY
DAYS AND BALMY EVENINGS. TAKE A SELECTION OF
SALADS, MAIN DISHES AND BREADS AND LET
EVERYONE HELP THEMSELVES.

Merguez Sausages with Iced Oysters

This is a truly wonderful taste sensation – revel in the French Christmas tradition of munching on a little hot sausage, then quelling the burning sensation with an ice-cold oyster. Merguez sausages come from North Africa and owe their flavour and colour to harissa, a hot chilli paste with subtle hints of coriander, caraway and garlic.

SERVES SIX

675g/1¹/₂lb merguez sausages

crushed ice for serving

24 oysters

2 lemons, cut into wedges, for squeezing

1 Prepare the barbecue. Once the flames have died down, position a lightly oiled grill rack over the coals to heat. When the coals are medium-hot, place the sausages on the rack. Grill them for 8 minutes, or until cooked through and golden, turning often.

2 Meanwhile, spread out the crushed ice on a platter and keep it chilled while you ready the oysters. Make sure all the oysters are closed, and discard any that aren't. Place them on the grill rack, a few at a time, with the deep-side down, so that as they open the juices will be retained in the lower shell. They will ease open after 3–5 minutes and must be removed from the heat immediately, so they don't start to cook.

3 Lay the oysters on the ice. When they have all eased open, get to work with a sharp knife, opening them fully if need be. Remove the oysters and place them with the juices on the deep half shells. Discard any oysters that fail to open. Serve immediately, with the hot, cooked sausages and with the lemon wedges.

Grilled Corn on the Cob

Keeping the husks on the corn protects the corn kernels and encloses the butter, so the flavours are contained. Fresh corn with husks intact are perfect, but banana leaves or a double layer of foil are also suitable.

SERVES SIX

3 dried chipotle chillies

7.5ml/1¹/₂ tsp lemon juice

45ml/3 tbsp chopped fresh flat leaf parsley

6 corn on the cob, with husks intact

FROM THE STORECUPBOARD

250g/9oz/generous 1 cup butter, softened

1 Heat a frying pan. Add the dried chillies and roast them by stirring them for 1 minute without letting them scorch. Put them in a bowl with almost boiling water to cover. Use a saucer to keep them submerged, and leave them to rehydrate for up to 1 hour. Drain, remove the seeds and chop the chillies finely. Place the butter in a bowl and add the chillies, lemon juice and parsley. Season to taste and mix well.

2 Peel back the husks from each cob without tearing them. Remove the silk. Smear about 30ml/2 tbsp of the chilli butter over each cob. Pull the husks back over the cobs, ensuring that the butter is well hidden. Put the rest of the butter in a pot, smooth the top and chill to use later. Place the cobs in a bowl of cold water and leave in a cool place for 1–3 hours; longer if that suits your work plan better.

3 Prepare the barbecue. Remove the corn cobs from the water and wrap in pairs in foil. Once the flames have died down, position a lightly oiled grill rack over the coals to heat. When the coals are medium-hot, or have a moderate coating of ash, grill the corn for 15–20 minutes. Remove the foil and cook them for about 5 minutes more, turning them often to char the husks a little. Serve hot, with the rest of the butter.

Butter Bean, Tomato and Red Onion Salad

Serve this salad with toasted pitta bread for a fresh summer lunch, or as an accompaniment to meat cooked on a barbecue.

SERVES FOUR

**2 x 400g/14oz cans
butter (lima) beans, rinsed
and drained**

**4 plum tomatoes,
roughly chopped**

1 red onion, finely sliced

FROM THE STORECUPBOARD

**45ml/3 tbsp herb-infused
olive oil**

salt and ground black pepper

1 Mix together the beans, tomatoes and onion in a large bowl. Season with salt and pepper, and stir in the oil.

2 Cover the bowl with clear film (plastic wrap) and chill for 20 minutes before serving.

VARIATIONS
• To make a tasty tuna salad, drain a 200g/7oz can tuna, flake the flesh and stir into the bean salad.
• For extra flavour and colour, stir in a handful of pitted black olives and a handful of chopped fresh parsley.
• To make a wholesome version of the Italian salad Panzanella, tear half a loaf of ciabatta into bite-size pieces and stir into the salad. Leave to stand for 20 minutes before serving.

Potato, Caraway Seed and Parsley Salad

Leaving the potatoes to cool in garlic-infused oil with the caraway seeds helps them to absorb plenty of flavour.

SERVES FOUR TO SIX

**675g/1¹/₂lb new potatoes,
scrubbed**

**15ml/1 tbsp caraway seeds,
lightly crushed**

**45ml/3 tbsp chopped
fresh parsley**

FROM THE STORECUPBOARD

**45ml/3 tbsp garlic-infused
olive oil**

salt and ground black pepper

1 Cook the potatoes in salted, boiling water for about 10 minutes, or until just tender. Drain thoroughly and transfer to a large bowl.

2 Stir the oil, caraway seeds and some salt and pepper into the hot potatoes, then set aside to cool. When the potatoes are almost cold, stir in the parsley and serve.

VARIATION
This recipe is also delicious made with sweet potatoes instead of new potatoes. Peel and roughly chop the sweet potatoes, then follow the recipe as before.

Warm Halloumi and Fennel Salad

The firm texture of halloumi cheese makes it perfect for the barbecue, as it keeps its shape very well. It is widely available in most large supermarkets and Greek delicatessens.

SERVES FOUR

200g/7oz halloumi cheese, thickly sliced

2 fennel bulbs, trimmed and thinly sliced

30ml/2 tbsp roughly chopped fresh oregano

FROM THE STORECUPBOARD

45ml/3 tbsp lemon-infused olive oil

salt and ground black pepper

1 Put the halloumi, fennel and oregano in a bowl and drizzle over the lemon-infused oil. Season with salt and black pepper to taste. (Halloumi is a fairly salty cheese, so be very careful when adding extra salt.)

2 Cover the bowl with clear film (plastic wrap) and chill for about 2 hours to allow the flavours to develop.

3 Place the halloumi and fennel on a griddle pan or over the barbecue, reserving the marinade, and cook for about 3 minutes on each side, until charred.

4 Divide the halloumi and fennel among four serving plates and drizzle over the reserved marinade. Serve immediately.

Pear and Blue Cheese Salad

A juicy variety of pear, such as a Williams, is just perfect in this dish. You can use any other blue cheese, such as Stilton or Gorgonzola, in place of the Roquefort if you prefer.

SERVES FOUR

1 Cut the pears into quarters and remove the cores. Thinly slice each pear quarter and arrange on a serving platter.

2 Slice the Roquefort as thinly as possible and place over the pears. Mix the oil and vinegar together and drizzle over the pears. Season with salt and pepper and serve.

COOK'S TIP Rich, dark balsamic vinegar has an intense yet mellow flavour. It is produced in Modena in the north of Italy and is widely available in most supermarkets.

4 ripe pears

115g/4oz Roquefort cheese

15ml/1 tbsp balsamic vinegar

FROM THE STORECUPBOARD

30ml/2 tbsp olive oil

salt and ground black pepper

Fresh Crab Sandwiches

There's not much to beat the taste of freshly cooked crab, but if you can't face dealing with live crabs, buy fresh cooked ones. Serve the crab meat with a bowl of rocket (arugula) and let everyone get in a mess cracking open the claws and making their own sandwiches.

SERVES SIX

3 live crabs, about 900g/ 2lb each

1 crusty wholegrain loaf, sliced

2 lemons, cut into quarters

FROM THE STORECUPBOARD

butter, for spreading

salt and ground black pepper

1 Lower the live crabs into a pan of cold water, then slowly bring to the boil. (This method is considered more humane than plunging the crabs into boiling water.) Cook the crabs for 5–6 minutes per 450g/1lb, then remove from the pan and set aside to cool.

2 Break off the claws and legs, then use your thumbs to ease the body out of the shell. Remove and discard the grey gills from the body and put the white meat in a bowl. Scrape the brown meat from the shell and add to the white meat.

3 Serve the crab meat, and the claws and legs with crab crackers, with slices of brown bread, butter and lemon wedges and let everyone make their own sandwiches.

Warm Pasta with Crushed Tomatoes and Basil

It doesn't matter which type of pasta you use for this recipe – any kind you have in the storecupboard will work well.

SERVES FOUR

6 small ripe tomatoes, halved

a small handful of fresh basil leaves

450g/1lb dried pasta shapes

FROM THE STORECUPBOARD

45ml/3 tbsp extra virgin olive oil

salt and ground black pepper

1 Put the halved tomatoes in a bowl and, using your hands, gently squash them until the juices start to run freely. Stir in the olive oil and tear in the basil leaves.

2 Season the tomatoes with salt and pepper and mix well to combine. Cover the bowl with clear film (plastic wrap) and chill for 2–3 hours, to allow the flavours to develop.

3 Remove the tomatoes from the refrigerator and allow them to return to room temperature.

4 Meanwhile, cook the pasta according to the instructions on the packet. Drain well, toss with the crushed tomato and basil mixture and serve immediately.

Roast Shallot Tart with Thyme

Tarts are perfect for a summer lunch or picnic, and sheets of ready-rolled puff pastry make tart-making incredibly easy.

SERVES FOUR

450g/1lb shallots, peeled and halved

30ml/2 tbsp fresh thyme leaves

375g/13oz packet ready-rolled puff pastry, thawed if frozen

FROM THE STORECUPBOARD

25g/1oz/2 tbsp butter

salt and ground black pepper

1 Preheat the oven to 190°C/375°F/Gas 5. Heat the butter in a large frying pan until foaming, then add the shallots. Season with salt and pepper and cook over a gentle heat for 10–15 minutes, stirring occasionally, until golden. Stir in the thyme, then remove from the heat and set aside.

2 Unroll the puff pastry on to a large baking sheet. Using a small, sharp knife, score a border all the way around, about 2.5cm/1in from the edge, without cutting all the way through the pastry.

3 Spread the shallots over the pastry, inside the border. Bake for 20–25 minutes, or until the pastry is golden and risen around the edges. Cut into squares and serve hot or warm.

Roasted Aubergines with Feta and Coriander

Aubergines take on a lovely smoky flavour when grilled on a barbecue. Choose a good quality Greek feta cheese for the best flavour.

SERVES SIX

3 medium aubergines (eggplants)

400g/14oz feta cheese

a small bunch of coriander (cilantro), roughly chopped

FROM THE STORECUPBOARD

60ml/4 tbsp extra virgin olive oil

salt and ground black pepper

1 Prepare a barbecue. Cook the aubergines for 20 minutes, turning occasionally, until charred and soft. Remove from the barbecue and cut in half lengthways.

2 Carefully scoop the aubergine flesh into a bowl, reserving the skins. Mash the flesh roughly with a fork.

3 Crumble the feta cheese, then stir into the mashed aubergine with the chopped coriander and olive oil. Season with salt and ground black pepper to taste.

4 Spoon the aubergine and feta mixture back into the skins and return to the barbecue for 5 minutes to warm through. Serve immediately.

Barbecued Sardines with Orange and Parsley

Sardines are ideal for the barbecue – the meaty flesh holds together, the skin crisps nicely and there are no lingering indoor cooking smells. Serve them with a selection of salads.

SERVES SIX

6 whole sardines, gutted

1 orange, sliced

a small bunch of fresh flat leaf parsley, chopped

FROM THE STORECUPBOARD

60ml/4 tbsp extra virgin olive oil

salt and ground black pepper

1 Arrange the sardines and orange slices in a single layer in a shallow, non-metallic dish. Sprinkle over the chopped parsley and season with salt and pepper.

2 Drizzle the olive oil over the sardines and orange slices and gently stir to coat well. Cover the dish with clear film (plastic wrap) and chill for 2 hours.

3 Meanwhile, prepare the barbecue. Remove the sardines and orange slices from the marinade and cook the fish over the barbecue for 7–8 minutes on each side, until cooked through. Serve immediately.

Soy Sauce and Star Anise Chicken

The pungent flavour of star anise penetrates the chicken breasts and adds a wonderful aniseedy kick to the smoky flavour of the barbecue. Serve with a refreshing salad.

SERVES FOUR

1 Put the chicken breast fillets in a shallow, non-metallic dish and add the star anise.

2 In a small bowl, whisk together the oil and soy sauce and season with black pepper to make a marinade.

3 Pour the marinade over the chicken and stir to coat each breast fillet all over. Cover the dish with clear film (plastic wrap) and chill for up to 8 hours.

4 Prepare a barbecue. Remove the chicken breasts from the marinade and cook for 8–10 minutes on each side, spooning over the marinade from time to time, until the chicken is cooked through. Serve immediately.

4 skinless chicken breast fillets

2 whole star anise

30ml/2 tbsp soy sauce

FROM THE STORECUPBOARD

45ml/3 tbsp olive oil

ground black pepper

Harissa-spiced Koftas

Serve these spicy koftas in pitta breads with sliced tomatoes, cucumber and mint leaves, with a drizzle of natural yogurt.

SERVES FOUR

450g/1lb/2 cups minced (ground) lamb

1 small onion, finely chopped

10ml/2 tsp harissa paste

FROM THE STORECUPBOARD

salt and ground black pepper

1 Place eight wooden skewers in a bowl of cold water and leave to soak for at least 10 minutes.

2 Put the lamb in a large bowl and add the onion and harissa. Mix well to combine, and season with plenty of salt and ground black pepper.

3 Using wet hands, divide the mixture into eight equal pieces and press on to the skewers in a sausage shape to make the koftas.

4 Prepare a barbecue. Cook the skewered koftas for about 10 minutes, turning occasionally, until cooked through. Serve immediately.

Cumin- and Coriander-rubbed Lamb

Rubs are quick and easy to prepare and can transform everyday cuts of meat such as chops into exciting and more unusual meals. Serve with a chunky tomato salad.

SERVES FOUR

30ml/2 tbsp ground cumin

30ml/2 tbsp ground coriander

8 lamb chops

FROM THE STORECUPBOARD

30ml/2 tbsp olive oil

salt and ground black pepper

1 Mix together the cumin, coriander and oil, and season with salt and pepper. Rub the mixture all over the lamb chops, then cover and chill for 1 hour.

2 Prepare a barbecue. Cook the chops for 5 minutes on each side, until lightly charred but still pink in the centre.

VARIATION *To make ginger- and garlic-rubbed pork, use pork chops instead of lamb chops and substitute the cumin and coriander with ground ginger and garlic granules. Increase the cooking time to 7–8 minutes each side.*

Hot Desserts

A HOT DESSERT MAKES THE PERFECT END TO A MEAL

AND CAN TAKE VERY LITTLE TIME TO PREPARE. A FEW

WELL-CHOSEN INGREDIENTS CAN BE TURNED INTO A

SUMPTUOUS, MOUTHWATERING TREAT WITH THE MINIMUM

OF EFFORT. MANY OF THE RECIPES IN THIS CHAPTER CAN

BE PREPARED IN ADVANCE AND SIMPLY POPPED IN THE

OVEN TO COOK WHILE YOU SERVE THE MAIN COURSE.

Plum and Almond Tart

To transform this tart into an extravagant dessert, dust with a little icing (confectioners') sugar and serve with a dollop of crème fraîche.

SERVES FOUR

1 Preheat the oven to 190°C/375°F/Gas 5. Unroll the pastry on to a large baking sheet. Using a small, sharp knife, score a border 5cm/2in from the edge of the pastry, without cutting all the way through.

2 Roll out the marzipan into a rectangle, to fit just within the pastry border, then lay it on top of the pastry, pressing down lightly with the tips of your fingers.

3 Scatter the sliced plums on top of the marzipan in an even layer and bake for 20–25 minutes, or until the pastry is risen and golden brown.

4 Carefully transfer the tart to a wire rack to cool slightly, then cut into squares or wedges and serve.

375g/13oz ready-rolled puff pastry, thawed if frozen

115g/4oz marzipan

6–8 plums, stoned and sliced

Baked Apples with Marsala

The Marsala cooks down with the juice from the apples and the butter to make a rich, sticky sauce. Serve these delicious apples with a spoonful of extra-thick cream.

SERVES SIX

1 Preheat the oven to 180°C/350°F/Gas 4. Using an apple corer, remove the cores from the apples and discard.

2 Place the apples in a small, shallow baking pan and stuff the figs into the holes in the centre of each apple.

3 Top each apple with a quarter of the butter and pour over the Marsala. Cover the pan tightly with foil and bake for about 30 minutes.

4 Remove the foil from the apples and bake for a further 10 minutes, or until the apples are tender and the juices have reduced slightly. Serve immediately with any remaining pan juices drizzled over the top.

4 medium cooking apples

50g/2oz/$^1/_3$ cup ready-to-eat dried figs

150ml/$^1/_4$ pint/$^2/_3$ cup Marsala

FROM THE STORECUPBOARD

50g/2oz/$^1/_4$ cup butter, softened

Grilled Peaches with Meringues

Ripe peaches take on a fabulous scented fruitiness when grilled with brown sugar, and mini meringues are the perfect accompaniment. Serve with crème fraîche flavoured with a little grated orange rind. When buying peaches or nectarines, choose fruit with an attractive rosy bloom, avoiding any that have a green-tinged skin or feel hard. Nectarines have a smoother skin than peaches and are actually a type of peach native to China.

SERVES SIX

2 egg whites

115g/4oz/¹/₂ cup soft light brown sugar, reserving 5ml/1 tsp for the peaches

pinch of ground cinnamon

6 ripe peaches, or nectarines

1 Preheat the oven to 140°C/275°F/Gas 1. Line two large baking sheets with baking parchment.

2 Whisk the egg whites until they form stiff peaks. Gradually whisk in the sugar and ground cinnamon until the mixture is stiff and glossy. Pipe 18 very small meringues on to the trays and bake for 40 minutes. Leave in the oven to cool.

3 Meanwhile, halve and stone (pit) the peaches or nectarines, sprinkling each half with a little sugar as it is cut. Grill (broil) for 4–5 minutes, until just beginning to caramelize.

4 Arrange the grilled peaches on serving plates with the meringues and serve immediately.

Summer Berries in Sabayon Glaze

This luxurious combination of summer berries under a light and fluffy liqueur sauce is lightly grilled to form a crisp, caramelized topping. Fresh or frozen berries can be used in this dessert. If you use frozen berries, defrost them in a sieve over a bowl to allow the juices to drip. Stir a little juice into the fruit before dividing among the dishes.

SERVES FOUR

1 Arrange the mixed summer berries or soft fruit in four individual flameproof dishes. Preheat the grill (broiler).

2 Whisk the yolks in a large bowl with the sugar and liqueur or wine. Place over a pan of hot water and whisk constantly until the mixture is thick, fluffy and pale.

3 Pour equal quantities of the yolk mixture into each dish. Place under the grill for 1–2 minutes, until just turning brown. Add an extra splash of liqueur, if you like, and serve immediately.

450g/1lb/4 cups mixed summer berries, or soft fruit

4 egg yolks

50g/2oz/¼ cup vanilla sugar or caster (superfine) sugar

120ml/4fl oz/½ cup liqueur, such as Cointreau or Kirsch, or a white dessert wine

Baked Ricotta Cakes with Red Sauce

These honey-flavoured desserts take only minutes to make from a few ingredients. The fragrant fruity sauce provides a contrast of both colour and flavour. The red berry sauce can be made a day in advance and chilled until ready to use. Frozen fruit doesn't need extra water, as it usually yields its juice easily on thawing.

SERVES FOUR

250g/9oz/generous 1 cup ricotta cheese

2 egg whites, beaten

60ml/4 tbsp scented honey, plus extra to taste

450g/1lb/4 cups mixed fresh or frozen fruit, such as strawberries, raspberries, blackberries and cherries

1 Preheat the oven to 180°C/350°F/Gas 4. Place the ricotta cheese in a bowl and break it up with a wooden spoon. Add the beaten egg whites and honey, and mix thoroughly until smooth and well combined.

2 Lightly grease four ramekins. Spoon the ricotta mixture into the prepared ramekins and level the tops. Bake for 20 minutes, or until the ricotta cakes are risen and golden.

3 Meanwhile, make the fruit sauce. Reserve about one-quarter of the fruit for decoration. Place the rest of the fruit in a pan, with a little water if the fruit is fresh, and heat gently until softened. Leave to cool slightly and remove any stones (pits) if using cherries.

4 Press the fruit through a sieve, then taste and sweeten with honey if it is too tart. Serve the sauce, warm or cold, with the ricotta cakes. Decorate with the reserved berries.

Apricot and Ginger Gratin

Made with tangy fresh apricots, this quick and easy dessert has a comforting, baked cheesecake-like flavour. For an even easier version of this delicious gratin, use 400g/14oz canned apricots in juice. Use juice from the can to beat into the cream cheese.

SERVES FOUR

1 Put the apricots in a pan with the sugar. Pour in 75ml/5 tbsp water and heat until barely simmering. Cover and cook very gently for 8–10 minutes, until they are tender but still holding their shape.

2 Preheat the oven to 200°C/400°F/Gas 6. Drain the apricots, reserving the syrup, and place in a large dish or divide among four individual ovenproof dishes. Set aside 90ml/6 tbsp of the syrup and spoon the remainder over the fruit.

3 Beat the cream cheese until softened, then gradually beat in the reserved syrup until smooth. Spoon the cheese mixture over the apricots. Sprinkle the biscuit crumbs over the cream cheese and juice mixture. Bake for 10 minutes, until the crumb topping is beginning to darken and the filling has warmed through. Serve immediately.

500g/1¹⁄₄ lb apricots, halved and stoned (pitted)

75g/3oz/scant ¹⁄₂ cup caster (superfine) sugar

200g/7oz/scant 1 cup cream cheese

75g/3oz gingernut biscuits (gingersnaps), crushed to crumbs

Deep-fried Cherries

Fresh fruit coated with a simple batter and then deep-fried is delicious and makes an unusual dessert. These succulent cherries are perfect sprinkled with sugar and cinnamon and served with a classic vanilla ice cream.

SERVES FOUR TO SIX

450g/1lb ripe red cherries, on their stalks

225g/8oz batter mix

1 egg

FROM THE STORECUPBOARD

vegetable oil, for deep-frying

1 Gently wash the cherries and pat dry with kitchen paper. Tie the stalks together with fine string to form clusters of four or five cherries.

2 Make up the batter mix according to the instructions on the packet, beating in the egg. Pour the vegetable oil into a deep-fat fryer or large, heavy pan and heat to 190°C/375°F.

3 Working in batches, half-dip each cherry cluster into the batter and then carefully drop the cluster into the hot oil. Fry for 3–4 minutes, or until golden. Remove the deep-fried cherries with a wire-mesh skimmer or slotted spoon and drain on a wire rack placed over crumpled kitchen paper, and serve immediately.

Hot Blackberry and Apple Soufflé

The deliciously tart flavours of blackberry and apple complement each other perfectly to make a light, mouthwatering and surprisingly low-fat, hot dessert. Running a table knife around the inside edge of the soufflé dishes before baking helps the soufflés to rise evenly without sticking to the rim of the dish. Make this dish in early autumn, when there are plentiful supplies of blackberries.

MAKES SIX

1 Preheat the oven to 200°C/400°F/Gas 6. Put a baking sheet in the oven to heat. Cook the blackberries and apple in a pan for 10 minutes, or until the juice runs from the blackberries and the apple has pulped down well. Press through a sieve into a bowl. Stir in 50g/2oz/¼ cup caster sugar. Set aside to cool.

2 Put a spoonful of the fruit purée into each of six 150ml/¼ pint/⅔ cup greased and sugared individual soufflé dishes and smooth the surface. Set the dishes aside.

3 Whisk the egg whites in a large bowl until they form stiff peaks. Gradually whisk in the remaining caster sugar. Fold in the remaining fruit purée and spoon the flavoured meringue into the prepared dishes. Level the tops with a palette knife (metal spatula) and run a table knife around the edge of each dish.

4 Place the dishes on the hot baking sheet and bake for 10–15 minutes, until the soufflés have risen well and are lightly browned. Dust the tops with a little sugar and serve immediately.

350g/12oz/3 cups blackberries

1 large cooking apple, peeled and finely diced

3 egg whites

150g/5oz/³/₄ cup caster (superfine) sugar, plus extra caster or icing (confectioners') sugar for dusting

Peach Pie

Fruit pies do not have to be restricted to the chunky, deep-dish variety. Here, juicy, ripe peaches are encased in crisp pastry to make a glorious puffed dome – simple but delicious. For a really crispy crust, glaze the pie with beaten egg yolk thinned with a little water before sprinkling with sugar. Serve the pie with good quality vanilla ice cream or clotted cream.

SERVES EIGHT

1 Blanch the peaches for 30 seconds. Drain, refresh in cold water, then peel. Halve, stone (pit) and slice the peaches.

2 Melt the butter in a large frying pan. Add the peach slices, then sprinkle with 15ml/1 tbsp water and the sugar. Cook for about 4 minutes, shaking the pan frequently, or until the sugar has dissolved and the peaches are tender. Set the pan aside to cool.

3 Cut the pastry into two pieces, one slightly larger than the other. Roll out on a lightly floured surface and, using plates as a guide, cut a 30cm/12in round and a 28cm/11in round. Place the pastry rounds on baking sheets lined with baking parchment, cover with clear film (plastic wrap) and chill for 30 minutes.

4 Preheat the oven to 200°C/400°F/Gas 6. Remove the clear film from the pastry rounds. Spoon the peaches into the middle of the larger round and spread them out to within 5cm/2in of the edge. Place the smaller pastry round on top. Brush the edge of the larger pastry round with water, then fold this over the top round and press to seal. Twist the edges together.

5 Lightly brush the pastry with water and sprinkle evenly with a little sugar. Make five or six small crescent-shape slashes on the top of the pastry. Bake the pie for about 45 minutes and serve warm.

6 large, firm ripe peaches

75g/3oz/6 tbsp caster (superfine) sugar, plus extra for glazing

450g/1lb puff pastry

FROM THE STORECUPBOARD

40g/1¹/₂oz/ 3 tbsp butter

EXTRAS

Brandy, peach liqueur or peach schnapps would be superb with the peaches in this pie: add 45ml/3 tbsp instead of the water in step 2.

Treacle Tart

The best chilled commercial shortcrust pastry makes light work of this old-fashioned favourite, with its sticky filling and twisted lattice topping. Smooth creamy custard is the classic accompaniment, but it is also delicious served with cream or ice cream. For a more textured filling, use wholemeal (whole-wheat) breadcrumbs or crushed cornflakes instead of the white breadcrumbs.

SERVES FOUR TO SIX

1 On a lightly floured surface, roll out three-quarters of the pastry to a thickness of 3mm/⅛in. Transfer to a 20cm/8in fluted flan tin (quiche pan) and trim off the overhang. Chill the pastry case (pie shell) for 20 minutes. Reserve the pastry trimmings.

2 Put a baking sheet in the oven and preheat to 200°C/400°F/Gas 6. To make the filling, warm the syrup in a pan until it melts. Grate the lemon rind and squeeze the juice.

3 Remove the syrup from the heat and stir in the breadcrumbs and lemon rind. Leave to stand for 10 minutes, then add more crumbs if the mixture is too thin and moist. Stir in 30ml/2 tbsp of the lemon juice, then spread the mixture evenly in the pastry case.

4 Roll out the reserved pastry and cut into 10–12 thin strips. Twist the strips into spirals, then lay half of them on the filling. Arrange the remaining strips at right angles to form a lattice. Press the ends on to the rim.

5 Place the tart on the hot baking sheet and bake for 10 minutes. Lower the oven temperature to 190°C/375°F/Gas 5. Bake for 15 minutes more, until golden. Serve warm.

350g/12oz (unsweetened) shortcrust pastry

260g/9¹/₂oz/generous ³/₄ cup golden (light corn) syrup

1 lemon

75g/3oz/1¹/₂ cups fresh white breadcrumbs

Caramelized Upside-down Pear Pie

In this gloriously sticky dessert, which is almost like the French classic *tarte tatin*, the pastry is baked on top of the fruit, which gives it a crisp and flaky texture. When inverted, the pie looks wonderful. Look for good-quality chilled pastry that you can freeze for future use. Serve with whipped cream, ice cream or just plain for a gloriously sticky dessert.

SERVES EIGHT

1 Peel, quarter and core the pears. Toss with some of the sugar in a bowl.

2 Melt the butter in a 27cm/10½in heavy, ovenproof omelette pan. Add the remaining sugar. When it changes colour, arrange the pears in the pan.

3 Continue cooking, uncovered, for 20 minutes, or until the fruit has completely caramelized.

4 Leave the fruit to cool in the pan. Preheat the oven to 200°C/400°F/Gas 6. Meanwhile, on a lightly floured surface, roll out the pastry to a round that is slightly larger than the diameter of the pan. Lay the pastry on top of the pears and then carefully tuck it in around the edge.

5 Bake for 15 minutes, then lower the oven temperature to 180°C/350°F/Gas 4. Bake for a further 15 minutes, or until the pastry is golden.

6 Let the pie cool in the pan for a few minutes. To unmould, run a knife around the pan's edge, then, using oven gloves, invert a plate over the pan and quickly turn the two over together.

7 If any pears stick to the pan, remove them gently with a palette knife (metal spatula) and replace them on the pie. The pie is best served warm.

5–6 firm, ripe pears

175g/6oz/scant 1 cup caster (superfine) sugar

225g/8oz (unsweetened) shortcrust pastry

FROM THE STORECUPBOARD

115g/4oz/¹/₂ cup butter

VARIATIONS

To make caramelized upside-down apple pie, replace the pears with eight or nine firm, full-flavoured eating apples – Cox's Orange Pippins would be a good choice. You will need more apples than pears, as they shrink during cooking.

Nectarines or peaches also work well, as does rhubarb. Rhubarb is tart, so you may need to add more sugar.

Blueberry and Almond Tart

This is a cheat's version of a sweet almond tart and the result is superb. Whisked egg whites and grated marzipan cook to form a light sponge under a tangy topping of contrasting blueberries. When whisking the egg whites for the filling, ensure all traces of yolk are removed – otherwise you won't be able to whisk them to their maximum volume.

SERVES SIX

**250g/9oz
(unsweetened)
shortcrust pastry**

**175g/6oz/generous
1 cup white marzipan**

**4 large (US extra large)
egg whites**

**130g/4¹/₂oz/
generous 1 cup
blueberries**

1 Preheat the oven to 200°C/400°F/Gas 6. Roll out the pastry and use to line a 23cm/9in round, loose-based flan tin (quiche pan). Line with greaseproof (waxed) paper and fill with baking beans, then bake for 15 minutes. Remove the beans and greaseproof paper and bake for a further 5 minutes. Reduce the oven temperature to 180°C/350°F/Gas 4.

2 Grate the marzipan. Whisk the egg whites until stiff. Sprinkle half the marzipan over them and fold in. Then fold in the rest.

3 Turn the mixture into the pastry case (pie shell) and spread it evenly. Sprinkle the blueberries over the top and bake for 20–25 minutes, until golden and just set. Leave to cool for 10 minutes before serving.

Baked Bananas with Ice Cream and Toffee Sauce

Bananas make one of the easiest of all desserts, just as welcome as a comforting winter treat as they are to follow a barbecue. For an extra sweet finishing touch, grate some plain (semisweet) chocolate on the bananas, over the sauce, just before serving. If baking on a barbecue, turn the bananas occasionally to ensure even cooking.

SERVES FOUR

4 large bananas

75g/3oz/scant $^1/_2$ cup light muscovado (brown) sugar

75ml/5 tbsp double (heavy) cream

4 scoops good-quality vanilla ice cream

1 Preheat the oven to 180°C/350°F/Gas 4. Put the unpeeled bananas in an ovenproof dish and bake for 15–20 minutes, until the skins are very dark and the flesh feels soft when squeezed.

2 Meanwhile, heat the light muscovado sugar in a small, heavy pan with 75ml/5 tbsp water until dissolved. Bring to the boil and add the double cream. Cook for 5 minutes, until the sauce has thickened and is toffee coloured. Remove from the heat.

3 Transfer the baked bananas in their skins to serving plates and split them lengthways to reveal the flesh. Pour some of the sauce over the bananas and top with scoops of vanilla ice cream. Serve any remaining sauce separately.

Roast Peaches with Amaretto

This is an excellent dessert to serve in summer, when peaches are at their juiciest and most fragrant. The apricot and almond flavour of the amaretto liqueur subtly enhances the sweet, fruity taste of ripe peaches. Serve with a spoonful of crème fraîche or whipped cream.

SERVES FOUR

1 Preheat the oven 190°C/375°F/Gas 5. Cut the peaches in half and prise out the stones (pits) with the point of the knife.

2 Place the peaches cut side up in a roasting pan. In a small bowl, mix the amaretto liqueur with the honey, and drizzle over the halved peaches, covering them evenly.

3 Bake the peaches for 20–25 minutes, or until tender. Place two peach halves on each serving plate and drizzle with the pan juices. Serve immediately.

4 ripe peaches

45ml/3 tbsp Amaretto di Sarone liqueur

45ml/3 tbsp clear honey

COOK'S TIP *You can cook these peaches over a barbecue. Place them on sheets of foil, drizzle over liqueur, then scrunch the foil around them to seal. Cook for 15–20 minutes.*

Passion Fruit Soufflés

These simplified soufflés are so easy and work beautifully. The passion fruit adds a tropical note to a favourite classic. The soufflés look very pretty sprinkled with icing (confectioners') sugar.

SERVES FOUR

**200ml/7fl oz/scant 1 cup
ready-made fresh custard**

3 passion fruits, halved

2 egg whites

FROM THE STORECUPBOARD

**knob (pat) of softened butter,
for greasing**

1 Preheat the oven to 200°C/400°F/Gas 6. Grease four 200ml/7fl oz/scant 1 cup ramekin dishes with the butter.

2 Pour the custard into a large mixing bowl. Scrape out the seeds and juice from the halved passion fruit and stir into the custard until well combined.

3 Whisk the egg whites until stiff, and fold a quarter of them into the custard. Carefully fold in the remaining egg whites, then spoon the mixture into the ramekin dishes.

4 Place the dishes on a baking sheet and bake for 8–10 minutes, or until the soufflés are well risen. Serve immediately.

Zabaglione

Light as air and wonderfully heady, this warm, wine egg custard is a much-loved Italian dessert. Traditionally made with Sicilian Marsala, other fortified wines such as Madeira or sweet sherry can be used.

SERVES FOUR

1 Place the egg yolks and sugar in a large heatproof bowl and whisk with an electric beater until the mixture is pale and thick.

2 Gradually add the Marsala, Madeira or sweet sherry to the egg mixture, 15ml/1 tbsp at a time, whisking well after each addition.

3 Place the bowl over a pan of gently simmering water and whisk for 5–7 minutes, until thick: when the beaters are lifted, they should leave a thick trail on the surface of the mixture. Do not be tempted to give up when beating the mixture, as the zabaglione will be too runny and will be likely to separate if it is underbeaten.

4 Pour into four warmed, stemmed glasses and serve immediately, with amaretti for dipping.

4 egg yolks

50g/2oz/¹/₄ cup caster (superfine) sugar

60ml/4 tbsp Marsala, Madeira or sweet sherry

amaretti biscuits, to serve

EXTRAS
Marinate chopped strawberries in a little extra Marsala, Madeira or sweet sherry for an hour or so. Sweeten with sugar, if you like, and spoon into glasses before you add the zabaglione.

Grilled Pineapple and Rum Cream

The sweeter and juicier the pineapple, the more delicious the pan juices will be in this tropical dessert. To test whether the pineapple is ripe, gently pull the green spiky leaves at the top of the fruit. If they come away easily, the fruit is ripe and ready to use.

SERVES FOUR

1 Heat the butter in a frying pan and add the pineapple. Cook over a moderate to high heat until the pineapple is starting to turn golden. Add the rum and allow to bubble for 1–2 minutes. Remove the pan from the heat and set aside to cool completely.

2 Whip the cream until it is soft but not stiff. Fold the pineapple and rum mixture evenly through the cream, then divide it between four glasses and serve.

115g/4oz pineapple, roughly chopped

45ml/3 tbsp dark rum

300ml/¹/₂ pint/1¹/₄ cups double (heavy) cream

FROM THE STORECUPBOARD

25g/1oz/2 tbsp butter

Warm Chocolate Zabaglione

Once you've tasted this sensuous dessert, you'll never regard cocoa in quite the same way again. The zabaglione can be dusted with icing (confectioners') sugar instead of extra cocoa, if you like. Serve with mini amaretti or other small, crisp biscuits (cookies).

SERVES SIX

6 egg yolks

150g/5oz/³/₄ cup caster (superfine) sugar

45ml/3 tbsp (unsweetened) cocoa powder, plus extra for dusting

200ml/7fl oz/scant 1 cup Marsala

1 Prepare a pan of simmering water and a heatproof bowl to fit on top. Place the egg yolks and sugar in the bowl and whisk, off the heat, until the mixture is pale and all the sugar has dissolved.

2 Add the cocoa and Marsala, then place the bowl over the simmering water. Beat with a hand-held electric mixer until the mixture is smooth, thick and foamy.

3 Pour quickly into tall glasses, dust lightly with cocoa and serve immediately, with amaretti or other dessert biscuits, if you like.

Hot Chocolate Rum Soufflés

Light as air, melt-in-the-mouth soufflés are always impressive, yet they are often based on the simplest store-cupboard ingredients. Serve them as soon as they are cooked for a fantastic finale to a special dinner party. For an extra indulgent touch, serve the soufflés with whipped cream flavoured with dark rum and grated orange rind.

SERVES SIX

50g/2oz/½ cup (unsweetened) cocoa powder

65g/2½oz/5 tbsp caster (superfine) sugar, plus extra caster or icing (confectioners') sugar for dusting

30ml/2 tbsp dark rum

6 egg whites

COOK'S TIP *When serving the soufflés at the end of a dinner party, prepare them just before the meal is served. Put them in the oven when the main course is finished and serve steaming hot.*

1 Preheat the oven to 190°C/375°F/Gas 3. Place a baking sheet in the oven to heat up.

2 Mix 15ml/1 tbsp of the cocoa with 15ml/1 tbsp of the sugar in a bowl. Grease six 250ml/8fl oz/1 cup ramekins. Pour the cocoa and sugar mixture into each of the dishes in turn, rotating them so that they are evenly coated.

3 Mix the remaining cocoa powder with the dark rum.

4 Whisk the egg whites in a clean, grease-free bowl until they form stiff peaks. Whisk in the remaining sugar. Stir a generous spoonful of the whites into the cocoa mixture to lighten it, then fold in the remaining whites.

5 Divide the mixture among the dishes. Place on the hot baking sheet, and bake for 13–15 minutes, or until well risen. Dust with caster or icing sugar before serving.

Cold Desserts

BECAUSE THEY CAN BE MADE IN ADVANCE, COLD DESSERTS
ARE THE PERFECT CHOICE FOR ENTERTAINING. ALL THE
RECIPES IN THIS CHAPTER HAVE AN ELEGANT SIMPLICITY
THAT GUARANTEES SUCCESS WITH EVEN THE MOST
SOPHISTICATED DINNER GUESTS. HOWEVER, THESE
DESSERTS ARE SO EASY TO PREPARE THAT YOU WILL WANT
TO SERVE THEM FOR EVERYDAY MEALS TOO.

Tropical Scented Fruit Salad

With its special colour and exotic flavour, this fresh fruit salad is perfect after a rich, heavy meal. For fabulous flavour and colour, try using three small blood oranges and three ordinary oranges. Other fruit that can be added include pears, kiwi fruit and bananas. Serve the fruit salad with whipping cream flavoured with 15g/½oz finely chopped drained preserved stem ginger.

SERVES FOUR TO SIX

1 Put the hulled and halved strawberries and peeled and segmented oranges into a serving bowl. Halve the passion fruit and using a teaspoon scoop the flesh into the bowl.

2 Pour the wine over the fruit and toss gently. Cover and chill in the refrigerator until ready to serve.

350–400g/12–14oz/ 3–3½ cups strawberries, hulled and halved

6 oranges, peeled and segmented

1–2 passion fruit

120ml/4fl oz/¹/₂ cup medium dry or sweet white wine

Juniper-scented Pears in Red Wine

More often used in savoury dishes than sweet, juniper berries have a dark blue, almost black colour with a distinct gin-like flavour. In this fruity winter dessert crushed juniper berries give the classic partnership of pears and red wine a slightly aromatic flavour. These pears are particularly good sprinkled with toasted almonds and whipped cream.

SERVES FOUR

1 Lightly crush the juniper berries using a pestle and mortar or with the end of a rolling pin. Put the berries in a pan with the sugar and wine and heat gently until the sugar dissolves.

2 Meanwhile, peel the pears, leaving them whole. Add them to the wine and heat until just simmering. Cover the pan and cook gently for about 25 minutes, until the pears are tender. Turn the pears once or twice to make sure they cook evenly.

3 Use a slotted spoon to remove the pears. Boil the syrup hard for a few minutes, until it is slightly reduced and thickened. If serving the pears hot, reheat them gently in the syrup, otherwise arrange them in a serving dish and spoon the syrup over.

30ml/2 tbsp juniper berries

50g/2oz/¹/₄ cup caster (superfine) sugar

600ml/1 pint/2¹/₂ cups red wine

4 large or 8 small firm pears, stalks intact

Oranges in Syrup

This recipe works well with most citrus fruits – for example, try pink grapefruit or sweet, perfumed clementines, which have been peeled but left whole. Serve the oranges with 300ml/½ pint/1¼ cups whipped cream flavoured with 5ml/1 tsp ground cinnamon, or 5ml/1 tsp ground nutmeg or with Greek (US strained plain) yogurt.

SERVES SIX

6 medium oranges

200g/7oz/1 cup sugar

100ml/3½ fl oz/ scant ¹/₂ cup fresh strong brewed coffee

50g/2oz/¹/₂ cup pistachio nuts, chopped (optional)

> **COOK'S TIP**
> *Choose a pan in which the oranges will just fit in a single layer – use a deep frying pan if you don't have a pan that is large enough.*

1 Finely pare, shred and reserve the rind from one orange. Peel the remaining oranges. Cut each one crossways into slices, then re-form them, with a cocktail stick (toothpick) through the centre.

2 Put the sugar in a heavy pan and add 50ml/2fl oz/¼ cup water. Heat gently until the sugar dissolves, then bring to the boil and cook until the syrup turns pale gold.

3 Remove from the heat and carefully pour 100ml/3½fl oz/ scant ½ cup freshly boiling water into the pan. Return to the heat until the syrup has dissolved in the water. Stir in the coffee.

4 Add the oranges and the rind to the coffee syrup. Simmer for 15–20 minutes, turning the oranges once during cooking. Leave to cool, then chill. Serve sprinkled with pistachio nuts, if using.

Fresh Fig Compote

A vanilla and coffee syrup brings out the wonderful flavour of figs – serve Greek (US strained plain) yogurt or vanilla ice cream with the poached fruit. A good selection of different honey is available – its aroma and flavour will be subtly scented by the plants surrounding the hives. Orange blossom honey works particularly well in this recipe, although any clear variety is suitable.

SERVES FOUR TO SIX

400ml/14fl oz/ 1²/₃ cups fresh brewed coffee

115g/4oz/¹/₂ cup clear honey

1 vanilla pod (bean)

12 slightly under-ripe fresh figs

1 Choose a frying pan with a lid, large enough to hold the figs in a single layer. Pour in the coffee and add the honey.

2 Split the vanilla pod lengthways and scrape the seeds into the pan. Add the vanilla pod, then bring to a rapid boil and cook until reduced to about 175ml/6fl oz/¾ cup.

3 Wash the figs and pierce the skins several times with a sharp skewer. Cut in half and add to the syrup. Reduce the heat, cover and simmer for 5 minutes. Remove the figs from the syrup with a slotted spoon and set aside to cool.

4 Strain the syrup over the figs. Allow to stand at room temperature for 1 hour before serving.

> **COOK'S TIP**
> *Figs come in three main varieties – red, white and black – and all three are suitable for cooking. They are sweet and succulent, and complement the stronger, more pervasive flavours of coffee and vanilla very well.*

Pistachio and Rose Water Oranges

This light and citrusy dessert is perfect to serve after a heavy main course, such as a hearty meat stew or a leg of roast lamb. Combining three favourite Middle Eastern ingredients, it is delightfully fragrant and refreshing. If you don't have pistachio nuts, use hazelnuts instead.

SERVES FOUR

1 Slice the top and bottom off one of the oranges to expose the flesh. Using a small serrated knife, slice down between the pith and the flesh, working round the orange, to remove all the peel and pith. Slice the orange into six rounds, reserving any juice. Repeat with the remaining oranges.

2 Arrange the orange rounds on a serving dish. Mix the reserved juice with the rose water and drizzle over the oranges. Cover the dish with clear film (plastic wrap) and chill for about 30 minutes. Sprinkle the chopped pistachio nuts over the oranges to serve.

4 large oranges

30ml/2 tbsp rose water

30ml/2 tbsp shelled pistachio nuts, roughly chopped

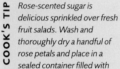

COOK'S TIP
Rose-scented sugar is delicious sprinkled over fresh fruit salads. Wash and thoroughly dry a handful of rose petals and place in a sealed container filled with caster (superfine) sugar for 2–3 days. Remove the petals before using the sugar.

Lychee and Elderflower Sorbet

The flavour of elderflowers is famous for bringing out the essence of gooseberries, but what is less well known is how wonderfully it complements lychees.

SERVES FOUR

175g/6oz/³/₄ cup caster sugar

400ml/14fl oz/1²/₃ cups water

500g/1¹/₄lb fresh lychees, peeled and stoned

15ml/1 tbsp elderflower cordial

dessert biscuits, to serve

> **COOK'S TIP**
> Switch the freezer to the coldest setting before making the sorbet – the faster the mixture freezes, the smaller the ice crystals that form and the better the final texture will be.

1 Place the sugar and water in a saucepan and heat gently until the sugar has dissolved. Increase the heat and boil for 5 minutes, then add the lychees. Lower the heat and simmer for 7 minutes. Remove from the heat and allow to cool.

2 Purée the fruit and syrup in a blender or food processor. Place a sieve over a bowl and pour the purée into it. Press through as much of the purée as possible with a spoon.

3 Stir the elderflower cordial into the strained purée, then pour the mixture into a freezerproof container. Freeze for 2 hours, until ice crystals start to form around the edges.

4 Remove the sorbet from the freezer and process briefly in a food processor or blender to break up the crystals. Repeat this process twice more, then freeze until firm. Transfer to the fridge for 10 minutes to soften slightly before serving in scoops, with biscuits.

Summer Fruit Brioche

Scooped-out, individual brioches make perfect containers for the fruity filling in this stylish, but simple dessert. If small brioches are not available, serve the fruit on slices cut from a large brioche. Any summer fruits can be used in this dessert – try raspberries, sliced peaches, nectarines, apricots, or pitted cherries. Serve with single (light) cream poured over.

SERVES FOUR

1 Preheat the grill (broiler). Slice the tops off the brioches and use a teaspoon to scoop out their centres, leaving a 1 cm/½in thick case. Lightly toast them, turning once and watching them carefully, as they will brown very quickly.

2 Put the strawberries in a pan with the sugar and add 60ml/4 tbsp water. Heat very gently for about 1 minute, until the strawberries are softened but still keep their shape. Remove the pan from the heat, stir in the raspberries and leave to cool.

3 Place the brioches on plates and pile the fruit mixture into them. Add plenty of juice to saturate the brioches and allow it to flood the plates. Place any extra fruit on the plates.

4 individual brioches

300g/11oz/ 2¹/₂ cups small ripe strawberries, halved

30ml/2 tbsp caster (superfine) sugar

115g/4oz/²/₃ cup raspberries

Rhubarb and Ginger Jellies

Made with bright pink, young rhubarb, these softly set jellies get the taste buds tingling. They are spiced with plenty of fresh ginger, which gives just a hint of zesty warmth. Pour the jelly into pretty glasses and serve it as it is or top it with spoonfuls of lightly whipped cream.

SERVES FIVE TO SIX

1kg/2¹/₄lb young rhubarb

200g/7oz/1 cup caster (superfine) sugar

50g/2oz fresh root ginger, finely chopped

15ml/1 tbsp powdered gelatine

1 Cut the rhubarb into 2cm/¾in chunks and place in a pan with the sugar and ginger. Pour in 450ml/¾ pint/scant 2 cups water and bring to the boil. Reduce the heat, cover and simmer gently for 10 minutes, until the rhubarb is very soft and pulpy.

2 Meanwhile, sprinkle the gelatine over 30ml/2 tbsp cold water in a small heatproof bowl. Leave to stand, without stirring, for 5 minutes, until the gelatine has become sponge-like in texture. Set the bowl over a small pan of hot water and simmer, stirring occasionally, until the gelatine has dissolved completely into a clear liquid. Remove from the heat.

3 Strain the cooked rhubarb through a fine sieve into a bowl. Stir in the dissolved gelatine until thoroughly mixed. Leave to cool slightly before pouring into serving glasses. Chill for at least 4 hours or overnight, until set.

Papayas in Jasmine Flower Syrup

The fragrant syrup can be prepared in advance, using fresh jasmine flowers from a house plant or the garden. You can also use fresh flowers as a garnish. The syrup tastes fabulous with papayas, but it is also good with all sorts of desserts. Try it with ice cream or spooned over lychees or mangoes.

SERVES FOUR

45ml/3 tbsp palm sugar or light muscovado (brown) sugar

20–30 jasmine flowers

2 ripe papayas

juice of 1 lime

1 Place 105ml/7 tbsp water in a small pan and add the sugar. Heat gently, stirring occasionally, until the sugar has dissolved, then simmer, without stirring, over a low heat for 4 minutes.

2 Pour into a bowl, leave to cool slightly, then add the jasmine flowers. Leave to steep for at least 20 minutes.

3 Peel the papayas and slice in half lengthways. Scoop out and discard the seeds. Place the papayas on serving plates and squeeze over the lime.

4 Strain the syrup into a clean bowl, discarding the flowers. Spoon the syrup over the papayas. If you like, decorate with a few fresh jasmine flowers.

Mango and Lime Fool

Canned mangoes are used here for convenience, but this zesty, tropical fruit fool tastes even better if made with fresh ones. Choose a variety with a good flavour, such as the fragrant Alphonso mango.

SERVES FOUR

400g/14oz can sliced mango, plus extra to garnish (optional)

grated rind of 1 lime, plus juice of $^1/_2$ lime

150ml/$^1/_4$ pint/$^2/_3$ cup double (heavy) cream

90ml/6 tbsp Greek (US strained plain) yogurt

1 Drain the canned mango slices and put them in a food processor, then add the grated lime rind and lime juice. Process until the mixture forms a smooth purée.

2 Alternatively, place the mango slices in a bowl and mash with a potato masher, then press through a sieve (strainer) into a bowl with the back of a wooden spoon. Stir in the lime rind and juice.

3 Pour the cream into a bowl and add the yogurt. Whisk until the mixture is thick and then quickly whisk in the mango mixture.

4 Spoon the fool into four tall cups or glasses and chill for at least 1 hour. Just before serving, decorate each glass with fresh mango slices, if you like.

Tangy Raspberry and Lemon Tartlets

You can make the pastry cases for these little tartlets in advance and store them in an airtight container until ready to serve.

SERVES FOUR

1 Preheat the oven to 190°C/375°F/Gas 5. Roll out the pastry and use to line four 9cm/3^1/$_2$in tartlet tins (muffin pans). Line each tin with a circle of baking parchment and fill with baking beans or uncooked rice.

2 Bake for 15–20 minutes, or until golden and cooked through. Remove the baking beans or rice and paper and take the pastry cases out of the tins. Leave to cool completely on a wire rack.

3 Set aside 12 raspberries for decoration and fold the remaining ones into the lemon curd. Spoon the mixture into the pastry cases and top with the reserved raspberries. Serve immediately.

175g/6oz ready-made short-crust pastry, thawed if frozen

120ml/8 tbsp good quality lemon curd

115g/4oz/^{2}/$_3$ cup fresh raspberries

Crispy Mango Stacks with Raspberry Coulis

This makes a very healthy yet stunning dessert – it is low in fat and contains no added sugar. However, if the raspberries are a little sharp, you may prefer to add a pinch of sugar to the purée.

SERVES FOUR

3 filo pastry sheets, thawed if frozen

2 small ripe mangoes

115g/4oz/²/₃ raspberries, thawed if frozen

FROM THE STORECUPBOARD

50g/2oz/¹/₄ cup butter, melted

1 Preheat the oven to 200°C/400°F/Gas 6. Lay the filo sheets on a clean work surface and cut out four 10cm/4in rounds from each. Brush each round with the melted butter and lay the rounds on two baking sheets. Bake for 5 minutes, or until crisp and golden. Place on wire racks to cool.

2 Peel the mangoes, remove the stones and cut the flesh into thin slices. Put the raspberries in a food processor with 45ml/3 tbsp water and process to a purée. Place a pastry round on each of four serving plates. Top with a quarter of the mango and drizzle with a little of the raspberry purée. Repeat until all the ingredients have been used, finishing with a layer of mango and a drizzle of raspberry purée.

Rhubarb and Ginger Trifles

Choose a good quality jar of rhubarb compote for this recipe; try to find one with large, chunky pieces of fruit.

SERVES FOUR

**12 gingernut biscuits
(gingersnaps)**

**50ml/2fl oz/¹/₄ cup rhubarb
compote**

**450ml/³/₄ pint/scant 2 cups
extra thick double (heavy)
cream**

1 Put the ginger biscuits in a plastic bag and seal. Bash the biscuits with a rolling pin until roughly crushed.

2 Set aside two tablespoons of crushed biscuits and divide the rest among four glasses.

3 Spoon the rhubarb compote on top of the crushed biscuits, then top with the cream. Place in the refrigerator and chill for about 30 minutes.

4 To serve, sprinkle the reserved crushed biscuits over the trifles and serve immediately.

Strawberry Cream Shortbreads

These pretty desserts are always popular. Serve them as soon as they are ready because the shortbread cookies will lose their lovely crisp texture if left to stand.

SERVES THREE

150g/5oz strawberries

450ml/³/₄ pint/scant 2 cups double (heavy) cream

6 round shortbread biscuits (cookies)

VARIATION

You can use any other berry you like for this dessert – try raspberries or blueberries. Two ripe, peeled peaches will also give great results.

1 Reserve three strawberries for decoration. Hull the remaining strawberries and cut them in half.

2 Put the halved strawberries in a bowl and gently crush using the back of a fork. (Only crush the berries lightly; they should not be reduced to a purée.)

3 Put the cream in a large, clean bowl and whip to form soft peaks. Add the crushed strawberries and gently fold in to combine. (Do not overmix.)

4 Halve the reserved strawberries, then spoon the strawberry and cream mixture on top of the shortbread cookies. Decorate each one with half a strawberry and serve immediately.

Blackberries in Port

Pour this rich fruit compote over ice cream or serve it with a spoonful of clotted cream to create an attractive, rich dessert. It's unbelievably quick and easy to make and is the perfect end to a dinner party. Blackberries can be found growing wild on hedgerows in late summer and there's nothing better than picking them yourself for this lovely dessert.

SERVES FOUR

300ml/¹/₂ pint/1¹/₄ cups ruby port

75g/3oz/6 tbsp caster (superfine) sugar

450g/1lb/4 cups blackberries

1 Pour the port into a pan and add the sugar and 150ml/¹/₄ pint/²/₃ cup water. Stir over a gentle heat with a wooden spoon until the sugar has dissolved.

2 Remove the pan from the heat and stir in the blackberries. Set aside to cool, then pour into a bowl and cover with clear film (plastic wrap). Chill until ready to serve.

Baby Summer Puddings

This classic English dessert is always a favourite, and serving it in individual portions with spoonfuls of clotted cream makes it extra special. White bread that is more than a day old actually works better than fresh bread. Slices of brioche make a wonderful alternative to white bread.

SERVES FOUR

6 white bread slices, crusts removed

450g/1lb/4 cups summer fruits

75g/3oz/6 tbsp caster (superfine) sugar

COOK'S TIP

You can enjoy this lovely dessert even in the winter. Use frozen summer fruits, which are available in supermarkets all year round. Simply thaw the fruits, then cook as if using fresh fruits.

1 Cut out four rounds from the bread slices, large enough to fit in the bottom of four 175ml/6fl oz/³/₄ cup dariole moulds.

2 Line the moulds with clear film (plastic wrap) and place a bread round in the base of each mould. Reserve two slices of bread and cut the remaining bread into slices and use to line the sides of the moulds, pressing to fit.

3 Put the summer fruits in a pan with the sugar and heat gently until the sugar has dissolved. Bring to the boil, then simmer gently for 2–3 minutes. Remove from the heat and leave to cool slightly, then spoon into the moulds.

4 Cut four rounds out of the remaining slices of bread to fit the top of the dariole moulds. Place the bread rounds on the fruit and push down to fit. Cover each dariole mould loosely with clear film and place a small weight on top.

5 Chill the desserts overnight, then turn out on to serving plates. Remove the clear film lining and serve immediately.

Raspberry Brûlée

Cracking through the caramelized sugary top of a crème brûlée to reveal the creamy custard underneath is always so satisfying. These ones have the added bonus of a deliciously rich, fruity custard packed with crushed raspberries.

SERVES FOUR

1 Tip the raspberries into a large bowl and crush with a fork. Add the custard and gently fold in until combined.

2 Divide the mixture between four 120ml/4fl oz/¹/₂ cup ramekin dishes. Cover each one with clear film (plastic wrap) and chill in the refrigerator for 2–3 hours.

3 Preheat the grill (broiler) to high. Remove the clear film from the ramekin dishes and place them on a baking sheet. Sprinkle the sugar over the custards and grill (broil) for 3–4 minutes, or until the sugar has caramelized.

4 Remove the custards from the grill and set aside for a few minutes to allow the sugar to harden, then serve.

115g/4oz fresh raspberries

300ml/¹/₂ pint/1¹/₄ cups ready-made fresh custard

75g/3oz caster (superfine) sugar

COOK'S TIP *You can now buy little gas blow torches for use in the kitchen. They make quick work of caramelizing the sugar on top of the brûlées – and are also fun to use!*

Portuguese Custard Tarts

Called *pastéis de nata* in Portugal, these tarts are traditionally served with a small strong coffee as a sweet breakfast dish, but they are equally delicious served as a pastry or dessert.

MAKES TWELVE

225g/8oz ready-made puff pastry, thawed if frozen

175ml/6fl oz/³⁄₄ cup fresh ready-made custard

30ml/2 tbsp icing (confectioners') sugar

1 Preheat the oven to 200°C/400°F/Gas 6. Roll out the pastry and cut out twelve 13cm/5in rounds. Line a 12-hole muffin tin (pan) with the pastry rounds. Line each pastry round with a circle of baking parchment and some baking beans or uncooked rice.

2 Bake the tarts for 10–15 minutes, or until the pastry is cooked through and golden. Remove the paper and baking beans or rice and set aside to cool.

3 Spoon the custard into the pastry cases and dust with the icing sugar. Place the tarts under a preheated hot grill (broiler) and cook until the sugar caramelizes. Remove from the heat and leave to cool before serving.

Baked Custard with Burnt Sugar

This delicious egg custard or crème brûlée is a rich indulgent dessert that can be prepared well in advance. You can buy vanilla sugar or make your own by placing a split vanilla pod (bean) in a jar of caster (superfine) sugar – the sugar will be ready to use after a couple of days.

SERVES SIX

1 Preheat the oven to 150°C/300°F/Gas 2. Place six 120ml/4fl oz/½ cup ramekins in a roasting pan or ovenproof dish and set aside while you prepare the vanilla custard.

2 Heat the double cream in a heavy pan over a gentle heat until it is very hot, but not boiling.

3 In a bowl, whisk the egg yolks and vanilla sugar until well blended. Whisk in the hot cream and strain into a large jug (pitcher). Divide the custard equally among the ramekins.

4 Pour enough boiling water into the roasting pan to come about halfway up the sides of the ramekins. Cover the pan with foil and bake for about 30 minutes, until the custards are just set. (Push the point of a knife into the centre of one; if it comes out clean, the custards are cooked.) Remove from the pan, cool, then chill.

5 Preheat the grill (broiler). Sprinkle the sugar evenly over the surface of the custards and grill (broil) for 30–60 seconds, until the sugar melts and caramelizes, taking care not to let it burn. Place in the refrigerator to chill and set the crust.

1 litre/1³/₄ pints/4 cups double (heavy) cream

6 egg yolks

90g/3¹/₂oz/¹/₂ cup vanilla sugar

75g/3oz/¹/₃ cup soft light brown sugar

COOK'S TIP *It is best to make the custards the day before you wish to eat them and chill overnight, so that they are really cold and firm.*

Passion Fruit Creams

These delicately perfumed creams are light with a fresh flavour from the passion fruit. Ripe passion fruit should look purple and wrinkled – choose fruit that are heavy for their size. When halved, the fragrant, sweet juicy flesh with small edible black seeds are revealed. These creams can be decorated with mint or geranium leaves and served with cream.

SERVES FIVE TO SIX

1 Preheat the oven to 180°C/350°F/Gas 4. Line the bases of six 120ml/4fl oz/½ cup ramekins with rounds of baking parchment and place them in a roasting pan.

2 Heat the cream to just below boiling point, then remove the pan from the heat. Sieve the flesh of four passion fruits and beat together with the sugar and eggs. Whisk in the hot cream and then ladle into the ramekins.

3 Half fill the roasting pan with boiling water. Bake the creams for 25–30 minutes, or until set, then leave to cool before chilling.

4 Run a knife around the insides of the ramekins, then invert them on to serving plates, tapping the bases firmly. Carefully peel off the baking parchment and chill in the refrigerator until ready to serve. Spoon on a little passion fruit flesh just before serving.

600ml/1 pint/2½ cups double (heavy) cream, or a mixture of single (light) and double (heavy) cream

6 passion fruits

30–45ml/2–3 tbsp vanilla sugar

5 eggs

Baked Caramel Custard

Many countries have their own version of this classic dessert. Known as *crème caramel* in France and *flan* in Spain, this chilled baked custard has a rich caramel flavour. By cooking the custard in a *bain-marie* or as here in a roasting pan with water, the mixture is cooked gently and the eggs are prevented from becoming tough or curdling. It is delicious served with fresh strawberries and thick cream.

SERVES SIX TO EIGHT

1 Put 175g/6oz/generous ¾ cup of the sugar in a small heavy pan with just enough water to moisten the sugar. Bring to the boil over a high heat, swirling the pan until the sugar has dissolved completely. Boil for about 5 minutes, without stirring, until the syrup turns a rich, dark caramel colour.

2 Working quickly, pour the caramel into a 1 litre/ 1¾ pint/4 cup soufflé dish. Holding the dish with oven gloves, carefully swirl it to coat the base and sides with the hot caramel mixture. Set aside to cool.

3 Preheat the oven to 160°C/325°F/Gas 3. In a bowl, whisk the eggs and egg yolks with the remaining sugar for 2–3 minutes, until smooth and creamy.

4 Heat the cream in a heavy pan until hot, but not boiling. Whisk the hot cream into the egg mixture and carefully strain the mixture into the caramel-lined dish. Cover tightly with foil.

5 Place the dish in a roasting pan and pour in just enough boiling water to come halfway up the side of the dish. Bake the custard for 40–45 minutes, until just set. To test whether the custard is set, insert a knife about 5cm/2in from the edge; if the blade comes out clean, the custard should be ready.

6 Remove the soufflé dish from the roasting pan and leave to cool for at least 30 minutes, then place in the refrigerator and chill overnight.

7 To turn out, carefully run a sharp knife around the edge of the dish to loosen the custard. Cover the dish with a serving plate and, holding them both together very tightly, invert the dish and plate, allowing the custard to drop down on to the plate.

8 Gently lift one edge of the dish, allowing the caramel to run down over the sides and on to the plate, then carefully lift off the dish. Serve immediately.

250g/9oz/1¹/₄ cups vanilla sugar

5 large (US extra large) eggs, plus 2 extra yolks

450ml/³/₄ pint/scant 2 cups double (heavy) cream

VARIATION

For a special occasion, make individual baked custards in ramekin dishes. Coat six to eight ramekins with the caramel and divide the custard mixture among them. Bake, in a roasting pan of water, for 25–30 minutes or until set. Thinly slice the strawberries and marinate them in a little sugar and a liqueur or dessert wine, such as Amaretto or Muscat wine.

Chocolate Banana Fools

This de luxe version of banana custard looks great served in glasses. It can be made a few hours in advance and chilled until ready to serve.

SERVES FOUR

1 Put the chocolate in a heatproof bowl and melt in the microwave on high power for 1–2 minutes. Stir, then set aside to cool. (Alternatively, put the chocolate in a heatproof bowl and place it over a pan of gently simmering water and leave until melted, stirring frequently.)

115g/4oz plain (semisweet) chocolate, chopped

300ml/¹⁄₂ pint/1¹⁄₄ cups fresh custard

2 bananas

2 Pour the custard into a bowl and gently fold in the melted chocolate to make a rippled effect.

3 Peel and slice the bananas and stir these into the chocolate and custard mixture. Spoon into four glasses and chill for 30 minutes–1 hour before serving.

Lemon Posset

This simple creamy dessert has distant origins, dating back to the Middle Ages. It is perfect for warm summer evenings and is particularly good served with crisp shortbread cookies.

SERVES FOUR

1 Gently heat the cream and sugar together until the sugar has dissolved, then bring to the boil, stirring constantly. Add the lemon juice and rind and stir until the mixture thickens.

2 Pour the mixture into four heatproof serving glasses and chill until just set, then serve.

600ml/1 pint/2¹⁄₂ cups double (heavy) cream

175g/6oz/scant 1 cup caster (superfine) sugar

grated rind and juice of 2 unwaxed lemons

COOK'S TIP
To make shortbread cookies, put 225g/8oz/1 cup chilled butter in a food processor and add 115g/4oz/²⁄₃ cup caster (superfine) sugar, 225g/8oz/2 cups plain (all-purpose) flour and 115g/4oz/²⁄₃ cup ground rice. Process to form a dough, then shape into a log 5cm/2in wide and wrap in clear film (plastic wrap). Chill for 30 minutes. Preheat the oven to 190°C/375°F/Gas 5. Cut the dough into thin slices, and bake for 15–20 minutes.

Chilled Chocolate and Espresso Mousse

Heady, aromatic espresso coffee adds a distinctive flavour to this smooth, rich mousse. For a special occasion, serve the mousse in stylish chocolate cups decorated with sprigs of mint, with mascarpone or clotted cream on the side.

SERVES FOUR

450g/1lb plain (semisweet) chocolate

45ml/3 tbsp freshly brewed espresso

4 eggs, separated

FROM THE STORECUPBOARD

25g/1oz/2 tbsp unsalted (sweet) butter

1 For each chocolate cup, cut a double thickness 15cm/6in square of foil. Mould it around a small orange, leaving the edges and corners loose to make a cup shape. Remove the orange and press the bottom of the foil case gently on a surface to make a flat base. Repeat to make four foil cups.

2 Break half the chocolate into small pieces and place in a bowl set over a pan of very hot water. Stir occasionally until the chocolate has completely melted.

3 Spoon the chocolate into the foil cups, spreading it up the sides with the back of a spoon to give a ragged edge. Chill for 30 minutes in the refrigerator, or until set hard. Gently peel away the foil, starting at the top edge.

4 To make the chocolate mousse, put the remaining chocolate and espresso into a bowl set over a pan of hot water and melt as before, until smooth and liquid. Stir in the butter, a little at a time. Remove the pan from the heat and then stir in the egg yolks.

5 Whisk the egg whites in a bowl until stiff, but not dry, then fold them into the chocolate mixture. Pour into a bowl and chill for at least 3 hours, or until the mousse is set. Scoop the chilled mousse into the chocolate cups just before serving.

Meringue Pyramid with Chocolate Mascarpone

This impressive cake makes a perfect centrepiece for a celebration buffet. Dust the pyramid with a little sieved icing (confectioners') sugar and sprinkle with just a few rose petals for simple but stunning presentation.

SERVES ABOUT TEN

200g/7oz plain (semisweet) chocolate

4 egg whites

150g/5oz/³⁄₄ cup caster (superfine) sugar

115g/4oz/³⁄₄ cup mascarpone cheese

1 Preheat the oven to 150°C/300°F/Gas 2. Line two large baking sheets with baking parchment or greaseproof (waxed) paper. Grate 75g/3oz of the chocolate.

2 Whisk the egg whites in a clean, grease-free bowl until they form stiff peaks. Gradually whisk in half the sugar, then add the rest and whisk until the meringue is very stiff and glossy. Add the grated chocolate and whisk lightly to mix.

3 Draw a 20cm/8in circle on the lining paper on one of the baking sheets, turn it upside down, and spread the marked circle evenly with about half the meringue. Spoon the remaining meringue in 28–30 teaspoonfuls on both baking sheets. Bake the meringue for 1–1½ hours, or until crisp and completely dried out.

4 Make the filling. Melt the remaining chocolate in a heatproof bowl over hot water. Cool slightly, then stir in the mascarpone. Cool the mixture until firm.

5 Spoon the chocolate mixture into a large piping (pastry) bag and use to sandwich the meringues together in pairs, reserving a small amount of filling for the pyramid.

6 Arrange the filled meringues on a serving platter, piling them up in a pyramid and keeping them in position with a few well-placed dabs of the reserved filling.

COOK'S TIP *The meringues can be made up to a week in advance and stored in a cool, dry place in an airtight container.*

Classic Chocolate Roulade

This rich, squidgy chocolate roll should be made at least eight hours before serving to allow it to soften. Expect the roulade to crack a little when you roll it up, and sprinkle with a little grated chocolate, if you like, as a final decoration. When melting chocolate, break it into even-sized pieces and place in a dry heatproof bowl over hot water. If the water is too hot the chocolate will turn grainy and scorch; if the chocolate is splashed with water it will harden and acquire a dull finish.

SERVES EIGHT

1 Preheat the oven to 180°C/350°F/Gas 4. Grease and line a 33 x 23cm/13 x 9in Swiss (jelly) roll tin (pan) with baking parchment.

2 Break the chocolate into squares and melt in a bowl over a pan of barely simmering water. Remove from the heat and leave to cool for about 5 minutes.

3 In a large bowl, whisk the sugar and egg yolks until light and fluffy. Stir in the melted chocolate.

4 Whisk the egg whites until stiff, but not dry, and then gently fold into the chocolate mixture.

5 Pour the chocolate mixture into the prepared tin, spreading it level with a palette knife (metal spatula). Bake for about 25 minutes, or until firm. Leave the cake in the tin and cover with a cooling rack, making sure that it does not touch the cake.

6 Cover the rack with a damp dishtowel, then wrap in clear film (plastic wrap). Leave in a cool place for 8 hours, preferably overnight.

7 Dust a sheet of greaseproof (waxed) paper with caster or icing sugar and turn out the roulade on to it. Peel off the lining paper.

8 To make the filling, whip the double cream until soft peaks form. Spread the cream over the roulade. Starting from one of the short ends, carefully roll it up, using the paper to help.

9 Place the roulade, seam side down, on to a serving plate and dust generously with more caster or icing sugar before serving.

200g/7oz plain (semisweet) chocolate

200g/7oz/1 cup caster (superfine) sugar, plus extra caster or icing (confectioners') sugar to dust

7 eggs, separated

300ml/¹⁄₂ pint/1¹⁄₄cups double (heavy) cream

COOK'S TIP

For a special dessert, decorate the roulade with swirls of whipped cream and chocolate coffee beans or with clusters of raspberries and mint leaves.

Cherry Chocolate Brownies

This is a modern version of the classic Black Forest gâteau. Choose really good-quality bottled fruits because this will make all the difference to the end result. Look out for bottled fruits at Christmas-time, in particular, when supermarket shelves are packed with different varieties. Other types of fruit will work equally well – try slices of orange bottled in liqueur or pears bottled in brandy.

SERVES FOUR

1 Using a sharp knife, carefully cut the brownies in half crossways to make two thin slices. Place one brownie square on each of four serving plates.

2 Pour the cream into a large bowl and whip until soft but not stiff, then divide half the whipped cream between the four brownie squares.

3 Divide half the cherries among the cream-topped brownies, then place the remaining brownie halves on top of the cherries. Press down lightly.

4 Spoon the remaining cream on top of the brownies, then top each one with more cherries and serve immediately.

4 chocolate brownies

300ml/^{1}/$_2$ pint/1^1/$_4$ cups double (heavy) cream

20–24 bottled cherries in Kirsch

Coffee Mascarpone Creams

For the best results, use good quality coffee beans and make the coffee as strong as possible. These little desserts are very rich so you need a really robust shot of coffee to give the desired result. They are particularly good served with a glass of liqueur or a cup of espresso.

SERVES FOUR

1 Put the mascarpone in a bowl and add the coffee. Mix well until smooth and creamy. Sift in the icing sugar and stir until thoroughly combined.

2 Spoon the mixture into little china pots or ramekin dishes and chill for 30 minutes before serving.

115g/4oz/^{1}/$_2$ cup mascarpone cheese

45ml/3 tbsp strong espresso coffee

45ml/3 tbsp icing (confectioners') sugar

VARIATION

You can flavour mascarpone with almost anything you like to make a quick but elegant dessert. Try replacing the coffee with the same quantity of orange juice, Marsala or honey.

Ice Creams and Frozen Desserts

ICE CREAMS AND ICED DESSERTS CAN MAKE A PERFECT,

REFRESHING END TO A MEAL. HOME-MADE ICES, WHETHER

A LIGHTLY PERFUMED SORBET, A CREAMY KULFI OR A RICH

AND CREAMY ICE CREAM GÂTEAU, ARE SURPRISINGLY

EASY TO MAKE AND A WONDERFUL TREAT TO SERVE

TO GUESTS AND FAMILY ALIKE.

Lemon Sorbet

This is probably the most classic sorbet of all. Refreshingly tangy and yet deliciously smooth, it quite literally melts in the mouth. Try to buy unwaxed lemons for recipes such as this one where the lemon rind is used. The wax coating can adversely affect the flavour of the rind.

200g/7oz/1 cup caster (superfine) sugar, plus extra for coating rind to decorate

4 lemons, well scrubbed

1 egg white

SERVES SIX

1 Put the sugar in a pan and pour in 300ml/½ pint/1¼ cups water. Bring to the boil, stirring occasionally until the sugar has just dissolved.

2 Using a swivel vegetable peeler, pare the rind thinly from two of the lemons so that it falls straight into the pan.

3 Simmer for 2 minutes without stirring, then take the pan off the heat. Leave to cool, then chill.

4 Squeeze the juice from all the lemons and add it to the syrup. Strain the syrup into a shallow freezerproof container, reserving the rind. Freeze the mixture for 4 hours, until it is mushy.

5 Process the sorbet (sherbet) in a food processor until it is smooth. Lightly whisk the egg white with a fork until it is just frothy. Replace the sorbet in the container, beat in the egg white and return the mixture to the freezer for 4 hours, or until it is firm.

6 Cut the reserved lemon rind into fine shreds and cook them in boiling water for 5 minutes, or until tender. Drain, then place on a plate and sprinkle generously with caster sugar. Scoop the sorbet into bowls or glasses and decorate with the sugared lemon rind.

Strawberry and Lavender Sorbet

A hint of lavender transforms a familiar strawberry sorbet into a perfumed dinner-party dessert. When buying strawberries look for plump, shiny fruit without any signs of staining or leakage at the bottom of the punnet – this suggests that the fruit at the bottom has been squashed. To hull strawberries, prise out the leafy top with a sharp knife or a specially designed strawberry huller.

SERVES SIX

1 Place the sugar in a pan and pour in 300ml/½ pint/1¼ cups water. Bring to the boil, stirring until the sugar has dissolved.

2 Take the pan off the heat, add the lavender flowers and leave to infuse (steep) for 1 hour. If time permits, chill the syrup in the refrigerator before using.

3 Process the strawberries in a food processor or in batches in a blender, then press the purée through a large sieve into a bowl.

4 Pour the purée into a freezerproof container, strain in the syrup and freeze for 4 hours, or until mushy. Transfer to a food processor and process until smooth. Whisk the egg white until frothy, and stir into the sorbet (sherbet). Spoon the sorbet back into the container and freeze until firm.

5 Serve in scoops, piled into tall glasses, and decorate with sprigs of lavender flowers.

150g/5oz/³/₄ cup
caster (superfine) sugar

6 fresh lavender
flowers, plus extra
to decorate

500g/1¹/₄lb/5 cups
strawberries, hulled

1 egg white

COOK'S TIP

The size of the lavender flowers can vary; if they are very small, you may need to use eight. To double check, taste a little of the cooled lavender syrup. If you think the flavour is too mild, add two or three more flowers, reheat and cool again before using.

Blackcurrant Sorbet

Wonderfully sharp and bursting with flavour, blackcurrants make a really fabulous sorbet. Blackcurrants are more acidic than white or redcurrants and are very rarely eaten raw. Taste the mixture after adding the syrup, and if you find it a little too tart, add a little more sugar before freezing.

SERVES SIX

500g/1¹/₄lb/5 cups blackcurrants, trimmed, plus extra to decorate

150g/5oz/³/₄ cup caster (superfine) sugar

1 egg white

1 Put the blackcurrants in a pan and add 150ml/¼ pint/²/₃ cup water. Cover the pan and simmer for 5 minutes, or until the fruit is soft. Cool, then process to a purée in a food processor or blender.

2 Set a large sieve over a bowl, pour the purée into the sieve, then press it through the mesh with the back of a spoon to form a smooth liquid.

3 Pour 200ml/7fl oz/scant 1 cup water into a clean pan. Add the sugar and bring to the boil, stirring until the sugar has dissolved. Pour the syrup into a bowl. Cool, then chill.

4 Mix the blackcurrant purée and sugar syrup together. Spoon into a freezerproof container and freeze until mushy. Lightly whisk the egg white until just frothy. Process the sorbet (sherbet) in a food processor until smooth, then return it to the container and stir in the egg white. Freeze for 4 hours, or until firm.

5 Transfer the sorbet to the refrigerator about 15 minutes before serving. Serve in scoops, decorated with the blackcurrant sprigs.

Damson Water Ice

Perfectly ripe damsons are sharp and full of flavour – if you can't find damsons, use another deep-red variety of plum or extra-juicy Victoria plums. To add an extra, nutty flavour to this mouthwatering ice, serve sprinkled with finely chopped toasted almonds.

SERVES SIX

500g/1¹/₄lb ripe damsons, washed

150g/5oz/³/₄ cup caster (superfine) sugar

1 Put the damsons into a pan and add 150ml/¼ pint/²/₃ cup water. Cover and simmer gently for 10 minutes, or until the damsons are tender.

2 Pour 300ml/½ pint/1¼ cups water into a second pan. Add the sugar and bring to the boil, stirring until the sugar has dissolved. Pour the syrup into a bowl, leave to cool, then chill.

3 Break up the cooked damsons in the pan with a wooden spoon and scoop out any free stones (pits). Pour the fruit and juices into a large sieve set over a bowl. Press the fruit through the sieve and discard the skins and any remaining stones from the sieve.

4 Pour the damson purée into a shallow plastic container. Stir in the syrup and freeze for 6 hours, beating once or twice to break up the ice crystals.

5 Spoon into tall serving glasses or dishes and serve the water ice with wafers.

VARIATION

Apricot water ice can be made in exactly the same way. Flavour the water ice with a little lemon or orange rind or add a broken cinnamon stick to the pan when poaching the fruit. Serve garnished with sprigs of mint or nasturtium flowers.

Peach and Cardamom Yogurt Ice

Make the most of spices that are familiar in savoury cooking by discovering their potential for sweet dishes. Cardamom, often used in Indian cooking, has a warm pungent aroma and a subtle lemon flavour. Although it is made with yogurt rather than cream, this ice cream has a luxurious velvety texture and it is a healthy choice, too.

SERVES FOUR

8 cardamom pods

6 peaches, total weight about 500g/1¼lb, halved and stoned (pitted)

75g/3oz/6 tbsp caster (superfine) sugar

200ml/7fl oz/scant 1 cup natural (plain) yogurt

1 Put the cardamom pods on a board and crush them with the base of a ramekin, or place in a mortar and crush with a pestle.

2 Chop the peaches coarsely and put them in a pan. Add the crushed cardamom pods, with their black seeds, the sugar and 30ml/2 tbsp water. Cover and simmer for 10 minutes, or until the fruit is tender. Leave to cool.

3 Process the peach mixture in a food processor or blender until smooth, then press through a sieve placed over a bowl.

4 Mix the yogurt into the sieved purée and pour into a freezerproof container. Freeze for 5–6 hours, until firm, beating once or twice with a fork, electric whisk, or in a processor to break up the ice crystals.

5 Scoop the ice cream on to a large platter and serve.

Summer Berry Frozen Yogurt

Any combination of summer fruits will work for this dish, as long as they are frozen, because this helps to create a chunky texture. Whole fresh or frozen berries make an attractive decoration.

SERVES SIX

350g/12oz/3 cups frozen summer fruits

200g/7oz/scant 1 cup Greek (US strained plain) yogurt

25g/1oz icing (confectioners') sugar

VARIATION *To make a rich and creamy ice cream, use double (heavy) cream in place of the yogurt. It's a lot less healthy but the taste is irresistible.*

1 Put all the ingredients into a food processor and process until combined but still quite chunky. Spoon the mixture into six 150ml/¼ pint/⅔ cup ramekin dishes.

2 Cover each dish with clear film (plastic wrap) and place in the freezer for about 2 hours, or until firm.

3 To turn out the frozen yogurts, dip the dishes briefly in hot water and invert them on to small serving plates. Tap the base of the dishes and the yogurts should come out. Serve immediately.

Raspberry Sherbet

Traditional sherbets are made in a similar way to sorbets but with added milk. This low-fat version is made from raspberry purée blended with sugar syrup and virtually fat-free fromage frais or yogurt.

SERVES SIX

175g/6oz/scant 1 cup caster (superfine) sugar

500g/1¼lb/3½ cups raspberries, plus extra, to serve

500ml/17fl oz/2¼ cups virtually fat-free fromage frais or yogurt

COOK'S TIP
To make the sherbet by hand, pour the raspberry purée into a freezerproof container and freeze for 4 hours, beating once with a fork, electric whisk or in a food processor to break up the ice crystals. Freeze, then beat again.

1 Put the sugar in a small pan with 150ml/¼ pint/⅔ cup water and bring to the boil, stirring until the sugar has dissolved completely. Pour into a jug (pitcher) and cool.

2 Put 350g/12oz/2½ cups of the raspberries in a food processor and blend to a purée. Press through a sieve into a large bowl and discard the seeds. Stir the sugar syrup into the raspberry purée and chill until very cold.

3 Add the fromage frais or yogurt to the chilled purée and whisk until smooth. Using an ice-cream maker, churn the mixture until it is thick but too soft to scoop. Scrape into a freezerproof container, then crush the remaining raspberries between your fingers and add to the ice cream. Mix lightly then freeze for 2–3 hours until firm. Scoop the ice cream into dishes and serve with extra raspberries.

Watermelon Ice

This simple, refreshing dessert is perfect after a hot, spicy meal. The aromatic flavour of kaffir lime leaves goes perfectly with watermelon.

SERVES FOUR TO SIX

90ml/6 tbsp caster (superfine) sugar

4 kaffir lime leaves, torn into small pieces

500g/1¼lb watermelon

1 Put the sugar and lime leaves in a pan with 105ml/7 tbsp water. Heat gently until the sugar has dissolved, then pour into a large bowl and set aside to cool.

2 Cut the watermelon into wedges with a large knife. Cut the flesh from the rind, remove the seeds and chop the flesh. Place the flesh in a food processor and process to a slush, then mix in the sugar syrup. Chill for 3–4 hours.

3 Strain the chilled mixture into a freezer container and freeze for 2 hours, then beat with a fork to break up the ice crystals. Return to the freezer and freeze for 3 hours more, beating at half-hourly intervals, then freeze until firm. Transfer the ice to the refrigerator about 30 minutes before serving.

Blackberry Ice Cream

There could scarcely be fewer ingredients in this delicious, vibrant ice cream, which is simple to make and ideal as a prepare-ahead dessert. Serve the ice cream with biscuits (cookies), such as shortbread or almond biscuits, to provide a delicious contrast in taste and texture.

SERVES FOUR TO SIX

500g/1¹/₄lb/5 cups blackberries, hulled, plus extra to decorate

75g/3oz/6 tbsp caster (superfine) sugar

300ml/¹/₂ pint/1¹/₄ cups whipping cream

crisp dessert biscuits (cookies), to serve

COOK'S TIP
Frozen blackberries can be used instead of fresh. You will need to increase the cooking time to 10 minutes and stir occasionally.

1 Put the blackberries into a pan, add 30ml/2 tbsp water and the sugar. Cover and simmer for 5 minutes, until just soft.

2 Tip the fruit into a sieve placed over a bowl and press it through the mesh, using a wooden spoon. Leave to cool, then chill.

3 Whip the cream until it is just thick but still soft enough to fall from a spoon, then mix it with the chilled fruit purée. Pour the mixture into a freezerproof container and freeze for 2 hours, or until it is part frozen.

4 Mash the mixture with a fork or process it in a food processor to break up the ice crystals. Return it to the freezer for 4 hours more, mashing or processing the mixture again after 2 hours.

5 Scoop the ice cream into dishes and decorate with extra blackberries. Serve with crisp dessert biscuits.

Coffee Ice Cream

This classic ice cream is always a favourite and, despite its simplicity, has an air of sophistication and elegance about it. If you have an ice cream maker, simply pour the mixture into it and churn until firm.

SERVES EIGHT

600ml/1 pint/2¹/₂ cups fresh ready-made custard

150ml/¹/₄ pint/²/₃ cup strong black coffee

300ml/¹/₂ pint/1¹/₄ cups double (heavy) cream

1 Put the custard in a large bowl and stir in the coffee. In a separate bowl, whip the cream until soft but not stiff and fold evenly into the coffee and custard mixture.

2 Pour the mixture into a freezerproof container and cover with a tight-fitting lid or clear film (plastic wrap) and freeze for about 2 hours.

3 Remove the ice cream from the freezer and beat with a fork to break up the ice crystals.

4 Return the ice cream to the freezer, freeze for a further 2 hours, then beat again. Return it to the freezer until completely frozen, then serve.

Kulfi

This favourite Indian ice cream is traditionally made by carefully boiling milk until it has reduced to about one-third of its original quantity. Although you can save time by using condensed milk, nothing beats the luscious result achieved by using the authentic method. When they are available, rose petals are a stylish decoration in addition to the pistachio nuts.

SERVES FOUR

1.5 litres/2¹/₂ pints/6¹/₄ cups full-fat (whole) milk

3 cardamom pods

25g/1oz/2 tbsp caster (superfine) sugar

50g/2oz/¹/₂ cup pistachio nuts, skinned

1 Pour the milk into a large, heavy pan. Bring to the boil, reduce the heat and simmer gently for 1 hour, stirring occasionally.

2 Put the cardamom pods in a mortar and crush them with a pestle. Add the pods and the seeds to the milk and continue to simmer, stirring frequently, for 1–1¹/₂ hours, or until the milk has reduced to about 475ml/16fl oz/2 cups. Strain the milk into a jug (pitcher), stir in the sugar and leave to cool.

3 Grind half the pistachios in a blender or nut grinder. Cut the remaining pistachios into thin slivers and set them aside for decoration. Stir the ground nuts into the milk mixture.

4 Pour the milk and pistachio mixture into four kulfi or lolly (popsicle) moulds. Freeze the mixture overnight or until firm.

5 To unmould the kulfi, half fill a plastic container or bowl with very hot water, stand the moulds in the water and count to ten. Immediately lift out the moulds and invert them on a baking sheet. Transfer the ice creams to individual plates and sprinkle sliced pistachios over the top.

Coconut Ice

The creamy taste and texture of this ice cream comes from the natural fat content of coconut as the mixture contains neither cream nor egg and is very refreshing. The lime adds a delicious tangy flavour as well as pretty green specks to the finished ice. Decorate with toasted coconut shavings or toasted desiccated (dry unsweetened shredded) coconut (this browns very quickly, so watch it constantly).

SERVES FOUR TO SIX

**115g/4oz/generous
¹/₄ cup caster
(superfine) sugar**

2 limes

**400ml/14fl oz can
coconut milk**

**toasted coconut
shavings, to
decorate (optional)**

COOK'S TIP
To make toasted coconut shavings, rinse the flesh from a coconut under cold water. Shave slices using a vegetable peeler, then toast under a moderate grill (broiler) until they are curled and the edges have turned golden.

1 Pour 150ml/¼ pint/²/₃ cup water in a small pan. Tip in the caster sugar and bring to the boil, stirring constantly until the sugar has completely dissolved. Remove the pan from the heat and leave the syrup to cool, then chill well.

2 Grate the rind from the limes finely, taking care to avoid the bitter pith. Squeeze out their juice and add to the pan of syrup with the rind. Add the coconut milk.

3 Pour the mixture into a freezerproof container and freeze for 5–6 hours, or until firm. Beat twice with a fork or electric whisk, or process in a food processor to break up the crystals. Scoop into dishes and decorate with toasted coconut shavings, if you like.

Gingered Semi-freddo

This Italian ice cream is rather like the original soft scoop ice cream. Made with a boiled sugar syrup rather than a traditional egg custard, and generously speckled with chopped stem ginger, this delicious ice cream will stay soft when frozen. For a really impressive dinner party dessert, serve the semi-freddo in plain (semisweet) chocolate cases.

SERVES SIX

1 Mix the sugar and 120ml/4fl oz/½ cup cold water in a pan and heat gently, stirring occasionally, until the sugar has dissolved.

2 Increase the heat and boil for 4–5 minutes, without stirring, until the syrup registers 119°C/238°F on a sugar thermometer. Alternatively, test by dropping a little of the syrup into a cup of cold water. Pour the water away and you should be able to mould the syrup into a small ball.

3 Put the egg yolks in a large heatproof bowl and whisk until frothy. Place the bowl over a pan of simmering water and whisk in the sugar syrup. Continue whisking until the mixture is very thick. Remove from the heat and whisk until cool.

4 Whip the cream and lightly fold it into the egg yolk mixture with the chopped stem ginger. Pour into a freezerproof container and freeze for 1 hour.

5 Stir the semi-freddo to bring any ginger that has sunk to the base of the container to the top, then return it to the freezer for 5–6 hours, until firm. Scoop into dishes or chocolate cases (*see* Cook's Tip). Decorate with slices of ginger and serve.

115g/4oz/generous
¹/₂ cup caster
(superfine) sugar

4 egg yolks

300ml/¹/₂ pint/1¹/₄
cups double (heavy)
cream

115g/4oz/²/₃ cup
drained stem
(preserved) ginger,
finely chopped, plus
extra slices, to decorate

COOK'S TIP
To make the cases, pour melted chocolate over squares of baking parchment and drape them over upturned glasses. Peel off the baking parchment when set.

Miniature Choc-ices

These little chocolate-coated ice creams make a fun alternative to the more familiar after-dinner chocolates, especially on hot summer evenings – although they need to be eaten quickly. Serve the choc-ices in fluted paper sweet (candy) cases. If you can, buy gold cases as they will contrast very prettily with the dark chocolate coating.

MAKES ABOUT TWENTY-FIVE

**750ml/1¹/₄ pints/
3 cups vanilla,
chocolate or
coffee ice cream**

**200g/7oz plain
(semisweet) chocolate,
broken into pieces**

**25g/1oz milk
chocolate, broken
into pieces**

**25g/1oz/¹/₄ cup
chopped hazelnuts,
lightly toasted**

1 Put a large baking sheet in the freezer for 10 minutes. Using a melon baller, scoop balls of ice cream and place these on the baking sheet. Freeze for at least 1 hour or until firm.

2 Line a second baking sheet with baking parchment and place in the freezer for 15 minutes. Melt the plain chocolate in a heatproof bowl set over a pan of gently simmering water. Melt the milk chocolate in a separate bowl.

3 Using a metal spatula, transfer the ice cream scoops to the parchment-lined sheet. Spoon a little plain chocolate over one scoop so that most of it is coated.

4 Sprinkle immediately with chopped nuts, before the chocolate sets. Coat half the remaining scoops in the same way, sprinkling each one with nuts before the chocolate sets. Spoon the remaining plain chocolate over all the remaining scoops.

5 Using a teaspoon, drizzle the milk chocolate over the choc-ices that are not topped with nuts. Freeze again until ready to serve.

White Chocolate Castles

With a little ingenuity, good-quality bought ice cream can masquerade as a culinary masterpiece – it's down to perfect presentation. For a professional finish, dust the castles and plates with a hint of cocoa powder or icing (confectioners') sugar.

SERVES SIX

225g/8oz white chocolate, broken into pieces

250ml/8fl oz/1 cup white chocolate ice cream

250ml/8fl oz/1 cup dark chocolate ice cream

115g/4oz/1 cup berries

1 Put the white chocolate in a heatproof bowl, set it over a pan of gently simmering water and leave until melted. Line a baking sheet with greaseproof (waxed) paper. Cut out six 30 x 13cm/12 x 5in strips of greaseproof paper, then fold each in half lengthways.

2 Stand a 7.5cm/3in pastry (cookie) cutter on the baking sheet. Roll one strip of paper into a circle and fit inside the cutter with the folded edge on the base paper. Stick the edges together with tape.

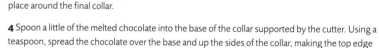

3 Remove the cutter and shape more paper collars in the same way, leaving the pastry cutter in place around the final collar.

4 Spoon a little of the melted chocolate into the base of the collar supported by the cutter. Using a teaspoon, spread the chocolate over the base and up the sides of the collar, making the top edge uneven. Carefully lift away the cutter.

5 Make five more chocolate cases in the same way, using the cutter for extra support each time. Leave the cases in a cool place or in the refrigerator to set.

6 Carefully peel away the paper from the sides of the chocolate cases, then lift the cases off the base. Transfer to serving plates.

7 Using a large melon baller or teaspoon, scoop the white and dark chocolate ice creams into the cases and decorate with berries. Serve immediately.

Caramel and Pecan Terrine

Frozen or long-life cream is a useful ingredient for making impressive desserts without having a mega shopping trip. Caramel and nuts transform cream to parfait in this recipe. Take care that the syrup does not become too dark, or the ice cream will taste bitter.

SERVES SIX

115g/4oz/generous ¹/₂ cup sugar

450ml/³/₄ pint/scant 2 cups double (heavy) cream

30ml/2 tbsp icing (confectioners') sugar

75g/3oz/³/₄ cup pecan nuts, toasted

COOK'S TIP

Watch the caramel syrup closely after removing it from the heat. If it starts to turn too dark, dip the base of the pan in cold water. If the syrup remains very pale, return the pan to the heat and cook it for a little longer.

1 Heat the sugar and 75ml/5 tbsp water in a small, heavy pan until the sugar dissolves. Boil rapidly until the sugar has turned pale golden. Remove the pan from the heat and leave to stand until the syrup turns a rich brown colour.

2 Pour 90ml/6 tbsp of the cream over the caramel. Heat to make a smooth sauce. Leave to cool.

3 Rinse a 450g/1lb loaf tin (pan), then line the base and sides with clear film (plastic wrap). Whip a further 150ml/¼ pint/²/₃cup of the cream with the icing sugar until it forms soft peaks. Whip the remaining cream separately and stir in the caramel sauce and the toasted pecan nuts.

4 Spoon one-third of the caramel cream into the prepared tin and spread with half the plain whipped cream. Spread half of the remaining caramel cream over the top, then top with the last of the plain cream. Finally, add the remaining caramel cream and level the surface. Freeze for 6 hours.

5 To serve, dip the tin in very hot water for 2 seconds, invert it on to a serving plate and peel away the film. Serve sliced.

White Chocolate and Brownie Torte

This delicious dessert is easy to make and guaranteed to appeal to just about everyone. If you can't buy good quality brownies, use a moist chocolate sponge or make your own. For extra decoration, put a few fresh summer berries such as strawberries or raspberries around the edge or on the centre of the torte.

SERVES TEN

300g/11oz white chocolate, broken into pieces

600ml/1 pint/2¹/₂ cups double (heavy) cream

250g/9oz rich chocolate brownies

(unsweetened) cocoa powder, for dusting

1 Dampen the sides of a 20cm/8in springform tin (pan) and line with a strip of greaseproof (waxed) paper. Put the chocolate in a small pan. Add 150ml/¼ pint/²/₃ cup of the cream and heat very gently until the chocolate has melted. Stir until smooth, then pour into a bowl and leave to cool.

2 Break the chocolate brownies into chunky pieces and sprinkle these over the base of the tin. Pack them down lightly to make a fairly dense base.

3 Whip the remaining cream until it forms peaks, then fold in the white chocolate mixture. Spoon into the tin to cover the layer of brownies, then tap the tin gently on the work surface to level the chocolate mixture. Cover and freeze overnight.

4 Transfer the torte to the refrigerator about 45 minutes before serving to soften slightly. Decorate with a light dusting of cocoa powder just before serving.

Soft Fruit and Meringue Gâteau

This recipe takes only five minutes to prepare but looks and tastes as though a lot of preparation went into it. The trick is to use really good vanilla ice cream. For a dinner party, slice the gâteau and place on individual plates, spoon ready-made strawberry or raspberry coulis around each slice and garnish with whole strawberries or raspberries.

SERVES SIX

1 Dampen a 900g/2lb loaf tin (pan) and line it with clear film (plastic wrap). If using strawberries, chop them into small pieces. Put them in a bowl and add the raspberries or redcurrants and icing sugar. Toss until the fruit is beginning to break up, but do not let it become mushy.

2 Put the ice cream in a bowl and break it up with a fork. Crumble the meringues into the bowl and add the soft fruit mixture.

3 Fold all the ingredients together until evenly combined and lightly marbled. Pack into the prepared tin and press down gently to level. Cover and freeze overnight. To serve, invert on to a plate, peel away the clear film and cut into slices.

400g/14oz/3¹/₂ cups mixed small strawberries, raspberries and/ or redcurrants

30ml/2 tbsp icing (confectioners') sugar

750ml/1¹/₄ pints/ 3 cups vanilla ice cream

6 meringue nests or 115g/4oz meringue

Cookies and Sweet Treats

HOME-BAKED COOKIES AND SWEET SNACKS ARE THE
ULTIMATE INDULGENCE BUT ARE VIEWED BY MANY AS
TAKING TOO MUCH TIME AND EFFORT. HOWEVER, WITH
JUST A FEW BASIC INGREDIENTS, YOU CAN WHIP UP
FABULOUS CAKES, COOKIES AND CANDIES IN MOMENTS.
TRY DELICIOUS TREATS SUCH AS CHOCOLATE BROWNIES,
CHEWY FLAPJACKS OR QUICK AND EASY TEABREAD.

All Butter Cookies

Crisp, buttery cookies are perfect with strawberries and cream or any creamy dessert or fruit compote. These biscuits or cookies are known as refrigerator biscuits as the mixture is chilled until it is firm enough to cut neatly into thin biscuits. The dough can be frozen and when thawed enough to slice, can be freshly baked, but do allow a little extra cooking time.

MAKES TWENTY-EIGHT TO THIRTY

1 Put the flour in a food processor. Add the butter and process until the mixture resembles coarse breadcrumbs. Add the icing sugar and vanilla, and process until the mixture comes together to form a dough. Knead lightly and shape into a thick sausage, 30cm/12in long and 5cm/2in in diameter. Wrap and chill for at least 1 hour, until firm.

2 Preheat the oven to 200°C/400°F/Gas 6. Grease two baking sheets. Using a sharp knife, cut 5mm/¼in thick slices from the dough and space them slightly apart on the baking sheet.

3 Bake for 8–10 minutes, alternating the position of the baking sheets in the oven halfway through cooking, if necessary, until the biscuits are cooked evenly and have just turned pale golden around the edges. Leave for 5 minutes, then transfer to a wire rack to cool. Serve dusted with icing sugar.

275g/10oz/2½ cups
plain (all-purpose) flour

90g/3½oz/scant
1 cup icing
(confectioners') sugar,
plus extra for dusting

10ml/2 tsp vanilla
essence (extract)

FROM THE
STORECUPBOARD

200g/7oz/scant
1 cup unsalted
(sweet) butter

Almond Cookies

These short, light cookies have a melt-in-the-mouth texture. Their simplicity means they are endlessly versatile – irresistible with tea or coffee and stylish with special desserts.

MAKES ABOUT TWENTY-FOUR

115g/4oz/1 cup plain (all-purpose) flour

175g/6oz/1¹/₂ cups icing (confectioners') sugar, plus extra for dusting

50g/2oz/¹/₂ cup chopped almonds, plus halved almonds to decorate

FROM THE STORECUPBOARD

115g/4oz/¹/₂ cup unsalted (sweet) butter, softened

COOK'S TIP *Use different-shaped cutters to make these cookies look even more interesting. Hearts, stars and crescents are three shapes that you might like to try.*

1 Preheat the oven to 180°C/350°F/Gas 4. Combine the flour, sugar and chopped almonds in a bowl.

2 Put the softened unsalted butter in the centre of the flour and nut mixture and use a blunt knife or your fingertips to draw the dry ingredients into the butter until a dough is formed. Shape the dough into a ball.

3 Place the dough on a lightly floured surface and roll it out to a thickness of about 3mm/¹/₈in. Using a 7.5cm/3in cookie cutter, cut out about 24 rounds, re-rolling the dough as necessary. Place the cookie rounds on baking sheets, leaving a little space between them. Bake the cookies for about 25 minutes, until pale golden.

4 Leave the cookies on the baking sheet for 10 minutes, then transfer to wire racks to cool. Dust thickly with sifted icing sugar before serving, decorated with halved almonds.

Chewy Flapjacks

Flapjacks are popular with adults and children alike and they are so quick and easy to make. For alternative versions of the basic recipe, stir in 50g/2oz/¼ cup finely chopped ready-to-eat dried apricots or sultanas (golden raisins). To make a really decadent treat, you can dip the cooled flapjack fingers into melted chocolate, to half cover.

MAKES TWELVE

1 Preheat the oven to 180°C/350°F/Gas 4. Line the base and sides of a 20cm/8in square cake tin (pan) with baking parchment.

2 Mix the butter, sugar and syrup in a pan and heat gently until the butter has melted. Add the oats and stir until all the ingredients are combined. Turn the mixture into the tin and level the surface.

3 Bake the flapjacks for 15–20 minutes, until just beginning to turn golden. Leave to cool slightly, then cut into fingers and remove from the tin. Store in an airtight container.

50g/2oz/¹/₄ cup caster (superfine) sugar

150g/5oz/generous ¹/₃ cup golden (light corn) syrup

250g/9oz/2¾ cups rolled oats

FROM THE STORECUPBOARD

175g/6oz/³/₄ cup unsalted (sweet) butter

Creamed Coconut Macaroons

Finely grated creamed coconut gives these soft-centred cookies a rich creaminess. Cooking the gooey mixture on baking parchment makes sure that the cookies are easily removed from the baking sheet. For a tangy flavour, add the grated rind of one lime to the mixture in step 2. The cooked macaroons can be stored in an airtight container for up to one week.

MAKES SIXTEEN TO EIGHTEEN

1 Preheat the oven to 180°C/350°F/Gas 4. Line a large baking sheet with baking parchment. Finely grate the creamed coconut.

2 Use an electric beater to whisk the egg whites in a large bowl until stiff. Whisk in the sugar, a little at a time, to make a stiff and glossy meringue. Fold in the grated creamed and desiccated coconut, using a large, metal spoon.

3 Place dessertspoonfuls of the mixture, spaced slightly apart, on the baking sheet. Bake for 15–20 minutes, until slightly risen and golden brown. Leave to cool on the parchment, then transfer to an airtight container.

50g/2oz creamed coconut, chilled

2 large (US extra large) egg whites

90g/3¹/₂oz/¹/₂ cup caster (superfine) sugar

75g/3oz/1 cup desiccated (dry unsweetened shredded) coconut

Orange and Pecan Scones

Serve these nutty orange scones with satiny orange or lemon curd or, for a simple, unsweetened snack, fresh and warm with unsalted (sweet) butter. Scones are best served on the day they are made, or they can be frozen. To freeze, place in an airtight container. To thaw, remove from the freezer and thaw at room temperature for an hour.

MAKES TEN

1 Preheat the oven to 220°C/425°F/Gas 7. Grease a baking sheet. Put the flour in a food processor with a pinch of salt and add the butter. Process the mixture until it resembles coarse breadcrumbs.

2 Add the orange rind. Reserve 30ml/2 tbsp of the orange juice and make the remainder up to 120ml/4fl oz/½ cup with water. Add the nuts and the juice mixture to the processor, process very briefly to a firm dough, adding a little water if the dough feels dry.

3 Turn the dough out on to a floured surface and roll out to 2cm/¾ in thick. Cut out scones using a round cutter and transfer them to the baking sheet. Re-roll the trimmings and cut more scones. Brush the scones with the reserved juice and bake for 15–20 minutes. Transfer to a wire rack to cool.

225g/8oz/2 cups self-raising (self-rising) flour

grated rind and juice of 1 orange

115g/4oz/1 cup pecan nuts, coarsely chopped

FROM THE STORECUPBOARD

50g/2oz/¹/₄ cup unsalted (sweet) butter, chilled and diced

salt

Quick and Easy Teabread

This succulent, fruity teabread can be served just as it is, or spread with a little butter. The loaf can be stored, tightly wrapped in foil or in an airtight container, for up to five days. A great way to get children to eat some fruit, this teabread is ideal for packed lunches, picnics, or simply served with a cup of tea for afternoon tea.

SERVES EIGHT

1 Put the fruit in a bowl. Add 150ml/¼ pint/⅔ cup boiling water and leave to stand for 30 minutes.

2 Preheat the oven to 180°C/350°F/Gas 4. Grease and line the base and long sides of a 450g/1lb loaf tin (pan).

3 Beat the main quantity of sugar and the egg into the fruit. Sift the flour into the bowl and stir until combined. Turn into the prepared tin and level the surface. Sprinkle with the remaining sugar.

4 Bake the teabread for about 50 minutes, until risen and firm to the touch. When the bread is cooked, a skewer inserted into the centre will come out without any sticky mixture on it. Leave the loaf in the tin for 10 minutes before turning out on to a wire rack to cool.

350g/12oz/2 cups
luxury mixed
dried fruit

75g/3oz/scant ¹/₃ cup
demerara (raw) sugar,
plus 15ml/1 tbsp

1 large (US extra
large) egg

175g/6oz/1¹/₂ cups
self-raising
(self-rising) flour

Cinnamon Pinwheels

These impressive sweet pastries go well with tea or coffee or as an accompaniment to ice cream and creamy desserts. If you find they turn soft during storage, re-crisp them briefly in the oven. Cinnamon is widely used in both sweet and savoury cooking: here ground cinnamon is used but it is also available as woody sticks. It has a delicious fragrant aroma and gives these simple-to-make pinwheels a warm spicy flavour.

MAKES TWENTY TO TWENTY-FOUR

50g/2oz/¹⁄₄ cup caster (superfine) sugar, plus a little extra for sprinkling

10ml/2 tsp ground cinnamon

250g/9oz puff pastry

beaten egg, to glaze

1 Preheat the oven to 220°C/425°F/Gas 7. Grease a large baking sheet. Mix the sugar with the cinnamon in a small bowl.

2 Roll out the pastry on a lightly floured surface to a 20cm/8in square and sprinkle with half the sugar mixture. Roll out the pastry to a 25cm/10in square so that the sugar is pressed into it.

3 Brush with the beaten egg and then sprinkle with the remaining sugar mixture. Loosely roll up the pastry into a log, brushing the end of the pastry with a little more egg to secure the edge in place.

4 Using a sharp knife, cut the log into thin slices and transfer them to the prepared baking sheet. Bake for 10 minutes, until golden and crisp. Sprinkle with more sugar and transfer to a wire rack to cool.

Almond Cigars

These simple, Moroccan-inspired pastries can be prepared in minutes. They are perfect served with strong black coffee or black tea, or as an after-dinner treat. They are also delicious served with traditional sweet Moroccan mint tea. To serve, the pastries look very pretty sprinkled with a little icing (confectioners') sugar as a simple finishing touch.

MAKES EIGHT TO TWELVE

250g/9oz marzipan

1 egg, lightly beaten

8–12 sheets filo pastry

FROM THE STORECUPBOARD

melted butter, for brushing

1 Knead the marzipan until soft and pliable, then put it in a mixing bowl and mix in the lightly beaten egg. Chill in the refrigerator for 1–2 hours.

2 Preheat the oven to 190°C/375°F/Gas 5. Lightly grease a baking sheet. Place a sheet of filo pastry on a piece of greaseproof (waxed) paper, keeping the remaining pastry covered with a damp cloth, and brush with the melted butter.

3 Shape 30–45ml/2–3 tbsp of the almond paste into a cylinder and place at one end of the pastry. Fold the pastry over to enclose the ends of the paste, then roll up to form a cigar shape. Place on the baking sheet and make 7–11 more cigars in the same way.

4 Bake the pastries in the preheated oven for about 15 minutes, or until golden brown in colour. Transfer to a wire rack to cool before serving.

Golden Ginger Macaroons

Macaroons are classic no-fuss biscuits – easy to whisk up in minutes from the minimum ingredients and always acceptable. A hint of ginger makes this recipe that bit different. For a darker colour and slightly richer flavour, use soft dark brown sugar instead. Bake these biscuits on non-stick baking trays or on a baking tray lined with baking parchment to prevent them from sticking.

MAKES EIGHTEEN TO TWENTY

1 Preheat the oven to 180°C/350°F/Gas 4. In a large, grease-free bowl, whisk the egg white until stiff and standing in peaks, but not dry and crumbly, then whisk in the brown sugar.

2 Sprinkle the ground almonds and ginger over the whisked egg white and gently fold them together.

3 Using two teaspoons, place spoonfuls of the mixture on baking trays, leaving plenty of space between each. Bake for about 20 minutes, until pale golden brown and just turning crisp.

4 Leave to cool slightly on the baking trays before transferring to a wire rack to cool completely.

1 egg white

75g/3oz/scant ¹/₂ cup soft light brown sugar

115g/4oz/1 cup ground almonds

5ml/1 tsp ground ginger

VARIATION Other ground nuts, such as hazelnuts or walnuts, are good alternatives to the almonds. Ground cinnamon or mixed (apple pie) spice can be used instead of the ginger, if liked.

Nutty Nougat

Nougat is an almost magical sweetmeat that emerges from honey-flavoured meringue made with boiled syrup. Since any other nuts or candied fruits can be used instead of almonds, as long as you have eggs, sugar and honey, you have the potential for making an impromptu gift or dinner-party treat.

MAKES ABOUT 500G/1¼ LB

1 Line a 17.5cm/7in square cake tin (pan) with rice paper. Place the sugar, honey or syrup and 60ml/4 tbsp water in a large, heavy pan and heat gently, stirring frequently, until the sugar has completely dissolved.

2 Bring the syrup to the boil and boil gently to the soft crack stage (when the syrup dropped into cold water separates into hard but not brittle threads) or 151°C/304°F on a sugar thermometer.

3 Meanwhile, whisk the egg white until very stiff, but not crumbly, then slowly drizzle in the syrup while whisking constantly.

4 Quickly stir in the nuts and pour the mixture into the prepared tin. Leave to cool but, before the nougat becomes too hard, cut it into squares. Store in an airtight container.

225g/8oz/generous 1 cup granulated sugar

225g/8oz/1 cup clear honey or golden (light corn) syrup

1 large (US extra large) egg white

115g/4oz/1 cup flaked (sliced) almonds or chopped pistachio nuts, roasted

Rich Chocolate Brownies

These brownies are packed with both milk and plain chocolate instead of adding sugar to the mixture. Serve them in small squares as they are very rich. When buying plain chocolate, bear in mind that the higher the percentage of cocoa solids, the higher the quality of the chocolate, and the less sugar it contains. The best quality has 70 per cent cocoa solids.

MAKES SIXTEEN

1 Preheat the oven to 180°C/350°F/Gas 4. Line the base and sides of a 20cm/8in square cake tin (pan) with baking parchment.

2 Break the plain chocolate and 90g/3½oz of the milk chocolate into pieces and put in a heatproof bowl with the butter. Melt over a pan of barely simmering water, stirring frequently.

3 Chop the remaining milk chocolate into chunky pieces. Stir the flour and eggs into the melted chocolate until combined. Stir in half the chopped milk chocolate and turn the mixture into the prepared tin, spreading it into the corners. Sprinkle with the remaining chopped chocolate.

4 Bake the brownies for 30–35 minutes, until risen and just firm to the touch. Leave to cool in the tin, then cut the mixture into squares. Store the brownies in an airtight container.

300g/11oz each plain (semisweet) and milk chocolate

75g/3oz/²/₃ cup self-raising (self-rising) flour

3 large (US extra large) eggs

FROM THE STORECUPBOARD

175g/6oz/³/₄ cup unsalted (sweet) butter

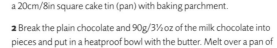

Rich Chocolate Biscuit Slice

This dark chocolate refrigerator cake is packed with crisp biscuit pieces and chunks of white chocolate for colour and flavour contrast. The slice is perfect served with strong coffee, either as a teatime treat or in place of dessert. Once set, cut the cake into slices and store the slices in an airtight container in the refrigerator until ready to serve.

SERVES EIGHT TO TEN

0275g/10oz fruit and nut plain (semisweet) chocolate

90g/3½oz digestive biscuits (graham crackers)

90g/3½oz white chocolate

FROM THE STORECUPBOARD

130g/4½oz/9 tbsp unsalted (sweet) butter

1 Grease and line the base and sides of a 450g/1lb loaf tin (pan) with baking parchment. Break the fruit and nut chocolate into pieces and place in a heatproof bowl with the butter. Place the bowl over a pan of barely simmering water and stir the chocolate gently until it is melted and smooth. Remove the bowl from the pan and leave to cool for 20 minutes.

2 Break the biscuits into small pieces. Finely chop the white chocolate. Stir the biscuits and white chocolate into the melted mixture until evenly combined. Turn the mixture into the prepared tin and pack down gently. Chill for about 2 hours, or until set. Cut the mixture into slices.

Chocolate and Prune Refrigerator Bars

Wickedly self-indulgent and very easy to make, these fruity chocolate bars will keep for 2–3 days in the refrigerator – if they don't all get eaten as soon as they are ready.

MAKES TWELVE BARS

250g/9oz good quality milk chocolate

115g/4oz digestive biscuits (graham crackers)

115g/4oz/¹/₂ cup ready-to-eat prunes

FROM THE STORECUPBOARD

50g/2oz/¹/₄ cup unsalted (sweet) butter

1 Break the chocolate into small pieces and place in a heatproof bowl. Add the butter and melt in the microwave on high for 1–2 minutes. Stir to mix and set aside. (Alternatively, place the bowl over a pan of gently simmering water and leave until melted, stirring frequently.)

2 Put the biscuits in a plastic bag and seal, then bash into small pieces with a rolling pin. Roughly chop the prunes and stir into the melted chocolate with the biscuits.

3 Spoon the chocolate and prune mixture into a 20cm/8in square cake pan and chill for 1–2 hours until set. Remove the cake from the refrigerator and, using a sharp knife, cut into 12 bars.

Blueberry Cake

Cake mixes make life very easy and are available in most supermarkets. Dust with icing (confectioners') sugar and serve for a simple dessert.

SERVES SIX TO EIGHT

220g/8oz packet sponge cake mix

1 egg, if needed

115g/4oz/1 cup blueberries

1 Preheat the oven to 190°C/375°F/Gas 5. Grease a 20cm/8in cake tin (pan). Make up the sponge cake mix according to the instructions on the packet, using the egg if required. Spoon the mixture into the prepared cake tin.

2 Bake the cake according to the instructions on the packet. Ten minutes before the end of the cooking time, sprinkle the blueberries over the top of the cake. (Work quickly so that the cake is out of the oven for as short a time as possible, otherwise it may sink in the middle.)

3 Leave the cake to cool in the tin for 2–3 minutes, then carefully remove from the tin and transfer to a wire rack. Leave to cool completely before serving.

Stuffed Prunes

Prunes and plain chocolate are delectable partners, especially when the dried fruit is soaked in Armagnac. Serve these sophisticated sweetmeats dusted with cocoa powder as a dinner-party treat with coffee.

MAKES ABOUT THIRTY

1 Put the prunes in a bowl and pour the Armagnac over. Stir, then cover with clear film (plastic wrap) and set aside for 2 hours, or until the prunes have absorbed the liquid.

2 Make a slit along each prune to remove the stone (pit), making a hollow for the filling, but leaving the fruit intact.

3 Heat the cream in a pan almost to boiling point. Put 115g/4oz of the chocolate in a bowl and pour over the hot cream.

4 Stir until the chocolate has melted and the mixture is smooth. Leave to cool, until it has the consistency of softened butter.

5 Fill a piping (pastry) bag with a small plain nozzle with the chocolate mixture. Pipe into the cavities of the prunes. Chill for about 20 minutes.

6 Melt the remaining chocolate in a heatproof bowl set over a pan of barely simmering water. Using a fork, dip the prunes, one at a time, into the chocolate to coat them generously. Place on baking parchment to set.

225g/8oz/
1 cup unpitted prunes

50ml/2fl oz/
¹⁄₄ cup Armagnac

150ml/¹⁄₂ pint/²⁄₃ cup
double (heavy) cream

350g/12oz plain
(semisweet) chocolate,
broken into squares

COOK'S TIP
Armagnac is a type of French brandy produced in the Gascogne region in the south-west of the country. It has a pale colour and a biscuity aroma. Other types of brandy can be used in this recipe.

Chocolate Truffles

Luxurious truffles are expensive to buy but very easy and fun to make. These rich melt-in-the-mouth treats are flavoured with coffee liqueur, but you could use whisky or brandy instead. The mixture can be rolled in cocoa powder or icing (confectioners') sugar instead of being dipped in melted chocolate. Remember to store the fresh-cream truffles in the refrigerator.

MAKES TWENTY-FOUR

1 Melt 225g/8oz of the plain chocolate in a heatproof bowl set over a pan of barely simmering water. Stir in the cream and liqueur, then chill the mixture for 4 hours, until firm.

2 Divide the mixture into 24 equal pieces and quickly roll each into a ball. Chill for about 1 hour, or until the truffles are firm again.

3 Melt the remaining plain, white or milk chocolate in separate small bowls. Using two forks, carefully dip eight of the truffles, one at a time, into the melted plain chocolate.

4 Repeat to cover the remaining 16 truffles with the melted white or milk chocolate. Place the truffles on a board or tray, covered with wax paper or foil. Leave to set before placing in individual mini paper cases or transferring to a serving dish.

350g/12oz plain (semisweet) chocolate

75ml/5 tbsp double (heavy) cream

30ml/2 tbsp coffee liqueur, such as Tia Maria, Kahlúa or Toussaint

225g/8oz good quality white or milk dessert chocolate

EXTRAS

Ring the changes by adding one of the following to the mixture:

GINGER
Stir in 40g/1½ oz/¼ cup finely chopped crystallized ginger.

CANDIED FRUIT
Stir in 50g/2oz/⅓ cup finely chopped candied fruit, such as pineapple and orange.

PISTACHIOS
Stir in 25g/1oz/¼ cup chopped skinned pistachio nuts.

HAZELNUTS
Roll each ball of chilled truffle mixture around a whole skinned hazelnut.

Chocolate Petit Four Cookies

Make these dainty cookies as stylish after-dinner snacks. If you do not have any amaretto liqueur, they will work well without it. Alternatively, you can substitute the same quantity of brandy or rum.

SERVES EIGHT

1 Preheat the oven according to the instructions on the cookie dough packet. Roll out the cookie dough on a floured surface to 1cm/^{1}/$_2$in thick. Using a 2.5cm/1in cutter, stamp out as many rounds from the dough as possible and transfer them to a lightly greased baking sheet. Bake for about 8 minutes, or until cooked through. Transfer to a wire rack to cool completely.

2 To make the filling, break the chocolate into small pieces and place in a heatproof bowl with the butter and Amaretto liqueur. Sit the bowl over a pan of gently simmering water and stir occasionally, until the chocolate has melted. Remove from the heat and set aside to cool.

3 Spread a small amount of the filling on the flat bottom of one of the cookies and sandwich together with another. Repeat until all the biscuits have been used.

350g/12oz carton chocolate chip cookie dough

115g/4oz plain (semisweet) chocolate

30ml/2 tbsp Amaretto di Sarone liqueur

FROM THE STORECUPBOARD

50g/2oz/^{1}/$_4$ cup butter

Praline Chocolate Bites

These delicate, mouthwatering little bites never fail to impress guests, but are quite simple to make. They are perfect for serving with coffee after dinner. Dust with icing sugar for a decorative finish.

SERVES FOUR

1 Put the sugar in a heavy pan with 90ml/6 tbsp water. Stir over a gentle heat until the sugar has dissolved. Bring the syrup to the boil and cook for about 5 minutes, without stirring, until the mixture is golden and caramelized.

2 Remove the pan from the heat and tip in the almonds, swirling the pan to immerse them in the caramel. Tip the mixture on to a lightly oiled baking sheet and set aside for 10–15 minutes, or until hardened. Meanwhile, melt the chocolate in a heatproof bowl set over a pan of simmering water.

3 Cover the hardened caramel mixture with clear film (plastic wrap) and break up with a rolling pin then place in a food processor. Process until finely chopped, then stir into the melted chocolate. Chill until set enough to roll into balls. Roll the mixture into 16 balls and place in mini paper cases to serve.

115g/4oz/1 cup caster (superfine) sugar

115g/4oz/^{2}/$_3$ cup whole blanched almonds

200g/7oz plain (semisweet) chocolate

COOK'S TIP The mixture for these bites can be made ahead and stored in the freezer for up to 2 weeks. To use, thaw the mixture at room temperature until soft enough to roll into balls.

Breads

THERE ARE FEW FOODS SO DELICIOUS AND COMFORTING
AS FRESHLY BAKED BREAD. THREE BASIC INGREDIENTS –
FLOUR, SALT AND YEAST – MIXED WITH WATER ARE ALL
THAT IS NEEDED TO MAKE A BASIC LOAF, WHILE THE
ADDITION OF A FOURTH INGREDIENT SUCH AS HERBS,
SUN-DRIED TOMATOES, OLIVE OIL OR MILK CAN
CREATE WONDERFUL, ENTICING VARIATIONS.

Scottish Morning Rolls

These soft, spongy bread rolls are irresistible while still warm and aromatic. Made with milk, rather than the more usual water, they have a rich flavour. In Scotland they are a firm favourite for breakfast with fried eggs and bacon. To speed up the rising time, place the rolls in the airing cupboard or on the top of the preheated oven.

MAKES TEN ROLLS

1 Grease two baking sheets. Sift the flour and salt together into a large bowl and make a well in the centre. Mix the yeast with the milk, then mix in 150ml/¼ pint/⅔ cup lukewarm water. Add to the centre of the flour and mix together to form a soft dough.

2 Knead the dough lightly in the bowl, then cover with lightly oiled clear film (plastic wrap) and leave to rise in a warm place for 1 hour, or until doubled in bulk. Turn the dough out on to a lightly floured surface and knock back (punch down).

3 Divide the dough into ten equal pieces. Knead lightly and, using a rolling pin, shape each piece of dough into a flat oval 10 x 7.5cm/ 4 x 3in, or a flat round 9cm/3½in.

4 Transfer to the prepared baking sheets, spaced well apart, and cover the rolls with oiled clear film. Leave to rise, in a warm place, for about 30 minutes.

5 Meanwhile, preheat the oven to 200°C/400°F/Gas 6. Press each roll in the centre with the three middle fingers to equalize the air bubbles and to help prevent blistering. Brush with milk and dust with flour. Bake for 15–20 minutes, or until lightly browned. Dust with more flour and cool slightly on a wire rack. Serve warm.

450g/1lb/4 cups unbleached strong white bread flour, plus extra for dusting

20g/³/₄oz fresh yeast

150ml/¹/₄ pint/²/₃ cup lukewarm milk, plus extra for glazing

FROM THE STORECUPBOARD

10ml/2 tsp salt

Panini all'Olio

Italian-style dough enriched and flavoured with extra virgin olive oil is versatile for making decorative rolls. Children will love helping to make and shape these rolls – they can try making twists, fingers or artichoke-shapes, or just about any shape they want. The rolls are sure to disappear as soon as they are cool enough to eat.

MAKES SIXTEEN ROLLS

450g/1lb/4 cups unbleached strong white bread flour

15g/½oz fresh yeast

60ml/4 tbsp extra virgin olive oil

FROM THE STORECUPBOARD

10ml/2 tsp salt

1 Lightly oil three baking sheets. Sift the flour and salt together in a large bowl and make a well in the centre. Measure 250ml/8fl oz/1 cup lukewarm water. Cream the yeast with half the water, then stir in the remainder. Add to the well with the oil and mix to a dough.

2 Turn the dough out on to a lightly floured surface and knead for 8–10 minutes, until smooth and elastic. Place in a lightly oiled bowl, cover with lightly oiled clear film (plastic wrap) and leave to rise in a warm place for about 1 hour, or until nearly doubled in bulk.

3 Turn the dough on to a lightly floured surface and knock back (punch down). Divide into 12 equal pieces and shape into rolls. To make twists, roll each piece of dough into a strip 30cm/12in long and 4cm/1½in wide. Twist each strip into a loose spiral and join the ends together to make a circle. Place on the baking sheets, spaced well apart. Brush lightly with olive oil, cover with lightly oiled clear film and leave to rise in a warm place for 20–30 minutes.

4 To make fingers, flatten each piece of dough into an oval and roll to about 23cm/9in long. Roll up from the wider end. Gently stretch the dough roll to 20–23cm/8–9in long. Cut in half. Place on the baking sheets, spaced well apart. Brush the dough with olive oil, cover with lightly oiled clear film and leave to rise in a warm place for 20–30 minutes.

5 To make artichoke-shapes, shape each piece of dough into a ball and space well apart on the baking sheets. Brush with oil, cover with lightly oiled clear film and leave to rise in a warm place for 20–30 minutes. Using scissors, snip 5mm/¼in deep cuts in a circle on the top of each ball, then make five larger horizontal cuts around the sides.

6 Preheat the oven to 200°C/400°F/Gas 6. Bake the rolls for 15 minutes.

French Baguette

Fine French flour is available from French delicatessens and superior supermarkets. If you cannot find any, try ordinary plain flour instead. Baguettes have a wide variety of uses: split horizontally and fill with meats, cheeses and salads; slice diagonally and toast the slices to serve with soup; or simply cut into chunks, spread with unsalted (sweet) butter and serve with French cheeses.

MAKES THREE LOAVES

500g/1¼lb/5 cups unbleached strong white bread flour

115g/4oz/1 cup fine French plain (all-purpose) flour

15g/½oz fresh yeast

FROM THE STORECUPBOARD

10ml/2 tsp salt

1 Sift the flours and salt into a bowl. Add the yeast to 550ml/18fl oz/2½ cups lukewarm water in another bowl and stir. Gradually beat in half the flour mixture to form a batter. Cover with clear film (plastic wrap) and leave for about 3 hours, or until nearly trebled in size.

2 Add the remaining flour a little at a time, beating with your hand. Turn out on to a lightly floured surface and knead for 8–10 minutes to form a moist dough. Place in a lightly oiled bowl, cover with lightly oiled clear film and leave to rise, in a warm place, for about 1 hour.

3 Knock back (punch down) the dough, turn out on to a floured surface and divide into three equal pieces. Shape each into a ball and then into a 15 x 7.5cm/6 x 3in rectangle. Fold the bottom third up lengthways and the top third down and press down. Seal the edges. Repeat two or three more times until each loaf is an oblong. Leave to rest in between folding for a few minutes.

4 Gently stretch each piece of dough into a 33–35cm/13–14in long loaf. Pleat a floured dishtowel on a baking sheet to make three moulds for the loaves. Place the loaves between the pleats, cover with lightly oiled clear film and leave to rise in a warm place for 45–60 minutes.

5 Preheat the oven to maximum, at least 230°C/450°F/Gas 8. Roll the loaves on to a baking sheet, spaced well apart. Slash the top of each loaf diagonally several times. Place at the top of the oven, spray the inside of the oven with water and bake for 20–25 minutes.

Rosemary Focaccia

If you do not need both loaves, freeze one for another time and warm it in the oven before serving. Sprinkle the loaves with finely chopped garlic, if you prefer.

MAKES TWO LOAVES

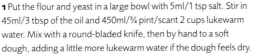

1 Put the flour and yeast in a large bowl with 5ml/1 tsp salt. Stir in 45ml/3 tbsp of the oil and 450ml/¾ pint/scant 2 cups lukewarm water. Mix with a round-bladed knife, then by hand to a soft dough, adding a little more lukewarm water if the dough feels dry.

2 Turn the dough out on to a lightly floured surface and knead for 10 minutes, until smooth and elastic. Put in a lightly oiled bowl and cover with oiled clear film (plastic wrap). Leave in a warm place for about 1 hour, until doubled in size.

3 Preheat the oven to 200°C/400°F/Gas 6. Turn out the dough on to a floured surface and cut in half. Roll out each half into a 25cm/10in round. Transfer to greased baking sheets, cover with lightly oiled clear film and leave for 20 minutes, until risen.

4 Press your fingers into the dough to make deep holes all over it about 3cm/1¼in apart. Leave for a further 5 minutes. Sprinkle with the rosemary and plenty of sea salt. Sprinkle with water to keep the crust moist and bake for 25 minutes, until pale golden. Remove from the oven and drizzle with the remaining olive oil. Transfer to a wire rack to cool.

675g/1¹/₂lb/4 cups strong white bread flour

15ml/1 tbsp easy-blend (rapid-rise) dried yeast

45ml/3 tbsp chopped fresh rosemary

FROM THE STORECUPBOARD

75ml/5 tbsp olive oil

Granary Cob

Mixing and shaping a simple round loaf is one of the most satisfying kitchen activities and the result is incomparably excellent. This bread is made with fresh yeast – it is a similar colour and texture to putty and should crumble easily when broken. For best results, buy fresh yeast in small quantities as required: it will keep for up to one month in the refrigerator.

MAKES ONE ROUND LOAF

450g/1lb/4 cups Granary (multigrain) or malthouse flour

15g/^{1}/$_2$oz fresh yeast

wheat flakes or cracked wheat, for sprinkling

FROM THE STORECUPBOARD

12.5ml/2^1/$_2$ tsp salt

1 Lightly flour a baking sheet. Mix the flour and 10ml/2 tsp of the salt together in a large bowl and make a well in the centre. Place in a very low oven for 5 minutes to warm.

2 Measure 300ml/½pint/1¼ cups lukewarm water. Mix the yeast with a little of the water, then blend in the rest. Pour the yeast mixture into the centre of the flour and mix to a dough.

3 Turn out on to a lightly floured surface and knead for about 10 minutes, until smooth and elastic. Place in a lightly oiled bowl, cover with lightly oiled clear film (plastic wrap) and leave to rise in a warm place for 1¼ hours, or until doubled in bulk.

4 Turn the dough out on to a lightly floured surface and knock back (punch down). Knead for 2–3 minutes, then roll into a ball. Place in the centre of the prepared baking sheet. Cover with an inverted bowl and leave to rise in a warm place for 30–45 minutes.

5 Preheat the oven to 230°C/450°F/Gas 8 towards the end of the rising time. Mix 30ml/2 tbsp water with the remaining salt and brush evenly over the bread. Sprinkle the loaf with wheat flakes or cracked wheat.

6 Bake the bread for 15 minutes, then reduce the oven temperature to 200°C/400°F/Gas 6 and bake for a further 20 minutes, or until the loaf is firm to the touch and sounds hollow when tapped on the base. Cool on a wire rack.

Grant Loaves

This quick and easy recipe was created by a baker called Doris Grant and was published in the 1940s. It is a dream for busy cooks as the dough requires no kneading and takes only a minute to mix. Nowadays we can make the recipe even quicker by using easy-blend yeast, which is added directly to the dry ingredients.

MAKES THREE LOAVES

1 Thoroughly grease three loaf tins (pans), each 21 x 11 x 6cm/ 8½ x 4½ x 2½in and set aside in a warm place. Sift the flour and salt together in a large bowl and warm slightly to take off the chill.

2 Sprinkle the dried yeast over 150ml/¼ pint/⅔ cup lukewarm water. After a couple of minutes, stir in the muscovado sugar. Leave the mixture for 10 minutes.

3 Make a well in the centre of the flour. Pour in the yeast mixture and add a further 900ml/1½ pints/3¾ cups lukewarm water. Stir to form a slippery dough. Mix for about 1 minute, working the dry ingredients from the sides into the middle.

4 Divide among the prepared tins, cover with oiled clear film (plastic wrap) and leave to rise in a warm place for 30 minutes, or until the dough has risen by about one-third to within 1cm/ ½in of the top of the tins.

5 Meanwhile, preheat the oven to 200°C/400°F/Gas 6. Bake for 40 minutes, or until the loaves are crisp and sound hollow when tapped on the base. Turn out on to a wire rack to cool.

1.3kg/3lb/12 cups wholemeal (whole-wheat) bread flour

15ml/1 tbsp easy-blend (rapid-rise) dried yeast

15ml/1 tbsp muscovado (molasses) sugar

FROM THE STORECUPBOARD

15ml/1 tbsp salt

Cottage Loaf

Create a culinary masterpiece from a few basic ingredients and experience the satisfaction of traditional baking. Serve this classic-shaped loaf to accompany home-made soup.

MAKES ONE LARGE ROUND LOAF

675g/1½lb/6 cups unbleached strong white bread flour

20g/¾oz fresh yeast

FROM THE STORECUPBOARD

10ml/2 tsp salt

1 Lightly grease two baking sheets. Sift the flour and salt together into a large bowl and make a well in the centre.

2 Mix the yeast in 150ml/¼ pint/⅔ cup lukewarm water until dissolved. Pour into the centre of the flour and add a further 250ml/8fl oz/1 cup lukewarm water, then mix to a firm dough.

3 Knead the dough on a lightly floured surface for 10 minutes, until it is smooth and elastic. Place in a lightly oiled bowl, cover with lightly oiled clear film (plastic wrap) and leave to rise in a warm place for about 1 hour.

4 Turn out on to a lightly floured surface and knock back (punch down). Knead for 2–3 minutes, then divide the dough into two-thirds and one-third and shape each piece into a ball. Place the balls of dough on the prepared baking sheets. Cover with inverted bowls and leave to rise in a warm place for 30 minutes.

5 Gently flatten the top of the larger round of dough and cut a cross in the centre, about 4cm/1½in across. Brush with a little water and place the smaller round on top. Carefully press a hole through the middle of the top ball, down into the lower part, using your thumb and first two fingers. Cover with lightly oiled clear film and leave to rest in a warm place for about 10 minutes.

6 Preheat the oven to 220°C/425°F/Gas 7 and place the bread on the lower shelf of the oven. Bake for 35–40 minutes, or until a rich golden brown colour. Cool on a wire rack before serving.

Split Tin

The deep centre split down this loaf gives it its name. The split tin loaf slices well for making thick-cut sandwiches, or for serving hearty chunks of bread to accompany robust cheese.

MAKES ONE LOAF

500g/1¼lb/5 cups unbleached strong white bread flour, plus extra for dusting

15g/½oz fresh yeast

60ml/4 tbsp lukewarm milk

FROM THE STORECUPBOARD

10ml/2 tsp salt

1 Grease a 900g/2lb loaf tin (pan). Sift the flour and salt into a bowl and make a well in the centre. Mix the yeast with 150ml/¼ pint/⅔ cup lukewarm water. Stir in another 150ml/¼ pint/⅔ cup lukewarm water. Pour the yeast mixture into the centre of the flour and using your fingers, mix in a little flour to form a smooth batter.

2 Sprinkle a little more flour from around the edge over the batter and leave in a warm place for about 20 minutes to "sponge". Add the milk and remaining flour; mix to a firm dough.

3 Place on a lightly floured surface and knead for about 10 minutes, until smooth and elastic. Place in a lightly oiled bowl, cover with lightly oiled clear film (plastic wrap) and leave to rise in a warm place for 1–1¼ hours, or until nearly doubled in bulk.

4 Knock back (punch down) the dough and turn out on to a lightly floured surface. Shape it into a rectangle, the length of the prepared tin. Roll the dough up lengthways, tuck the ends under and place, seam side down, in the tin. Cover the loaf and leave to rise in a warm place for about 20–30 minutes.

5 Using a sharp knife, make one deep central slash. Dust the top of the loaf with a little sifted flour. Leave for 10–15 minutes. Meanwhile, preheat the oven to 230°C/450°F/Gas 8. Bake for 15 minutes, then reduce the oven temperature to 200°C/400°F/Gas 6. Bake for 20–25 minutes, until golden and it sounds hollow when tapped on the base. Cool on a wire rack.

Poppy-seeded Bloomer

This long, crusty loaf gets its fabulous flavour from poppy seeds. Cut into thick slices, the bread is perfect for mopping up the cooking juices of hearty stews, or for absorbing good dressing on summery salads. A variety of seeds can be used to add flavour, texture and colour to this loaf – try sunflower, pumpkin or sesame seeds as an alternative to the poppy seeds. Brushing the loaf with the salted water before baking helps to give it a crisp, crusty finish.

MAKES ONE LARGE LOAF

1 Lightly grease a baking sheet. Sift the flour and 10ml/2 tsp salt together into a large bowl and make a well in the centre.

2 Measure 450ml/¾ pint/scant 2 cups lukewarm water and stir about a third of it into the yeast in a bowl. Stir in the remaining water and pour into the centre of the flour. Mix, gradually incorporating the surrounding flour, to a firm dough.

3 Turn out on to a lightly floured surface and knead the dough very well, for at least 10 minutes, until smooth and elastic. Place the dough in a lightly oiled bowl, cover with lightly oiled clear film (plastic wrap) and leave to rise, at cool room temperature (about 15–18 C/60–65 F), for 5–6 hours, or until doubled in bulk.

4 Knock back (punch down) the dough, turn out on to a lightly floured surface and knead it thoroughly for about 5 minutes. Return the dough to the bowl and re-cover. Leave to rise, at cool room temperature, for a further 2 hours or slightly longer.

5 Knock back again and repeat the thorough kneading. Leave the dough to rest for 5 minutes, then roll out on a lightly floured surface into a rectangle 2.5cm/1in thick. Roll the dough up from one long side and shape it into a square-ended, thick baton shape about 33 x 13cm/13 x 5in.

6 Place the loaf, seam side up, on a lightly floured baking sheet. Cover with lightly oiled clear film and leave to rest for 15 minutes. Turn the loaf over and place on the greased baking sheet. Plump the loaf up by tucking the dough under the sides and ends. Using a sharp knife, cut six diagonal slashes on the top.

7 Leave to rest, covered, in a warm place, for 10 minutes. Meanwhile, preheat the oven to 230°C/450°F/Gas 8.

8 Mix the remaining salt with 30ml/2 tbsp water and brush this glaze over the bread. Sprinkle with poppy seeds.

9 Spray the oven with water, bake the bread immediately for 20 minutes, then reduce the oven temperature to 200°C/400°F/Gas 6. Bake for 25 minutes more, or until golden and it sounds hollow when tapped on the base. Transfer to a wire rack to cool.

675g/1½lb/6 cups unbleached strong white bread flour

15g/½oz fresh yeast

poppy seeds, for sprinkling

FROM THE STORECUPBOARD

12.5ml/2½ tsp salt

COOK'S TIP The traditional cracked, crusty appearance of this loaf is difficult to achieve in a domestic oven. However, you can get a similar result by spraying the oven with water before baking. If the underneath of the loaf is not very crusty at the end of baking, turn it over on the baking sheet, switch off the heat and leave it in the oven for a further 5–10 minutes.

Traditional Irish Soda Bread

Irish soda bread contains no yeast and therefore does not need to be left to rise, so it is quick and easy to make. It is best eaten on the day that it is made, preferably while still warm. You can bake a loaf in the morning, ready to take on a picnic to serve with cheese and salads.

SERVES FOUR TO SIX

450g/1lb plain wholemeal (all-purpose whole-wheat) flour

10ml/2 tsp bicarbonate of soda (baking soda)

400ml/14fl oz/1²/₃ cups buttermilk

FROM THE STORECUPBOARD

5ml/1 tsp salt

1 Preheat the oven to 200°C/400°F/Gas 6. Place the flour in a large bowl and stir in the bicarbonate of soda and salt. Make a well in the centre.

2 Gradually pour the buttermilk into the well, beating in the flour from around the edges to form a soft, not sticky, dough.

3 Turn the dough out on to a lightly floured surface and knead for 5 minutes, until smooth. Shape into a 20cm/8in round and place on a lightly greased baking sheet.

4 Using a sharp knife, cut a deep cross on the top of the dough and bake for 30–35 minutes, or until slightly risen and cooked through. Cool slightly on a wire rack before serving.

Spring Onion Flatbreads

Use these flatbreads to wrap around barbecue-cooked meat and chunky vegetable salads, or serve with tasty dips such as hummus. They're at their best as soon as they're cooked.

MAKES SIXTEEN

1 Place the flour in a large mixing bowl and stir in the salt, yeast and spring onions. Make a well in the centre and pour in 300ml/¹/₂ pint/1¹/₄ cups hand hot water. Mix to form a soft, but not sticky, dough.

2 Turn out the dough on to a floured work surface and knead for about 5 minutes, until smooth. Put the dough back in the bowl, cover with a damp dishtowel and leave in a warm place until doubled in size.

3 Knock back (punch down) the dough to get rid of any excess air and turn out on to a floured work surface. Divide the dough into 16 pieces and roll each piece into a smooth ball. Roll out each ball to a 13cm/5in round.

4 Heat a large frying pan until hot. Dust off any excess flour from one dough round and place in the frying pan. Cook for about 1 minute, then flip over and cook for a further 30 seconds. Repeat with the remaining dough rounds.

450g/1lb/4 cups strong white bread flour, plus extra for dusting

7g/¹/₄ oz packet easy-blend (rapid-rise) dried yeast

4 spring onions (scallions), finely chopped

FROM THE STORECUPBOARD

5ml/1 tsp salt

VARIATION

To make garlic flatbreads, use 2 finely chopped garlic cloves in place of the chopped spring onions. To add extra bite, mix in 1 finely chopped fresh red chilli as well.

Pitta Bread

Soft, slightly bubbly pitta bread is a pleasure to make. It can be eaten in a variety of ways, such as Mediterranean-style filled with salad or little chunks of meat cooked on the barbecue, or it can be torn into pieces and dipped in savoury dips such as hummus or tzatziki. Chop any leftover bread and incorporate into the Lebanese salad *fattoush* with parsley, mint, tomatoes and cucumber.

MAKES TWELVE

500g/1¼lb/5 cups strong white bread flour, or half white and half wholemeal (whole-wheat)

12.5ml/2½ tsp easy-blend (rapid-rise) dried yeast

FROM THE STORECUPBOARD

15ml/1 tbsp olive oil

15ml/1 tbsp salt

1 Combine the flour, yeast and salt. Combine the oil and 250ml/8fl oz/1 cup water, then add half of the flour mixture, stirring in the same direction, until the dough is stiff. Knead in the remaining flour. Place the dough in a clean bowl, cover with a clean dishtowel and leave in a warm place for at least 30 minutes and up to 2 hours.

2 Knead the dough for 10 minutes, or until smooth. Lightly oil the bowl, place the dough in it, cover again and leave to rise in a warm place for about 1 hour, or until doubled in size.

3 Divide the dough into 12 equal pieces. With lightly floured hands, flatten each piece, then roll out into a round measuring about 20cm/8in and about 4mm–1cm/¼–½in thick. Keep the rolled breads covered while you make the remaining pittas.

4 Heat a heavy frying pan over a medium-high heat. When hot, lay one piece of flattened dough in the pan and cook for 15–20 seconds. Turn it over and cook the second side for about 1 minute.

5 When large bubbles start to form on the bread, turn it over again. It should puff up. Using a clean dishtowel, gently press on the bread where the bubbles have formed. Cook for a total of 3 minutes, then remove the pitta from the pan. Repeat with the remaining dough. Wrap the pitta breads in a clean dishtowel, stacking them as each one is cooked. Serve the pittas hot while they are soft and moist.

VARIATION
To bake the breads, preheat the oven to 220°C/425°F/Gas 7. Fill an unglazed or partially glazed dish with hot water and place in the bottom of the hot oven. Alternatively, arrange a handful of unglazed tiles in the base of the oven. Use either a non-stick baking sheet or a lightly oiled baking sheet and heat in the oven for a few minutes. Place two or three pieces of flattened dough on to the hot baking sheet and place in the hottest part of the oven. Bake for 2–3 minutes until puffed up. Repeat with the remaining dough.

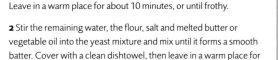

Yemeni Sponge Flat Breads

These flat breads, known as *lahuhs* and made from a batter, are bubbly and soft. They are eaten with soups but are also good with salads, dips or cheese.

SERVES FOUR

1 Measure 500ml/17fl oz/generous 2 cups lukewarm water. In a bowl, dissolve the dried yeast in about 75ml/5 tbsp of the water. Leave in a warm place for about 10 minutes, or until frothy.

2 Stir the remaining water, the flour, salt and melted butter or vegetable oil into the yeast mixture and mix until it forms a smooth batter. Cover with a clean dishtowel, then leave in a warm place for about 1 hour, until doubled in size.

3 Stir the thick, frothy batter and, if it seems too thick to ladle out, add a little extra water. Cover and leave the batter to stand in a warm place for about 1 hour.

4 Cook the flat breads in a non-stick frying pan. Ladle 45–60ml/ 3–4 tbsp of batter (or less for smaller breads) into the pan and cook over a low heat until the top is bubbling and the colour has changed. (Traditionally these breads are cooked on only one side, but they can be turned over and the second side cooked for just a moment, if you like.)

5 Remove the cooked flat bread from the frying pan with a spatula and keep warm in a clean dishtowel. Continue cooking until you have used up all the remaining batter.

15ml/1 tbsp dried active yeast

350g/12oz/ 3 cups plain (all-purpose) flour

FROM THE STORECUPBOARD

50g/2oz/¹/₄ cup butter, melted, or 60ml/4 tbsp vegetable oil

5ml/1 tsp salt

COOK'S TIP *Use two or three frying pans at the same time so that the flat breads are ready together and so can be eaten piping hot.*

West Indian Flat Breads

Eclectic Caribbean food is influenced by a wide range of international cultures. It is the Anglo-Indian connection that brought the Indian flat bread called roti to Trinidad in the West Indies. Serve these simple-to-make breads straight from the pan to accompany spicy seafood chowders, curries, or any other dish that has plenty of sauce for mopping up.

MAKES EIGHT ROTIS

1 Mix the flour, baking powder and salt together in a large bowl and make a well in the centre. Gradually mix in 300ml/½ pint/1¼ cups water to make a firm dough.

2 Knead on a lightly floured surface until smooth. Place in a lightly oiled bowl, cover with lightly oiled clear film (plastic wrap). Leave to stand for 20 minutes.

3 Divide the dough into eight equal pieces and roll each one on a lightly floured surface into an 18cm/7in round. Brush the surface of each round with a little of the clarified butter or ghee, fold in half and half again. Cover the folded rounds with lightly oiled clear film (plastic wrap) and leave for 10 minutes.

4 Take one roti and roll out on a lightly floured surface into a round about 20–23cm/8–9in in diameter. Brush both sides with some clarified butter or ghee.

5 Heat a griddle or heavy frying pan, add the roti and cook for about 1 minute. Turn over and cook for 2 minutes, then turn over again and cook for 1 minute. Wrap in a clean dishtowel to keep warm while cooking the remaining rotis. Serve warm.

450g/1lb/4 cups atta or fine wholemeal (whole-wheat) flour

5ml/1 tsp baking powder

FROM THE STORECUPBOARD

115–150g/4–5oz/8–10 tbsp clarified butter or ghee, melted

5ml/1 tsp salt

Tandoori Rotis

Indian flat breads are fun to make at home: these may not be strictly authentic in terms of cooking method, but they taste fantastic. This bread would normally be baked in a tandoor, a clay oven that is heated with charcoal or wood. The oven becomes extremely hot, cooking the bread in minutes. The rotis are ready when light brown bubbles appear on the surface.

MAKES SIX ROTIS

350g/12oz/3 cups atta or fine wholemeal (whole-wheat) flour

FROM THE STORECUPBOARD

30–45ml/2–3 tbsp melted ghee or butter, for brushing

5ml/1 tsp salt

1 Sift the flour and salt into a large bowl. Add 250ml/8fl oz/1 cup water and mix to a soft dough. Knead on a lightly floured surface for 3–4 minutes, until smooth. Place the dough in a lightly oiled mixing bowl, cover with lightly oiled clear film (plastic wrap) and leave to rest for 1 hour.

2 Turn out on to a lightly floured surface. Divide the dough into six pieces and shape each piece into a ball. Press out into a larger round with the palm of your hand, cover with lightly oiled clear film (plastic wrap) and leave to rest for 10 minutes.

3 Meanwhile, preheat the oven to 230°C/450°F/Gas 8. Place three baking sheets in the oven to heat. Roll the rotis into 15cm/6in rounds, place two on each baking sheet and bake for 8–10 minutes. Brush with ghee or butter and serve warm.

Preserves, Pickles, Relishes and Sauces

SWEET AND SAVOURY PRESERVES, CONDIMENTS AND
SAUCES CAN ADD THE FINISHING TOUCH TO A SIMPLE DISH.
A SPOONFUL OF FRUIT JAM OR JELLY CAN TRANSFORM A
PLAIN SCONE INTO TEATIME TREAT, WHILE PIQUANT
PICKLES AND RELISHES CAN ENLIVEN BREAD AND CHEESE,
AND A FLAVOURSOME SAUCE CAN TURN SIMPLY COOKED
FISH INTO A REALLY SPECIAL MEAL.

Bramble Jelly

The tart, fruity flavour of wild blackberries makes this jelly one of the best, especially for serving with hot buttered toast or English muffins. When picking the fruit, include a small proportion of red unripe berries for a good set. Redcurrant jelly is made in the same way, but with less sugar. Reduce the quantity to 350g/12oz/1½ cups of sugar for every 600ml/ 1 pint/2½ cups of fruit juice.

900g/2lb/ 8 cups blackberries

juice of 1 lemon

about 900g/2lb/ 4 cups caster (superfine) sugar

MAKES 900G/2LB

1 Put the blackberries and lemon juice into a large pan (use a preserving pan with two handles if possible). Add 300ml/½ pint/1¼ cups water. Cover the pan and cook for 15–30 minutes, or until the blackberries are very soft.

2 Ladle into a jelly bag or a large sieve lined with muslin (cheesecloth) and set over a large mixing bowl. Leave the fruit to drip overnight to obtain the maximum amount of juice. Do not disturb or squeeze the bag or the jelly will be cloudy.

3 Discard the fruit pulp. Measure the juice and allow 450g/1lb/2 cups sugar to every 600ml/ 1 pint/2½ cups juice. Place the juice and sugar in a large, heavy pan and bring to the boil, stirring constantly until the sugar has dissolved.

4 Boil the mixture rapidly until the jelly registers 105°C/220°F on a sugar thermometer, or test for setting by spooning a small amount on to a chilled saucer (keep a saucer in the freezer for this purpose). Chill for 3 minutes, then push the mixture with your finger: if wrinkles form on the surface of the jelly, it is ready.

5 Skim off any scum and immediately pour the jelly into warm sterilized jars. Cover and seal immediately, then label when the jars are cold.

Strawberry Jam

This is the classic fragrant preserve for English afternoon tea, served with freshly baked scones and clotted cream. It is also extremely good stirred into plain yogurt for breakfast. When choosing strawberries for making jam, pick undamaged, slightly under-ripe fruit if possible – the pectin content will be high and ensure a good set.

MAKES ABOUT 1.3KG/3LB

1kg/2¼lb/8 cups small strawberries

900g/2lb/4 cups granulated sugar

juice of 2 lemons

1 Layer the strawberries and sugar in a large bowl. Cover and leave overnight.

2 The next day, scrape the strawberries and their juice into a large, heavy pan. Add the lemon juice. Gradually bring to the boil over a low heat, stirring until the sugar has dissolved.

3 Boil steadily for 10–15 minutes, or until the jam registers 105°C/220°F on a sugar thermometer. Alternatively, test for setting by spooning a small amount on to a chilled saucer. Chill for 3 minutes, then push the jam with your finger: if wrinkles form on the surface, it is ready. Cool for 10 minutes.

4 Stir the jam before pouring it into warm sterilized jars, filling them right to the top. Cover with waxed paper discs immediately, but do not seal with lids until the jam is completely cold.

COOK'S TIP *For best results when making jam, don't wash the strawberries unless absolutely necessary. Instead, brush off any dirt, or wipe the strawberries with a damp cloth. If you have to wash any, pat them dry and then spread them out on a clean dishtowel to dry.*

Spiced Poached Kumquats

Warm cinnamon and star anise make a heady combination with the full citrus flavour of kumquats. Star anise is an attractive spice: it is an eight-pointed star that contains tiny aniseed-flavoured, amber coloured seeds. The kumquats go well with rich meats, such as roast pork or baked ham, or with punchy goat's milk cheese. They are also good with desserts and ice creams.

SERVES SIX

1 Cut the kumquats in half and discard the pips (seeds). Place the kumquats in a pan with the caster sugar, 150ml/¼ pint/⅔ cup water and the cinnamon stick and star anise. Cook over a gentle heat, stirring until the sugar has dissolved.

2 Increase the heat, cover the pan and boil the mixture for about 8–10 minutes, until the kumquats are tender. To bottle the kumquats, spoon them into warm, sterilized jars, seal and label.

3 If you want to serve the spiced kumquats soon after making them, let the mixture cool, then chill it.

**450g/1lb/
4 cups kumquats**

**115g/4oz/
¹/₂ cup caster
(superfine) sugar**

1 small cinnamon stick

1 star anise

Three-fruit Marmalade

Bitter marmalade oranges have a powerful flavour and plenty of setting power to make an excellent preserve. Known as Seville oranges, they are usually only available for a short time in January – but sweet oranges can be used in this recipe if necessary.

MAKES 2.25KG/5LB

1 Wash the fruit, halve, and squeeze their juice. Pour into a large heavy pan or preserving pan. Tip the pips (seeds) and pulp into a square of muslin (cheesecloth), gather the sides into a bag and tie the neck. Tie the bag to the pan handle so that it dangles in the juice.

2 Remove and discard the membranes and pith from the citrus skins and cut the rinds into slivers. Add to the pan with 1.75 litres/3 pints/7½ cups water. Heat until simmering and then cook gently for 2 hours. Test the rinds for softness by pressing a cooled piece with a finger.

3 Lift out the muslin bag, squeezing out the juice into the pan. Discard the bag. Stir the sugar into the pan and heat very gently, stirring occasionally, until the sugar has dissolved.

4 Bring the mixture to the boil and boil for 10–15 minutes, or until the marmalade registers 105°C/220°F on a sugar thermometer. Alternatively, test the marmalade for setting by pouring a small amount on to a chilled saucer. Chill for 3 minutes, then push the marmalade with your finger: if wrinkles form on the surface, it is ready. Cool for 15 minutes.

5 Stir the marmalade and pour it into warm, sterilized jars. Cover with waxed paper discs. Seal and label when completely cold. Store in a cool dark cupboard.

**2 Seville
(Temple) oranges**

2 lemons

1 grapefruit

**1.5kg/3lb 6oz/
6³/₄ cups
granulated sugar**

COOK'S TIP

Allow the marmalade to cool slightly before potting so that it is thick enough to stop the fruit from sinking in the jars.

Preserved Lemons

These are widely used in Middle Eastern cooking, for which only the peel is used and not the pulp. In this recipe the lemons are cut into wedges instead of being preserved whole, in traditional style. The wedges are more practical for potting and they are also easy to prepare before use.

MAKES TWO JARS

1 Wash the lemons well and cut each into six to eight wedges. Press a generous amount of sea salt into the cut surfaces, pushing it into every crevice.

2 Pack the salted lemon wedges into two 1.2 litre/2 pint/5 cup sterilized jars. To each jar, add 30–45ml/2–3 tbsp salt and 90ml/ 6 tbsp lemon juice, then top up with boiling water to cover the lemons. (If using larger jars, use more lemon juice and less water.)

3 Cover the jars and leave to stand for 2–4 weeks before serving.

4 To serve, rinse the preserved lemons well to remove some of the salty flavour, then pull off and discard the flesh. Cut the lemon peel into strips or leave in chunks and use as you like.

10 unwaxed lemons

**about 200ml/
7fl oz/scant 1 cup
fresh lemon juice or a
combination of fresh
and preserved**

FROM THE
STORECUPBOARD

sea salt

Middle Eastern Pickle

Beetroot brings attractive colour and its inimitable sweet, slightly earthy flavour to this Middle Eastern speciality. The pickle is delicious with falafel or cold roast beef. When buying beetroot, choose firm, unblemished, small- to medium-sized specimens. If you buy beetroot with green tops, reserve them and cook like spinach for a tasty vegetable accompaniment.

MAKES FOUR JARS

**1kg/2¹/₄lb
young turnips**

**3–4 raw
beetroot (beets)**

juice of 1 lemon

FROM THE
STORECUPBOARD

**about 45ml/3 tbsp
kosher salt or
coarse sea salt**

1 Wash, but do not peel the turnips and beetroot. Then cut them into slices about 5mm/¼in thick. Put the salt in a bowl with about 1.5 litres/2½ pints/6¼ cups water, stir and leave on one side until the salt has completely dissolved.

2 Sprinkle the beetroot with lemon juice and divide among four 1.2 litre/2 pint/5 cup sterilized jars. Top with the sliced turnips, packing them in very tightly. Pour over the brine, making sure that the vegetables are completely covered.

3 Seal the jars and leave in a cool place for seven days for the flavours to develop before serving.

Horseradish and Beetroot Sauce

This is a traditional Jewish speciality. Known as *chrain,* it is often eaten at Pesah, the Passover meal, for which horseradish is one of the traditional bitter flavours. However, it complements a variety of foods and dishes of many different cooking styles, including roast meats and grilled fish.

SERVES ABOUT EIGHT

1 Put the horseradish and beetroot in a bowl and mix together, then season with sugar, vinegar and salt to taste.

2 Spoon the sauce into a sterilized jar, packing it down firmly, and seal. Store in the refrigerator, where it will keep for up to 2 weeks.

150g/5oz grated fresh horseradish

2 cooked beetroot (beets), grated

15ml/1 tbsp sugar

15–30ml/1–2 tbsp red wine vinegar

FROM THE STORECUPBOARD

salt

COOK'S TIP

Fresh horseradish is very potent and should be handled with care as it can make the skin burn as well as the eyes run. Wear fine rubber gloves to protect your hands.

Yellow Pepper and Coriander Relish

Relishes are quick and easy to make and they are delicious with cold meats and cheese or as a sandwich filler. Here the ingredients are lightly cooked, then processed to a chunky consistency. Red or orange (bell) peppers will work just as well as yellow as they all have a sweet flavour. Don't use green peppers though, because they are not sweet.

SERVES FOUR TO SIX

1 Seed and coarsely chop the peppers. Heat the oil in a frying pan and gently cook the peppers, stirring frequently, for 8–10 minutes, until lightly coloured.

2 Meanwhile, seed the chilli and slice it as thinly as possible. Transfer the peppers and cooking juices to a food processor and process lightly until chopped. Transfer half the peppers to a bowl. Using a sharp knife, chop the fresh coriander, then add to the food processor and process briefly.

3 Tip the contents of the food processor into the bowl with the rest of the peppers and add the chilli and salt. Mix well, cover and chill until ready to serve.

3 large yellow (bell) peppers

1 large mild fresh red chilli

small handful of fresh coriander (cilantro)

FROM THE STORECUPBOARD

45ml/3 tbsp sesame oil

salt

COOK'S TIP *Other flavoured oils, such as lemon- or garlic-infused oil, can be used in place of the sesame oil.*

Hot Mango Salsa

For sweet, tangy results, select a really juicy, ripe mango for this salsa – it is not worth making the salsa with a firm, unripe mango as it will not taste as good as it should. Keep an unripe mango in the fruit bowl for a few days until it has ripened. This fruity salsa is a delicious accompaniment to chargrilled or barbecued chicken or fish.

SERVES FOUR TO SIX

1 To prepare the mango, cut the flesh off on either side of the flat stone (pit). Peel and finely dice the mango halves and cut off and chop the flesh that still clings to the stone.

2 Finely grate the lime rind and squeeze the juice. Seed and finely shred the fresh red chilli.

3 Finely chop the onion and mix it in a bowl with the mango, lime rind, 15ml/1 tbsp lime juice, the chilli and a little salt. Cover and chill until ready to serve.

1 medium ripe mango

1 lime

1 large mild fresh red chilli

¹/₂ small red onion

FROM THE
STORECUPBOARD

salt

Harissa

This simplified version of harissa – the classic spicy North African sauce – is extremely quick to make. It can be served as a dip with wedges of Middle Eastern flat bread, as a condiment with couscous and other North African dishes, or as a flavouring to spice up meat and vegetable stews. This basic spice blend goes very well with other aromatic herbs and spices so you can vary the flavour by adding chopped fresh coriander (cilantro) or a pinch of caraway seeds along with the lemon juice, if you like.

SERVES FOUR TO SIX

1 Put the paprika, cayenne pepper, ground cumin and 250ml/8fl oz/ 1 cup water in a large, heavy pan.

2 Bring the spice mixture to the boil, then immediately remove the pan from the heat.

3 Stir in the lemon juice to taste and allow to cool completely before serving or using.

45ml/3 tbsp paprika

2.5–5ml/^{1}/$_2$–1 tsp cayenne pepper

1.5ml/^{1}/$_4$ tsp ground cumin

juice of ^{1}/$_4$–^{1}/$_2$ lemon

Aioli

This classic, creamy garlic mayonnaise from France is simple to make and absolutely delicious. Serve it with salads or as a dip with crudités, with potato wedges, or as a quick sauce for pan-fried salmon. Try to use extra virgin olive oil for this mayonnaise if you can – it has a rich and delicious flavour that really makes this sauce special.

SERVES FOUR TO SIX

1 Put the garlic cloves in a mortar, add a pinch of salt and pound to a smooth paste with a pestle.

2 Transfer the garlic paste to a bowl. Add the egg yolks and whisk for about 30 seconds, until creamy. Whisk in the olive oil, drop by drop, until the mixture begins to thicken, then add the oil in a slow drizzle until the mixture is thick and creamy.

3 Beat in the lemon juice and seasoning to taste. Serve immediately or cover with clear film (plastic wrap) and chill in the refrigerator until ready to use. Allow the aioli to return to room temperature before serving.

4 large garlic cloves, peeled

2 egg yolks

250ml/8fl oz/1 cup extra virgin olive oil

15–30ml/1–2 tbsp lemon juice

FROM THE STORECUPBOARD

salt

Roasted Garlic Sauce

A roasted garlic sauce has plenty of robust flavour without the harshness of some uncooked garlic sauces and dressings. This one keeps well in the refrigerator for several days. Serve it as an accompaniment to barbecued burgers or sausages, grilled steaks, lamb chops or pork steaks – the possibilities are endless.

SERVES SIX TO EIGHT

6 large heads of garlic

2 slices white bread, about 90g/3¹/₂oz

30–45ml/2–3 tbsp lemon juice

FROM THE STORECUPBOARD

120ml/4fl oz/¹/₂ cup olive oil

salt

1 Preheat the oven to 200°C/400°F/Gas 6. Slice the tops off the garlic and place the bulbs on a sheet of foil. Spoon over 30ml/2 tbsp of the oil and sprinkle with salt. Wrap the foil over the garlic and bake for 1 hour, until soft. Open out the foil and leave the garlic to cool.

2 Discard the crusts from the bread. Soak the bread in water for 1 minute, then squeeze dry and place in a food processor. Squeeze the garlic flesh into the processor. Process to a smooth paste.

3 Add 30ml/2 tbsp lemon juice with a little salt and pepper. With the machine running, gradually add the remaining oil in a thin stream to make a smooth paste. Check the seasoning, adding more lemon juice if needed. Turn into a bowl, cover and chill until required.

Watercress Sauce

This pretty green sauce is refreshingly tart and peppery. It is delicious served as an accompaniment to poached fish, or as a dip for simply grilled prawns (shrimp). Do not prepare the sauce more than a few hours ahead of serving, as the watercress will discolour the sauce. This peppery green sauce can also be made with rocket (arugula) leaves instead of the watercress.

SERVES SIX TO EIGHT

200g/7oz watercress leaves

300g/11oz/1¹/₄ cups mayonnaise

15–30ml/1–2 tbsp freshly squeezed lemon juice

FROM THE STORECUPBOARD

200g/7oz/scant 1 cup unsalted (sweet) butter

salt and ground black pepper

1 Remove the tough stems from the watercress leaves and finely chop the leaves by hand or in a food processor. Add the mayonnaise and the freshly squeezed lemon juice and process to mix.

2 Melt the unsalted butter, then add to the watercress mixture, a little at a time, processing or whisking in a bowl until the butter has been fully incorporated and the sauce is thick and smooth. Season to taste with salt and pepper, then cover and chill in the refrigerator for at least an hour before serving.

EXTRAS
Garlic makes a delicious addition to this sauce. Peel and finely chop 1–2 garlic cloves and combine with the chopped watercress leaves, mayonnaise and lemon juice, before adding the melted butter in step 2.

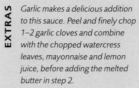

Shallots in Balsamic Vinegar

These whole shallots cooked in balsamic vinegar and herbs are a modern variation on pickled onions, but they have a much more gentle, smooth flavour. They are delicious served with cold pies, meats and cheese. A combination of bay leaves and thyme are used here but rosemary, oregano or marjoram sprigs would work just as well.

SERVES SIX

1 Put the unpeeled shallots in a bowl, cover with boiling water and leave for 2 minutes for the skins to loosen. Drain and peel the shallots, leaving them whole.

2 Put the sugar, bay leaves or thyme and vinegar in a heavy pan and bring to the boil. Add the shallots, cover and simmer gently for about 40 minutes, until the shallots are just tender.

3 Transfer the mixture to a sterilized jar, seal and label, then store in a cool, dark place. Alternatively, drain and transfer to a serving dish. Leave to cool, then chill until ready to serve.

500g/1¼lb shallots

30ml/2 tbsp muscovado (molasses) sugar

several bay leaves or fresh thyme sprigs

300ml/½ pint/ 1¼ cups balsamic vinegar

Barbecue Sauce

A wide selection of ready-made barbecue sauces are available in the supermarkets, but they really don't compare with the home-made variety. This 10-minute version can be used to transform baked or grilled chicken, sausages or fish into an interesting meal that needs no more than a mixed salad and baked potatoes as accompaniments.

SERVES FOUR TO SIX

1 Tip the cans of chopped tomatoes with herbs or garlic into a medium, heavy pan and add the finely chopped onion, black treacle and Worcestershire sauce.

2 Bring to the boil and cook, uncovered, until the mixture is thickened and pulpy, stirring frequently with a wooden spoon to stop the sauce catching on the base of the pan. Season lightly with salt and plenty of freshly ground black pepper and transfer to a serving dish or jug (pitcher). Serve the sauce warm or cold.

2 x 400g/14 oz cans chopped tomatoes with herbs or garlic

1 onion, finely chopped

15ml/1 tbsp black treacle (molasses)

45ml/3 tbsp Worcestershire sauce

FROM THE STORECUPBOARD

salt and ground black pepper

Mixed Herb and Peppercorn Sauce

This lovely, refreshing sauce relies on absolutely fresh herbs (any combination will do) and good-quality olive oil for its fabulous flavour. Make it a day in advance, to allow the flavours to mingle. Serve the sauce with simply cooked fish such as salmon or with grilled beef or lamb steaks.

SERVES FOUR TO SIX

1 Crush the cumin seeds using a mortar and pestle. Alternatively, put the seeds in a small bowl and pound them with the end of a rolling pin. Add the pink or green peppercorns and pound a little to break them up slightly.

2 Remove any tough stalks from the herbs. Put the herbs in a food processor with the cumin seeds, peppercorns, oil and salt and process until the herbs are finely chopped, scraping the sauce down from the sides of the bowl if necessary.

3 Turn the sauce into a small serving dish, cover with clear film (plastic wrap) and chill until ready to serve.

10ml/2 tsp cumin seeds

15ml/1 tbsp pink or green peppercorns in brine, drained and rinsed

25g/1oz/1 cup fresh mixed herbs, such as parsley, mint, chives and coriander (cilantro)

FROM THE STORECUPBOARD

45ml/3 tbsp lemon-infused olive oil

salt

Healthy Juices and Smoothies

THERE IS SOMETHING REALLY ENTICING ABOUT FRESHLY
MADE BLENDED DRINKS AND HEALTHY JUICES. THEY CAN BE
CLEANSING, FRESH OR ZESTY, SMOOTH AND CREAMY OR
RICH AND DECADENT — BUT WHAT THEY ALL HAVE IN
COMMON IS A WONDERFULLY MOREISH QUALITY THAT
MAKES YOU FEEL THAT EVERY GLASSFUL IS A TREAT.

Leafy Apple Lift-off

This delicious blend of fruit and fresh green leaves is refreshing and healthy. The leaves are robustly flavoured and have a peppery, pungent taste. To prepare the leaves, discard any damaged and discoloured ones and rinse thoroughly in cold water to remove any grit. To prevent the juice from being watery, dry the leaves in a salad spinner or on kitchen paper before juicing.

SERVES ONE

1 Quarter the apple. Using a juice extractor, juice the fruit and watercress, rocket or spinach.

2 Add the lime juice to the apple, grape and leaf mixture and stir thoroughly to blend all the ingredients together. Pour the juice into a tall glass and serve immediately.

1 eating apple

150g/5oz white grapes

25g/1oz watercress, rocket (arugula) or spinach

15ml/1 tbsp lime juice

Fennel Fusion

The hearty combination of raw vegetables and apples makes a surprisingly delicious juice that is packed with natural goodness and is a truly wonderful pick-me-up. Use the remaining cabbage and fennel to make a really crunchy salad – slice and dress with French dressing or simply with olive oil, herb vinegar and plenty of freshly ground black pepper and sea salt to taste.

SERVES ONE

1 Coarsely slice the red cabbage and the fennel bulb and quarter the eating apples. Using a juice extractor, juice the vegetables and fruit.

2 Add the lemon juice to the red cabbage, fennel and apple mixture and stir thoroughly to blend all the ingredients together. Pour into a glass and serve immediately.

$^1/_2$ small red cabbage

$^1/_2$ fennel bulb

2 eating apples

15ml/1 tbsp lemon juice

Tropical Calm

This deliciously scented juice is packed with goodness to cleanse and calm the system. Orange fruits such as cantaloupe melons and papayas are rich in the phytochemical betacarotene, which is a valuable anti-oxidant and is thought to have many health-promoting properties.

SERVES ONE

1 papaya

¹/₂ cantaloupe melon

90g/3¹/₂oz seedless white grapes

1 Halve the papaya, remove the seeds and skin, then cut the flesh into coarse slices. Halve the melon, remove the seeds, cut into quarters, slice the flesh away from the skin and cut into chunks.

2 Using a juicer, juice the prepared fruit. Alternatively, blend the fruit in a food processor or blender for a thicker juice. Serve immediately.

Strawberry Soother

Relax with this comforting blend of just two fruits – it is rich in vitamin C and fabulous flavour. It's a perfect drink for summer when sweet strawberries, peaches and necatarines are in season.

SERVES ONE

225g/8oz/2 cups strawberries

1 peach or nectarine

1 Hull the strawberries. Using a sharp knife, quarter the peach or nectarine and pull out the stone (pit). Cut the flesh into coarse slices or chunks.

2 Using a juice extractor, juice the fruit. Alternatively, place the fruit in a food processor or blender and process until smooth. Serve immediately.

Carrot Revitalizer

This vibrant combination of vegetables and fruit makes a lively, health-giving drink. Carrots yield generous quantities of sweet juice, which goes perfectly with the sharp flavour of pear and the zesty taste of orange. This powerful drink will nourish and stimulate the system.

SERVES ONE

1 Scrub and trim the carrots and quarter the apples. Peel the orange and cut into rough segments.

2 Using a juice extractor, juice the carrots and fruit, pour into a glass and serve immediately.

3 carrots

2 apples

1 orange

Purple Pep

Jewel-coloured beetroot juice is well known for its detoxifying properties so this juice makes the perfect choice when you've been over-doing it. It offers an excellent supply of valuable nutrients that are essential for good health.

SERVES ONE

3 carrots

115g/4oz beetroot (beet)

25g/1oz baby spinach, washed and dried

2 celery sticks

1 Scrub and trim the carrots and beetroot. Using a sharp knife, cut the beetroot into large chunks.

2 Using a juice extractor, juice the carrots, beetroot, spinach and celery, then pour into a glass and serve immediately.

Tomato and Cucumber Juice with Basil

Some herbs don't juice well, losing their aromatic flavour and turning muddy and dull. Basil, on the other hand, is an excellent juicer, keeping its distinctive fresh fragrance. It makes the perfect partner for mild, refreshing cucumber and the ripest, juiciest tomatoes you can find. Try using cherry tomatoes for an extra sweet flavour.

SERVES TWO

¹/₂ cucumber, peeled

a handful of fresh basil

350g/12oz tomatoes

1 Quarter the cucumber lengthways. There's no need to remove the seeds. Push it through a juicer with the basil, then do the same with the tomatoes.

2 Pour the tomato, basil and cucumber juice over ice cubes in one tall or two short glasses and echo the herb flavour by adding a few basil sprigs for decoration.

Beetroot, Ginger and Orange Juice

Despite its firmness, beetroot can be juiced raw and its intense flavour goes perfectly with tangy citrus fruits and fresh root ginger. It has the highest sugar content of any vegetable and makes a delicious juice with a vibrant colour and rich but refreshing taste.

SERVES ONE

1 Scrub the beetroot, then trim them and cut into quarters. Push half the beetroot through a vegetable juicer, followed by the ginger and the remaining beetroot and pour the juice into a jug (pitcher).

2 Squeeze the juice from the orange, using a citrus juicer or by hand, and pour into the beetroot juice. Stir to combine.

3 Pour the juice over ice cubes in a glass or clear glass cup and serve immediately to enjoy the full benefit of all the nutrients. (Do not let the ice cubes melt into the juice or they will dilute its flavour.)

200g/7oz raw beetroot (beets)

1cm/$^1\!/_2$in piece fresh root ginger, peeled

1 large orange

Melon Pick-me-up

Spicy fresh root ginger is delicious with melon and pear in this reviving and invigorating concoction. Charentais or Galia melon can be used instead of the cantaloupe melon in this recipe. To enjoy fresh root ginger at its best, buy it in small quantities and keep in a cool, dry place for up to a week. As it ages, the root will dry out and become hard.

SERVES ONE

1 Quarter the cantaloupe melon, remove the seeds using a teaspoon or a sharp knife, and carefully slice the flesh away from the skin, reserving any juice. Quarter the pears and reserve any juice.

2 Using a juice extractor, juice the melon flesh and juice, quartered pears and juice and the fresh root ginger. Pour the juice into a tall glass and serve immediately.

$^{1}/_{2}$ **cantaloupe melon**

2 pears

2.5cm/1in piece of fresh root ginger

Apple Shiner

This refreshing fusion of sweet apple, honeydew melon, red grapes and lemon provides a reviving burst of energy and a feel-good sensation. Serve as a drink or use to pour over muesli (granola) for a quick and healthy breakfast.

SERVES ONE

1 eating apple

$^{1}/_{2}$ **honeydew melon**

90g/3$^{1}/_{2}$oz red grapes

15ml/1 tbsp lemon juice

1 Quarter the apple and remove the core. Cut the melon into quarters, remove the seeds and slice the flesh away from the skin.

2 Using a juice extractor, juice the apple, melon and grapes. Alternatively, process the fruit in a food processor or blender for 2–3 minutes, until smooth. Pour the juice into a long, tall glass, stir in the lemon juice and serve immediately.

Citrus Sparkle

Zesty citrus fruits are packed with vitamin C, which is necessary for a healthy immune system. Pink grapefruit have a sweeter flavour than the yellow varieties – in fact, the pinker they are, the sweeter they are likely to be. For a lighter drink to serve two, divide the juice between two glasses and top up with sparkling mineral water or soda water (club soda) and ice cubes.

SERVES ONE

1 Cut the pink grapefruit and orange in half and squeeze out the juice using a citrus fruit squeezer.

2 Pour the juice into a glass, stir in 15ml/1 tbsp lemon juice, add the remaining lemon juice if required and serve immediately.

1 pink grapefruit

1 orange

30ml/2 tbsp freshly squeezed lemon juice

Hum-zinger

Aromatic tropical fruits make a drink that is bursting with flavour and energy. Enjoy a glass first thing in the morning to kick-start your day.

SERVES ONE

$^1/_2$ pineapple, peeled

1 small mango, peeled and stoned (pitted)

$^1/_2$ small papaya, seeded and peeled

1 Remove any "eyes" left in the pineapple, then cut all the fruit into fairly coarse chunks.

2 Using a juice extractor, juice the fruit. Alternatively, use a food processor or blender and process for about 2–3 minutes until smooth. Pour into a glass and serve immediately.

2 pink grapefruit, halved

2 ripe pears

Grapefruit and Pear Juice

This deliciously refreshing rose-tinged blend will keep you bright-eyed and bushy-tailed. Its sharp yet sweet flavour is perfect for breakfast or as a pick-me-up when energy levels are flagging. If the grapefruit are particularly tart, serve the juice with a little bowl of brown sugar, or even brown sugar stirrers.

SERVES TWO

1 Take a thin slice from one grapefruit half and halve it. Cut a few thin slices of pear. Squeeze the juice from the grapefruit halves, then the pears using a juicer.

2 Combine the fruit juices and pour into two glasses. Add a few ice cubes to each glass and decorate with the grapefruit and pear slices. Serve immediately.

Strawberry Apple Slush

Sweet, juicy strawberries make a delicately fragrant juice, with a consistency that's not too thick and not too thin. The addition of apple juice and just a hint of vanilla creates a tantalizing treat that's perfect for sipping on a lazy summer's afternoon.

SERVES TWO

300g/11oz/2³/₄ cups ripe strawberries

2 small, crisp eating apples

10ml/2 tsp vanilla syrup

1 Reserve a couple of strawberries and hull the remaining ones. Roughly chop the apples and push all the fruits through a juicer. Stir in the vanilla syrup.

2 Half-fill two tall glasses with crushed ice. Pour over the juice, decorate with the reserved strawberries (slicing them if you like) and serve immediately.

Honey and Watermelon Tonic

This refreshing juice will help to cool the body, calm the digestion and cleanse the system, and may even have aphrodisiac qualities. On hot days add ice cubes to keep the juice cool. The distinctive pinkish-red flesh of the watermelon gives this tonic a beautiful hue – decorate with a few fresh mint leaves to provide a stunning colour contrast.

SERVES FOUR

1 Cut the watermelon flesh into chunks, cutting away the skin and discarding the black seeds. Place in a large bowl, pour the chilled water over and leave to stand for 10 minutes.

2 Tip the mixture into a large sieve set over a bowl. Using a wooden spoon, press gently on the fruit to extract all the liquid.

3 Stir in the lime juice and sweeten to taste with honey. Pour into a jug (pitcher) or glasses and serve.

1 watermelon

1 litre/1³/₄ pints/ 4 cups chilled still mineral water

juice of 2 limes

clear honey, to taste

Cranberry, Ginger
and Cinnamon Spritzer

Partially freezing fruit juice gives it a refreshingly slushy texture.
The combination of cranberry and apple juice is tart and clean. Add
a few fresh or frozen cranberries to decorate each glass, if you like.

SERVES FOUR

600ml/1 pint/2^1/$_2$ cups
chilled cranberry juice

150ml/^{1}/$_4$ pint/^{2}/$_3$ cup clear
apple juice

4 cinnamon sticks

about 400ml/14fl oz/
1^2/$_3$ cups chilled ginger ale

1 Pour the cranberry juice into a shallow freezerproof container and freeze for about 2 hours, or until a thick layer of ice crystals has formed around the edges.

2 Mash the semi-frozen juice with a fork to break up the ice, then return the mixture to the freezer for a further 2–3 hours or until it is almost solid.

3 Pour the apple juice into a small pan, add two cinnamon sticks and bring to just below boiling point. Pour into a jug (pitcher) and leave to cool, then remove the cinnamon sticks and set them aside. Cool, then chill the juice.

4 Spoon the cranberry ice into a food processor or blender. Add the cinnamon-flavoured apple juice and process briefly until slushy. Pile the mixture into cocktail glasses, top up with chilled ginger ale, decorate with cinnamon sticks and serve immediately.

Lavender Orange Lush

This fragrant, lavender-scented juice is guaranteed to perk up a jaded palate in no time at all. It has a heavenly aroma and distinct yet subtle taste. Make plenty and keep it in the refrigerator. Use extra lavender sprigs as fun stirrers or a pretty garnish.

SERVES FOUR TO SIX

10–12 lavender flowers

45ml/3 tbsp caster (superfine) sugar

8 large oranges

1 Pull the lavender flowers from their stalks and put them into a bowl with the sugar and 120ml/4fl oz/$^1/_2$ cup boiling water. Stir briskly until the sugar has dissolved, then leave the lavender to steep for 10 minutes.

2 Squeeze the oranges using a citrus juicer and pour the juice into a jug (pitcher). Strain the lavender syrup into the juice and chill. Serve poured over ice.

Ice Cool Currant

Intensely flavoured blackcurrants, whizzed in a blender with crushed ice, make a drink so thick and slushy that you might want to serve it with long spoons. If you have a glut of blackcurrants, make a double quantity of the juice and store it in the refrigerator for up to a week, ready to blend with ice.

SERVES TWO

125g/4¹/₄oz/generous 1 cup blackcurrants

60ml/4 tbsp light muscovado (brown) sugar

good pinch of mixed (apple pie) spice (optional)

VARIATION *Redcurrants or a mixture of redcurrants and blackcurrants could also be used instead of blackcurrants if you like. The juice will have a lighter taste.*

1 Put the blackcurrants and sugar in a pan. (There is no need to string the blackcurrants first.) Add the mixed spice, if using, and pour in 100ml/3¹/₂fl oz/scant ¹/₂ cup water. Bring the mixture to the boil and cook for 2–3 minutes, or until the blackcurrants are completely soft.

2 Press the mixture through a sieve into a bowl, pressing the pulp with the back of a dessertspoon to extract as much juice as possible. Set aside to cool completely.

3 Put 225g/8oz crushed ice in a food processor or blender with the cooled juice and process for about 1 minute until slushy and thoroughly mixed. Scrape the drink into tall glasses and serve immediately.

Lemon Float

Traditional lemonade made with freshly squeezed lemons and served with scoops of ice cream and soda water makes the ultimate refresher. The lemonade can be stored in the refrigerator for up to two weeks, so make a double batch when the weather is hot.

SERVES FOUR

6 lemons

200g/7oz/1 cup caster (superfine) sugar

8 scoops vanilla ice cream

1 Finely grate the rind from the lemons, then squeeze out the juice using a citrus juicer. Put the rind in a bowl with the sugar and pour over 600ml/1 pint/2^1/$_2$ cups boiling water. Stir until the sugar dissolves, then leave to cool.

2 Stir the lemon juice into the cooled syrup. Strain and chill for several hours. To serve, put a scoop of ice cream in each glass, then half-fill with the lemonade and add plenty of lemon slices. Top up with soda water (club soda) and add another scoop of ice cream to each glass and serve immediately.

Blue Lagoon

Blueberries are not only an excellent source of betacarotene and vitamin C, but they are also rich in flavonoids, which help to cleanse the system. Mixed with other dark red fruits, such as blackberries and grapes, they make a highly nutritious and extremely delicious blend that can be stored in the refrigerator and enjoyed throughout the day.

SERVES ONE

90g/3¹/₂oz/scant 1 cup blackcurrants or blackberries

150g/5oz red grapes

130g/4¹/₂oz/generous 1 cup blueberries

1 If using blackcurrants, gently pull the stalks through the tines of a fork to remove the fruit, then remove the stalks from the grapes.

2 Push all the fruits through a juicer, saving a few for decoration. Place some ice in a medium glass and pour over the juice. Decorate with the reserved fruit and serve.

Strawberry and Banana Smoothie

The blend of perfectly ripe bananas and strawberries creates a drink that is both fruity and creamy, with a luscious texture. Papaya, mango or pineapple can be used instead of strawberries for a tropical drink. Popular with adults and children alike, this is a great way to get children to enjoy fruit – much healthier than commercial milkshakes, too.

SERVES FOUR

1 Hull the strawberries. Peel the bananas and chop them into fairly large chunks.

2 Put the fruit in a food processor or blender. Process to a thick, coarse purée, scraping down the sides of the goblet as necessary.

3 Add the skimmed milk and ice cubes, crushing the ice first unless you have a heavy-duty processor. Process until smooth and thick. Pour into tall glasses and top each with strawberry slices to decorate. Serve immediately.

200g/7oz/1³/₄ cups
strawberries, plus
extra, sliced,
to decorate

2 ripe bananas

300ml/¹/₂ pint/1¹/₄
cups skimmed milk

10 ice cubes

EXTRAS *For a rich and velvety drink, add 120ml/ 4fl oz/¹/₂ cup coconut milk and process as above. Reduce the volume of milk to 175ml/6fl oz/³/₄ cup.*

Raspberry and Orange Smoothie

Sharp-sweet raspberries and zesty oranges taste fabulous combined with the light creaminess of yogurt. This smoothie takes just minutes to prepare, making it perfect for breakfast – or any other time of the day. If you like a really tangy drink add freshly squeezed lemon or lime juice to taste.

SERVES TWO TO THREE

1 Place the raspberries and yogurt in a food processor or blender and process for about 1 minute, until smooth and creamy.

2 Add the orange juice to the raspberry and yogurt mixture and process for about 30 seconds, or until thoroughly combined. Pour into tall glasses and serve immediately.

COOK'S TIP *For a super-chilled version, use frozen raspberries or a combination of frozen summer berries such as strawberries, redcurrants and blueberries instead of fresh. You may need to blend the raspberries and yogurt slightly longer for a really smooth result.*

250g/9oz/1¹/₂ cups
fresh raspberries,
chilled

200ml/7fl oz/scant
1 cup natural (plain)
yogurt, chilled

300ml/¹/₂pint/1¹/₄
cups freshly squeezed
orange juice, chilled

New York Egg Cream

No one knows precisely why this legendary drink is called egg cream, but some say it was a witty way of describing richness at a time when no one could afford to put both expensive eggs and cream together in a drink. Use full-fat (whole) milk for a really creamy taste. Dust a little cocoa powder over the top of the egg cream before serving, if you like.

SERVES ONE

45–60ml/3–4 tbsp good quality chocolate syrup

120ml/4fl oz/¹/₂ cup chilled milk

175ml/6fl oz/³/₄ cup chilled sparkling mineral water

1 Carefully pour the chocolate syrup into the bottom of a tall glass avoiding dripping any on the inside of the glass.

2 Pour the chilled milk into the glass on to the chocolate syrup.

3 Gradually pour the chilled sparkling mineral water into the glass, sip up any foam that rises to the top of the glass and carefully continue to add the remaining chilled sparkling mineral water. Stir well before drinking.

COOK'S TIP *An authentic egg cream is made with an old-fashioned seltzer dispenser that you press and spritz. In any case, you can use soda water (club soda) rather than mineral water, if you like.*

Banana and Maple Flip

This satisfying drink is packed with so much goodness that it makes a complete breakfast in a glass – great for when you're in a hurry. Be sure to use a really fresh free-range egg. The glass can be decorated with a slice of orange or lime to serve.

SERVES ONE

1 small banana, peeled
and halved

50ml/2fl oz/¼ cup thick Greek
(US strained plain) yogurt

1 egg

30ml/2 tbsp maple syrup

1 Put the peeled and halved banana, thick Greek yogurt, egg and maple syrup in a food processor or blender. Add 30ml/ 2 tbsp chilled water.

2 Process the ingredients constantly for about 2 minutes, or until the mixture turns a really pale, creamy colour and has a nice frothy texture.

3 Pour the banana and maple flip into a tall, chilled glass and serve immediately. Decorate the glasses with an orange or lime slice, if you like.

To chill the drinking glass quickly, place it in the freezer while you are preparing the drink.

For a hint of sharpness, add 5ml/1 tsp lemon or lime juice or use a slightly tangy yogurt.

Chocolate Brownie Milkshake

This truly indulgent drink is so simple, yet utterly rich and luxurious, so take a quiet moment to yourself and just sit back, relax and enjoy. For an even more indulgent treat, spoon over whipped cream and sprinkle with grated chocolate to serve.

SERVES ONE

40g/1¹/₂oz chocolate brownies

200ml/7fl oz/scant 1 cup full cream (whole) milk

2 scoops vanilla ice cream

1 Crumble the chocolate brownies into a food processor or blender and add the milk. Blend until the mixture is smooth.

2 Add the ice cream to the chocolate milk mixture and blend until the shake is really smooth and frothy. Pour into a tall glass and serve immediately.

Peppermint Candy Crush

The next time you see peppermint candy canes that are on sale at Christmas time, buy a few sticks and make this fun kid's drink . All you need to do is whizz up the candy with some milk and freeze until slushy, so it's ready and waiting for thirsty youngsters.

SERVES FOUR

90g/3¹/₂oz pink peppermint candy canes, plus four extra to serve

750ml/1¹/₄ pints/3 cups milk

a few drops of pink food colouring (optional)

1 While the candy canes are still in their wrappers, break into small bits using a rolling pin. (If it is unwrapped, put the candy in a polythene bag before you crush it.) Tip the pieces into a food processor or blender.

2 Pour the milk over the candy and add a few drops of pink food colouring, if using. Process until the cane is broken up into tiny pieces, then pour the mixture into a shallow freezer container and freeze for 2 hours, or until frozen around the edges.

3 Beat the mixture with a fork, breaking up the semi-frozen areas and stirring them into the centre. Re-freeze and repeat the process once or twice more until the mixture is slushy. Spoon into tall glasses and serve with candy cane stirrers.

Drinks

FROM CHILLED COCKTAILS AND ICY SHAKES TO WINTER
WARMERS, THERE ARE MANY UNUSUAL DRINKS YOU
CAN MAKE WITH JUST THREE OR FOUR INGREDIENTS.
YOU'LL NEED A SPECIAL ELECTRIC JUICER TO MAKE
SOME OF THE JUICES BUT ALL THE OTHER DRINKS CAN
BE WHIPPED UP IN AN INSTANT USING ORDINARY
KITCHEN EQUIPMENT. WARM YOURSELF UP WITH A CUP
OF CARDAMOM HOT CHOCOLATE OR A RUM AND STAR
ANISE HOT TODDY OR TRY A REFRESHING SEA BREEZE
OR MARGARITA COCKTAIL.

Cardamom Hot Chocolate

Hot chocolate is a wonderful treat at any time of day – for breakfast with a warm croissant, as a teatime treat on a cold winter afternoon or before bed to help you sleep. Adding spicy cardamom gives this hot chocolate an extra rich, fragrant aroma.

SERVES FOUR

900ml/1½ pints/3¾ cups milk

2 cardamom pods, bruised

200g/7oz plain (semisweet) chocolate, broken into pieces

1 Put the milk in a pan with the cardamom pods and bring to the boil. Add the chocolate and whisk until melted.

2 Using a slotted spoon, remove the cardamom pods and discard. Pour the hot chocolate into heatproof glasses, mugs or cups and serve with whipped cream.

Atole

This drink, rather like a thick milkshake in consistency, is made from Mexican cornflour (masa harina) and flavoured with piloncillo (Mexican unrefined brown sugar). Ground cinnamon and/or fresh fruit purées are often added before serving, and some recipes introduce ground almonds.

SERVES SIX

1 Combine the milk with 600ml/ 1 pint/2½ cups cold water. Put the masa harina in a heavy pan and gradually beat in the milk and water mixture to make a smooth paste.

2 Place the pan over a moderate heat, add the vanilla pod and bring the mixture to the boil, stirring constantly until it thickens. Beat in the sugar and stir until the sugar has dissolved. Remove from the heat, discard the vanilla and serve.

200g/7oz/1³/₄ cups white masa harina

600ml/1 pint/ 2¹/₂ cups milk

1 vanilla pod (bean)

50g/2oz/¹/₄ cup piloncillo or soft dark brown sugar

EXTRAS *Process 115g/4oz/ 1 cup strawberries, chopped pineapple or orange segments in a food processor or blender until smooth, then press the purée through a sieve. Stir the purée into the corn mixture and return the pan to the heat until warmed through. Remove the vanilla pod and serve.*

Café de Olla

This spiced black coffee is one of the most popular drinks in Mexico. The name means out of the pot, which refers to the heavy earthenware cooking pot, or *olla*, in which the coffee is made. Piloncillo is the local unrefined brown sugar, but any soft dark brown sugar can be used. French or Viennese roast coffees work particularly well in this hot drink.

SERVES FOUR

115g/4oz/¹/₂ cup piloncillo or soft dark brown sugar

4 cinnamon sticks, each about 15cm/ 6in long

50g/2oz/²/₃ cup freshly ground coffee, from dark-roast coffee beans

1 Pour 1 litre/1¾ pints/4 cups water into a pan. Add the sugar and cinnamon sticks. Heat gently, stirring occasionally to make sure that the sugar dissolves, then bring to the boil. Boil rapidly for about 20 minutes, until the syrup has reduced by one-quarter.

2 Add the ground coffee to the syrup and stir well, then bring the liquid back to the boil. Remove from the heat, cover the pan and leave to stand for about 5 minutes.

3 Strain the coffee through a fine sieve (strainer), and pour into cups.

Vanilla Caffè Latte

This luxurious vanilla and chocolate version of the classic coffee drink can be served at any time of the day topped with whipped cream, with cinnamon sticks to stir and flavour the drink. Caffè latte is a popular breakfast drink in Italy and France, and is now widely available elsewhere.

SERVES TWO

1 Pour the milk into a small pan and bring to the boil, then remove from the heat. Mix the espresso or very strong coffee with 500ml/16fl oz/ 2 cups of the boiled milk in a large heatproof jug (pitcher). Sweeten with vanilla sugar to taste.

2 Return the remaining boiled milk in the pan to the heat and add the 45ml/3 tbsp vanilla sugar. Stir constantly until dissolved. Bring to the boil, then reduce the heat. Add the dark chocolate and continue to heat, stirring constantly until all the chocolate has melted and the mixture is smooth and glossy.

3 Pour the chocolate milk into the jug of coffee and whisk thoroughly. Serve in tall mugs or glasses topped with whipped cream and with cinnamon sticks to stir.

700ml/24fl oz/scant 3 cups milk

250ml/8fl oz/1 cup espresso or very strong coffee

45ml/3 tbsp vanilla sugar, plus extra to taste

115g/4oz dark (bittersweet) chocolate, grated

Frothy Hot Chocolate

Real hot chocolate doesn't come as a powder in a packet – it is made with the best chocolate you can afford, whisked in hot milk until really frothy. This recipe uses dark (bittersweet) chocolate, but for a special treat you could use Mexican chocolate, which is flavoured with almonds, cinnamon and vanilla, and sweetened with sugar. All the ingredients are crushed together in a special mortar, and heated over coals. The powdered mixture is then shaped into discs, which can be bought in specialist stores.

SERVES FOUR

1 Pour the milk into a pan. Split the vanilla pod lengthways using a sharp knife to reveal the seeds, and add it to the milk; the vanilla seeds and the pod will flavour the milk.

2 Add the chocolate. The amount to use depends on personal taste – start with a smaller amount if you are unsure of the flavour and taste at the beginning of step 3, adding more if necessary.

3 Heat the chocolate milk gently, stirring until all the chocolate has melted and the mixture is smooth, then whisk with a wire whisk until the mixture boils. Remove the vanilla pod from the pan and divide the drink among four mugs or heatproof glasses. Serve the hot chocolate immediately.

1 litre/1³/₄pints/ 4 cups milk

50–115g/2–4oz dark (bittersweet) chocolate, grated

1 vanilla pod (bean)

Cuba Libre

Rum and coke takes on a much livelier, citrus flavour in this vibrant Caribbean cocktail that's sure to put you in the mood to party. The refreshing flavour and aroma of freshly squeezed limes is the dominant taste in this blend, and the dark rum really packs a punch when combined with the sweet, syrupy cola drink.

SERVES EIGHT

9 limes

250ml/8fl oz/1 cup dark rum

800ml/1¹/₃ pints/3¹/₂ cups cola drink

1 Thinly slice one lime then, using a citrus juicer, squeeze the juice from the rest of the limes.

2 Put plenty of ice cubes into a large glass jug (pitcher), tucking the lime slices around them, then pour in the lime juice.

3 Pour the rum into the jug and stir well with a long-handled spoon. Top up with cola drink and serve immediately in tall glasses with stirrers.

Tropical Fruit Royale

Based on the Kir Royale, a blend of champagne and crème de cassis, this elegant cocktail is made with tropical fruits and sparkling wine. Remember to blend the fruits ahead of time to give the mango ice cubes time to freeze.

SERVES SIX

1 Peel the mangoes, cut the flesh off the stone (pit), then put the flesh in a food processor or blender. Process until smooth, scraping the mixture down from the sides of the bowl.

2 Fill an ice cube tray with a good half of the mango purée and freeze for 2 hours until solid.

3 Cut six wedges from one or two of the passion fruits and scoop the pulp from the rest into the remaining mango purée. Process until well blended.

4 Spoon the mixture into six stemmed glasses. Divide the mango ice cubes among the glasses, top up with sparkling wine and add the passion fruit wedges. Serve with stirrers.

2 large mangoes

6 passion fruit

sparkling wine

Lemon Vodka

Very similar to the deliciously moreish Italian liqueur, Limoncello, this lemon vodka should be drunk in small quantities due to its hefty alcoholic punch. Blend the sugar, lemons and vodka and keep in a bottle in the refrigerator, ready for pouring over crushed ice, or topping up with soda or sparkling water.

SERVES TWELVE TO FIFTEEN

10 large lemons

275g/10oz/generous 1¼ cups caster (superfine) sugar

250ml/8fl oz/1 cup vodka

1 Squeeze the lemons using a citrus juicer. Pour the juice into a jug (pitcher), add the sugar and whisk well until all the sugar has dissolved.

2 Strain the sweetened lemon juice into a clean bottle or narrow-necked jar and add the vodka. Shake the mixture well to combine and chill for up to 2 weeks.

3 To serve, fill small glasses with ice and pour over the lemon vodka or pour into larger, ice-filled glasses and top up with chilled soda water (club soda).

Quick Bloody Mary

Using vodka flavoured with chilli gives this drink the perfect spicy kick. You can make your own chilli vodka, simply by slipping a fresh red chilli into a bottle of vodka and leaving the flavours to infuse.

SERVES FOUR

250ml/8fl oz/1 cup chilli vodka

1.2 litres/2 pints/5 cups tomato juice

5ml/1 tsp celery salt

FROM THE STORECUPBOARD

2.5ml/¹/₂ tsp ground black pepper

1 Quarter-fill four tall glasses with a handful of ice cubes and pour over the chilli vodka. (If there's a chilli in the bottle, be careful not to pour it out!)

2 Pour the tomato juice into a jug (pitcher) and add the celery salt and pepper. Stir well to combine.

3 Pour the flavoured tomato juice over the vodka, mix well using a long-handled spoon or stirrer, and serve with a stick of celery in each glass.

Gin Fizz

The combination of sourness and fizziness in this 19th-century recipe is what makes it so refreshing.

SERVES ONE

1 Shake the gin, lemon juice and sugar with ice until the sugar is properly dissolved. Pour out into a frosted, tall, narrow glass half-filled with ice, and top up with soda.

2 Add two straws. There should be a little less soda than the other combined ingredients.

2 measures/3 tbsp gin

juice of half a large lemon

5ml/1 tsp caster (superfine) sugar

soda water

Sea Breeze

One of today's most requested cocktails, Sea Breeze was one of the first popular cocktails to use cranberry juice. Ocean Spray is one of the most famous brands, but the supermarkets nearly all have a proprietary version.

SERVES ONE

2 measures/3 tbsp vodka

2 measures/3 tbsp grapefruit juice

3 measures/4$^{1}/_2$ tbsp cranberry juice

1 Shake all the ingredients well with plenty of ice, and pour everything into a chilled highball glass.

2 Add a wedge of lime and a few cranberries.

Perfect Manhattan

When making Manhattans it's a matter of preference whether you use sweet vermouth, dry vermouth or a mixture of the two. Both of the former require a dash of Angostura bitters. The last, given here, is such a harmoniously balanced mixture that it doesn't need it.

SERVES ONE

2 measures/3 tbsp rye whiskey

¹⁄₄ measure/1 tsp dry vermouth

¹⁄₄ measure/1 tsp sweet red vermouth

1 Pour the whiskey and vermouths into a bar glass half-full of ice. Stir well for 30 seconds to mix and chill.

2 Strain on the rocks or straight up into a chilled cocktail glass.

3 Pare away a small strip of lemon rind. Tie it into a knot to help release the oils from the rind, and drop it into the cocktail.

4 Add a maraschino cherry with its stalk left intact. As any Manhattan drinker wil tell you, the cherry is essential.

Margarita

With the Tequila Sunrise, Margarita, created in Tijuana in the late 1940s, is probably the best-known tequila cocktail of them all. Its saltiness and sourness make it a great aperitif. Some recipes use lemon juice instead of lime, but lime juice sharpens its bite.

SERVES ONE

1 1/2 measures/6 tsp silver tequila

1/2 measure/2 tsp Cointreau

juice of a lime

FROM THE STORECUPBOARD

salt

1 Rub the rim of a cocktail glass with a wedge of fresh lime, and then dip it in fine salt.

2 Shake the tequila, Cointreau and lime juice with ice, and strain into the prepared glass. Garnish with a twist of cucumber rind or a half-slice of lime.

Brandy Alexander

One of the greatest cocktails of them all, Alexander can be served at the end of a grand dinner with coffee as a creamy digestif, or as the first drink of the evening at a cocktail party, since the cream in it helps to line the stomach. It was possibly originally made with gin rather than brandy, and the cream was sweetened, but the formula below is undoubtedly the best of all possible worlds.

SERVES ONE

1 measure/1¹/₂ tbsp cognac

1 measure/1¹/₂ tbsp brown crème de cacao

1 measure/1¹/₂ tbsp double (heavy) cream

1 Shake the ingredients thoroughly with ice, and strain into a cocktail glass.

2 Scatter ground nutmeg, or grate a little whole nutmeg, on top. Alternatively, sprinkle with grated dark chocolate.

Spritzer

The most famous white wine cocktail is this simple fizzy creation. Everyone who drinks spritzers seems to have his or her own preferred proportions, but this recipe should be reliable. The point is that the drink is lower in alcohol than a standard glass of wine.

SERVES ONE

3 measures/4^{1}/$_{2}$ tbsp dry white wine

4 measures/6 tbsp soda water

1 Half-fill a highball glass with cracked ice, and add the wine and soda.

2 Garnish with mixed summer berries if you like, but the drink doesn't really need them.

Nutritional Information

The nutritional analysis below is **per portion**, unless otherwise stated.

p62 Zingy Papaya, Lime and Ginger Salad
Energy 58Kcal/245kJ; Protein 1g; Carbohydrate 14g, of which sugars 14g; Fat 0g, of which saturates 0g; Cholesterol 0mg; Calcium 33mg; Fibre 3.1g; Sodium 900mg.

p63 Cantaloupe Melon with Grilled Strawberries
Energy 36Kcal/150kJ; Protein 1g; Carbohydrate 8g, of which sugars 8g; Fat 0g, of which saturates 0g; Cholesterol 0mg; Calcium 18mg; Fibre 1g; Sodium 100mg.

p64 Crunchy Oat Cereal
Energy 438Kcal/1823kJ; Protein 7g; Carbohydrate 36g, of which sugars 10g; Fat 31g, of which saturates 8g; Cholesterol 27mg; Calcium 46mg; Fibre 3.4g; Sodium 100mg.

p65 Cranachan Energy 284Kcal/1182kJ; Protein 12g; Carbohydrate 14g, of which sugars 8g; Fat 22g, of which saturates 10g; Cholesterol 6mg; Calcium 251mg; Fibre 2.3g; Sodium 100mg.

p66 Porridge
Energy 115Kcal/488kJ; Protein 3.6g; Carbohydrate 20.9g, of which sugars 0g; Fat 2.5g, of which saturates 0g; Cholesterol 0mg; Calcium 16mg; Fibre 2g; Sodium 300mg.

p67 Eggy Bread Panettone
Energy 465Kcal/1934kJ; Protein 7g; Carbohydrate 37g, of which sugars 26g; Fat 33g, of which saturates 11g; Cholesterol 210mg; Calcium 58mg; Fibre 0.5g; Sodium 300mg.

p68 Chocolate Brioche Sandwiches Energy 365Kcal/1530kJ; Protein 7g;

Carbohydrate 40g, of which sugars 19g; Fat 18g, of which saturates 0g; Cholesterol 1mg; Calcium 81mg; Fibre 1.3g; Sodium 300mg.

p68 Roast Bananas with Greek Yogurt and Honey
Energy 222Kcal/926kJ; Protein 9g; Carbohydrate 18g, of which sugars 17g; Fat 14g, of which saturates 7g; Cholesterol 0mg; Calcium 194mg; Fibre 0.7g; Sodium 100mg.

p70 Apricot Turnovers
Energy 291Kcal/1225kJ; Protein 3g; Carbohydrate 43g, of which sugars 22g; Fat 14g, of which saturates 0g; Cholesterol 0mg; Calcium 35mg; Fibre 0g; Sodium 200mg.

p71 Warm Pancakes with Caramelized Pears Energy 858Kcal/3590kJ; Protein 14g; Carbohydrate 103g, of which sugars 62g; Fat 46g, of which saturates 22g; Cholesterol 177mg; Calcium 285mg; Fibre 5.3g; Sodium 200mg.

p72 Smoked Salmon and Chive Omelette
Energy 234Kcal/974kJ; Protein 22g; Carbohydrate 0g, of which sugars 0g; Fat 16g, of which saturates 5g; Cholesterol 478mg; Calcium 79mg; Fibre 0g; Sodium 900mg.

p73 Quick Kedgeree
Energy 396Kcal/1654kJ; Protein 19g; Carbohydrate 32g, of which sugars 6g; Fat 21g, of which saturates 2g; Cholesterol 248mg; Calcium 69mg; Fibre 0.8g; Sodium 700mg.

p74 Jugged Kippers Energy 202Kcal/845kJ; Protein 11.9g; Carbohydrate 13.1g, of which sugars 2g; Fat 11.8g, of which saturates 4.8g; Cholesterol 87mg; Calcium 59mg; Fibre 1.5g; Sodium 650mg.

p75 Scotch Pancakes with Bacon and Maple Syrup
Per pancake: Energy 302Kcal/1265kJ; Protein 13g; Carbohydrate 32g, of which sugars 18g; Fat 15g, of which saturates 4g; Cholesterol 43mg; Calcium 60mg; Fibre 0.9g; Sodium 1.0g.

p76 Croque-monsieur
Energy 417Kcal/1750kJ; Protein 27g; Carbohydrate 36g, of which sugars 2g; Fat 19g, of which saturates 11g;

Cholesterol 73mg; Calcium 498mg; Fibre 1.1g; Sodium 1.1g.

p76 Eggs Benedict
Energy 279Kcal/1158kJ; Protein 16g; Carbohydrate 0g, of which sugars 0g; Fat 24g, of which saturates 12g; Cholesterol 369mg; Calcium 52mg; Fibre 0g; Sodium 700mg.

p80 Hummus
Energy 125Kcal/523kJ; Protein 6g; Carbohydrate 9g, of which sugars 0g; Fat 7g, of which saturates 1g; Cholesterol 0mg; Calcium 92mg; Fibre 3.1g; Sodium 100mg.

p81 Baba Ghanoush
Energy 395Kcal/1635kJ; Protein 13g; Carbohydrate 5g, of which sugars 4g; Fat 3g, of which saturates 5g; Cholesterol 0mg; Calcium 92mg; Fibre 8.1g; Sodium 100mg.

p82 Cannellini Bean Pâté
Energy 252Kcal/1635kJ; Protein 13g; Carbohydrate 21g, of which sugars 2g; Fat 13g, of which saturates 4g; Cholesterol 12mg; Calcium 120mg; Fibre 7.6g; Sodium 900mg.

p83 Chicken Liver and Brandy Pâté
Energy 263Kcal/1091kJ; Protein 16g; Carbohydrate 0g, of which sugars 0g; Fat 20g, of which saturates 12g; Cholesterol 170mg; Calcium 91mg; Fibre 0g; Sodium 400mg.

p84 Peperonata
Energy 140Kcal/583kJ; Protein 2g; Carbohydrate 8g, of which sugars 8g; Fat 11g, of which saturates 2g; Cholesterol 0mg; Calcium 19mg; Fibre 2.0g; Sodium 100mg.

p84 Artichoke and Cumin Dip Energy 37Kcal/155kJ; Protein 2g; Carbohydrate 2g, of which sugars 1g; Fat 3g, of which saturates 0g; Cholesterol 0mg; Calcium 29mg; Fibre 0.1g; Sodium 100mg.

p86 Sweet and Salty Vegetable Crisps
Energy 64Kcal/265kJ; Protein 1g; Carbohydrate 3g, of which sugars 3g; Fat 0g, of which saturates 1g; Cholesterol 0mg; Calcium 8mg; Fibre 0.7g; Sodium 100mg.

p87 Sizzling Prawns
Energy 109Kcal/450kJ; Protein 2g; Carbohydrate 1g, of which sugars 0g; Fat 11g, of which

saturates 2g; Cholesterol 17mg; Calcium 8mg; Fibre 0.1g; Sodium 100mg.

p88 Potted shrimps
Energy 326Kcal/1389kJ; Protein 11g; Carbohydrate 0g, of which sugars 0g; Fat 31g, of which saturates 26g; Cholesterol 170mg; Calcium 91mg; Fibre 0g; Sodium 400mg.

p88 Marinated Feta with Lemon and Oregano
Energy 803Kcal/3308kJ; Protein 8g; Carbohydrate 1g, of which sugars 1g; Fat 85g, of which saturates 18g; Cholesterol 35mg; Calcium 199mg; Fibre 0g; Sodium 700mg.

p90 Mushroom Caviar
Energy 101Kcal/417kJ; Protein 3g; Carbohydrate 23g, of which sugars 92g; Fat 9g, of which saturates 1g; Cholesterol 0mg; Calcium 14mg; Fibre 1.7g; Sodium 100mg.

p91 Brandade of Salt Cod
Energy 627Kcal/2583kJ; Protein 10g; Carbohydrate 1g, of which sugars 1g; Fat 64g, of which saturates 20g; Cholesterol 57mg; Calcium 96mg; Fibre 0.1g; Sodium 100mg.

p92 Chopped Egg and Onions Energy 245Kcal/1017kJ; Protein 12g; Carbohydrate 3g, of which sugars 2g; Fat 20g, of which saturates 5g; Cholesterol 389mg; Calcium 70mg; Fibre 0.5g; Sodium 200mg.

p92 Israeli Cheese with Green Olives
Energy 252Kcal/1040kJ; Protein 4g; Carbohydrate 0g, of which sugars 0g; Fat 26g, of which saturates 16g; Cholesterol 53mg; Calcium 116mg; Fibre 0.5g; Sodium 800mg.

p94 Bacon-rolled Enokitake Mushrooms
Energy 116Kcal/483kJ; Protein 9g; Carbohydrate 1g, of which sugars 0g; Fat 9g, of which saturates 3g; Cholesterol 27mg; Calcium 10mg; Fibre 1.2g; Sodium 500mg.

p95 Walnut and Goat's Cheese Bruschetta
Energy 520Kcal/2159kJ; Protein 16g; Carbohydrate 26g, of which sugars 7g; Fat 42g, of which saturates 13g; Cholesterol 47mg; Calcium 113mg; Fibre 0.6g; Sodium 500mg.

p98 Spanish Salted Almonds
Energy 206Kcal/853kJ; Protein 8g; Carbohydrate 2g, of which sugars 1g; Fat 19g, of which saturates 1g; Cholesterol 0mg; Calcium 80mg; Fibre 2.5g; Sodium 300mg.

p99 Golden Gruyère and Basil Tortillas
Energy 430Kcal/1795kJ; Protein 20g; Carbohydrate 33g, of which sugars 1g; Fat 25g, of which saturates 13g; Cholesterol 58mg; Calcium 613mg; Fibre 1.3g; Sodium 700mg.

p100 Polenta Chips
Per chip: Energy 35Kcal/144kJ; Protein 1g; Carbohydrate 3g, of which sugars 0g; Fat 2g, of which saturates 1g; Cholesterol 4mg; Calcium 20mg; Fibre 0.1g; Sodium 100mg.

p101 Parmesan Tuiles
Energy 48Kcal/199kJ; Protein 4g; Carbohydrate 0g, of which sugars 0g; Fat 3g, of which saturates 2g; Cholesterol 11mg; Calcium 118mg; Fibre 0g; Sodium 100mg.

p102 Yogurt Cheese in Olive Oil Energy 1927kcal/7943kJ; Protein 32g; Carbohydrate 10g, of which sugars 10g; Fat

201g, of which saturates 47g; Cholesterol 0mg; Calcium 758mg; Fibre 0.0g; Sodium 400mg.

p103 Eggs Mimosa
Energy 77Kcal/318kJ; Protein 4g; Carbohydrate 0g, of which sugars 0g; Fat 7g, of which saturates 2g; Cholesterol 116mg; Calcium 18mg; Fibre 0.5g; Sodium 100mg.

p104 Marinated Smoked Salmon with Lime and Coriander Energy 65Kcal/271kJ; Protein 9g; Carbohydrate 0g, of which sugars 0g; Fat 3g, of which saturates 1g; Cholesterol 12mg; Calcium 9mg; Fibre 0g; Sodium 600mg.

p104 Blinis with Caviar and Crème Fraîche
Energy 96Kcal/398kJ; Protein 2g; Carbohydrate 5g, of which sugars 3g; Fat 8g, of which saturates 5g; Cholesterol 39mg; Calcium 19mg; Fibre 0.2g; Sodium 200mg.

p106 Marinated Anchovies
Energy 112Kcal/469kJ; Protein 14g; Carbohydrate 1g, of which sugars 1g; Fat 6g, of which saturates 1g; Cholesterol 35mg; Calcium 172mg; Fibre 0.1g; Sodium 500mg.

p107 Chilli Prawn Skewers
Energy 51Kcal/215kJ; Protein 7g; Carbohydrate 5g, of which sugars 4g; Fat 0g, of which saturates 0g; Cholesterol 78mg; Calcium 37mg; Fibre 0.3g; Sodium 700mg.

p108 Salt Cod and Potato Fritters
Energy 718Kcal/2980kJ; Protein 21.1g; Carbohydrate 33.1g, of which sugars 1.9g; Fat 56.5g, of which saturates 8.3g; Cholesterol 165mg; Calcium 67mg; Fibre 1.6g; Sodium 196mg.

p109 Asian-style Crab Cakes Energy 70Kcal/209kJ; Protein 6g; Carbohydrate 2g, of which sugars 0g; Fat 4g, of which saturates 1g; Cholesterol 20mg; Calcium 4mg; Fibre 0.1g; Sodium 100mg.

p110 Crab and Water-chestnut Wontons Energy 41Kcal/175kJ; Protein 6g; Carbohydrate 4g, of which sugars 1g; Fat 0g, of which saturates 0g; Cholesterol 21mg; Calcium 36mg; Fibre 0.1g; Sodium 300mg.

p110 Chilli-spiced Chicken Wings Energy 428Kcal/1781kJ; Protein 30g; Carbohydrate 12g, of which sugars 4g; Fat 29g, of which saturates 6g; Cholesterol 129mg; Calcium 60mg; Fibre 0.3g; Sodium 200mg.

p112 Vietnamese Spring Rolls with Pork
Energy 218Kcal/910kJ; Protein 20g; Carbohydrate 3g, of which sugars 0g; Fat 14g, of which saturates 1g; Cholesterol 0mg; Calcium 2mg; Fibre 0g; Sodium 400mg.

p113 Curried Lamb Samosas
Energy 57Kcal/238kJ; Protein 4g; Carbohydrate 1g, of which sugars 0g; Fat 4g, of which saturates 2g; Cholesterol 18mg; Calcium 8mg; Fibre 0g; Sodium 100mg.

p116 Avocado Soup Energy 301Kcal/1240kJ; Protein 4g; Carbohydrate 5g, of which sugars 3g; Fat 30g, of which saturates 7g; Cholesterol 45mg; Calcium 86mg; Fibre 2.5g; Sodium 600mg.

p117 Vichyssoise
Energy 186kcal/781kJ; Protein 5g; Carbohydrate 16g, of which sugars 4g; Fat 4g, of which saturates 2g; Cholesterol 17mg; Calcium 8mg; Fibre 0.1g; Sodium 100mg.

p118 Avgolemono
Energy 117Kcal/495kJ; Protein 7g; Carbohydrate 15g, of which sugars 1g; Fat 4g, of which saturates 1g; Cholesterol 116mg; Calcium 26mg; Fibre 0.6g; Sodium 400mg.

p119 Simple Cream of Onion Soup Energy 499kcal/2073kJ; Protein 4g; Carbohydrate 21g, of which sugars 15g; Fat 45g, of which saturates 28g; Cholesterol 118mg; Calcium 89mg; Fibre 3.5g; Sodium 600mg.

p120 Capelletti in Broth
Energy 130Kcal/551kJ; Protein 6g; Carbohydrate 22g, of which sugars 1g; Fat 3g, of which saturates 1g; Cholesterol 5mg; Calcium 68mg; Fibre 1g; Sodium 600mg.

p120 Tiny Pasta in Broth
Energy 86Kcal/366kJ; Protein 4g; Carbohydrate 15g, of which sugars 1g; Fat 2g, of which saturates 1g; Cholesterol 2mg; Calcium 33mg; Fibre 0.8g; Sodium 500mg.

p122 Potato and Roasted Garlic Broth
Energy 122Kcal/515 kJ; Protein 5g; Carbohydrate 25g, of which sugars 1g; Fat 1g, of which saturates 0g; Cholesterol 0mg; Calcium 12mg; Fibre 2.2g; Sodium 900mg.

p123 Winter Squash Soup with Tomato Salsa
Energy 255Kcal/1059kJ; Protein 3g; Carbohydrate 18g, of which sugars 12g; Fat 19g; of which saturates 3g; Cholesterol 0mg; Calcium 86mg; Fibre 3.1g; Sodium 100mg.

p124 Butter Bean, Sun-dried Tomato and Pesto Soup
Energy 305Kcal/1276kJ; Protein 14g; Carbohydrate 23g, of which sugars 3g; Fat 18g, of which saturates 4g; Cholesterol 8mg; Calcium 136mg; Fibre 7.5g; Sodium 1.5g.

p125 Stilton and Watercress Soup Energy 162Kcal/671kJ; Protein 8g; Carbohydrate 1g, of which sugars 1g; Fat 14g, of which saturates 9g; Cholesterol 38mg; Calcium 169mg; Fibre 0.6g; Sodium 400mg.

p126 Curried Cauliflower Soup Energy 137Kcal/579kJ; Protein 11g; Carbohydrate 14g, of which sugars 12g; Fat 5g, of which saturates 2g; Cholesterol 11mg; Calcium 268mg; Fibre 2.3g; Sodium 200mg.

p127 Tuscan Bean Soup
Energy 209Kcal/877kJ; Protein 8g; Carbohydrate 19g, of which sugars 9g; Fat 12g, of which saturates 2g; Cholesterol 0mg; Calcium 79mg; Fibre 6.6g; Sodium 500mg.

p128 Pea Soup with Garlic
Energy 208Kcal/874kJ; Protein 14g; Carbohydrate 22g, of which sugars 6g; Fat 8g, of which saturates 4g; Cholesterol 13mg; Calcium 81mg; Fibre

11.7g; Sodium 700mg.

p129 Star-gazer Vegetable Soup Energy 102Kcal/425kJ; Protein 4g; Carbohydrate 19g, of which sugars 9g; Fat 1g, of which saturates 0g; Cholesterol 0mg; Calcium 44mg; Fibre 3.0g; Sodium 700mg.

p132 Baked Eggs with Creamy Leeks Energy 219Kcal/905kJ; Protein 9g; Carbohydrate 2g, of which sugars 2g; Fat 19g, of which saturates 10g; Cholesterol 261mg; Calcium 61g; Fibre 1.2g; Sodium 100mg.

p133 Red Onion and Olive Pissaladière Energy 436Kcal/1815kJ; Protein 6g; Carbohydrate 37g, of which sugars 6g; Fat 31g, of which saturates 2g; Cholesterol 0mg; Calcium 77mg; Fibre 1.5g; Sodium 500mg.

p134 Figs with Prosciutto and Roquefort Energy 192Kcal/808kJ; Protein 10g; Carbohydrate 19g, of which sugars 19g; Fat 9g, of which saturates 5g; Cholesterol 17mg; Calcium 142mg; Fibre 1.7g; Sodium 700mg.

p135 Pea and Mint Omelette Energy 216Kcal/898kJ; Protein 17g; Carbohydrate 2g, of which sugars 1g; Fat 15g, of which saturates 5g; Cholesterol 469mg; Calcium 87mg; Fibre 1.3g; Sodium 400mg.

p136 Warm Penne with Fresh Tomatoes and Basil Energy 556Kcal/2356kJ; Protein 16g; Carbohydrate 99g, of which sugars 7g; Fat 14g, of which saturates 2g; Cholesterol 0mg; Calcium 46mg; Fibre 5.1g; Sodium 100mg.

p137 Broccoli and Chilli Spaghetti Energy 675Kcal/ 2835kJ; Protein 16g; Carbohydrate 67g, of which sugars 5g; Fat 40g, of which saturates 6g; Cholesterol 0mg; Calcium 86mg; Fibre 5.5g; Sodium 100mg.

p138 Grilled Aubergine, Mint and Couscous Salad Energy 264Kcal/1101kJ; Protein 5g; Carbohydrate 35g, of which sugars 5g; Fat 12g, of which saturates 2g; Cholesterol 0mg; Calcium 39mg; Fibre 4.5g; Sodium 200mg.

p139 Marinated Courgette and Flageolet Bean Salad Energy 155Kcal/647kJ; Protein 8g; Carbohydrate 11g, of which sugars 2g; Fat 9g, of which saturates 1g; Cholesterol 0mg; Calcium 57mg; Fibre 4.7g; Sodium 300mg.

p140 Roasted Pepper and Hummus Wrap Energy 370Kcal/1533kJ; Protein 11g; Carbohydrate 53g, of which sugars 14g; Fat 14g, of which saturates 1g; Cholesterol 0mg; Calcium 101mg; Fibre 6g; Sodium 800mg.

p140 Focaccia with Sardines and Roast Tomatoes Energy 507Kcal/2134kJ; Protein 29g; Carbohydrate 54g, of which sugars 5g; Fat 21g, of which saturates 4g; Cholesterol 20mg; Calcium 205mg; Fibre 3.1g; Sodium 800mg.

p142 Jansson's Temptation Energy 688kcal/2859kJ; Protein 15g; Carbohydrate 51g, of which sugars 1g; Fat 49g, of which saturates 29g; Cholesterol 134mg; Calcium 182mg; Fibre 4.6g; Sodium 1g.

p143 Crisp Fried Whitebait Energy 591Kcal/2446kJ; Protein 22g; Carbohydrate 6g, of which sugars 0g; Fat 53g, of which saturates 0g; Cholesterol 0mg; Calcium 968mg; Fibre 0.2g; Sodium 300mg.

p144 Seared Tuna Niçoise Energy 325Kcal/1358kJ; Protein 39g; Carbohydrate 0g, of which sugars 0g; Fat 18g, of which saturates 4g; Cholesterol 158mg; Calcium 42mg; Fibre 0g; Sodium 200mg.

p144 Creamy Parmesan-Baked Eggs Energy 194Kcal/803kJ; Protein 11g; Carbohydrate 0g, of which sugars 0g; Fat 17g, of which saturates 8g; Cholesterol 280mg; Calcium 98mg; Fibre 0g; Sodium 200mg.

p146 Toasted Sourdough with Goat's Cheese Energy 414Kcal/1722kJ; Protein 13g; Carbohydrate 20g, of which sugars 2g; Fat 32g, of which saturates 11g; Cholesterol 44mg; Calcium 127mg; Fibre 0.7g; Sodium 600mg.

p147 Steak and Blue Cheese Sandwiches Energy 816Kcal/ 3418kJ; Protein 64g; Carbohydrate 52g, of which sugars 3g; Fat 41g, of which saturates 19g; Cholesterol 174mg; Calcium 434mg; Fibre 2.3g; Sodium 1.8g.

p148 Spicy Chorizo Sausage and Spring Onion Hash Energy 442Kcal/1843kJ; Protein 23g; Carbohydrate 23g, of which sugars 6g; Fat 29g, of which saturates 11g; Cholesterol 0mg; Calcium 41mg; Fibre 1.8g; Sodium 800mg.

p149 Baked Sweet Potatoes with Leeks and Gorgonzola Energy 352Kcal/1474kJ; Protein 10g; Carbohydrate 45g, of which sugars 24g; Fat 16g, of which saturates 7g; Cholesterol 26mg; Calcium 223mg; Fibre 7.2g; Sodium 700mg.

p152 Mussels in White Wine Energy 300Kcal/1252kJ; Protein 17g; Carbohydrate 5g, of which sugars 1g; Fat 13g, of which saturates 7g; Cholesterol 87mg; Calcium 83mg; Fibre 0.4g; Sodium 800mg.

p153 Crab and Cucumber Wraps Energy 310Kcal/1312kJ; Protein 15g; Carbohydrate 59g, of which sugars 2g; Fat 3g, of which saturates 0g; Cholesterol 25mg; Calcium 117mg; Fibre 2.4g; Sodium 200mg.

p154 Scallops with Fennel and Bacon Energy 452Kcal/1870kJ; Protein 20g; Carbohydrate 4g, of which sugars 3g; Fat 40g, of which saturates 22g; Cholesterol 108mg; Calcium 114mg; Fibre 3.6g; Sodium 800mg.

p155 Prawn and New Potato Stew Energy 271Kcal/1147kJ; Protein 22g; Carbohydrate 35g, of which sugars 6g; Fat 6g, of which saturates 2g; Cholesterol 219mg; Calcium 113mg; Fibre 2.9g; Sodium 1.5g.

p156 Haddock with Fennel Butter Energy 220Kcal/921kJ; Protein 29g; Carbohydrate 1g, of which sugars 1g; Fat 11g, of which saturates 7g; Cholesterol 81mg; Calcium 123mg; Fibre 0.3g; Sodium 200mg.

p157 Baked Salmon with Caraway Seeds Energy 665Kcal/2758kJ; Protein 51g; Carbohydrate 0g, of which sugars 0g; Fat 34g, of which saturates 20g; Cholesterol 186mg; Calcium 61mg; Fibre 0g; Sodium 300mg.

p158 Sea Bass in a Salt Crust Energy 200Kcal/842kJ; Protein 39g; Carbohydrate 0g, of which sugars 0g; Fat 5g, of which saturates 1g; Cholesterol 160mg; Calcium 261mg; Fibre 0g; Sodium 2.2g.

p159 Roast Cod wrapped in Prosciutto Energy 342Kcal/1427kJ; Protein 38g; Carbohydrate 3g, of which sugars 3g; Fat 20g, of which saturates 4g; Cholesterol 98mg; Calcium 25mg; Fibre 1g; Sodium 400mg.

p160 Grilled Hake with Lemon and Chilli Energy 206Kcal/862kJ; Protein 27g; Carbohydrate 0g, of which sugars 0g; Fat 11g, of which saturates 2g; Cholesterol 35mg; Calcium 26mg; Fibre 0g; Sodium 300mg.

p161 Trout with grilled Serrano Ham Energy 236Kcal/980kJ; Protein 19g; Carbohydrate 0g, of which sugars 0g; Fat 18g, of which saturates 9g; Cholesterol 43mg; Calcium 7mg; Fibre 0g; Sodium 1.2g.

p162 Tonno con Piselli Energy 329kcal/1379kJ; Protein 30g; Carbohydrate 23g, of which sugars 8g; Fat 14g, of which saturates 4g; Cholesterol 40mg; Calcium 83mg; Fibre 6.8g; Sodium 600mg.

p163 Filo-wrapped Fish Energy 509Kcal/2135kJ; Protein 36.2g; Carbohydrate 37.2g, of which sugars 10.4g; Fat 25.1g, of which saturates 4.2g; Cholesterol 75mg; Calcium 137mg; Fibre 5g; Sodium 192mg.

p164 Poached Fish in Spicy Tomato Sauce Energy 217Kcal/915kJ; Protein 36g; Carbohydrate 7g, of which sugars 3g; Fat 5g, of which saturates 2g; Cholesterol 94mg; Calcium 33mg; Fibre 1.1g; Sodium 400mg.

p165 Fish with Tomato and Pine Nuts Energy 308Kcal/1294kJ; Protein 42g;

Carbohydrate 6g, of which sugars 3g; Fat 13g, of which saturates 2g; Cholesterol 80mg; Calcium 94mg; Fibre 1.0g; Sodium 400mg.

p167 Baked Salmon with Green Sauce Energy 1044Kcal/4323kJ; Protein 51.6g; Carbohydrate 1.4g, of which sugars 1.2g; Fat 92.4g, of which saturates 28.5g; Cholesterol 231mg; Calcium 135mg; Fibre 0.7g; Sodium 558mg.

p168 Teriyaki Salmon Energy 618Kcal/2558kJ; Protein 31g; Carbohydrate 2g, of which sugars 2g; Fat 54g, of which saturates 7g; Cholesterol 75mg; Calcium 36mg; Fibre 0g; Sodium 1.4g.

p169 Roast Mackerel in Spicy Chermoula Paste Energy 591Kcal/2449kJ; Protein 39g; Carbohydrate 6g, of which sugars 4g; Fat 46g, of which saturates 9g; Cholesterol 108mg; Calcium 66mg; Fibre 1.1g; Sodium 200mg.

p170 Pan-fried Skate Wings Energy 160Kcal/671kJ; Protein 23g; Carbohydrate 0g, of which sugars 0g; Fat 7g, of which saturates 4g; Cholesterol 18mg; Calcium 64mg; Fibre 0.1g; Sodium 300mg.

p171 Sea Bass with Parsley and Lime Butter Energy 213Kcal/890kJ; Protein 29g; Carbohydrate 0g, of which sugars 0g; Fat 11g, of which saturates 5g; Cholesterol 138mg; Calcium 199mg; Fibre 0.1g; Sodium 200mg.

p174 Beef Patties with Onions and Peppers Energy 339Kcal/1416 kJ; Protein 30g; Carbohydrate 15g, of which sugars 11g; Fat 18g, of which saturates 6g; Cholesterol 70mg; Calcium 60mg; Fibre 4.0g; Sodium 100mg.

p175 Steak with Warm Tomato Salsa Energy 175Kcal/736kJ; Protein 25g; Carbohydrate 3g, of which sugars 7g; Fat 3g, of which

saturates 69g; Cholesterol 69mg; Calcium 18mg; Fibre 0.9g, Sodium 100mg.

p176 Meatballs in Tomato Sauce Energy 309Kcal/1290kJ; Protein 22g; Carbohydrate 12g, of which sugars 7g; Fat 20g, of which saturates 8g; Cholesterol 70mg; Calcium 89mg; Fibre 2.0g; Sodium 800mg.

p177 Beef Cooked in Red Wine Energy 244Kcal/1021kJ; Protein 24g; Carbohydrate 1g, of which sugars 0g; Fat 7g, of which saturates 3g; Cholesterol 69mg; Calcium 14mg; Fibre 0.1g; Sodium 100mg.

p178 Pan-fried Gaelic steaks Energy 738Kcal/3062kJ; Protein 54.1g; Carbohydrate 1.3g, of which sugars 1.3g; Fat 54.2g, of which saturates 31.6g; Cholesterol 226mg; Calcium 49mg; Fibre 0g; Sodium 200mg.

p179 Thai-style Rare Beef and Mango Salad Energy 316Kcal/1330kJ; Protein 28g; Carbohydrate 22g, of which sugars 22g; Fat 14g, of which saturates 4g; Cholesterol 57mg; Calcium 26mg; Fibre 3.9g; Sodium 900mg.

p180 North African Lamb Energy 412Kcal/1716 kJ; Protein 34g; Carbohydrate 16g, of which sugars 14g; Fat 24g, of which saturates 11g; Cholesterol 127mg; Calcium 36mg; Fibre 2.7g; Sodium 200mg.

p181 Lamb Steaks with Redcurrant Glaze Energy 301Kcal/1258kJ; Protein 24g; Carbohydrate 12g, of which sugars 12g; Fat 17g, of which saturates 8g; Cholesterol 94mg; Calcium 10mg; Fibre 0.0g; Sodium 100mg.

p182 Lamb Chops with a Mint Jelly Crust Energy 201Kcal/845kJ; Protein 22g; Carbohydrate 11g, of which sugars 2g; Fat 8g, of which saturates 3g; Cholesterol 67mg; Calcium 41mg; Fibre 0.3g; Sodium 300mg.

p183 Marinated Lamb with Oregano and Basil Energy 251Kcal/1042kJ; Protein 21g; Carbohydrate 0g, of which sugars 0g; Fat 19g, of which saturates 5g; Cholesterol 67mg; Calcium 29mg; Fibre 0g; Sodium 1.2g.

p184 Roast Shoulder of Lamb with Whole Garlic Cloves Energy 296Kcal/1244kJ; Protein 28g; Carbohydrate 19g, of which sugars 2g; Fat 13g, of which saturates 6g; Cholesterol

90mg; Calcium 16mg; Fibre 1.4g; Sodium 100mg.

p185 Roast Leg of Lamb with Rosemary and Garlic Energy 223Kcal/931kJ; Protein 28g; Carbohydrate 0g, of which sugars 0g; Fat 12g, of which saturates 4g; Cholesterol 99mg; Calcium 9mg; Fibre 0g; Sodium 100mg.

p186 Sweet-and-sour Lamb Energy 237Kcal/988kJ; Protein 20g; Carbohydrate 8g, of which sugars 8g; Fat 13g, of which saturates 4g; Cholesterol 74mg; Calcium 13mg; Fibre 0g; Sodium 200mg.

p187 Roast Lamb with Figs Energy 446Kcal/1859kJ; Protein 33g; Carbohydrate 11g, of which sugars 11g; Fat 27g, of which saturates 11g; Cholesterol 125mg; Calcium 39mg; Fibre 1.2g; Sodium 200mg.

p188 Paprika Pork Energy 249Kcal/1049kJ; Protein 31g; Carbohydrate 15g, of which sugars 8g; Fat 8g, of which saturates 2g; Cholesterol 88mg; Calcium 44mg; Fibre 3.0g; Sodium 300mg.

p189 Pork Kebabs Energy 218Kcal/916kJ; Protein 28g; Carbohydrate 8g, of which sugars 8g; Fat 8g, of which saturates 3g; Cholesterol 79mg; Calcium 22mg; Fibre 0.5g; Sodium 400mg.

p190 Fragrant Lemon Grass and Ginger Pork Patties Energy 187Kcal/782kJ; Protein 24g; Carbohydrate 0g, of which sugars 0g; Fat 10g, of which saturates 2g; Cholesterol 71mg; Calcium 8mg; Fibre 0g; Sodium 200mg.

p191 Pan-fried Gammon with Cider Energy 448Kcal/1860kJ; Protein 40g; Carbohydrate 1g, of which sugars 1g; Fat 30g, of which saturates 11g; Cholesterol 72mg; Calcium 26mg; Fibre 0g; Sodium 2.1g.

p192 Caramelized Onion and Sausage Tarte Tatin Energy 569Kcal/2368kJ; Protein 16g; Carbohydrate 37g, of which sugars 6g; Fat 41g, of which saturates 7g; Cholesterol 42mg; Calcium 143mg; Fibre 1.6g; Sodium 1.2g.

p193 Roast Pork with Juniper Berries and Bay Energy 238Kcal/1003kJ; Protein 42g; Carbohydrate 0g, of which sugars 0g; Fat 8g, of which saturates 2g; Cholesterol

126mg; Calcium 11mg; Fibre 0g; Sodium 200mg.

p194 Sticky Glazed Pork Ribs Energy 622Kcal/2605kJ; Protein 64g; Carbohydrate 16g, of which sugars 14g; Fat 34g, of which saturates 12g; Cholesterol 218mg; Calcium 78mg; Fibre 0g; Sodium 200mg.

p194 Chinese Spiced Pork Chops Energy 231Kcal/961kJ; Protein 27g; Carbohydrate 1g, of which sugars 0g; Fat 13g, of which saturates 4g; Cholesterol 76mg; Calcium 31mg; Fibre 0g; Sodium 500mg.

p198 Pot-roasted Chicken with Preserved Lemons Energy 280Kcal/1180kJ; Protein 36g; Carbohydrate 19g, of which sugars 1g; Fat 7g, of which saturates 1g; Cholesterol 135mg; Calcium 15mg; Fibre 1.5g; Sodium 200mg.

p199 Honey Mustard Chicken Energy 244Kcal/1028kJ; Protein 27g; Carbohydrate 12g, of which sugars 12g; Fat 10g, of which saturates 2g; Cholesterol 130mg; Calcium 33mg; Fibre 0.7g; Sodium 400mg.

p200 Drunken Chicken Energy 343Kcal/1437kJ; Protein 39g; Carbohydrate 1g, of which sugars 1g; Fat 11g, of which saturates 3g; Cholesterol 158mg; Calcium 38mg; Fibre 0.1g; Sodium 100mg.

p201 Soy-marinated Chicken Energy 67Kcal/703kJ; Protein 34g; Carbohydrate 4g, of which sugars 3g; Fat 2g, of which saturates 0g; Cholesterol 88mg; Calcium 36mg; Fibre 1.7g; Sodium 500mg.

p202 Stir-fried Chicken with Thai Basil Energy 209Kcal/878kJ; Protein 31g; Carbohydrate 5g, of which sugars 5g; Fat 7g, of which saturates 1g; Cholesterol 88mg; Calcium 22mg; Fibre 1.3g; Sodium 200mg.

p203 Crème Fraîche and Coriander Chicken

Energy 164Kcal/682kJ; Protein 16g; Carbohydrate 0g, of which sugars 0g; Fat 11g, of which saturates 5g; Cholesterol 96mg; Calcium 18mg; Fibre 0g; Sodium 200mg.

p204 Chicken Escalopes with Lemon and Serrano Ham Energy 253Kcal/1058kJ; Protein 36g; Carbohydrate 0g, of which sugars 0g; Fat 12g, of which saturates 6g; Cholesterol 109mg; Calcium 9mg; Fibre 0g; Sodium 500mg.

p205 Roast Chicken with Herb Cheese, Chilli and Lime Stuffing Energy 220Kcal/921kJ; Protein 29g; Carbohydrate 0g, of which sugars 0g; Fat 12g, of which saturates 6g; Cholesterol 131mg; Calcium 27mg; Fibre 0g; Sodium 200mg.

p206 Tandoori Chicken Energy 592Kcal/2479kJ; Protein 44g; Carbohydrate 7g, of which sugars 4.5g; Fat 11.4g, of which saturates 1.1g; Cholesterol 105mg; Calcium 54mg; Fibre 0.4g; Sodium 826mg.

p207 Roast Chicken with Black Pudding and Sage Energy 297Kcal/1246kJ; Protein 36g; Carbohydrate 5g, of which sugars 0g; Fat 15g, of which saturates 7g; Cholesterol 161mg; Calcium 87mg; Fibre 0g; Sodium 500mg.

p208 Spatchcock Poussins with Herb Butter Energy 810Kcal/3364kJ; Protein 51g; Carbohydrate 1g, of which sugars 0g; Fat 67g, of which saturates 29g; Cholesterol 341mg; Calcium 38mg; Fibre 0.3g; Sodium 400mg.

p209 Chilli-spiced Poussin Energy 337Kcal/1403kJ; Protein 25g; Carbohydrate 0g, of which sugars 0g; Fat 27g, of which saturates 6g; Cholesterol 131mg; Calcium 28mg; Fibre 0g; Sodium 200mg.

p210 Turkey Patties Energy 155Kcal/651kJ; Protein 26g; Carbohydrate 1g, of which sugars 1g; Fat 5g, of which saturates 1g; Cholesterol 79mg; Calcium 11mg; Fibre 0.1g; Sodium 100mg.

p211 Guinea Fowl with Whisky Sauce Energy 449Kcal/1866kJ; Protein 34g; Carbohydrate 1g, of which sugars 1g; Fat 29g, of which saturates 13g; Cholesterol 51mg; Calcium 56mg; Fibre 0g; Sodium 200mg.

p212 Pheasant Cooked in Port with Mushrooms Energy 457Kcal/1902kJ; Protein 31g; Carbohydrate 9g, of which sugars 9g; Fat 24g, of which saturates 11g; Cholesterol 263mg; Calcium 46mg; Fibre 0.8g; Sodium 200mg.

p213 Roast Pheasant with Sherry and Mustard Sauce Energy 393Kcal/1632kJ; Protein 30g; Carbohydrate 3g, of which sugars 3g; Fat 23g, of which saturates 11g; Cholesterol 263mg; Calcium 39mg; Fibre 0g; Sodium 400mg.

p214 Marmalade and Soy Roast Duck Energy 273Kcal/1144kJ; Protein 32g; Carbohydrate 8g, of which sugars 7g; Fat 13g, of which saturates 4g; Cholesterol 144mg; Calcium 20mg; Fibre 0g; Sodium 700mg.

p215 Duck with Plum Sauce Energy 334Kcal/1405kJ; Protein 33g; Carbohydrate 22g, of which sugars 21g; Fat 13g, of which saturates 4g; Cholesterol 144mg; Calcium 48mg; Fibre 2.8g; Sodium 100mg.

p218 Minty Courgette Linguine Energy 580Kcal/2442kJ; Protein 15g; Carbohydrate 87g, of which sugars 4g; Fat 21g, of which saturates 3g; Cholesterol 0mg; Calcium 61mg; Fibre 4.4g; Sodium 100mg.

p219 Pasta with Roast Tomatoes and Goat's Cheese Energy 749Kcal/3156kJ; Protein 28g; Carbohydrate 95g, of which sugars 12g; Fat 31g, of which saturates 13g; Cholesterol 49mg; Calcium 419mg; Fibre 6.5g; Sodium 500mg.

p220 Linguine with Anchovies and Capers Energy 527Kcal/2228kJ; Protein 15g; Carbohydrate 85g, of which sugars 3g; Fat 16g, of which saturates 2g; Cholesterol 4mg; Calcium 48mg; Fibre 3.5g; Sodium 300mg.

p220 Home-made Potato Gnocchi Energy 683Kcal/2892kJ; Protein 24g; Carbohydrate 136g, of which sugars 4g; Fat 8g, of which saturates 2g; Cholesterol 232mg; Calcium 164mg; Fibre 8.2g; Sodium 2.1g.

p222 Spaghettini with Roasted Garlic Energy 637Kcal/2670kJ; Protein 14g; Carbohydrate 77g, of which sugars 4g; Fat 33g, of which saturates 5g; Cholesterol 2mg; Calcium 53mg; Fibre 3.1g; Sodium 100mg.

p223 Spaghetti with Lemon Energy 450Kcal/1895kJ; Protein 11g; Carbohydrate 65g, of which sugars 3g; Fat 18g, of which saturates 3g; Cholesterol 0mg; Calcium 23mg; Fibre 2.6g; Sodium 100mg.

p224 Linguine with Rocket Energy 652Kcal/2729kJ; Protein 18g; Carbohydrate 66g, of which sugars 4g; Fat 37g, of which saturates 8g; Cholesterol 17mg; Calcium 225mg; Fibre 2.9g; Sodium 100mg.

p225 Tagliatelle with Vegetable Ribbons Energy 308Kcal/1292kJ; Protein 9g; Carbohydrate 42g, of which sugars 7g; Fat 13g, of which saturates 2g; Cholesterol 0mg; Calcium 76mg; Fibre 2.4g; Sodium 360mg.

p226 Spaghetti with Raw Tomato and Ricotta Sauce Energy 530Kcal/2230kJ; Protein 14g; Carbohydrate 69g, of which sugars 7g; Fat 24g, of which saturates 5g; Cholesterol 14mg; Calcium 100mg; Fibre 3.8g; Sodium 100mg.

p227 Farfalle with Tuna Energy 572Kcal/2433kJ; Protein 27g; Carbohydrate 89g, of which sugars 8g; Fat 15g, of which saturates 4g; Cholesterol 37mg; Calcium 63mg; Fibre 5.4g; Sodium 800mg.

p228 Fettuccine all'Alfredo Energy 697Kcal/2917kJ; Protein 16g; Carbohydrate 67g, of which sugars 3g; Fat 42g, of which saturates 26g; Cholesterol 107mg; Calcium 172mg; Fibre 2.7g; Sodium 200mg.

p229 Pansotti with Walnut Sauce Energy 550Kcal/2282kJ; Protein 11g; Carbohydrate 24g, of which sugars 2g; Fat 47g, of which saturates 13g; Cholesterol 41mg; Calcium 136mg; Fibre 1.9g; Sodium 200mg.

p230 Fettuccine with Butter and Parmesan Energy 560Kcal/2362kJ; Protein 22g; Carbohydrate 76g, of which sugars 3g; Fat 21g, of which saturates 12g; Cholesterol 53mg; Calcium 322mg; Fibre 3.1g; Sodium 300mg.

p231 Penne with Cream and Smoked Salmon Energy 475Kcal/2005kJ; Protein 18g; Carbohydrate 67g, of which sugars 3g; Fat 17g, of which saturates 9g; Cholesterol 48mg; Calcium 64mg; Fibre 2.7g; Sodium 200mg.

p232 Oven-baked Porcini Risotto Energy 288Kcal/1218kJ; Protein 6g; Carbohydrate 52g, of which sugars 2g; Fat 8g, of which saturates 1g; Cholesterol 0mg; Calcium 43mg; Fibre 1.6g; Sodium 100mg.

p233 Persian Baked Rice Energy 573Kcal/2389kJ; Protein 11g; Carbohydrate 91g, of which sugars 1g; Fat 18g, of which saturates 7g; Cholesterol 27mg; Calcium 54mg; Fibre 0.9g; Sodium 200mg.

p234 Rosemary Risotto with Borlotti Beans Energy 362Kcal/1517 kJ; Protein 11g; Carbohydrate 38g, of which sugars 4g; Fat 20g, of which saturates 8g; Cholesterol 19mg; Calcium 80mg; Fibre 65g; Sodium 900mg.

p235 Pancetta and Broad Bean Risotto Energy 526Kcal/2211kJ; Protein 18g; Carbohydrate 72g, of which sugars 4g; Fat 21g, of which saturates 6g; Cholesterol 29mg; Calcium 81mg; Fibre 3.4g; Sodium 2.4g.

p236 Mussel Risotto Energy 348Kcal/459kJ; Protein 15g; Carbohydrate 31g, of which sugars 4g; Fat 19g, of which saturates 7g; Cholesterol 351mg; Calcium 83mg; Fibre 6.5g; Sodium 700mg.

p237 Crab Risotto

Rum and Star Anise Hot Toddy

Hot toddies are normally made with whisky but rum works really well too and produces a deliciously warming drink that's perfect for a cold winter evening – or even a winter afternoon after a hearty walk out in the freezing cold countryside. You can also flavour this toddy with different spices such as a vanilla pod (bean) or cinnamon stick.

SERVES FOUR

300ml/¹/₂ pint/1¹/₄ cups dark rum

45ml/3 tbsp caster (superfine) sugar

1 star anise

1 Pour the rum into a heatproof jug (pitcher) and add the sugar and star anise. Pour in 450ml/³/₄ pint/scant 2 cups boiling water and stir thoroughly until the sugar has dissolved.

2 Carefully pour the hot toddy into heatproof glasses or mugs and serve immediately.

Energy 345Kcal/1458kJ;
Protein 20g; Carbohydrate 54g,
of which sugars 0g; Fat 7g, of
which saturates 1g; Cholesterol
54mg; Calcium 35mg; Fibre
0.3g; Sodium 900mg.

p238 Coconut Rice
Energy 472Kcal/2009kJ;
Protein 8g; Carbohydrate 114g,
of which sugars 16g; Fat 1g, of
which saturates 0g; Cholesterol
0mg; Calcium 40mg; Fibre
0.6g; Sodium 400mg.

p239 Savoury Ground Rice
Energy 333Kcal/1392kJ;
Protein 7g; Carbohydrate 59g,
of which sugars 4g; Fat 7g, of
which saturates 4g; Cholesterol
18mg; Calcium 111mg; Fibre
1.5g; Sodium 100mg.

**p242 Aubergines with
Cheese Sauce** Energy
509Kcal/2111kJ; Protein 22g;
Carbohydrate 13g, of which
sugars 7g; Fat 41g, of which
saturates 19g; Cholesterol
80mg; Calcium 640mg; Fibre
2.2g; Sodium 900mg.

p243 Mushroom Stroganoff
Energy 318Kcal/1316kJ;
Protein 10g; Carbohydrate
13g, of which sugars 7g; Fat
26g, of which saturates 13g;
Cholesterol 56mg; Calcium
194mg; Fibre 2.7g; Sodium
400mg.

**p244 Red Onion and Goat's
Cheese Pastries**
Energy 554Kcal/2308kJ; Protein
13g; Carbohydrate 48g, of which
sugars 8g; Fat 36g, of which
saturates 6g; Cholesterol 27mg;
Calcium 128mg; Fibre 1.6g;
Sodium 500mg.

**p245 Baked Leek and Potato
Gratin** Energy 574Kcal/2394kJ;
Protein 20g; Carbohydrate 43g,
of which sugars 5g; Fat 37g, of
which saturates 23g; Cholesterol
108mg; Calcium 257mg; Fibre
4.6g; Sodium 300mg.

p246 Mushroom Polenta
Energy 518Kcal/2155kJ; Protein
19g; Carbohydrate 46g, of which
sugars 0g; Fat 26g, of which
saturates 16g; Cholesterol 69mg;

Calcium 333mg; Fibre 2.5g;
Sodium 400mg.

**p247 Tomato and Tapenade
Tarts** Energy 603Kcal/2512kJ;
Protein 9g; Carbohydrate 50g,
of which sugars 5g; Fat 43g, of
which saturates 7g; Cholesterol
21mg; Calcium 117mg; Fibre
1.7g; Sodium 800mg.

p248 Stuffed Baby Squash
Energy 469Kcal/1951kJ;
Protein 14g; Carbohydrate
48g, of which sugars 1g; Fat
24g, of which saturates 10g;
Cholesterol 36mg; Calcium
316mg; Fibre 2g; Sodium
300mg.

**p249 Roasted Peppers with
Halloumi and Pine Nuts**
Energy 361Kcal/1504kJ;
Protein 18g; Carbohydrate
16g, of which sugars 16g; Fat
26g, of which saturates 12g;
Cholesterol 58mg; Calcium
105mg; Fibre 4.3g; Sodium
400mg.

**p250 Spicy Chickpea
Samosas** Energy 580Kcal/
2437kJ; Protein 20g;
Carbohydrate 72g, of which
sugars 12g; Fat 24g, of which
saturates 6g; Cholesterol
17mg; Calcium 91mg; Fibre
8.3g; Sodium 500mg.

**p251 Tofu and Pepper
Kebabs** Energy 177Kcal/738kJ;
Protein 10g; Carbohydrate 13g,
of which sugars 12g; Fat 10g, of
which saturates 2g; Cholesterol
0mg; Calcium 342mg; Fibre
3.6g; Sodium 800mg.

**p252 Mixed Bean and
Tomato Chilli**
Energy 216Kcal/911kJ; Protein
12g; Carbohydrate 30g, of
which sugars 6g; Fat 6g, of
which saturates 2g; Cholesterol
10mg; Calcium 47mg; Fibre
8.9g; Sodium 1g.

**p253 Cheese and Tomato
Soufflés** Energy 317Kcal/
1319kJ; Protein 19g;
Carbohydrate 6g, of which
sugars 3g; Fat 25g, of which
saturates 10g; Cholesterol
203mg; Calcium 395mg; Fibre
0.1g; Sodium 600mg.

**p254 Classic Margherita
Pizza** Energy 552Kcal/2317kJ;
Protein 22g; Carbohydrate 59g,
of which sugars 4g; Fat 27g, of
which saturates 12g;
Cholesterol 46mg; Calcium
362mg; Fibre 2.4g; Sodium
800mg.

**p255 Cheesy Leek and
Couscous Cake** Energy
474Kcal/1973kJ; Protein 19g;
Carbohydrate 41g, of which

sugars 2g; Fat 27g, of which
saturates 12g; Cholesterol
49mg; Calcium 408mg; Fibre
2.2g; Sodium 500mg.

**p256 Potato and Onion
Tortilla** Energy 512Kcal/2132kJ;
Protein 15g; Carbohydrate 40g,
of which sugars 5g; Fat 34g, of
which saturates 6g; Cholesterol
285mg; Calcium 73mg; Fibre
3.7g; Sodium 100mg.

p257 Spiced Lentils
Energy 326Kcal/1372kJ; Protein
24g; Carbohydrate 34g, of which
sugars 4g; Fat 11g, of which
saturates 7g; Cholesterol 35mg;
Calcium 235mg; Fibre 6.2g,
Sodium 800mg.

**p258 Roast Acorn Squash
with Spinach and
Gorgonzola** Energy 317Kcal/
1312kJ; Protein 12g;
Carbohydrate 10g, of which
sugars 2g; Fat 25g, of which
saturates 12g; Cholesterol
45mg; Calcium 404mg; Fibre
3.6g; Sodium 1g.

**p259 Creamy Red Lentil
Dhal** Energy 156Kcal/658kJ;
Protein 9g; Carbohydrate 21g,
of which sugars 1g; Fat 4g, of
which saturates 0g; Cholesterol
0mg; Calcium 27mg; Fibre
1.8g; Sodium 200mg.

**p260 Wild Mushroom and
Fontina Tart**
Energy 508Kcal/2110kJ;
Protein 14g; Carbohydrate 25g,
of which sugars 1g; Fat 40g, of
which saturates 15g;
Cholesterol 63mg; Calcium
309mg; Fibre 2.0g; Sodium
500mg.

**p261 Parmigiana di
Melanzane** Energy 218Kcal/
904kJ; Protein 7g;
Carbohydrate 5g, of which
sugars 4g; Fat 19g, of which
saturates 5g; Cholesterol 13mg;
Calcium 168mg; Fibre 2.8g;
Sodium 200mg.

**p264 Japanese-style
Spinach with Toasted
Sesame Seeds**
Energy 51Kcal/210kJ; Protein
4g; Carbohydrate 2g, of which
sugars 2g; Fat 3g, of which
saturates 0g; Cholesterol 0mg;
Calcium 213mg; Fibre 2.6g;
Sodium 600mg.

**p265 Braised Lettuce and
Peas with Spring Onions**
Energy 206Kcal/851kJ; Protein
8g; Carbohydrate 17g, of which
sugars 8g; Fat 12g, of which
saturates 7g; Cholesterol 27mg;
Calcium 109mg; Fibre 6.5g;
Sodium 100mg.

p266 Asparagus with Lemon

Sauce Energy 84Kcal/349kJ;
Protein 6g; Carbohydrate 7g, of
which sugars 4g; Fat 3g, of which
saturates 1g; Cholesterol 90mg;
Calcium 58mg; Fibre 2.9g;
Sodium 100mg.

p267 Caramelized Shallots
Energy 109Kcal/450kJ; Protein
1g; Carbohydrate 10g, of which
sugars 8g; Fat 7g, of which
saturates 4g; Cholesterol 18mg;
Calcium 23mg; Fibre 1.2g;
Sodium 100mg.

**p268 Green Beans with
Almond Butter and Lemon**
Energy 192Kcal/790kJ; Protein
4g; Carbohydrate 4g, of which
sugars 3g; Fat 18g, of which
saturates 7g; Cholesterol 27mg;
Calcium 65mg; Fibre 2.9g;
Sodium 200mg.

**p268 Garlicky Green Salad
with Raspberry Dressing**
Energy 83Kcal/344kJ; Protein
1g; Carbohydrate 1g, of which
sugars 1g; Fat 9g, of which
saturates 1g; Cholesterol 0mg;
Calcium 14mg; Fibre 0.5g;
Sodium 100mg.

**p270 Cauliflower with Garlic
Crumbs** Energy
289Kcal/1201kJ; Protein 8g;
Carbohydrate 18g, of which
sugars 4g; Fat 21g, of which
saturates 3g; Cholesterol 0mg;
Calcium 61mg; Fibre 4.0g;
Sodium 200mg.

**p271 Summer Squash and
Baby New Potatoes in Warm
Dill Sour Cream**
Energy 261Kcal/1093kJ;
Protein 5g; Carbohydrate 27g,
of which sugars 9g; Fat 15g, of
which saturates 9g; Cholesterol
45mg; Calcium 129mg; Fibre
2.7g; Sodium 100mg.

**p272 Minty Broad Beans with
Lemon** Energy 118Kcal/493kJ;
Protein 7g; Carbohydrate 9g, of
which sugars 2g; Fat 7g, of which
saturates 1g; Cholesterol 0mg;
Calcium 35mg; Fibre 69g;
Sodium 100mg.

p272 Gingered Carrot Salad
Energy 82Kcal/339kJ; Protein
1g; Carbohydrate 7g, of which

sugars 7g; Fat 7g, of which
saturates 1g; Cholesterol 0mg;
Calcium 70mg; Fibre 2.1g;
Sodium 100mg.

**p274 Baked Winter Squash
with Tomatoes**
Energy 139Kcal/583kJ; Protein
4g; Carbohydrate 12g, of which
sugars 10g; Fat 9g, of which
saturates 1g; Cholesterol 0mg;
Calcium 98mg; Fibre 3.9g;
Sodium 100mg.

**p275 Stewed Okra with
Tomatoes and Coriander**
Energy 79Kcal/332 kJ; Protein
7g; Carbohydrate 9g, of which
sugars 8g; Fat 2g, of which
saturates 1g; Cholesterol 0mg;
Calcium 355mg; Fibre 8.7g;
Sodium 100mg.

**p276 Roast Asparagus with
Crispy Prosciutto**
Energy 141Kcal/582kJ; Protein
7g; Carbohydrate 2g, of which
sugars 2g; Fat 11g, of which
saturates 3g; Cholesterol 18mg;
Calcium 38mg; Fibre 1.5g;
Sodium 400mg.

p277 Garlicky Roasties
Energy 324Kcal/1356kJ;
Protein 6g; Carbohydrate 45g,
of which sugars 2g; Fat 14g, of
which saturates 2g; Cholesterol
0mg; Calcium 15mg; Fibre
3.9g; Sodium 100mg.

p278 Leek Fritters
Energy 331Kcal/1380kJ;
Protein 11g; Carbohydrate 34g,
of which sugars 6g; Fat 17g, of
which saturates 3g; Cholesterol
116mg; Calcium 84mg; Fibre
5.5g; Sodium 100mg.

p279 Deep-fried Artichokes
Energy 111Kcal/459kJ; Protein
2g; Carbohydrate 2g, of which
sugars 1g; Fat 11g, of which
saturates 2g; Cholesterol 0mg;
Calcium 24mg; Fibre 0g;
Sodium 100mg.

**p280 Stir-fried Broccoli with
Soy Sauce and Sesame
Seeds** Energy 130Kcal/538kJ;
Protein 6g; Carbohydrate 4g, of
which sugars 2g; Fat 10g, of
which saturates 2g; Cholesterol
0mg; Calcium 267mg; Fibre

4.4g; Sodium 600mg.

**p281 Stir-fried Brussel
Sprouts with Bacon and
Caraway Seeds**
Energy 130Kcal/542kJ; Protein
7g; Carbohydrate 5g, of which
sugars 3g; Fat 10g, of which
saturates 2g; Cholesterol 9mg;
Calcium 40mg; Fibre 4.6g;
Sodium 300mg.

**p282 Bocconcini with
Fennel and Basil**
Energy 243Kcal/1008kJ;
Protein 14g; Carbohydrate 0g,
of which sugars 0g; Fat 21g, of
which saturates 11g; Cholesterol
44mg; Calcium 282mg; Fibre
0g; Sodium 400mg.

**p283 Noodles with Sesame-
roasted Spring Onions**
Energy 268Kcal/1121kJ;
Protein 3g; Carbohydrate 50g,
of which sugars 3g; Fat 3g, of
which saturates 1g; Cholesterol
0mg; Calcium 51mg; Fibre
0.5g; Sodium 400mg.

p284 Spicy Potato Wedges
Energy 205Kcal/860kJ; Protein
4g; Carbohydrate 30g, of which
sugars 1g; Fat 9g, of which
saturates 1g; Cholesterol 0mg;
Calcium 16mg; Fibre 2.2g;
Sodium 100mg.

**p284 Crisp and Golden
Roast Potatoes with Goose
Fat and Garlic**
Energy 202Kcal/848kJ; Protein
4g; Carbohydrate 30g, of which
sugars 1g; Fat 1g, of which
saturates 0.8g; Cholesterol
7mg; Calcium 10mg; Fibre
2.6g; Sodium 100mg.

**p286 Tomato and Aubergine
Gratin** Energy 229Kcal/952kJ;
Protein 6g; Carbohydrate 6g, of
which sugars 6g; Fat 20g, of
which saturates 5g; Cholesterol
9mg; Calcium 125mg; Fibre 40g;
Sodium 100mg.

p287 Bubble and Squeak
Energy 205Kcal/854kJ; Protein
3g; Carbohydrate 23g, of which
sugars 4g; Fat 12g, of which
saturates 1g; Cholesterol 0mg;
Calcium 30mg; Fibre 2.8g;
Sodium 100mg.

p288 Cheesy Creamy Leeks
Energy 333Kcal/1376kJ;
Protein 9g; Carbohydrate 6g,
of which sugars 5g; Fat 30g,
of which saturates 17g;
Cholesterol 70mg; Calcium
205mg; Fibre 4.4g; Sodium
200mg.

**p289 Creamy Polenta with
Dolcelatte** Energy 271Kcal/
1130kJ; Protein 11g;
Carbohydrate 21g, of which
sugars 7g; Fat 16g, of which

saturates 6g; Cholesterol 23mg;
Calcium 274mg; Fibre 0.4g;
Sodium 400mg.

**p290 Fennel, Potato and
Garlic Mash**
Energy 374Kcal/1560kJ; Protein
7g; Carbohydrate 38g, of which
sugars 4g; Fat 23g, of which
saturates 6g; Cholesterol 17mg;
Calcium 73mg; Fibre 6.2g;
Sodium 100mg.

p291 Champ
Energy 445Kcal/1858kJ;
Protein 8g; Carbohydrate
49g, of which sugars 7g; Fat
25g, of which saturates 16g;
Cholesterol 66mg; Calcium
143mg; Fibre 3.7g; Sodium
200mg.

**p294 Sour Cucumber with
Fresh Dill**
Energy 18Kcal/75kJ; Protein
1g; Carbohydrate 2g, of which
sugars 2g; Fat 0g, of which
saturates 0g; Cholesterol 0mg;
Calcium 50mg; Fibre 0.9g;
Sodium 100mg.

**p295 Beetroot with Fresh
Mint** Energy 75Kcal/314kJ;
Protein 2g; Carbohydrate 10g,
of which sugars 9g; Fat 3g, of
which saturates 0g; Cholesterol
0mg; Calcium 41mg; Fibre
2.4g; Sodium 100mg.

**p296 Globe Artichokes with
Green Beans and Garlic
Dressing** Energy 371kcal/
1528kJ; Protein 4g;
Carbohydrate 5g, of which
sugars 3g; Fat 38g, of which
saturates 6g; Cholesterol 0mg;
Calcium 60mg; Fibre 1.2g;
Sodium 100mg.

**p297 Halloumi and Grape
Salad** Energy 274Kcal/1139kJ;
Protein 10g; Carbohydrate 9g,
of which sugars 9g; Fat 22g, of
which saturates 10g;
Cholesterol 14mg; Calcium
241mg; Fibre 0.6g; Sodium 1g.

**p298 Watermelon and Feta
Salad** Energy 211Kcal/884kJ;
Protein 8g; Carbohydrate 16g,
of which sugars 15g; Fat 13g, of
which saturates 5g; Cholesterol
23mg; Calcium 145mg; Fibre
1.1g; Sodium 700mg.

**p299 Tomato, Bean and
Fried Basil Salad**
Energy 201Kcal/837kJ; Protein
6g; Carbohydrate 13g, of which
sugars 3g; Fat 14g, of which
saturates 2g; Cholesterol 0mg;
Calcium 30mg; Fibre 4.5g;
Sodium 400mg.

**p300 Moroccan Date,
Orange and Carrot Salad**
Energy 147Kcal/619kJ; Protein
4g; Carbohydrate 26g, of which

sugars 25g; Fat 4g, of which
saturates 0g; Cholesterol 0mg;
Calcium 98mg; Fibre 4.9g;
Sodium 100mg.

**p301 Pink Grapefruit and
Avocado Salad**
Energy 216Kcal/892kJ; Protein
2g; Carbohydrate 8g, of which
sugars 7g; Fat 20g, of which
saturates 3g; Cholesterol 6mg;
Calcium 34mg; Fibre 3.8g;
Sodium 100mg.

p302 Turnip Salad
Energy 107Kcal/443kJ; Protein
2g; Carbohydrate 8g, of which
sugars 7g; Fat 8g, of which
saturates 5g; Cholesterol 23mg;
Calcium 82mg; Fibre 2.4g;
Sodium 100mg.

p302 Moroccan Carrot Salad
Energy 85Kcal/350kJ; Protein
0g; Carbohydrate 4g, of which
sugars 4g; Fat 8g, of which
saturates 1g; Cholesterol 0mg;
Calcium 18mg; Fibre 1.3g;
Sodium 100mg.

**p304 Warm Chorizo and
Spinach Salad**
Energy 273Kcal/1127kJ;
Protein 8g; Carbohydrate 2g,
of which sugars 2g; Fat 26g, of
which saturates 6g; Cholesterol
0mg; Calcium 96mg; Fibre
1.2g; Sodium 300mg.

p305 Potato and Olive Salad
Energy 296Kcal/1246kJ; Protein
5g; Carbohydrate 48g, of which
sugars 4g; Fat 11g, of which
saturates 2g; Cholesterol 0mg;
Calcium 40mg; Fibre 3.3g;
Sodium 300mg.

**p306 Asparagus, Bacon
and Leaf Salad**
Energy 239Kcal/989kJ; Protein
13g; Carbohydrate 5g, of which
sugars 5g; Fat 19g, of which
saturates 4g; Cholesterol 19mg;
Calcium 54mg; Fibre 2.7g;
Sodium 800mg.

**p307 Anchovy and Roasted
Pepper Salad**
Energy 86Kcal/366kJ; Protein
6g; Carbohydrate 12g, of which
sugars 11g; Fat 2g, of which
saturates 0g; Cholesterol 8mg;
Calcium 57mg; Fibre 4.0g;

Sodium 500mg.

p310 Merguez Sausages with Iced Oysters Energy 353Kcal/1469kJ; Protein 25g; Carbohydrate 5g, of which sugars 3g; Fat 26g, of which saturates 11g; Cholesterol 23mg; Calcium 56mg; Fibre 0g; Sodium 800mg.

p311 Grilled Corn on the Cob Energy 445Kcal/1846kJ; Protein 5g; Carbohydrate 24g, of which sugars 3g; Fat 37g, of which saturates 22g; Cholesterol 89mg; Calcium 16mg; Fibre 2.7g; Sodium 300mg.

p312 Butter Bean, Tomato and Red Onion Salad Energy 227Kcal/955kJ; Protein 11g; Carbohydrate 27g, of which sugars 7g; Fat 9g, of which saturates 1g; Cholesterol 0mg; Calcium 40mg; Fibre 8.9g; Sodium 100mg.

p312 Potato, Caraway Seed and Parsley Salad Energy 129Kcal/541kJ; Protein 2g; Carbohydrate 18g, of which sugars 1g; Fat 6g, of which saturates 1g; Cholesterol 0mg; Calcium 19mg; Fibre 1.2g; Sodium 100mg.

p314 Warm Halloumi and Fennel Salad Energy 209Kcal/863kJ; Protein 8g; Carbohydrate 2g, of which sugars 2g; Fat 19g, of which saturates 8g; Cholesterol 35mg; Calcium 200mg; Fibre 1.8g; Sodium 800mg.

p315 Pear and Blue Cheese Salad Energy 197Kcal/822kJ; Protein 6g; Carbohydrate 16g, of which sugars 16g; Fat 12g, of which saturates 6g; Cholesterol 26mg; Calcium 170mg; Fibre 3.5g; Sodium 600mg.

p316 Fresh Crab Sandwiches Energy 392Kcal/1636kJ; Protein 27g; Carbohydrate 28g, of which sugars 2g; Fat 20g, of which saturates 9g; Cholesterol 107mg; Calcium 74mg; Fibre 3.3g; Sodium 900mg.

p317 Warm Pasta with Crushed Tomatoes and Basil Energy 481Kcal/2038kJ; Protein 14g; Carbohydrate 88g, of which sugars 5g; Fat 11g, of which saturates 2g; Cholesterol 0mg; Calcium 40mg; Fibre 4.3g; Sodium 100mg.

p318 Roast Shallot Tart with Thyme Energy 441Kcal/1851kJ; Protein 7g; Carbohydrate 45g, of which sugars 8g; Fat 29g, of which saturates 3g; Cholesterol 13mg; Calcium 131mg; Fibre 1.6g; Sodium 400mg.

p319 Roasted Aubergines with Feta and Coriander Energy 248Kcal/1028kJ; Protein 11g; Carbohydrate 3g, of which sugars 3g; Fat 21g, of which saturates 10g; Cholesterol 47mg; Calcium 252mg; Fibre 2.0g; Sodium 1g.

p320 Barbecued Sardines with Orange and Parsley Energy 324Kcal/1353kJ; Protein 31g; Carbohydrate 2g, of which sugars 2g; Fat 21g, of which saturates 5g; Cholesterol 0mg; Calcium 144mg; Fibre 0.6g; Sodium 200mg.

p321 Soy Sauce and Star Anise Chicken Energy 210Kcal/880kJ; Protein 30g; Carbohydrate 1g, of which sugars 1g; Fat 10g, of which saturates 2g; Cholesterol 88mg; Calcium 11mg; Fibre 0.0g; Sodium 600mg.

p322 Harissa-spiced Koftas Energy 180Kcal/750kJ; Protein 23g; Carbohydrate 2g, of which sugars 1g; Fat 9g, of which saturates 4g; Cholesterol 83mg; Calcium 18mg; Fibre 0.2g; Sodium 300mg.

p323 Cumin- and Coriander-Rubbed Lamb Energy 264Kcal/1098kJ; Protein 29g; Carbohydrate 0g, of which sugars 0g; Fat 17g, of which saturates 6g; Cholesterol 104mg; Calcium 33mg; Fibre 0g; Sodium 200mg.

p326 Plum and Almond Tart Energy 491Kcal/2061kJ; Protein 7g; Carbohydrate 61g, of which sugars 28g; Fat 27g, of which saturates 0g; Cholesterol 0mg; Calcium 84mg; Fibre 1.9g; Sodium 300mg.

p327 Baked Apples with Marsala Energy 215Kcal/901kJ; Protein 1g; Carbohydrate 22g, of which sugars 22g; Fat 11g, of which saturates 7g; Cholesterol 27mg; Calcium 40mg; Fibre 3.3g; Sodium 100mg.

p328 Grilled Peaches with Meringues Energy 123Kcal/526kJ; Protein 2g; Carbohydrate 31g, of which sugars 31g; Fat 0g, of which saturates 0g; Cholesterol 0mg; Calcium 24mg; Fibre 2.3g; Sodium 100mg.

p329 Summer Berries in Sabayon Glaze Energy 217Kcal/914kJ; Protein 4g; Carbohydrate 29g, of which sugars 29g; Fat 6g, of which saturates 2g; Cholesterol 202mg; Calcium 72mg; Fibre 3.4g; Sodium 100mg.

p330 Baked Ricotta Cakes with Red Sauce Energy 176Kcal/741kJ; Protein 8g; Carbohydrate 21g, of which sugars 21g; Fat 7g, of which saturates 4g; Cholesterol 31mg; Calcium 173mg; Fibre 1.4g; Sodium 100mg.

p331 Apricot and Ginger Gratin Energy 414Kcal/1731kJ; Protein 4g; Carbohydrate 44g, of which sugars 35g; Fat 26g, of which saturates 16g; Cholesterol 48mg; Calcium 94mg; Fibre 2.4g; Sodium 200mg.

p332 Deep-fried Cherries Energy 146Kcal/612kJ; Protein 4g; Carbohydrate 18g, of which sugars 10g; Fat 7g, of which saturates 2g; Cholesterol 61mg; Calcium 65mg; Fibre 1.0g; Sodium 100mg.

p333 Hot Blackberry and Apple Soufflé Energy 128Kcal/543kJ; Protein 2g; Carbohydrate 31g, of which sugars 31g; Fat 0g, of which saturates 0g; Cholesterol 0mg; Calcium 28mg; Fibre 2.2g; Sodium 100mg.

p334 Peach Pie Energy 321Kcal/1347kJ; Protein 4g; Carbohydrate 39g, of which sugars 19g; Fat 18g, of which saturates 3g; Cholesterol 11mg; Calcium 42mg; Fibre 1.7g; Sodium 200mg.

p335 Treacle Tart Energy 416Kcal/1749kJ; Protein 4g; Carbohydrate 66g, of which sugars 35g; Fat 17g, of which saturates 0g; Cholesterol 0mg; Calcium 46mg; Fibre 1.3g; Sodium 300mg.

p336 Caramelized Upside-down Pear Pie Energy 322Kcal/1347kJ; Protein 1g; Carbohydrate 37g, of which sugars 25g; Fat 20g, of which saturates 7g; Cholesterol 31mg; Calcium 18mg; Fibre 0.8g; Sodium 100mg.

p338 Blueberry and Almond Tart Energy 316Kcal/1324kJ; Protein 6g; Carbohydrate 41g, of which sugars 23g; Fat 16g, of which saturates 0g; Cholesterol 0mg; Calcium 41mg; Fibre 1.5g; Sodium 100mg.

p339 Baked Bananas with Ice Cream and Toffee Sauce Energy 368Kcal/1545kJ; Protein 4g; Carbohydrate 55g, of which sugars 52g; Fat 16g, of which saturates 10g; Cholesterol 40mg; Calcium 81mg; Fibre 1.1g; Sodium 400mg.

p340 Roast Peaches with Amaretto Energy 111Kcal/472kJ; Protein 2g; Carbohydrate 24g, of which sugars 24g; Fat 0g, of which saturates 0g; Cholesterol 0mg; Calcium 11mg; Fibre 2.3g; Sodium 100mg.

p341 Passion Fruit Soufflés Energy 57Kcal/243kJ; Protein 4g; Carbohydrate 9g, of which sugars 6g; Fat 1g, of which saturates 1g; Cholesterol 4mg; Calcium 72mg; Fibre 0.4g; Sodium 100mg.

p342 Zabaglione Energy 131Kcal/548kJ; Protein 3g; Carbohydrate 14g, of which sugars 14g; Fat 5g, of which saturates 2g; Cholesterol 202mg; Calcium 26mg; Fibre 0.0g; Sodium 100mg.

p343 Grilled Pineapple and Rum Cream Energy 454Kcal/1869kJ; Protein 1g; Carbohydrate 4g, of which sugars 4g; Fat 45g, of which saturates 28g; Cholesterol 116mg; Calcium 43mg; Fibre 0.3g; Sodium 100mg.

p344 Warm Chocolate Zabaglione Energy 228Kcal/959kJ; Protein 4g; Carbohydrate 29g, of which sugars 29g; Fat 7g, of which saturates 3g; Cholesterol 202mg; Calcium 38mg; Fibre 0.8g; Sodium 100mg.

p345 Hot Chocolate Rum Soufflés Energy 91Kcal/382kJ; Protein 4g; Carbohydrate 12g,

of which sugars 11g; Fat 2g, of which saturates 1g; Cholesterol 0mg; Calcium 14mg; Fibre 1.0g; Sodium 100mg.

p348 Tropical Scented Fruit Salad Energy 97Kcal/410kJ; Protein 2g; Carbohydrate 19g, of which sugars 19g; Fat 0g, of which saturates 0g; Cholesterol 0mg; Calcium 89mg; Fibre 3.6g; Sodium 100mg.

p349 Juniper-scented Pears in Red Wine Energy 251Kcal/1057kJ; Protein 1g; Carbohydrate 38g, of which sugars 38g; Fat 0g, of which saturates 0g; Cholesterol 0mg; Calcium 39mg; Fibre 5.5g; Sodium 100mg.

p350 Oranges in Syrup Energy 236Kcal/1001kJ; Protein 3g; Carbohydrate 48g, of which sugars 48g; Fat 5g, of which saturates 1g; Cholesterol 0mg; Calcium 82mg; Fibre 3.0g; Sodium 100mg.

p350 Fresh Fig Compote Energy 156Kcal/667kJ; Protein 2g; Carbohydrate 38g, of which sugars 38g; Fat 0g, of which saturates 0g; Cholesterol 0mg; Calcium 67mg; Fibre 2.5g; Sodium 100mg.

p352 Pistachio and Rose Water Oranges Energy 94Kcal/400kJ; Protein 3g; Carbohydrate 18g, of which sugars 18g; Fat 2g, of which saturates 0g; Cholesterol 0mg; Calcium 102mg; Fibre 3.7g; Sodium 100mg.

p353 Lychee and Elderflower Sorbet Energy 249Kcal/1063kJ; Protein 1g; Carbohydrate 65g, of which sugars 65g; Fat 0g, of which saturates 0g; Cholesterol 0mg; Calcium 12mg; Fibre 0.9g; Sodium 100mg.

p354 Summer Fruit Brioche Energy 206Kcal/868kJ; Protein 4g; Carbohydrate 37g, of which sugars 20g; Fat 6g, of which saturates 2g; Cholesterol 5mg; Calcium 59mg; Fibre 1.5g; Sodium 200mg.

p355 Rhubarb and Ginger Jellies Energy 179Kcal/765kJ; Protein 2g; Carbohydrate 45g, of which sugars 44g; Fat 0g, of which saturates 0g; Cholesterol 0mg; Calcium 193mg; Fibre 2.8g; Sodium 100mg.

p356 Papayas in Jasmine Flower Syrup Energy 251Kcal/1057kJ; Protein 1g; Carbohydrate 38g, of which sugars 38g; Fat 0g, of which saturates 0g; Cholesterol 0mg; Calcium 39mg; Fibre 5.5g; Sodium 100mg.

p357 Mango and Lime Fool Energy 289Kcal/1204kJ; Protein 2g; Carbohydrate 21g, of which sugars 21g; Fat 22g, of which saturates 14g; Cholesterol 51mg; Calcium 62mg; Fibre 0.7g; Sodium 0mg.

p358 Tangy Raspberry and Lemon Tartlets Energy 206Kcal/868kJ; Protein 4g; Carbohydrate 37g, of which sugars 20g; Fat 6g, of which saturates 2g; Cholesterol 5mg; Calcium 59mg; Fibre 1.5g; Sodium 200mg.

p359 Crispy Mango Stacks with Raspberry Coulis Energy 189Kcal/791kJ; Protein 3g; Carbohydrate 21g, of which sugars 13g; Fat 11g, of which saturates 7g; Cholesterol 27mg; Calcium 18mg; Fibre 3.0g; Sodium 100mg.

p360 Rhubarb and Ginger Trifles Energy 690Kcal/2852kJ; Protein 4g; Carbohydrate 26g, of which sugars 13g; Fat 34g, of which saturates 39g; Cholesterol 154mg; Calcium 99mg; Fibre 0.6g; Sodium 100mg.

p361 Strawberry Cream Shortbreads Energy 890Kcal/3673kJ; Protein 4g; Carbohydrate 22g, of which sugars 10g; Fat 88g, of which saturates 55g; Cholesterol 225mg; Calcium 105mg; Fibre 1.0g; Sodium 100mg.

p362 Blackberries in Port Energy 220Kcal/923kJ; Protein 1g; Carbohydrate 34g, of which sugars 34g; Fat 0g, of which saturates 0g; Cholesterol 0mg; Calcium 51mg; Fibre 3.5g; Sodium 100mg.

p362 Baby Summer Puddings Energy 212Kcal/904kJ; Protein 5g; Carbohydrate 48g, of which sugars 23g; Fat 1g, of which saturates 0g; Cholesterol 0mg; Calcium 72mg; Fibre 1.9g; Sodium 300mg.

p364 Raspberry Brûlée Energy 152Kcal/649kJ; Protein 3g; Carbohydrate 34g, of which sugars 30g; Fat 2g, of which saturates 1g; Cholesterol 6mg; Calcium 114mg; Fibre 0.7g; Sodium 100mg.

p365 Portuguese Custard Tarts Energy 90Kcal/379kJ; Protein 2g; Carbohydrate 11g, of which sugars 4g; Fat 5g, of which saturates 0g; Cholesterol 1mg; Calcium 31mg; Fibre 0.0g; Sodium 100mg.

p366 Baked Custard with Burnt Sugar Energy 992Kcal/4099kJ; Protein 6g; Carbohydrate 31g, of which sugars 31g; Fat 95g, of which saturates 57g; Cholesterol 430mg; Calcium 114mg; Fibre 0g; Sodium 0mg.

p367 Passion Fruit Creams Energy 602Kcal/2487kJ; Protein 8g; Carbohydrate 10g, of which sugars 10g; Fat 59g, of which saturates 35g; Cholesterol 330mg; Calcium 81mg; Fibre 0.5g; Sodium 100mg.

p368 Baked Caramel Custard Energy 481Kcal/1999kJ; Protein 7g; Carbohydrate 34g, of which sugars 34g; Fat 36g, of which saturates 21g; Cholesterol 292mg; Calcium 62mg; Fibre 0g; Sodium 100mg.

p370 Chocolate Banana Fools Energy 265Kcal/1180kJ; Protein 5g; Carbohydrate 42g, of which sugars 37g; Fat 10g, of which saturates 6g; Cholesterol 8mg; Calcium 117mg; Fibre 1.3g; Sodium 100mg.

p370 Lemon Posset Energy 917Kcal/3801kJ; Protein 2g; Carbohydrate 49g, of which sugars 49g; Fat 81g, of which saturates 50g; Cholesterol 206mg; Calcium 79mg; Fibre 0g; Sodium 100mg.

p372 Chilled Chocolate and Espresso Mousse Energy 710Kcal/2974kJ; Protein 13g; Carbohydrate 71g, of which sugars 70g; Fat 43g, of which saturates 24g; Cholesterol 253mg; Calcium 74mg; Fibre 2.8g; Sodium 100mg.

p373 Meringue Pyramid with Chocolate Mascarpone Energy 216Kcal/907kJ; Protein 3g; Carbohydrate 28g, of which sugars 28g; Fat 11g, of which saturates 7g; Cholesterol 12mg; Calcium 20mg; Fibre 0.5g; Sodium 100mg.

p375 Classic Chocolate Roulade Energy 434Kcal/1815kJ; Protein 9g; Carbohydrate 43g, of which sugars 43g; Fat 26g, of which saturates 15g; Cholesterol 208mg; Calcium 72mg; Fibre 0.7g; Sodium 100mg.

p376 Cherry Chocolate Brownies Energy 522Kcal/2159kJ; Protein 3g; Carbohydrate 23g, of which sugars 12g; Fat 47g, of which saturates 27g; Cholesterol 128mg; Calcium 62mg; Fibre 0.5g; Sodium 100mg.

p376 Coffee Mascarpone Creams Energy 146Kcal/604kJ; Protein 1g; Carbohydrate 5g, of which sugars 5g; Fat 14g, of which saturates 9g; Cholesterol 27mg; Calcium 29mg; Fibre 0g; Sodium 100mg.

p380 Lemon Sorbet Energy 135Kcal/577kJ; Protein 1g; Carbohydrate 35g, of which sugars 35g; Fat 0g, of which saturates 0g; Cholesterol 0mg; Calcium 6mg; Fibre 0g; Sodium 100mg.

p381 Strawberry and Lavender Sorbet Energy 123Kcal/522kJ; Protein 1g; Carbohydrate 31g, of which sugars 31g; Fat 0g, of which saturates 0g; Cholesterol 0mg; Calcium 16mg; Fibre 0.9g; Sodium 100mg.

p382 Blackcurrant Sorbet Energy 124Kcal/529kJ; Protein 1g; Carbohydrate 32g, of which sugars 32g; Fat 0g, of which saturates 0g; Cholesterol 0mg; Calcium 53mg; Fibre 3g; Sodium 100mg.

p383 Damson Water Ice Energy 130Kcal/555kJ; Protein 0g; Carbohydrate 34g, of which sugars 34g; Fat 0g, of which saturates 0g; Cholesterol 0mg; Calcium 23mg; Fibre 1.5g; Sodium 100mg.

p384 Peach and Cardamom Yogurt Ice Energy 155Kcal/659kJ; Protein 4g; Carbohydrate 33g, of which sugars 33g; Fat 2g, of which saturates 0g; Cholesterol 1mg; Calcium 126mg; Fibre 1.9g; Sodium 100mg.

p385 Summer Berry Frozen Yogurt Energy 74Kcal/311kJ; Protein 3g; Carbohydrate 10g, of which sugars 10g; Fat 3g, of which saturates 2g; Cholesterol 0mg; Calcium 61mg; Fibre 0.7g; Sodium 100mg.

p386 Raspberry Sherbet
Energy 179Kcal/763kJ; Protein
8g; Carbohydrate 39g, of which
sugars 39g; Fat 0g, of which
saturates 0g; Cholesterol 1mg;
Calcium 132mg; Fibre 2.3g;
Sodium 100mg.

p387 Watermelon Ice
Energy 85Kcal/363kJ; Protein
0g; Carbohydrate 22g, of which
sugars 22g; Fat 0g, of which
saturates 0g; Cholesterol 0mg;
Calcium 7mg; Fibre 0.1g;
Sodium 100mg.

p388 Blackberry Ice Cream
Energy 391Kcal/1621kJ; Protein
3g; Carbohydrate 28g, of which
sugars 28g; Fat 30g, of which
saturates 19g; Cholesterol 79mg;
Calcium 97mg; Fibre 3.9g;
Sodium 100mg.

p389 Coffee Ice Cream
Energy 164Kcal/686kJ; Protein
3g; Carbohydrate 13g, of which
sugars 9g; Fat 11g, of which
saturates 7g; Cholesterol 32mg;
Calcium 115mg; Fibre 0g;
Sodium 100mg.

p390 Kulfi
Energy 334Kcal/1389kJ;
Protein 14g; Carbohydrate 24g,
of which sugars 24g; Fat 20g, of
which saturates 10g; Cholesterol
53mg; Calcium 455mg; Fibre
0.6g; Sodium 200mg.

p391 Coconut Ice
Energy 137Kcal/583kJ; Protein
0g; Carbohydrate 35g, of which
sugars 35g; Fat 0g, of which
saturates 0g; Cholesterol 0mg;
Calcium 33mg; Fibre 0g; Sodium
100mg.

p392 Gingered Semi-freddo
Energy 397Kcal/1694kJ; Protein
3g; Carbohydrate 28g, of which
sugars 28g; Fat 31g, of which
saturates 18g; Cholesterol
203mg; Calcium 45mg; Fibre 0g;
Sodium 100mg.

p393 Miniature Choc-ices
Energy 106Kcal/442kJ; Protein
2g; Carbohydrate 12g, of which
sugars 11g; Fat 6g, of which
saturates 3g; Cholesterol 8mg;
Calcium 36mg; Fibre 0.3g;
Sodium 100mg.

**p394 White Chocolate
Castles** Energy
352Kcal/1476kJ; Protein 6g;
Carbohydrate 43g, of which
sugars 42g; Fat 18g, of which
saturates 11g; Cholesterol
22mg; Calcium 198mg; Fibre
0.5g; Sodium 100mg.

**p395 Caramel and Pecan
Terrine** Energy
553Kcal/2292kJ; Protein 2g;
Carbohydrate 27g, of which
sugars 27g; Fat 49g, of which
saturates 26g; Cholesterol
103mg; Calcium 46mg; Fibre
0.6g; Sodium 100mg.

**p396 White Chocolate and
Brownie Torte** Energy
572Kcal/2374kJ; Protein 5g;
Carbohydrate 35g, of which
sugars 25g; Fat 47g, of which
saturates 27g; Cholesterol
103mg; Calcium 130mg; Fibre
0.4g; Sodium 100mg.

**p397 Soft Fruit and
Meringue Gâteau**
Energy 331Kcal/1392kJ;
Protein 6g; Carbohydrate 52g,
of which sugars 50g; Fat 12g, of
which saturates 8g; Cholesterol
30mg; Calcium 143mg; Fibre
1.4g; Sodium 100mg.

p400 All Butter Cookies
Energy 99Kcal/419kJ; Protein
1g; Carbohydrate 11g, of which
sugars 3g; Fat 6g, of which
saturates 4g; Cholesterol 16mg;
Calcium 15mg; Fibre 0.3g;
Sodium 100mg.

p401 Almond Cookies
Energy 94Kcal/394kJ; Protein
1g; Carbohydrate 12g, of which
sugars 8g; Fat 5g, of which
saturates 3g; Cholesterol 11mg;
Calcium 13mg; Fibre 0.3g;
Sodium 100mg.

p402 Chewy Flapjacks
Energy 276Kcal/1038kJ; Protein
3g; Carbohydrate 29g, of which
sugars 14g; Fat 14g, of which
saturates 8g; Cholesterol 34mg;
Calcium 16mg; Fibre 1.4g;
Sodium 100mg.

**p403 Creamed Coconut
Macaroons** Energy
83Kcal/344kJ; Protein 1g;
Carbohydrate 6g, of which
sugars 6g; Fat 10g, of which
saturates 5g; Cholesterol 29mg;
Calcium 7mg; Fibre 0.6g;
Sodium 100mg.

**p404 Orange and Pecan
Scones** Energy
192Kcal/806kJ; Protein
3g; Carbohydrate 18g, of which
sugars 1g; Fat 12g, of which
saturates 3g; Cholesterol 12mg;
Calcium 87mg; Fibre 1.2g;
Sodium 100mg.

**p405 Quick and Easy
Teabread** Energy
239Kcal/1017kJ; Protein 4g;
Carbohydrate 56g, of which
sugars 40g; Fat 1g, of which
saturates 0g; Cholesterol 32mg;
Calcium 116mg; Fibre 1.6g;
Sodium 600mg.

p406 Cinnamon Pinwheels
Energy 45Kcal/189kJ; Protein
1g; Carbohydrate 6g, of which
sugars 2g; Fat 2g, of which
saturates 0g; Cholesterol 5mg;
Calcium 9mg; Fibre 0.0g;
Sodium 100mg.

p407 Almond Cigars
Energy 171Kcal/721kJ; Protein
4g; Carbohydrate 28g, of which
sugars 22g; Fat 5g, of which
saturates 1g; Cholesterol 29mg;
Calcium 25mg; Fibre 0.8g;
Sodium 100mg.

**p408 Golden Ginger
Macaroons** Energy
59kCal/248kJ; Protein 2g;
Carbohydrate 5g, of which
sugars 5g; Fat 4g, of which
saturates 0g; Cholesterol 13mg;
Calcium 20mg; Fibre 0.5g;
Sodium 100mg.

p408 Nutty Nougat
Energy 2251Kcal/9514kJ; Protein
28g; Carbohydrate 416g, of
which sugars 413g; Fat 64g, of
which saturates 5g; Cholesterol
312mg; Calcium 25mg; Fibre
0.8g; Sodium 100mg.

**p410 Rich Chocolate
Brownies**
Energy 213Kcal/892kJ; Protein
4g; Carbohydrate 14g, of which
sugars 11g; Fat 16g, of which
saturates 10g; Cholesterol
77mg; Calcium 67mg; Fibre
0.3g; Sodium 100mg.

**p411 Rich Chocolate Biscuit
Slice** Energy 408Kcal/1711kJ;
Protein 3g; Carbohydrate 36g,
of which sugars 30g; Fat 29g, of
which saturates 18g; Cholesterol
44mg; Calcium 55mg; Fibre
1.1g; Sodium 100mg.

**p412 Chocolate and Prune
Refrigerator Bars**
Energy 198Kcal/829kJ; Protein
2g; Carbohydrate 22g, of which
sugars 16g; Fat 12g, of which
saturates 7g; Cholesterol 18mg;
Calcium 59mg; Fibre 0.9g;
Sodium 100mg.

p413 Blueberry Cake
Energy 240Kcal/1005kJ;
Protein 3g; Carbohydrate 28g,
of which sugars 17g; Fat 14g, of
which saturates 3g; Cholesterol
56mg; Calcium 36mg; Fibre
0.6g; Sodium 200mg.

p414 Stuffed Prunes
Energy 98Kcal/411kJ; Protein

1g; Carbohydrate 10g, of which
sugars 10g; Fat 6g, of which
saturates 4g; Cholesterol 8mg;
Calcium 9mg; Fibre 0.7g;
Sodium 100mg.

p415 Chocolate Truffles
Energy 143Kcal/596kJ; Protein
2g; Carbohydrate 15g, of which
sugars 15g; Fat 9g, of which
saturates 5g; Cholesterol 5mg;
Calcium 32mg; Fibre 0.4g;
Sodium 100mg.

**p416 Chocolate Petit Four
Cookies** Energy
366Kcal/1533kJ; Protein 4g;
Carbohydrate 43g, of which
sugars 26g; Fat 21g, of which
saturates 11g; Cholesterol
15mg; Calcium 47mg; Fibre
1.4g; Sodium 200mg.

**p416 Praline Chocolate
Bites** Energy 544Kcal/2280kJ;
Protein 9g; Carbohydrate 64g,
of which sugars 63g; Fat 30g, of
which saturates 10g; Cholesterol
3mg; Calcium 88mg; Fibre
3.4g; Sodium 100mg.

p420 Scottish Morning Rolls
Energy 165Kcal/701kJ; Protein
6g; Carbohydrate 35g, of which
sugars 1g; Fat 1g, of which
saturates 0g; Cholesterol 2mg;
Calcium 2mg; Fibre 1.4g;
Sodium 200mg.

p421 Panini all'Olio Energy
121Kcal/510kJ; Protein 3g;
Carbohydrate 21g, of which
sugars 0g; Fat 3g, of which
saturates 0g; Cholesterol 0mg;
Calcium 40mg; Fibre 0.9g;
Sodium 200mg.

p422 French Baguette
Energy 702Kcal/3285kJ; Protein
23g; Carbohydrate 155g, of
which sugars 3g; Fat 3g, of
which saturates 0g; Cholesterol
0mg; Calcium 289mg; Fibre
6.4g; Sodium 1.3g.

p423 Rosemary Focaccia
Energy 1504Kcal/6349kJ;
Protein 42g; Carbohydrate
255g, of which sugars 5g; Fat
42g, of which saturates 6g;
Cholesterol 0mg; Calcium
490mg; Fibre 10.5g; Sodium
100mg.

p424 Granary Cob
Per loaf: Energy 1403Kcal/
5965kJ; Protein 59g;
Carbohydrate 288g, of which
sugars 9g; Fat 10g, of which
saturates 1g; Cholesterol 0mg;
Calcium 176mg; Fibre 40.5g;
Sodium 4.9g.

p425 Grant Loaves Per loaf:
Energy 1371Kcal/5831kJ;
Protein 57g; Carbohydrate
282g, of which sugars 14g; Fat
10g, of which saturates 1g;
Cholesterol 0mg; Calcium
17.1mg; Fibre 39g; Sodium 2g.

p426 Cottage Loaf
Per loaf: Energy 2312Kcal/
9839kJ; Protein 80g;
Carbohydrate 508g, of which
sugars 9g; Fat 10g, of which
saturates 1g; Cholesterol 0mg;
Calcium 951mg; Fibre 20.9g;
Sodium 4g.

p427 Split Tin
Per loaf: Energy
1770kcal/7527kJ; Protein 65g;
Carbohydrate 380g, of which
sugars 10g; Fat 10g, of which
saturates 3g; Cholesterol 8mg;
Calcium 784mg; Fibre 15.5g;
Sodium 4g.

**p429 Poppy-seeded
Bloomer** Per loaf: Energy
2310Kcal/9828kJ; Protein 82g;
Carbohydrate 508g, of which
sugars 9g; Fat 15g, of which
saturates 2g; Cholesterol 0mg;
Calcium 1140mg; Fibre 20.9g;
Sodium 4.9g.

**p430 Traditional Irish Soda
Bread** Energy 257Kcal/1093kJ;
Protein 12g; Carbohydrate 5g,
of which sugars 2g; Fat 0g, of
which saturates 0g; Cholesterol
11mg; Calcium 109mg; Fibre
6.8g; Sodium 800mg.

**p430 Spring Onion
Flatbreads** Energy
97Kcal/414kJ; Protein 3g;
Carbohydrate 21g, of which
sugars 0g; Fat 0g, of which
saturates 0g; Cholesterol 0mg;
Calcium 41mg; Fibre 0.9g;
Sodium 100mg.

p432 Pitta Bread
Energy 151Kcal/641kJ; Protein

5g; Carbohydrate 31g, of which
sugars 1g; Fat 2g, of which
saturates 0g; Cholesterol 0mg;
Calcium 59mg; Fibre 1.3g;
Sodium 500mg.

**p433 Yemeni Sponge Flat
Breads** Energy 393Kcal/1660kJ;
Protein 9g; Carbohydrate 68g, of
which sugars 1g; Fat 11g, of
which saturates 7g; Cholesterol
27mg; Calcium 126mg;
Fibre 2.7g; Sodium 600mg.

**p434 West Indian Flat
Breads** Energy
316Kcal/1322kJ; Protein 7g;
Carbohydrate 36g, of which
sugars 1g; Fat 17g, of which
saturates 10g; Cholesterol
44mg; Calcium 27mg; Fibre
5.1g; Sodium 300mg.

p435 Tandoori Rotis
Energy 218Kcal/922kJ; Protein
7g; Carbohydrate 37g, of which
sugars 1g; Fat 5g, of which
saturates 3g; Cholesterol 11mg;
Calcium 23mg; Fibre 5.3g;
Sodium 400mg.

p438 Bramble Jelly
Per 15ml/1 tbsp: Energy
63Kcal/268kJ; Protein 0g;
Carbohydrate 17g, of which
sugars 17g; Fat 0g, of which
saturates 0g; Cholesterol 0mg;
Calcium 8mg; Fibre 0g; Sodium
0mg.

p439 Strawberry Jam
Per 15ml/1 tbsp: Energy
42Kcal/161kJ; Protein 0g;
Carbohydrate 11g, of which
sugars 11g; Fat 0g, of which
saturates 0g; Cholesterol 0mg;
Calcium 3mg; Fibre 0.1g;
Sodium 0mg.

**p440 Spiced Poached
Kumquats**
Energy 108Kcal/459kJ; Protein
1g; Carbohydrate 27g, of which
sugars 0g; Fat 0g, of which
saturates 0g; Cholesterol 0mg;
Calcium 21mg; Fibre 2.9g;
Sodium 100mg.

p440 Three-fruit Marmalade
Per jar: Energy 1225Kcal/
5223kJ; Protein 1324g;
Carbohydrate 324g, of which
sugars 324g; Fat 0g, of which
saturates 0g; Cholesterol 0mg;
Calcium 71mg; Fibre 0.1g;
Sodium 2.2g.

p442 Preserved Lemons
Per jar: Energy 41Kcal/174kJ;
Protein 2g; Carbohydrate 7g,
of which sugars 7g; Fat 1g, of
which saturates 0g; Cholesterol
0mg; Calcium 71mg; Fibre
0.1g; Sodium 2.2g.

p443 Middle Eastern Pickles
Per jar: Energy 86Kcal/365kJ;
Protein 4g; Carbohydrate 18g,

of which sugars 17g; Fat 1g, of
which saturates 0g; Cholesterol
0mg; Calcium 137mg; Fibre
7.4g; Sodium 4.5g.

**p444 Horseradish and
Beetroot Sauce** Energy
28Kcal/121kJ; Protein 1g;
Carbohydrate 6g, of which
sugars 5g; Fat 0g, of which
saturates 0g; Cholesterol 0mg;
Calcium 28mg; Fibre 1.5g;
Sodium 100mg.

**p445 Yellow Pepper and
Coriander Relish**
Energy 77Kcal/324kJ; Protein
1g; Carbohydrate 6g, of which
sugars 5g; Fat 6g, of which
saturates 1g; Cholesterol 0mg;
Calcium 12mg; Fibre 1.7g;
Sodium 100mg.

p446 Hot Mango Salsa
Energy 18Kcal/76kJ; Protein
0g; Carbohydrate 4g, of which
sugars 4g; Fat 0g, of which
saturates 0g; Cholesterol 0mg;
Calcium 6mg; Fibre 0.7g;
Sodium 100mg.

p447 Harissa
Energy 35Kcal/148kJ; Protein
2g; Carbohydrate 4g, of which
sugars 0g; Fat 2g, of which
saturates 0g; Cholesterol 0mg;
Calcium 23mg; Fibre 0.0g;
Sodium 100mg.

p448 Aioli
Energy 400Kcal/1646kJ;
Protein 1g; Carbohydrate 0g, of
which sugars 0g; Fat 7g, of
which saturates 75g; Cholesterol
10mg; Calcium 10mg; Fibre
0.1g; Sodium 100mg.

p449 Roasted Garlic Sauce
Energy 184Kcal/761kJ; Protein
3g; Carbohydrate 9g, of which
sugars 1g; Fat 15g, of which
saturates 2g; Cholesterol 0mg;
Calcium 17mg; Fibre 1.1g;
Sodium 100mg.

p450 Watercress Sauce
Energy 451Kcal/1856kJ;
Protein 1g; Carbohydrate 1g, of
which sugars 1g; Fat 49g, of
which saturates 16g; Cholesterol
98mg; Calcium 50mg; Fibre
0.4g; Sodium 300mg.

**p451 Shallots in Balsamic
Vinegar** Energy 59Kcal/247kJ;
Protein 1g; Carbohydrate 12g,
of which sugars 10g; Fat 0g, of
which saturates 0g; Cholesterol
0mg; Calcium 25mg; Fibre
1.2g; Sodium 100mg.

p452 Barbecue Sauce
Energy 31Kcal/132kJ; Protein
1g; Carbohydrate 7g, of which
sugars 6g; Fat 0g, of which
saturates 0g; Cholesterol 0mg;
Calcium 42mg; Fibre 0.8g;
Sodium 100mg.

**p453 Mixed Herb and
Peppercorn Sauce**
Energy 50Kcal/207kJ; Protein
0g; Carbohydrate 0g, of which
sugars 0g; Fat 6g, of which
saturates 1g; Cholesterol 0mg;
Calcium 15mg; Fibre 0g;
Sodium 100mg.

p456 Leafy Apple Lift-off
Energy 169Kcal/719kJ; Protein
2g; Carbohydrate 41g, of which
sugars 41g; Fat 1g, of which
saturates 0g; Cholesterol 0mg;
Calcium 69mg; Fibre 4.2g;
Sodium 100mg.

p456 Fennel Fusion
Energy 127Kcal/539kJ; Protein
3g; Carbohydrate 29g, of which
sugars 29g; Fat 1g, of which
saturates 0g; Cholesterol 0mg;
Calcium 96mg; Fibre 7.9g;
Sodium 100mg.

p458 Tropical Calm
Energy 149Kcal/633kJ; Protein
3g; Carbohydrate 34g, of which
sugars 26g; Fat 1g, of which
saturates 0g; Cholesterol 0mg;
Calcium 118mg; Fibre 5.7g;
Sodium 100mg.

p458 Strawberry Soother
Energy 111Kcal/471kJ; Protein
3g; Carbohydrate 26g, of which
sugars 26g; Fat 0g, of which
saturates 0g; Cholesterol 0mg;
Calcium 50mg; Fibre 4.4g;
Sodium 100mg.

p459 Carrot Revitalizer
Energy 232Kcal/981kJ; Protein
4g; Carbohydrate 55g, of which
sugars 54g; Fat 1g, of which
saturates 0g; Cholesterol 0mg;
Calcium 137mg; Fibre 11.9g;
Sodium 100mg.

p459 Purple Pep
Energy 136Kcal/571kJ; Protein
4g; Carbohydrate 29g, of which
sugars 27g; Fat 1g, of which
saturates 0g; Cholesterol 0mg;
Calcium 150mg; Fibre 9.1g;
Sodium 200mg.

**p460 Tomato and Cucumber
Juice with Basil**
Energy 41Kcal/175kJ; Protein
2g; Carbohydrate 7g, of which
sugars 6g; Fat 1g, of which
saturates 0g; Cholesterol 0mg;

Calcium 51mg; Fibre 2.2g; Sodium 100mg.

p461 Beetroot, Ginger and Orange Juice
Energy 155Kcal/666kJ; Protein 6g; Carbohydrate 34g, of which sugars 31g; Fat 1g, of which saturates 0g; Cholesterol 0mg; Calcium 134mg; Fibre 7.1g; Sodium 100mg.

p462 Melon Pick-me-up
Energy 189Kcal/799kJ; Protein 3g; Carbohydrate 45g, of which sugars 45g; Fat 1g, of which saturates 0g; Cholesterol 0mg; Calcium 95mg; Fibre 10.2g; Sodium 100mg.

p462 Apple Shiner
Energy 228Kcal/970kJ; Protein 4g; Carbohydrate 56g, of which sugars 56g; Fat 1g, of which saturates 0g; Cholesterol 0mg; Calcium 57mg; Fibre 5.1g; Sodium 100mg.

p463 Citrus Sparkle
Energy 167Kcal/705kJ; Protein 5g; Carbohydrate 38g, of which sugars 38g; Fat 0g, of which saturates 0g; Cholesterol 0mg; Calcium 167mg; Fibre 7.4g; Sodium 100mg.

p463 Hum-zinger
Energy 227Kcal/975kJ; Protein 3g; Carbohydrate 55g, of which sugars 51g; Fat 1g, of which saturates 0g; Cholesterol 0mg; Calcium 95mg; Fibre 8.6g; Sodium 100mg.

p464 Grapefruit and Pear Juice Energy 140Kcal/597kJ; Protein 2g; Carbohydrate 33g, of which sugars 33g; Fat 1g, of which saturates 0g; Cholesterol 0mg; Calcium 78mg; Fibre 6.9g; Sodium 100mg.

p465 Strawberry Apple Slush Energy 95Kcal/400kJ; Protein 2g; Carbohydrate 23g, of which sugars 23g; Fat 0g, of which saturates 0g; Cholesterol 0mg; Calcium 28mg; Fibre 3.5g; Sodium 100mg.

p466 Honey and Watermelon Tonic
Energy 96Kcal/399kJ; Protein 1g; Carbohydrate 22g, of which

sugars 22g; Fat 10g, of which saturates 0g; Cholesterol 0mg; Calcium 19mg; Fibre 0.3g; Sodium 100mg.

p467 Cranberry, Ginger and Cinnamon Spritzer
Energy 121Kcal/512kJ; Protein 8g; Carbohydrate 29g, of which sugars 8g; Fat 0g, of which saturates 0g; Cholesterol 0mg; Calcium 3mg; Fibre 0g; Sodium 100mg.

p468 Lavender Orange Lush
Energy 133Kcal/568kJ; Protein 3g; Carbohydrate 32g, of which sugars 32g; Fat 0g, of which saturates 0g; Cholesterol 0mg; Calcium 132mg; Fibre 4.8g; Sodium 100mg.

p469 Ice Cool Currant
Energy 126Kcal/539kJ; Protein 1g; Carbohydrate 35g, of which sugars 35g; Fat 0g, of which saturates 0g; Cholesterol 0mg; Calcium 54mg; Fibre 2.3g; Sodium 100mg.

p470 Lemon Float
Energy 345Kcal/1461kJ; Protein 3g; Carbohydrate 70g, of which sugars 69g; Fat 8g, of which saturates 5g; Cholesterol 19mg; Calcium 91mg; Fibre 0.1g; Sodium 100mg.

p471 Blue Lagoon
Energy 148Kcal/630kJ; Protein 3g; Carbohydrate 36g, of which sugars 36g; Fat 0g, of which saturates 0g; Cholesterol 0mg; Calcium 127mg; Fibre 8.3g; Sodium 100mg.

p472 Strawberry and Banana Smoothie Energy 85Kcal/360kJ; Protein 4g; Carbohydrate 18g, of which sugars 17g; Fat 0g, of which saturates 0g; Cholesterol 2mg; Calcium 103mg; Fibre 1.1g; Sodium 100mg.

p472 Raspberry and Orange Smoothie Energy 110Kcal/466kJ; Protein 5g; Carbohydrate 18g, of which sugars 18g; Fat 2g, of which saturates 1g; Cholesterol 7mg; Calcium 164mg; Fibre 2.2g; Sodium 100mg.

p474 New York Egg Cream
Energy 271Kcal/1132kJ; Protein 6g; Carbohydrate 20g, of which sugars 19g; Fat 19g, of which saturates 1g; Cholesterol 7mg; Calcium 207mg; Fibre 0g; Sodium 100mg.

p475 Banana and Maple Flip
Energy 376Kcal/1573kJ; Protein 12g; Carbohydrate 58g, of which sugars 52g; Fat 12g, of which saturates 5g; Cholesterol 240mg; Calcium 141mg; Fibre 0.9g; Sodium 100mg.

p476 Chocolate Brownie Milkshake Energy 454Kcal/1899kJ; Protein 12g; Carbohydrate 50g, of which sugars 36g; Fat 24g, of which saturates 14g; Cholesterol 47mg; Calcium 344mg; Fibre 0.8g; Sodium 300mg.

p477 Peppermint Candy Crush Energy 175Kcal/743kJ; Protein 6g; Carbohydrate 32g, of which sugars 32g; Fat 3g, of which saturates 2g; Cholesterol 11mg; Calcium 227mg; Fibre 0g; Sodium 100mg.

p480 Rum and Star Anise Hot Toddy Energy 200Kcal/833kJ; Protein 0g; Carbohydrate 12g, of which sugars 12g; Fat 0g, of which saturates 0g; Cholesterol 0mg; Calcium 1mg; Fibre 0g; Sodium 100mg.

p481 Cardamom Hot Chocolate Energy 359Kcal/1567kJ; Protein 10g; Carbo-hydrate 42g, of which sugars 42g; Fat 18g, of which saturates 11g; Cholesterol 6mg; Calcium 127mg; Fibre 0g; Sodium 100mg.

p482 Atole Energy 197Kcal/838kJ; Protein 4g; Carbohydrate 44g, of which sugars 13g; Fat 2g, of which saturates 1g; Cholesterol 6mg; Calcium 127mg; Fibre 0g; Sodium 100mg.

p482 Café de Olla
Energy 149Kcal/634kJ; Protein 1g; Carbohydrate 34g, of which sugars 30g; Fat 2g, of which saturates 0g; Cholesterol 0mg; Calcium 25mg; Fibre 0g; Sodium 100mg.

p484 Vanilla Caffè Latte
Energy 545Kcal/2299kJ; Protein 15g; Carbohydrate 77g, of which sugars 76g; Fat 22g, of which saturates 13g; Cholesterol 24mg; Calcium 445mg; Fibre 1.4g; Sodium 200mg.

p485 Frothy Hot Chocolate
Energy 223Kcal/942kJ; Protein 10g; Carbohydrate 25g, of which sugars 25g; Fat 10g, of which saturates 6g; Cholesterol 16mg; Calcium 307mg; Fibre 0.5g; Sodium 100mg.

p486 Cuba Libre
Energy 109Kcal/454kJ; Protein 0g; Carbohydrate 11g, of which sugars 11g; Fat 0g, of which saturates 0g; Cholesterol 0mg; Calcium 9mg; Fibre 0g; Sodium 100mg.

p487 Tropical Fruit Royale
Energy 94Kcal/396kJ; Protein 1g; Carbohydrate 13g, of which sugars 13g; Fat 0g, of which saturates 0g; Cholesterol 0mg; Calcium 15mg; Fibre 2.0g;

Sodium 100mg.

p488 Lemon Vodka
Energy 111Kcal/470kJ; Protein 0g; Carbohydrate 20g, of which sugars 20g; Fat 0g, of which saturates 0g; Cholesterol 0mg; Calcium 10mg; Fibre 0g; Sodium 100mg.

p489 Quick Bloody Mary
Energy 171Kcal/722kJ; Protein 2g; Carbohydrate 9g, of which sugars 9g; Fat 0g, of which saturates 0g; Cholesterol 0mg; Calcium 30mg; Fibre 1.8g; Sodium 1.2g.

p490 Gin Fizz
Energy 200Kcal/840kJ; Protein 0g; Carbohydrate 28g, of which sugars 7g; Fat 0g, of which saturates 0g; Cholesterol 0mg; Calcium 11mg; Fibre 0g; Sodium 100mg.

p491 Sea Breeze
Energy 135Kcal/566kJ; Protein 0g; Carbohydrate 10g, of which sugars 4g; Fat 0g, of which saturates 0g; Cholesterol 0mg; Calcium 6mg; Fibre 0g; Sodium 100mg.

p492 Perfect Manhattan
Energy 106Kcal/440kJ; Protein 0g; Carbohydrate 1g, of which sugars 1g; Fat 0g, of which saturates 0g; Cholesterol 0mg; Calcium 1mg; Fibre 0g; Sodium 100mg.

p493 Margarita Energy 90Kcal/376kJ; Protein 0g; Carbohydrate 4g, of which sugars 4g; Fat 0g, of which saturates 0g; Cholesterol 0mg; Calcium 3mg; Fibre 0g; Sodium 100mg.

p494 Brandy Alexander
Energy 218Kcal/894kJ; Protein 0g; Carbohydrate 8g, of which sugars 8g; Fat 12g, of which saturates 8g; Cholesterol 31mg; Calcium 11mg; Fibre 0g; Sodium 100mg.

p495 Spritzer Energy 30Kcal/124kJ; Protein 0g; Carbohydrate 0g, of which sugars 0g; Fat 0g, of which saturates 0g; Cholesterol 0mg; Calcium 9mg; Fibre 0.1g; Sodium 100mg.

Index

A

accompaniments 50–3
aioli 47, 448
alcohol 36, 45
  brandy Alexander 494
  Cuba libre 486
  desserts 49, 327, 329, 340,
    343, 345, 349, 362–3
  fish dishes 152
  gin fizz 490
  lemon vodka 488
  margarita 493
  meat dishes 177, 178, 191
  perfect Manhattan 492
  poultry dishes 83, 200, 211,
    213
  quick bloody Mary 489
  rum and star anise hot
    toddy 480
  sea breeze 491
  spritzer 495
almond cigars 407
anchovy and roasted pepper
  salad 307
apples 18
  apple and thyme mash 50
  apple sauce 46
  apple shiner 462
  baked apples with Marsala 327
  hot blackberry and apple
    soufflé 333
  leafy apple lift-off 456–7
  strawberry apple slush 465
apricot and ginger gratin 331
apricot turnovers 70
aromatics 30–3
artichokes
  artichoke and cumin
    dip 84–5
  deep-fried artichokes 279
  globe artichokes with green
    beans and garlic dressing
    296
arugula see rocket
asparagus
  asparagus with crispy
    prosciutto 276
  asparagus with lemon
    sauce 266
  asparagus, bacon and leaf
    salad 306

atole 482–3
aubergines 20
  aubergines with cheese
    sauce 242
  baba ghanoush 81
  grilled aubergine, mint and
    couscous salad 138
  parmigiana di melanzane 261
  roasted aubergines with feta
    and coriander 319
  tomato and aubergine
    gratin 286
avgolemono 118
avocado
  avocado and cumin salsa 48
  avocado and pink grapefruit
    salad 301
  avocado soup 116

B

baba ghanoush 81
bacon-rolled enokitake
  mushrooms 94
bananas
  banana and maple flip 475
  banana and strawberry
    smoothie 472–3
  banana chocolate
    fools 370–1
  bananas with Greek yogurt
    and honey 68–9
  bananas with ice cream and
    toffee sauce 339
barbecues 14, 57
  barbecue sauce 452
  barbecued sardines with
    orange and parsley 320
basil 50, 99, 136, 183, 202–3,
  282, 299, 317, 460
beans 21
  butter bean, sun-dried
    tomato and pesto soup 124
  butter bean, tomato and red
    onion salad 312–13
  cannellini bean pâté 82
  globe artichokes with beans
    and garlic dressing 296
  green beans with almond
    butter and lemon 268–9
  marinated courgette and
    flageolet bean salad 139
  minty broad beans with
    lemon 272–3
  mixed bean and tomato
    chilli 252
  pancetta and broad bean
    risotto 235
  rosemary risotto with borlotti
    beans 234
  tomato, bean and fried basil
    salad 299
  Tuscan bean soup 127
beef 26, 44
  beef cooked in red wine 177

beef patties with onions and
  peppers 174
  meatballs in tomato
    sauce 176
  pan-fried Gaelic steaks 178
  steak and blue cheese
    sandwiches 147
  steak with warm tomato
    salsa 175
  Thai-style rare beef and
    mango salad 179
beetroot
  beetroot and horseradish
    sauce 444
  beetroot with fresh mint 295
  beetroot, ginger and orange
    juice 461
black pudding and sage with
  roast chicken 207
blackberries
  blackberries in port 362–3
  blackberry and apple
    soufflé 333
  blackberry ice cream 388
blackcurrant sorbet 382
blinis with caviar and crème
  fraîche 104–5
blueberries
  blueberry and almond
    tart 338
  blueberry cake 413
bouquet garni 28
bramble jelly 438
bread 53, 67, 405, 418–35
breakfast menus 55
broccoli 20
  broccoli and chilli
    spaghetti 137
  stir-fried broccoli with soy
    sauce and sesame
    seeds 280
Brussels sprouts
  creamy stir-fried Brussels
    sprouts 53
  stir-fried Brussels sprouts
    with bacon and caraway
    seeds 281
bubble and squeak 287
buying ingredients 6–7

C

cabbage 20
  stir-fried cabbage with
    hazelnuts 53
cakes 43, 413
caramel and pecan terrine 395
caraway seeds 157, 281, 312–13
cardamom 32, 49, 384, 481
carrots
  carrot revitalizer 459
  gingered carrot salad 272–3
  Moroccan carrot salad 303
  Moroccan date, orange and
    carrot salad 300

cauliflower 20
  cauliflower with garlic
    crumbs 270
  curried cauliflower soup 126
celeriac and parsnips,
  honey-fried 53
cheese 22–3
  aubergines with cheese
    sauce 242
  baked ricotta cakes with red
    sauce 330
  baked sweet potatoes with
    leeks and Gorgonzola 149
  blue cheese dip 48
  bocconcini with fennel and
    basil 282
  cheese and tomato
    soufflés 253
  cheesy creamy leeks 288
  cheesy leek and couscous
    cake 255
  coffee mascarpone creams
    376–7
  creamy Parmesan-baked
    eggs 144–5
  creamy polenta with
    Dolcelatte 289
  croque-monsieur 76–7
  crushed potatoes with pine
    nuts and Parmesan 50
  fettuccine with butter and
    Parmesan 230
  figs with prosciutto and
    Roquefort 134
  golden Gruyère and basil
    tortillas 99
  grilled polenta with
    Gorgonzola 52
  halloumi and grape salad 297
  Israeli cheese with green
    olives 92–3
  marinated feta with lemon
    and oregano 88–9
  Marsala mascarpone 49
  meringue pyramid with
    chocolate mascarpone 373
  Parmesan and parsley
    mash 50
  Parmesan tuiles 101
  parmigiana di melanzane 261
  pasta with roast tomatoes
    and goat's cheese 219
  pear and blue cheese
    salad 315
  red onion and goat's cheese
    pastries 244
  roast acorn squash with
    spinach and Gorgonzola 258
  roast chicken with herb
    cheese, chilli and lime
    stuffing 205
  roasted aubergines with feta
    and coriander 319
  roasted peppers with

halloumi and pine nuts 249
soft polenta with Cheddar
   cheese and thyme 52
soft polenta with Parmesan
   and sage 52
spaghetti with raw tomato
   and ricotta sauce 226
steak and blue cheese
   sandwiches 147
Stilton and watercress
   soup 125
toasted sourdough with
   goat's cheese 146
tomato and tapenade
   tarts 247
walnut and goat's cheese
   bruschetta 95
warm halloumi and fennel
   salad 314
watermelon and feta
   salad 298
wild mushroom and Fontina
   tart 260
yogurt cheese in olive oil 102
chermoula 33, 169
cherries, deep-fried 332
cherry chocolate brownies 376–7
chicken 27, 44
   chicken escalopes with
      lemon and Serrano
      ham 204
   chicken liver and brandy
      pâté 83
   chilli-spiced chicken
      wings 110–11
   chilli-spiced poussin 209
   crème fraîche and coriander
      chicken 202–3
   drunken chicken 200
   honey mustard chicken 199
   pot-roasted chicken with
      preserved lemons 198
   roast chicken with black
      pudding and sage 207
   roast chicken with herb
      cheese, chilli and lime
      stuffing 205
   soy sauce and star anise
      chicken 321
   soy-marinated chicken 201
   spatchcock poussins with
      herb butter 208
   stir-fried chicken with Thai
      basil 202–3
   tandoori chicken 206
chickpea samosas 250
chillies 20, 30, 37, 44
   broccoli and chilli
      spaghetti 137
   chilli and spring onion
      noodles 51
   chilli prawn skewers 107
   chilli-spiced chicken
      wings 110–11
   chilli-spiced poussin 209
   fried chilli polenta
      triangles 52
   grilled hake with lemon and
      chilli 160

mixed bean and tomato
   chilli 252
chocolate 35
   cardamom hot chocolate 481
   chilled chocolate and
      espresso mousse 372
   chocolate and prune
      refrigerator bars 412
   chocolate banana fools 370–1
   chocolate brioche
      sandwiches 68–9
   chocolate brownie
      milkshake 476
   chocolate fudge sauce 48
   chocolate petit four
      cookies 416–17
   chocolate truffles 415
   classic chocolate
      roulade 374–5
   frothy hot chocolate 485
   hot chocolate rum
      soufflés 345
   meringue pyramid with
      chocolate mascarpone 373
   miniature choc-ices 393
   New York egg cream 474
   praline chocolate
      bites 416–17
   rich chocolate biscuit
      slice 411
   rich chocolate brownies 410
   toffee chocolate sauce 48
   warm chocolate
      zabaglione 344
   white chocolate and brownie
      torte 396
   white chocolate castles 394
cinnamon 32, 49, 51, 406, 467
coconut 36
   coconut ice 391
   coconut macaroons 403
   coconut rice 51, 238
coffee 35
   café de olla 482–3
   chilled chocolate and
      espresso mousse 372
   coffee ice cream 389
   coffee mascarpone
      creams 376–7
   vanilla caffè latte 484
condiments 37
cookies 42, 43, 400, 401,
   416–17
cooking techniques 14–17
coriander 29, 31, 45, 51,
   104–5, 202–3, 275, 323
corn 21, 311
cottage loaf 426
courgette 139, 218
couscous 40
   cheesy leek and couscous
      cake 255
   grilled aubergine, mint and
      couscous salad 138
crab
   crab and cucumber
      wraps 153
   crab and water chestnut
      wontons 110–11

crab risotto 237
crab sandwiches 316
cranachan 65
cranberry, ginger and cinnamon
   spritzer 467
cranberry sauce, quick 46
cream 22, 49
   baked eggs with creamy
      leeks 132
   cheesy creamy leeks 288
   creamy Parmesan-baked
      eggs 144–5
   sour cream and chive dip 48
   summer squash and baby
      new potatoes in warm dill
      sour cream 271
crème fraîche 22
   blinis with caviar and crème
      fraîche 104–5
   crème fraîche and coriander
      chicken 202–3
croque-monsieur 76–7
crunchy oat cereal 64
cucumber
   cucumber and crab
      wraps 153
   cucumber and tomato juice
      with basil 460
   cucumber with fresh dill 294
cumin 31, 45, 48, 84–5, 323
currants 181, 382, 469, 471
custard 42
   baked caramel
      custard 368–9
   baked custard with burnt
      sugar 366
   Portuguese custard tarts 365

D
dairy produce 22–3
damson water ice 383
dill 271, 294
dinner menu 56
dips 48, 84–5
dressings 45, 268–9, 296
duck 27
   duck with plum sauce 215

E
eggplants see aubergines
eggs 23
   avgolemono 118
   baked eggs with creamy
      leeks 132
   chopped egg and
      onions 92–3
   creamy Parmesan-baked
      eggs 144–5
   easy egg-fried rice 51
   eggs Benedict 76–7
   eggs mimosa 103
   eggy bread panettone 67
   pea and mint omelette 135
   smoked salmon and chive
      omelette 72
elderflower and lychee
   sorbet 353
equipment 10–13

F
fennel
   fennel and bacon with
      scallops 154
   fennel and basil with
      bocconcini 282
   fennel and halloumi
      salad 314
   fennel butter and
      haddock 156
   fennel fusion 456–7
   fennel, potato and garlic
      mash 290
figs 19, 134, 187, 350–1
fish 16, 24–5, 44
   anchovy and roasted pepper
      salad 307
   baked salmon with caraway
      seeds 157
   baked salmon with green
      sauce 166–7
   barbecued sardines with
      orange and parsley 320
   brandade of salt cod 91
   crisp fried whitebait 143
   farfalle with tuna 227
   filo-wrapped fish 163
   fish with pine nuts 165
   focaccia with sardines and
      roast tomatoes 140–1
   grilled hake with lemon and
      chilli 160
   haddock and fennel
      butter 156
   Jansson's temptation 142
   jugged kippers 74
   linguine with anchovies and
      capers 220–1
   marinated anchovies 106
   marinated smoked salmon
      with lime and
      coriander 104–5
   pan-fried skate wings with
      capers 170
   penne with cream and
      smoked salmon 231
   poached fish in spicy tomato
      sauce 164
   quick kedgeree 73
   roast cod wrapped in
      prosciutto with vine
      tomatoes 159
   roast mackerel with spicy
      chermoula paste 169
   salt cod and potato
      fritters 108

sea bass in a salt crust 158
sea bass with parsley and
  lime butter 171
seared tuna Niçoise 144–5
smoked salmon and chive
  omelette 72
teriyaki salmon 168
tonno con piselli 162
trout with grilled Serrano
  ham 161
flapjacks 402
flour 38
French baguette 422
fruit 18–19
  baby summer puddings 362–3
  baked ricotta cakes with red
    sauce 330
  citrus sparkle 463
  dried 36
  frozen 42
  hum-zinger 463
  soft fruit and meringue
    gâteau 397
  summer berries in sabayon
    glaze 329
  summer berry frozen
    yogurt 385
  summer fruit brioche 354
  tropical calm 458
  tropical fruit royale 487
  tropical scented fruit
    salad 348

G
garlic 33, 39, 44
  cauliflower with garlic
    crumbs 270
  crisp and golden roast
    potatoes with goose fat
    and garlic 284–5
  crushed potatoes with garlic
    and basil 50
  fennel, potato and garlic
    mash 290
  garlicky green salad with
    raspberry dressing 268–9
  garlicky roasties 277
  globe artichokes with green
    beans and garlic
    dressing 296
  pea soup with garlic 128
  potato and roasted garlic
    broth 122
  roast leg of lamb with
    rosemary and garlic 185
  roast shoulder of lamb with

whole garlic cloves 184
roasted garlic sauce 449
rosemary and garlic
  marinade 45
spaghettini with roasted
  garlic 222
ginger 32, 33
  apricot and ginger gratin 331
  cranberry, ginger and
    cinnamon spritzer 467
  fragrant lemon grass and
    ginger pork patties 190
  ginger and soy marinade 45
  gingered carrot salad 272–3
  gingered semi-freddo 392
  golden ginger
    macaroons 408–9
  rhubarb and ginger
    jellies 355
  rhubarb and ginger trifles 360
  zingy papaya, lime and
    ginger salad 62
gooseberry relish 46
granary cob 424
Grant loaves 425
grapefruit 301, 464
grapes 19, 297
guinea fowl with whisky
  sauce 211

H
haddock and fennel butter 156
harissa 33, 322, 447
herbs 28–9, 47, 453
honey 35
  honey and watermelon
    tonic 466
  honey and wholegrain
    mustard dressing 45
  honey-fried parsnips and
    celeriac 53
  honey mustard chicken 199
  roast bananas with Greek
    yogurt and honey 68–9
horseradish and beetroot
  sauce 444
hummus 80, 140–1

I
ice cool currant 469
ice cream 339, 388–92
  miniature choc ices 393
Irish soda bread 430–1

J
Jansson's temptation 142
Japanese-style spinach with
  toasted sesame seeds 264
jugged kippers 74
juniper 193, 349

K
kedgeree, quick 73
kulfi 390
kumquats, spiced poached 440–1

L
lamb 27
  cumin-and-coriander rubbed

lamb 323
curried lamb samosas 113
lamb chops with a mint jelly
  crust 182
lamb steaks with redcurrant
  glaze 181
marinated lamb with oregano
  and basil 183
North African lamb 180
roast lamb with figs 187
roast leg of lamb with
  rosemary and garlic 185
roast shoulder of lamb with
  whole garlic cloves 184
sweet-and-sour lamb 186
lavender and strawberry
  sorbet 381
lavender orange lush 468
leafy apple lift-off 456–7
leeks 21
  baked eggs with creamy
    leeks 132
  baked leek and potato
    gratin 245
  baked sweet potatoes with
    leeks and Gorgonzola 149
  cheesy creamy leeks 288
  cheesy leek and couscous
    cake 255
  leek fritters 278
  vichyssoise 117
lemon grass and ginger pork
  patties 190
lemons 18
  asparagus with lemon
    sauce 266
  avgolemono 118
  chicken escalopes with
    lemon and Serrano
    ham 204
  crushed potatoes with
    parsley and lemon 50
  green beans with almond
    butter and lemon 268–9
  grilled hake with lemon and
    chilli 160
  lemon float 470
  lemon mayonnaise 47
  lemon posset 370–1
  lemon sorbet 380
  lemon vodka 488
  marinated feta with lemon
    and oregano 88–9
  minty broad beans with
    lemon 272–3
  pot-roasted chicken with
    preserved lemons 198
  preserved lemons 36, 442
  spaghetti with lemon 223
  tangy raspberry and lemon
    tartlets 358
lentils 41
  creamy red lentil dhal 259
  spiced lentils 258
lettuce and peas with spring
  onions 265
lime 62, 104–5, 171, 205, 357
lychee and elderflower
  sorbet 353

M
mangoes 19
  crispy mango stacks with
    raspberry coulis 359
  hot mango salsa 446
  mango and lime fool 357
  Thai-style rare beef and
    mango salad 179
maple and banana flip 475
maple syrup and bacon with
  Scotch pancakes 75
marinades 37, 45, 88–9, 104–5,
  106, 139, 183, 201
marmalade 35
  marmalade and soy roast
    duck 214
  three-fruit marmalade 440–1
marzipan 42
  almond cigars 407
  blueberry and almond
    tart 338
  plum and almond tart 326
mayonnaise 47
meat 16, 26–7
meatballs in tomato sauce 176
melons 19
  cantaloupe melon with
    grilled strawberries 63
  honey and watermelon
    tonic 466
  melon pick-me-up 462
  watermelon and feta
    salad 298
  watermelon ice 387
menus 54–9
meringues 328, 397
  meringue pyramid with
chocolate mascarpone 373
mint 135, 138, 182, 295
  minty broad beans with
    lemon 272–3
  minty courgette linguine 218
mushrooms 21, 41
  bacon-rolled enokitake
    mushrooms 94
  mushroom caviar 90
  mushroom polenta 246
  mushroom stroganoff 243
  oven-baked porcini
    risotto 232
  wild mushroom and Fontina
    tart 260
mussel risotto 236
mussels in white wine 152
mustard 31, 37

honey mustard chicken 199
mustard cheese sauce 46
roast pheasant with sherry
    and mustard sauce 213

N
New York egg cream 474
noodles 40
    chilli and spring onion
        noodles 51
    noodles with sesame-roasted
        spring onions 283
    soy and sesame egg
        noodles 51
    spicy peanut noodles 51
nuts 36
    almond cookies 401
    caramel and pecan
        terrine 395
    chocolate brioche
        sandwiches 68–9
    crushed potatoes with pine
        nuts and Parmesan 50
    fish with tomato and pine
        nuts 165
    green beans with almond
        butter and lemon 268–9
    green beans with almond
        butter and lemon 268–9
    nutty nougat 408–9
    orange and pecan scones 404
    pansotti with walnut
        sauce 229
    parsley and walnut pesto 47
    pistachio and rose water
        oranges 352
    roasted peppers with
        halloumi and pine nuts 249
    Spanish salted almonds 98
    spicy peanut noodles 51
    walnut and goat's cheese
        bruschetta 95

O
oats 64, 65, 66, 402
oils 39, 44, 102
okra with tomatoes and
    coriander 275
olives 41, 92–3, 133, 305
onions 21
    beef patties with onions
        and peppers 174
    braised lettuce and peas with
        spring onions 265
    butter bean, tomato and red
        onion salad 312–13

caramelized onion and
    sausage tarte tatin 192
caramelized shallots 267
champ 291
chilli and spring onion
    noodles 51
chopped egg and onions
    92–3
coriander and spring onion
    rice 51
noodles with sesame-roasted
    spring onions 283
potato and onion tortilla 256
red onion and goat's cheese
    pastries 244
red onion and olive
    pissaladière 133
roast shallot tart with
    thyme 318
shallots in balsamic
    vinegar 451
simple cream of onion
    soup 119
spicy chorizo sausage and
    spring onion hash 148
spring onion flatbreads 430–1
oranges 18
    barbecued sardines with
        orange and parsley 320
    beetroot, ginger and orange
        juice 461
    lavender orange lush 468
    Moroccan date, orange and
        carrot salad 300
    orange and pecan
        scones 404
    orange and tarragon
        dressing 45
    oranges in syrup 350–1
    pistachio and rose water
        oranges 352
    raspberry and orange
        smoothie 472–3
oregano 88–9, 183
oysters with merguez
    sausages 310

P
pancakes with caramelized
    pears 71
panini all'olio 421
papaya, lime and ginger
    salad 62
papayas in jasmine flower
    syrup 356
parmigiana di melanzane 261
parsley 50, 171, 320, 312–13
    parsley and walnut pesto 47
parsnips and celeriac,
    honey-fried 53
passion fruit 19
    passion fruit creams 367
    passion fruit soufflés 341
pasta 40
    broccoli and chilli
        spaghetti 137
    cappelletti in broth 120–1
    farfalle with tuna 227
    fettuccine all'Alfredo 228

fettuccine with butter
    and Parmesan 230
linguine with anchovies and
    capers 220–1
linguine with rocket 224
minty courgette linguine 218
pansotti with walnut
    sauce 229
pasta sauces 43
pasta with roast tomatoes
    and goat's cheese 219
penne with cream and
    smoked salmon 231
spaghetti with lemon 223
spaghetti with raw tomato
    and ricotta sauce 226
spaghettini with roasted
    garlic 222
tagliatelle with vegetable
    ribbons 225
tiny pasta in broth 120–1
warm pasta with crushed
    tomatoes and basil 317
warm penne with fresh
    tomatoes and basil 136
pastry 42
peaches 19
    peach and cardamom yogurt
        ice 384
    peach pie 334
    peaches with Amaretto 340
    peaches with meringues 328
pears 18
    caramelized upside-down
        pear pie 336–7
    juniper-scented pears in red
        wine 349
    pear and blue cheese
        salad 315
    warm pancakes with
        caramelized pears 71
peas 21
    braised lettuce and peas with
        spring onions 265
    pea and mint omelette 135
    pea soup with garlic 128
    tonno con piselli 162
peppermint candy crush 477
peppers 20
    anchovy and roasted pepper
        salad 307
    beef patties with onions and
        peppers 174
    peperonata 84–5
    roasted pepper and hummus
        wrap 140–1
    roasted peppers with
        halloumi and pine nuts 249
    tofu and pepper kebabs 251
    yellow pepper and coriander
        relish 445
Persian baked rice 233
pesto 37, 47, 50
    butter bean, sun-dried
        tomato and pesto soup 124
pheasant 27
    pheasant cooked in port with
        mushrooms 212
    roast pheasant with sherry

and mustard sauce 213
pickle, Middle Eastern 443
picnic menu 59
pineapples 19
    grilled pineapple and rum
        cream 343
pistachio and rose water
    oranges 352
pitta bread 432
pizza 43
    classic margherita pizza 254
plum and almond tart 326
plum sauce with duck 215
polenta 40
    creamy polenta with
        Dolcelatte 289
    fried chilli polenta
        triangles 52
    mushroom polenta 246
    polenta chips 100
    soft polenta 52
    soft polenta with Cheddar
        cheese and thyme 52
    soft polenta with Parmesan
        and sage 52
poppy-seeded bloomer 428–9
pork 26
    asparagus, bacon and leaf
        salad 306
    bacon-rolled enokitake
        mushrooms 94
    chicken escalopes with
        lemon and Serrano ham 204
    Chinese spiced pork
        chops 194–5
    croque-monsieur 76–7
    eggs Benedict 76–7
    figs with prosciutto and
        Roquefort 134
    fragrant lemon grass and
        ginger pork patties 190
    pan-fried gammon with
        cider 191
    pancetta and broad bean
        risotto 235
    paprika pork 188
    pork kebabs 189
    roast asparagus with crispy
        prosciutto 276
    roast cod wrapped in
        prosciutto with vine
        tomatoes 159
    roast pork with juniper
        berries and bay 193
    scallops with fennel and
        bacon 154

Scotch pancakes with bacon and maple syrup 75
sticky glazed pork ribs 194–5
stir-fried Brussels sprouts with bacon and caraway seeds 281
trout with grilled Serrano ham 161
Vietnamese spring rolls with pork 112
porridge 66
Portuguese custard tarts 365
potatoes 20
  baked leek and potato gratin 245
  baked sweet potatoes with leeks and Gorgonzola 149
  bubble and squeak 287
  champ 291
  crisp and golden roast potatoes with goose fat and garlic 284–5
  crushed potatoes 50
  fennel, potato and garlic mash 290
  garlicky roasties 277
  home-made potato gnocchi 220–1
  Jansson's temptation 142
  mashed potatoes 50
  potato and olive salad 305
  potato and onion tortilla 256
  potato and roasted garlic broth 122
  potato, caraway seed and parsley salad 312–13
  prawn and new potato stew 155
  salt cod and potato fritters 108
  spicy potato wedges 284–5
  summer squash and baby new potatoes in warm dill sour cream 271
  vichyssoise 117
potted shrimps with cayenne pepper 88–9
poultry 16, 27
praline chocolate bites 416–17
praline cream 49
prawn and new potato stew 155
prune and chocolate refrigerator bars 412
prunes, stuffed 414

R
raspberries
  raspberry and lemon tartlets 358
  raspberry and orange smoothie 472–3
  raspberry and vanilla sauce 48
  raspberry brûlée 364
  raspberry coulis with crispy mango stacks 359
  raspberry dressing with garlicky green salad 268–9
  raspberry sherbet 386
red wine and bay marinade 45
rhubarb 19, 355, 360
rice 17, 40, 41, 43
  coconut rice 51, 238
  coriander and spring onion rice 51
  crab risotto 237
  easy egg-fried rice 51
  mussel risotto 236
  pancetta and bean risotto 235
  Persian baked rice 233
  porcini risotto 232
  quick kedgeree 73
  rosemary risotto with borlotti beans 234
  savoury ground rice 239
  star anise and cinnamon rice 51
rocket pesto 47
rocket with linguine 224
rosemary 45, 49, 185, 234, 423
rum and cinnamon cream 49
rum and star anise hot toddy 480

S
sage 28, 52, 207
salt 31, 108, 158
satay sauce, quick 46
sauces 37, 46, 48
Scotch pancakes with bacon and maple syrup 75
Scottish morning rolls 418
sea bass in a salt crust 158
sea bass with parsley and lime butter 171
sesame 51, 264, 280, 283
shellfish 25
  Asian-style crab cakes 109
  chilli prawn skewers 107
  crab and cucumber wraps 153
  crab and water chestnut wontons 110–11
  crab risotto 237
  fresh crab sandwiches 316
  merguez sausages with iced oysters 310
  mussel risotto 236
  mussels in white wine 152
  potted shrimps with cayenne pepper 88–9
  prawn and new potato stew 155
  scallops with fennel and bacon 154
  sizzling prawns 87
short-cut ingredients 42–3

skate wings with capers 170
smoked salmon and chive omelette 72
soda bread 430–1
sourdough with goat's cheese 146
soy sauce 37, 45, 51, 201, 214, 280, 321
Spanish salted almonds 98
spices 15, 30–3
spinach 21, 258, 264, 304
split tin loaf 427
stock 44
strawberries
  strawberries with cantaloupe melon 63
  strawberry and banana smoothie 472–3
  strawberry and lavender sorbet 381
  strawberry apple slush 465
  strawberry cream shortbreads 361
  strawberry jam 439
  strawberry soother 458
sugar 34
summer al fresco lunch menu 59
Sunday lunch menu 58
supper menu 56
sweet-and-sour lamb 186

T
tandoori chicken 206
tandoori rotis 435
teabread, quick and easy 405
teriyaki salmon 168
Thai-style rare beef and mango salad 179
thyme 50, 52, 318
toffee sauce 339
tofu and pepper kebabs 251
tomatoes 20, 37, 41
  baked winter squash with tomatoes 274
  butter bean, sun-dried tomato and pesto soup 124
  butter bean, tomato and red onion salad 312–13
  cheese and tomato soufflés 253
  easy tomato sauce 46
  fish with tomato and pine nuts 165
  focaccia with sardines and roast tomatoes 140–1
  meatballs in tomato sauce 176
  mixed bean and tomato chilli 252
  pasta with roast tomatoes and goat's cheese 219
  poached fish in spicy tomato sauce 164
  roast cod wrapped in prosciutto with vine tomatoes 159
  spaghetti with raw tomato and ricotta sauce 226
  steak with warm tomato salsa 175

  stewed okra with tomatoes and coriander 275
  tomato and aubergine gratin 286
  tomato and cucumber juice with basil 460
  tomato and tapenade tarts 247
  tomato, bean and fried basil salad 299
  warm pasta with crushed tomatoes and basil 317
  warm penne with fresh tomatoes and basil 136
  winter squash soup with tomato salsa 123
treacle tart 335
turkey patties 210
turnip salad in sour cream 302

V
vanilla 48, 484
vegetables 17, 20–1, 41, 44
  purple pep 459
  star-gazer vegetable soup 129
  sweet and salty vegetable crisps 86
  tagliatelle with vegetable ribbons 225
vichyssoise 117
Vietnamese spring rolls with pork 112

W
walnut and goat's cheese bruschetta 95
watercress and Stilton soup 125
watercress sauce 450
West Indian flat breads 434

Y
yellow pepper and coriander relish 445
Yemeni sponge flat breads 433
yogurt
  cranachan 65
  peach and cardamom yogurt ice 384
  roast bananas with Greek yogurt and honey 68–9
  summer berry frozen yogurt 385
  yogurt cheese in olive oil 102

Z
zabaglione 342
  chocolate zabaglione 344